EUROPEANS IN THE WORLD
Volume Two
Sources on Cultural Contact from 1650 to the Present

James R. Lehning
University of Utah

and

Megan Armstrong
University of Utah

Prentice
Hall

Upper Saddle River, New Jersey 07458

Library of Congress Cataloging-in-Publication Data

Europeans in the world: sourcers on cultural contact/[compiled] by Megan Armstrong and James R. Lehning.
  p.cm.
  Includes bibliographical references.
  Contents: v. 1. From antiquity to 1700—v. 2. From 1650 to the present.
  ISBN 0-13-091269-7 (v. 1)—ISBN 0-13-091260-3 (v. 2)
  1. Civilization, Western. 2. Europe—Civilization. 3. Europe—Intellectual life. 4. Europe—History. I. Armstrong, Megan II. Lehning, James R.
  CB245.#E75 2002
  909'.09821—dc21

                                                                              2001037443

VP, Editorial Director: Charlyce Jones-Owen
Senior Acquistions Editor: Charles Cavaliere
Editorial Assistant: Adrienne Paul
Senior Managing Editor: Jan Stephan
Production Liaison: Fran Russello
Project Manager: Russell Jones (Pine Tree Composition)
Prepress and Manufacturing Buyer: Tricia Kenny
Art Director: Jayne Conte
Cover Designer: Kiwi Design
Cover Image: "Panorama of Durbar Procession". By permission of the British Library
Marketing Manager: Claire Rehwinkel

Cartography in this book configured by Maryland Cartographics, Oxford, Maryland
This book was set in 10/12 Baskerville by Pine Tree Composition
and was printed and bound by Courier Companies, Inc.
The cover was printed by Phoenix Color Corp.

 © 2002 by Pearson Education, Inc.
Upper Saddle River, New Jersey 07458

Printed in the United States of America

10 9 8 7 6 5 4 3 2 1

ISBN 0-13-091260-3

Pearson Education Limited, *London*
Pearson Education Australia, Pte. Limited, *Sydney*
Pearson Education Singapore, Pte. Ltd.
Pearson Education North Asia Ltd., *Hong Kong*
Pearson Education Canada, Ltd., *Toronto*
Pearson Educación de Mexico, S.A. de C.V.
Pearson Education—Japan, *Tokyo*
Pearson Education Malaysia, Pte. Ltd.
Pearson Education, Upper Saddle River, *New Jersey*

For Charles Lehning

CONTENTS

Chapter 16 Pacific Exploration, 1768–1850   41

Chapter 17 African Exploration, 1820–1885   61

Chapter 18 The Expansion of European Empires, 1783–1900   82

Chapter 19 Race and Science, 1850–1904   104

Chapter 24 Independence Movements, 1945–1965   210

Chapter 25 The Globalization of the World Economy, 1900–1999   233

Chapter 26 Postcolonialism, 1970–Present   258

Credits   275

ACKNOWLEDGEMENTS

The authors would like to acknowledge friends and colleagues who helped in the completion of this work. In particular, we would like to thank Faith Childress, Elizabeth Clement, Nadja Durbach, Ipek Giencel Sezgin, Ray Gunn, Eric Hinderaker, Rebecca Horn, Isabel Moreira, Bradley Parker, Luise Poulton, Richard Raiswell, Wes Sasaki-Uemura, Janet Theiss, Peter Von Sivers, and Anand Yang for their advice and assistance.

We would also like to thank Charles Cavaliere of Prentice Hall for his support and advice throughout this project, and the staff at Prentice Hall for helping produce the book.

No acknowledgment would be complete without mentioning our colleagues who were gracious enough to review these volumes. They are: Jack M. Balcer, Ohio State University; Sara E. Chapman, Oakland University; Carol E. Harrison, Kent State University; and Larissa J. Taylor, Colby College. We thank them for their efforts in fulfilling this critical responsibility.

PREFACE

In the last generation, undergraduate history curricula in North American colleges and universities have increasingly become concerned with teaching national, thematic, and continental histories in a global context. There has been a growing recognition that civilizations are not airtight containers, as they have been thought of in the past, but rather that contact between civilizations is an important aspect of historical processes. Journals that focus on the history of European interaction with the rest of the globe, such as the Journal of World History and Itinerario: The European Journal of Overseas History, have been developed and become normal reading for historians—no matter what their specific interests. These changes have affected many of the staple courses in the curriculum, such as Western Civilization; have led to new courses, such as World Civilization; and have also led to more specialized courses on topics such as Travel, Exploration, Imperialism, and Colonialism.

At the same time, more and more college and university teachers attempt to use primary sources in their classes. Theses sources act as a way of teaching the craft of the historian through exposure to the words and phrases of people who lived in the past, as well as allowing the student to see the raw material from which historical accounts are developed, which makes those accounts more meaningful.

Europeans in the World is primary source reader which focuses on the relations between European civilization and the rest of the world and covers chronologically, in two volumes, the period from Antiquity to the late twentieth century. It presents excerpts from primary source texts, both written documents and visual images, which where possible, express multiple voices about the ways in which European civilization interacted with the civilizations of other parts of the world. The texts presented here cover themes such as politics, gender, religion, and ethnicity in non-European parts of the world. The readings not only include such standard accounts as J. A. Hobson's *Imperialism*, but also accounts by Catholic religious men and women such as Marie de l'Incarnation (*Letters*) and Matteo Ricci (*Journals*), unusual European travelers such as Mary Kingsley (*Travels in West Africa*), and by colonial subjects such as Mohandas K. Gandhi (*Hind Swaraj*).

Because textbooks typically treat the subject sparingly, each volume begins with a schematic account of European contact with the rest of the world which is aimed at providing a context for the selected documents. The volume introductions also include a suggestion of the the themes that may be found in the documents, as well as a guide to the student on how to read them. The documents themselves are divided into topical chapters arranged in roughly chronological order. Each of these chapters begins with a discussion of the specific events and themes that mark the chapter, and there are brief introductions to each document that provides background information about the author and about the document itself. At the end of each chapter are suggestions for further reading, recommended Web sites, and study questions to assist the student in further exploring the topic.

Europeans in the World therefore presents college and university teachers of history with materials that can be used to increase the sense in their students of the importance of contact throughout its history between the West and the rest of the world. It allows and understanding that this contact at times not only imposed Western institutions and values on those parts of the world, but also affected the development of Western Civilization.

James R. Lehning
Megan Armstrong

INTRODUCTION

Cultural interaction has been one of the most important forces in shaping Western culture from its beginnings. The documents selected for this volume focus attention on different faces of cultural interaction from the early modern period to the present. They shed light in particular on the cultural impact of conquest and trade on European and non-European societies, the rise of imperial powers and colonization, and the influence of Eastern intellectual and spiritual traditions upon Western philosophy, religion, legal systems, science, and literature. They also raise questions about Western assumptions about human nature, specifically with regard to gender roles, spirituality, and race. To give students some appreciation for the richness and variety of historical sources, we include travel accounts, memoirs, economic records, novels, laws, and ethnographic reports. Most of the documents in this reader were written by Europeans, primarily by European men. Whenever possible, however, we have included accounts written by non-Europeans, by both European and non-European women, and by individuals of different socioeconomic status so that students can compare and contrast differing perspectives on cultural interaction.

The documents are arranged both chronologically and thematically. The first section covers the period from the colonization of the New World and the creation of an Atlantic economic complex in the seventeenth century to the eighteenth century Enlightenment. The exploration of the Pacific and Africa by Europeans in the eighteenth and nineteenth centuries is the subject of the second section. Next, the consolidation of European imperial control of Asia and Africa is considered. The fourth section covers a number of ways in which Europeans dealt with their dominance of other parts of the world, from the literary, scholarly, and artistic assumptions of Orientalism to the late-nineteenth-century development of anthropology as an academic discipline whose subject matter was not only the non-European world, but also human nature itself. Finally, in the fifth section, the decline of European imperial power is examined, along with the reorientation of relations between Europe and the rest of the world that have come with the end of European empires.

THE EXPERIENCE OF THE NEW WORLD AND ITS IMPACT ON EUROPE

The discovery of the New World opened a new area for European contact with non-Europeans. By a century and a half after Columbus's first landfall at Hispaniola, present-day Haiti, a small but growing collection of European settlements were scattered along the Atlantic coasts of North and South America and on the islands of the Caribbean. In the seventeenth and eighteenth centuries, these settlements became part of an Atlantic trade complex that linked Europe, Africa, and the New World. In North America, English and French colonies produced furs and timber for export. Farther south, crops suited to the warmer climate and in growing demand in Europe began to be produced. In 1611, the first tobacco crop was planted in Virginia, and shipments grew dramatically over the next several decades, providing the colony with a valuable export crop. A system known as the "headright" system, by which new arrivals in the colony received fifty acres of land, and those who financed the passage of others received fifty acres for them, allowed a rapid expansion of tobacco cultivation, as well as an incentive for the importation of new settlers as indentured servants to provide labor. Other crops proved suitable for the tropical areas of the New World. Sugarcane was first introduced there in the mid-1540s: production reached 2,500 metric tons by the 1560s, then doubled again by 1580. By 1630, production was up to more than twenty thousand tons, about ten times that of any other sugar colony. In the 1640s a "sugar revolution" came to the English islands of Barbados and Jamaica in the eastern Caribbean and later, in the last decades of the seventeenth century, to the French colony of Saint-Domingue. In the early eighteenth century, cacao began to be produced in Brazil, and beginning in the 1790s, another crop, coffee, became a major export crop of that country.

The high mortality caused after contact among the indigenous population by exposure to European disease and the difficulties of providing labor through the system of indentured service made it difficult for the colonizers to find adequate labor for these crops, either among the native population or new migrants from Europe. Portuguese, and later Dutch, trading posts on the coast of West Africa provided the solution through the development of the slave trade. Portugal, with its existing colonies on the African coast, was able to draw on slavery as a source for a growing plantation system in Brazil, and slave ships from other European countries were also soon plying the Atlantic. Settlements in the New World tropics therefore also included a growing number of Africans, brought forcibly from their homelands to provide the labor force for an increasingly complex plantation economy that bound together Europe, North and South America, and Africa. Slavery became predominant between Brazil and the middle Atlantic colonies in North America, and on the Caribbean islands. In Saint Domingue, in 1740, 82 percent of the population was slave, only 8 percent European, and the remainder "free people of color."

As a consequence of the opening of the New World and the development of this Atlantic economic complex, Europeans experienced increased contact with Africans as well as Native Americans. This provided grist for the participants in the intellectual movement that marked late seventeenth- and eighteenth-century European thought, the Enlightenment. An extension of the principles of rational inquiry characteristic of the Scientific Revolution of the seventeenth century into areas of study having to do with man and civilization, the Enlightenment was a collection of different approaches within a general commitment to nature and rationality. The fundamental tests of any institutions were whether they were natural and rational, and the *philosophes* of the Enlightenment emerged as persistent critics of the political, legal, and religious institutions of their time, each of which seemed to fail these tests.

In this context, the increased knowledge that came to Europe about the peoples of Africa and the Americas provided an opportunity for European intellectuals to refine and place a distinct new cast on the traditional theme of the Noble Savage, the idealized image of humans uncorrupted by civilization. Especially when coupled with the persistent theme of human progress that marked eighteenth-century European thought, the uncivilized inhabitants of Africa and the Americas were models of what Europeans had been, and also what they might be if their own civilization was reformed to the prescriptions of the *philosophes*.

EXPLORATION: THE OPENING OF THE PACIFIC AND SUB-SAHARAN AFRICA TO EUROPEANS

As industrial development and political revolution in Europe undercut the Atlantic complex, the eighteenth-century struggle for power between the great powers of Europe led to a series of wars that had implications elsewhere in the world. The most important of these, the Seven Years' War (1756–1763), was the first global war, with actions not only in Europe but also in North America, Africa, the Caribbean, and India. The British defeat of France in this war marked the apogee of British imperial power: with Spain and Portugal in decline, France no longer a major factor in North America, and the British navy dominant in the Atlantic and in the Mediterranean Sea, Britain was able to exert its power and authority throughout the world.

The immediate aftermath of the British victory in the Seven Years' War was to open the way for a major British effort to expand its knowledge of the parts of the world that had either remained unknown or were badly understood by Europeans. This meant further attempts to discover the Northwest Passage through North America into the Pacific, a project undertaken over the next seventy-five years from both the Atlantic and Pacific sides of the continent. It also led to attempts to explore the great expanse of the Pacific Ocean, still, in 1763, relatively unknown to Europeans and the object more of speculation than of certain knowledge.

The voyages led by the British naval officer James Cook accumulated an extraordinary amount of information, and began to turn the Pacific Ocean into an area well known to Europeans. Cook and later explorers undertook a number of important operations: scientific experiments, such as the plotting of the transit of the planet Venus that first took Cook to Tahiti; gathering plant and animal life specimens of the area and generating descriptions of the geological formations and climatic conditions encountered; information on the inhabitants of the islands; and mapping of the coastlines and hydrographic conditions of the area. By the early nineteenth century, the Pacific was frequently visited by European ships. Some came to trade with the peoples of the islands, some brought European settlers such as the convicts who settled Australia or the missionaries who came to try to convert the islanders to European religions, and some exploited the rich whaling waters of the Southern Pacific fishery.

Soon after the opening of the Pacific to European ships, another part of the world began to be investigated by Europeans. Earlier phases of European expansion had planted colonies or merchant communities on the coast of Africa, from the French colony of Senegal on the tip of West Africa around to the Portuguese colony of Angola and Dutch and British holdings in South Africa. There had also been longstanding European contact with the Ottoman Empire, which controlled the territories of the eastern Mediterranean Sea and North Africa. But at the beginning of the nineteenth century, Europeans had only begun to penetrate into the African continent itself.

The focal point for this penetration, as it developed in the course of the nineteenth century, was the Nile River. Beginning just before the turn of the century with a French expedition to Egypt led by Napoleon Bonaparte, Europeans began to push up the river from Alexandria. Soon after, others attempted to reach the river from the east by entering the continent from the Indian Ocean. The massive difficulties of these expeditions, which not only involved tremendous logistical problems but also dealings with the inhabitants of the Nile valley and their conflicts, as well as the necessity of surviving the different climate and disease conditions of Africa, meant that progress was slow. Only in the third quarter of the century, when a number of concerted pushes were made by David Livingstone, Richard Burton, John Hanning Speke, and Samuel Baker, was the Nile traveled by Europeans from its mouth to its sources.

The area west of the Nile River also became an object of interest for Europeans during the nineteenth century, at least partially because it was thought that the Niger River, which opened into the Gulf of Guinea, might be a part of the Nile system. In the 1820s and 1830s, several expeditions entered West Africa, both from the north, following the caravan routes across the Sahara from the Mediterranean coast, and from the south, going overland from near the mouth of the Niger. The goal of these expeditions was the commercial city of Timbuctoo, in the middle of West Africa, which had not been seen by Europeans but was reputed to be awash in the wealth of Africa. When it was finally reached by the English army officer Gordon Laing in 1826, it proved to be a great disappointment, its trade disrupted by local disputes, especially the Islamic holy wars that marked West African history for much of the nineteenth century. These local conditions also made exploration difficult, and, with the final resolution of the route of the Niger in 1830 by Richard Lander, further exploration of West Africa slowed. The French made a slow and measured advance inland from Senegambia in the 1850s and 1860s, but it was only in the 1880s that exploration picked up again, with a push up the Congo River by the French explorer Savorgnan de Brazza, the *New York Herald Tribune* reporter H. M. Stanley, and the agents of King Leopold II of Belgium as he extended the territories claimed by the International Congo Association.

THE NEW EUROPEAN EMPIRES OF THE NINETEENTH CENTURY

Exploration led to political control only gradually. If the Seven Years' War had consolidated British power around the world, it was soon dealt a damaging defeat in the War of American Independence (1776-1783). Not only were the North American colonies that revolted against rule from London valuable possessions and trading partners with the Mother Country; but also the conflict between Britain and its colonies provided the opportunity for France to return to the battle against its long time enemy as an ally of the rebellious American colonies. French naval power made possible the decisive defeat of the British army at Yorktown in 1781, which made clear to the British that they would never be able to regain effective control of the colonies. The Treaty of Paris, which ended the war and acknowledged the independence of the United States of America, seemingly destroyed British imperial power a scant two decades after its apogee at the end of the Seven Years' War.

But if the independence of the United States undercut formal British control of North America, it did not mean that the advantages of empire could not be recouped in other ways. Over the next century, Britain in particular established a series of commercial links with the rest of the world which gave it important economic benefits even without the political ties that bound the thirteen North American colonies to England before 1783 and which had been the usual pattern of empire for several centuries. This "informal empire" or "imperialism of free trade" began at the end of the War of American Independence, with the provisions of the peace treaty that established commercial ties between Britain and the United States, saving the American market for British manufacturers. With the British navy able to bring its power to bear on any recalcitrant settlement in Africa and Asia, and British diplomats inventing a series of justifications for British intervention, this made Britain the most important and influential European power in those parts of the world that remained nominally independent of any empire.

The informal predominance of Great Britain in Asia and Africa did not go uncontested by other powers, which had their own merchants attempting to establish trade with the Pacific Islands, Asia, and the interior of Africa. For much of the nineteenth century, the continental powers had little inclination to pursue political control in the rest of the world, and were content to attempt to safeguard the interests of their own subjects through diplomacy. The absence of any force on the scene capable of standing up to the British navy, and the frequent desire to join with Britain to gain advantages for all European powers, meant that British claims usually stood for lack of a serious objection.

In the last third of the nineteenth century, however, this began to change. The exploration of the Nile Basin and West Africa, and the development of the International Congo Association, founded in 1878 by King Leopold II of Belgium and the explorer H. M. Stanley, brought Africa to the attention of Europeans, and a number of explorers made claims for their countries as they moved into the interior of the continent. The unification of Germany in 1871 had brought diplomatic predominance in continental Europe to that country and its forceful chancellor, Otto von Bismarck. In the 1870s Bismarck's Germany and a resurgent France refused to accept British claims to control over large parts of Africa, and in 1885 the growing number of colonial issues finally led to an international Congress, held in Berlin, to resolve issues about imperial expansion in Africa.

The Berlin Congress agreed upon the rules for European imperial expansion into Africa, and by 1905 virtually the entire continent had been divided up between the European powers. There were small Italian, Portuguese, and German possessions, but the principal empires were the British, which extended with only a few interruptions from the Cape of Good Hope to Egypt, and the French, which dominated West Africa and had only been prevented from extending eastward to the Indian Ocean by the British possessions in the Sudan.

EUROPEAN VERSIONS OF THE OTHER: ORIENTALISM, TRAVEL, RACE, FICTION, ETHNOGRAPHY

The exploration of the Pacific basin and consolidation of European empires in Africa meant that, by the nineteenth century and continuing into the twentieth, non-European influences had gained a major place in European civilization. In a variety of ways, Europeans dealt with the presence, in Europe, of non-Europeans and artifacts of the non-European world. We may view this influence as a process in which Europeans sifted through in different ways the ideas, peoples, and products of the non-European world. The result was that non-European influences became apparent in a variety of genres and forms of intellectual and cultural activity in Europe itself. The producers of these cultural works acted themselves as interpreters of the non-European world to

Europeans. They brought to this task not only their experience of the non-European world, but also their assumptions and forms of expression drawn from European culture. In a wide variety of ways, therefore, Europeans created versions of the non-European for European culture.

This European expansion took place at a time when ideas about race were assuming great importance in European culture. European perceptions of the peoples they met on Pacific islands, in North Africa, Asia, and sub-Saharan Africa were influenced by, and influenced in turn, the ways in which the category of race was discussed and interpreted in Europe itself. These views on race were to some extent concerned with distinctions within Europe itself, But these questions took on an added significance when applied to the relationship between European peoples and those coming under European control in the nineteenth century. The justifications for European power were found in a hardening of European perceptions of race, and by the second half of the century, these drew sharp distinctions between Europeans and others. The characteristics attributed to each race not only justified European dominance, but also led to theorizing about the relative merits of maintaining racial purity or allowing mixing of two races. Such questions about the relationships between different races also seemed to lead naturally to the scientific discoveries of the century. The claims of Charles Darwin and others about the evolution of the natural world were adopted as models for the development of races, and this provided a way of placing the different races of the world in a relationship to each other.

Before the end of the eighteenth century, the most significant part of the non-European world, the territory across the Mediterranean Sea and east of Arabia, was becoming the subject of a field of study, what became known as Orientalism. Beginning in the 1780s, European scholars undertook the study of Oriental languages and culture, a process encouraged by the pragmatic needs of governments that were having increased contact with those territories as the eastern Mediterranean became an area of great interest to European diplomats, and as India became an important British colony. These scholarly interests had the paradoxical effect of placing the cultural heritages of these regions in the control of Europeans, as political control by European powers became more important in the course of the nineteenth century; at the same time, however, Orientalist scholars acquired a respect for that cultural heritage, and became advocates with both imperial administrations and colonial subjects for the preservation and study of at least some version of North African, Middle Eastern, and Indian languages and literatures.

Orientalist scholarship also increased the awareness of those languages and literatures among Europeans. It was even more widely diffused, especially in the first half of the nineteenth century, by the frequency among European intellectuals of trips around the Mediterranean basin, through Greece, around the eastern Mediterranean and across North Africa to Algeria and Morocco, and then to northern Europe or England through Spain. These travels provided a wide range of experiences for the poets, novelists, and journalists who undertook them, as they observed and sometimes participated in the activities of the peoples who lived in these territories. These experiences also became the basis for a wide range of expressions once these men had returned to Europe. For better or for worse, and in ignorance or well informed about Oriental cultures, they produced a version of the East that was a mainstay of nineteenth-century European culture.

This was especially the case among artists, and a school of Orientalist art developed at the beginning of the nineteenth century, taking as its subject matter the observations of the peoples, religion, and institutions of North Africa and the Middle East. The shepherds and cultivators of the desert, the communities in which they lived, the mosques in which they prayed, and the courts from which their princes ruled were all portrayed on canvases hung in European art museums and collected by wealthy Europeans. As with other cultural forms, these paintings, portraying pastoral scenes as well as decadence and indulgence, provided Europeans who did not themselves visit the Orient with an image of the place and its residents.

European discussions of race were often based on speculation or on information drawn from Europe itself. But the nineteenth century saw an increase in the direct experience of the non-European world by Europeans. Improvements in communication and the increasing European presence around the world opened up opportunities for Europeans to visit parts of Africa, Asia, or the Pacific that had only recently become accessible at all to Europeans. One important way in which these voyages were communicated to other Europeans, and became part of the common fund of European knowledge about the rest of the world, was through the publication of accounts by travelers of their experiences abroad. Travelers had always attempted to profit from their journeys, and spread information, by publishing books recounting the wonders they had seen, and this practice continued into the nineteenth century. These accounts at the beginning of the century drew heavily on the scientific practice of published accounts of voyages of discovery, such as works by the Pacific explorers Cook and Bougainville or the more scientifically oriented journals of Joseph Banks and Charles Darwin. As the century went on, however, and less scientifically oriented travelers began to publish accounts, they assumed a distinctive form that separated them from other kinds of writing about the rest of the world. Certainly these travelers did not have an easy time of it, as they worked their way up the Nile, through West Africa, or across the provinces of China. Travel removed them from the familiar world, and placed them in isolation away from other Europeans and at times away from the power and protection of European governments. Travel writing not only collected, often in haphazard ways, information and insight about other parts of the world, but it also expressed both the decentering of the world for travelers, as they left Europe behind, and their view of how a European should be treated when traveling elsewhere in the world.

Although travel accounts purported to be accurate, both about the events of the trip and the observations made about non-Europeans and the territories visited, fiction made such claims only indirectly. There was no necessary requirement that novelists who wrote about other parts of the world had actually visited the places they described; this often turned out to be the case, as they were able to describe characters, plots, and locations that were believable for their readers. Naval and army officers, missionaries, idle travelers, and colonial officials all used their experiences as the basis for fictional representations of the rest of the world. The detail that these writers could utilize provided a powerful effect, legitimizing the version of the non-European world that they presented. Even the descriptions of faraway parts of the European empires presented in juvenile literature proved significant in giving Europeans a vision of the rest of the world.

But if some fiction explicitly utilized the world outside of Europe as the locale for its characters and plot, the effect of European contact with the rest of the world was even more pervasive. Non-European settings and characters were ways in which novelists could break European norms of behavior. Exotic places such as the islands of the Pacific, the heart of China, or the interior of Africa were spaces in which European authors could imagine their own triumph. As European power spread into other parts of the world, the fictional representations of European interactions with the inhabitants of those places became more directly concerned with the exercise of European power.

Racial theorists, novelists, and travel writers all made claims to some form of accuracy about the peoples of the rest of the world and their interpretations of the relationship between Europeans and those peoples. In the second half of the nineteenth century, an academic discipline developed whose principal subject matter was the customs and characteristics of non-Europeans. Initially known as ethnography, and then in the 1870s adopting the name of anthropology, this discipline claimed to be a "science of man." In its pretensions to scientific knowledge about what its practioners called "culture" and in its perceptions of the peoples who became its subject matter, anthropology was influenced by the general approach of Europeans to the rest of the world, the hierarchical ordering of civilizations, with Europe at the top, that marked Enlightenment and nineteenth-century theorizing.

Anthropology developed its own specific way of addressing these problems, for it was concerned with finding a way of definitively resolving the major questions that occupied nineteenth-century Europeans about the similarities and differences between themselves and the peoples they had been meeting as they explored and conquered the rest of the world. That conquest, by the turn of the twentieth century, opened the way for the development of a methodology, participant observer fieldwork, that anthropologists claimed gave them unique insights into other cultures. Protected by European colonial power in ways that earlier travelers could only dream about, twentieth-century anthropologists fine-tuned their ability to visit, observe, and interpret the cultures of others around the world. In many instances this produced catalogs of the habits and customs of other peoples; it also provided the material for further theorizing about the nature of man, a question with profound consequences for the ways in which Europeans viewed themselves and their relationship to the inhabitants of their colonies. By providing a body of seemingly solid evidence about other cultures, the discipline of anthropology interpreted the rest of the world for those who dismissed the claims of racial theorists, travelers, and novelists, and became, in the twentieth century, a significant force in the preparation and training of those Europeans who would go around the world to administer the European empires.

THE END OF THE EUROPEAN EMPIRES
AND THE CREATION OF THE POSTCOLONIAL WORLD

The ability of nineteenth-and early twentieth-century Europeans to travel in other parts of the world in relative safety, to live there if they chose to do so, and to seek their own fortunes in Asia, Africa, and the Pacific was a product of the extraordinary power that European states had come to exert over those areas of the world by the late nineteenth century. Even though different European powers approached their imperial stewardship in different ways, they all actively sought to develop some form of cooperative relationship with the peoples whom they governed. This was in fact a necessity, given the need for some cooperation by indigenous elites in maintaining European power in the colonies. Imperial powers therefore began, even if only in limited ways, to open their own educational systems and cultures to some of their colonial subjects. Indigenous elites became educated not only in European-type schools in their own countries, but also spent time in imperial capitals such as Paris and London, and attended the elite universities—Paris, London, Oxford, Cambridge—of the imperial powers.

This exposure of indigenous elites to European life familiarized them with European ideologies such as liberalism and nationalism. It created the incongruous situation in which they began to think of their own countries in European terms, as potential nation-states, and demanded for themselves the same political and civil rights that were becoming normal parts of European political life. The principles of equality and democracy that had been so explosive in nineteenth-century Europe were to prove equally so in the European colonies. At the turn of the century, Great Britain moved to grant greater autonomy to its colonies in which white settlers predominated, beginning the process that would turn South Africa, Australia, New Zealand, and Canada into members of the Commonwealth of Nations. At the same time, movements seeking greater autonomy within the British Empire were organized in India.

Such efforts initially had little impact. Colonial troops were brought to Europe during the First World War and fought for the security of Britain, France, Germany, or Italy. Although the peace settlement after the war led to some reshuffling of imperial possessions, as Germany's colonies became "protectorates" of Great Britain, and the financial consequences of the war shifted economic dominance of the developed world into the hands of the United States, the European dominance of the rest of the world seemed unchanged. The voices of Ho Chi Minh calling for greater autonomy of Indochina within the French empire or Mohandas Gandhi seeking the same for India in the British empire remained relatively unheard by colonial administrators, European political leaders, or the European public, who had grown up with the empires and assumed they would remain a part of their world.

The effect of the Second World War on European empires, however, proved catastrophic. France was quickly defeated by Germany in 1940, and its own internal divisions between those who collaborated with the German occupier and those who followed Charles de Gaulle in resistance were mirrored in the colonies. Britain was reduced to a small island struggling to maintain its own security against the apparently overwhelming power of Germany, and its fleet, the guarantor of its world power, proved unable to resist the naval advances of Japan in the Pacific in the early years of the war. Everywhere colonial subjects viewed the spectacle of their imperial masters in disarray, fighting among themselves, and at times replaced by non-Europeans. The war therefore undercut the aura of European imperial power. The wartime destruction of the European infrastructure and economy also seriously damaged the ability of the European imperial powers to find the resources to maintain their empires.

The Second World War also changed the structure of diplomacy in ways that undercut the European empires. Although the European powers, whether defeated like Germany and Italy, or victorious like Great Britain and France, were faced with the task of postwar reconstruction, two new powers, peripheral to Europe, began to assume preeminence in world diplomacy. The United States of America had intervened in Europe in 1941 as in 1917, but this time it remained in Europe, first as an occupying power and then as leader of an alliance that drew together most of Western Europe. The Soviet Union also emerged from the war and the postwar settlement as a major world power, controlling by the end of the 1940s a range of satellites in Eastern Europe and exerting influence in other countries around the world through its position as the unchallenged leader of the world communist movement. While facing each other during the Cold

War, both these powers were adamantly opposed to the imperial pretensions of the European powers. The major imperial powers, Great Britain and France, found little sympathy from their American ally for their attempts to reestablish and maintain control in
their colonies, a point made in the diplomacy surrounding the French war in Algeria
(1954-1962) and the French and British intervention in Suez in 1956. Smaller imperial
countries, such as Belgium and Portugal, found it even more difficult to maintain their
colonies. The Soviet Union, meanwhile, used its own resources to provide materiel and
diplomatic support for movements for independence throughout the empires, and Soviet funds and weapons made possible the military attempts by colonies to gain independence that marked the 1950s and early 1960s.

With remarkable rapidity, the European colonial empires dissolved in the two
decades after the end of World War II. France proved unable to defeat the Viet Minh
in Vietnam in Southeast Asia. It negotiated a withdrawal in 1954, only to be replaced
by the United States, which would attempt to maintain a government of its own choos-
ing until 1973. Having ended its own Indochinese war, France soon found itself fighting again in Algeria in North Africa. With grants of independence to Tunisia and
Morocco in 1956, and the victory of the Algerians in 1962, the French Empire came to
an end. Great Britain was facing similar challenges, being forced to grant independence to India in 1947, followed by similar grants to a number of Asian and African
colonies over the next decade. The early 1960s saw the final end of the British Empire, as agreements were reached with virtually all the remaining colonies to grant
them independence. By the time Portugal finally relinquished its African colonies in
the 1970s, the great empires of the previous century not only had ended, but also
seemed anachronistic to many.

Decolonization did not mean a severing of all ties between Europe and its former
colonies, but rather a reconstruction of these ties in ways that recognized the political independence of the colonies while maintaining, or even deepening, the economic links
between them. Beginning before the movement for independence of colonies, the
world economy had been becoming more and more global, with trade expanding to
reach more frequently over the boundaries of older trade regions. Steamships and railroads had begun this process in the late nineteenth century, and by the period between
the wars there were significant trade and financial links between most parts of the world.
The collapse of the European empires after 1945 did not end these economic structures, only the political systems that had eased their implementation.

The reconstruction of world economic patterns in the second half of the twentieth century, therefore, was reminiscent of patterns before the formalization of empire
in the nineteenth century. The economies of most former colonies were built around
the production of commodities for export to the imperial center. Many of the newly
independent states of Asia and Africa therefore found themselves needing to sell the
products of their own economies to the developed world in order to earn foreign exchange and were dependent on European powers for scientific, technical, and administrative expertise. In the eyes of some leaders of these new nations, this situation
indicated that political independence was only a partial solution to their problems
and that world leaders needed to recognize the continued economic dominance of
the former colonies by the former imperial powers, and take steps to change this situation as well.

Independence had, however, given the former colonies the possibility of developing and implementing diplomatic strategies that could counter this economic de-

pendence. In some instances, such as the Organization of Petroleum Exporting Countries (OPEC), which was able to control much of the supply of oil to the developed world, they were temporarily successful in gaining control of their resources and raising prices on world markets. But as the U.S.–led intervention in Kuwait in 1990 indicated, the developed world was still able to use its military and diplomatic power to maintain some form of control over resources its own economies required.

Military intervention remained rare, however, and there was some sympathy in the developed countries for the economic needs of the former colonies after 1945, as well as recognition of the dependence of the developed world on predictable supplies of commodities such as oil from parts of the less-developed world. This resulted in the formation of international organizations devoted to stabilizing the international economy and providing assistance to the former colonies as they attempted to diversify their own economies. Such organizations, while in some instances providing badly needed assistance, have also increased the interdependence of the global economy, making it more and more difficult for any one nation to maintain isolation from that global economy. The global economic recession of the 1970s deepened this dependency by forcing heavier borrowing and increasing the links between the economies of the former colonies and the financial institutions of the developed world. As the century came to an end, therefore, leaders of both developed and less-developed countries still sought to find ways of reducing economic differences between their countries without disrupting the economic growth that all countries in the world depended on for political and social stability.

Economic relationships were not the only kind that continued between the European powers and their former colonies after independence. The experience of empire had profoundly affected both the colonies and the imperial powers, and after independence the interconnections of colonial and imperial cultures continued. In many instances imperial powers attempted to maintain special relationships with their former colonies, as the British Commonwealth and the French Community. European universities continued to have large student contingents from the former colonies. European capitals were themselves marked by the influence of empire, as the prevalence of Indian restaurants in London, Vietnamese restaurants in Paris, and Indonesian restaurants in Amsterdam indicated the continued influence of now-dissolved empires.

The economic prosperity of postwar Western Europe and the continuation of rights of emigration between the former colonies and the European metropoles also contributed to the development of another highly significant form of continued contact, the migration of non-Europeans to Europe, introducing a new awareness of ethnic difference and diversity into West European nations. West Germany encouraged an influx of Turkish immigrants, called *gastarbeiter* (guest workers), in the 1950s and 1960s to fill the labor shortage it faced during the Economic Miracle of that era and, although the immigration ended with the recession of the 1970s, a significant number of Turkish citizens and their German-born children remained. Great Britain and France also received an influx of migrants, encouraged both by prospects for employment in Europe and also by provisions of the independence agreements that gave them immigration rights. Especially in the industrial regions and cities of Western Europe, significant numbers of people of Caribbean, Pacific, Asian, and African descent collected, facing not only poverty and poor housing conditions, but also discrimination and public rhetoric that urged them to "return home" even though increasingly they had been born in Europe.

The presence of a significant number of people of non-European descent became, in the 1980s and 1990s, one of the most important political and cultural issues in Europe. Right-wing politicians found that attacking immigration appealed to many voters, especially those suffering through the European transition from an industrial economy to one based on high technology. European ideas about race and nationality made it difficult for some Europeans to accept the citizenship of immigrants or their children. Religious differences, especially between a supposedly Christian or secularized Europe and Islamic immigrants, raised seemingly impossible barriers to acceptance, even though European nations had their own histories of religious differences.

The experience of colonialism remained important for non-Europeans as well, a point increasingly made in the 1980s by artists, novelists, and filmmakers who took as their subject matter the contact between Europe and its former colonies. In many instances individuals who experienced migration and discrimination in Europe were working out the cultural implications of the dramatically increased contact between Europeans and non-Europeans. The centuries of contact, conquest, and negotiation between Europe and other parts of the world had, by the end of the twentieth century, produced a world in which it was impossible to avoid the influence of non-Europeans on Europe, and of Europe on the rest of the world.

THEMATIC ISSUES IN THE STUDY OF EUROPEAN CONTACT WITH THE WORLD

The documents presented in this volume describe specific instances of the relationship between Europeans and the peoples who lived in other parts of the world. They are the evidence from which historians' accounts of this relationship are built. Understanding what they have to say is the basic purpose of reading them critically. Such a reading involves understanding the specific context, in time and place, in which the document was created, and the perspectives and biases of the author. The introductions to each document are intended to provide the information needed for this understanding. They will tell you who the author of the document was (whether an individual or an institution), when the document was created, and what the circumstances were that led to its creation. This information should be kept in mind as you read and discuss the document. The documents themselves express a number of different kinds of information about the relationship between Europeans and the rest of the world. Drawing the full meaning from them therefore means examining them in terms of these themes.

As Europeans and non-Europeans met each other, they noticed different *physical characteristics* about each other and about the places in which they met. These characteristics helped to define the similarities and the differences between the participants in contact, and over time became important aspects of the ongoing interactions between Europeans and non-Europeans. Skin color, facial features, and stature helped these groups distinguish themselves from each other. Similarly, the ships on which Europeans arrived, the military camps and churches that they established, or the trading caravans in which they moved became areas in which Europeans attempted to control the extent and nature of the transactions between themselves and the indigenous peoples of the lands they visited. Rivers, forests, sacred places, and native villages, on the other hand, were places in which these relations might be reversed, and Europeans would become dependent on those peoples for assistance and protection. How these characteristics were defined, therefore, is a significant part of the process of cultural contact.

The documents presented here virtually always express in some way the relationships of *power* between Europe and the rest of the world. This might be in terms of the obvious diplomatic or institutional aspects of politics. But contact between Europeans and non-Europeans involved assumptions each party made about the their ability to influence each other, a less formal but still important aspect of power. The documents also describe the agency of the European and that of the non-European, another aspect of a political relationship. Describing Europeans as capable of great feats, while non-Europeans are either invisible or passive, is a further way of expressing these relationships.

The documents also describe *economic relationships* between Europeans and non-Europeans. Even though Europeans thought about and traveled to other parts of the world for a wide range of reasons, they often saw the non-European world in economic terms, whether as a potential market for European goods, as a source of raw materials for European industry, as a potential destination for emigration from Europe, or as a source of commodities that Europeans desired for their own consumption. When Europeans traveled to other parts of the world, they purchased or simply seized goods, services, and even people for their own use. Indigenous peoples often did the same, as complaints by ship captains about thefts by Pacific islanders and the need many explorers felt to give gifts to the peoples they met indicate. Such transactions could be crucial to the way the relationship between non-Europeans and Europeans developed, and paying attention to them is an important part of understanding these documents.

The Europeans who traveled around the world, and the people they met as they did so, rarely lived in completely egalitarian worlds. Ship crews and land expeditions were made up of individuals who had different social positions at home, and these continued in the course of the travels. Non-European societies were also differentiated in specific ways. Contrasts in *social status* among both Europeans and non-Europeans were expressed at times in the expectations that individuals had of others, both in their own parties and from others, and in the demands they made of others. Participants in the interactions described in these documents thus revealed their own assumptions about how societies were supposed to work, and these also helped determine the outcome of the interaction between Europeans and non-Europeans, as each side interpreted the actions and demands of the other in terms of their own understanding of social structure.

The interactions between Europeans and non-Europeans were also affected by assumptions about *religion* and *spirituality*. Europeans, whether missionaries or not, were convinced that their faith, Christianity, was the true religion, although differences between Protestant denominations and Catholicism often surfaced in Africa and Asia. These beliefs justified the enforced conversion of non-Europeans and their political and economic subjugation to European powers, as well as the condemnation of indigenous religious practices. These religions, however, provided a basis for indigenous peoples to resist European incursions, a resistance also encouraged by the conflicts between European missionaries of different denominations and the inability of European religions to fulfill the promises made by their missionaries.

The documents included here also express assumptions about *gender*. In both European and non-European societies, men and women had differing roles, privileges, and powers, to a large extent culturally constructed. These are reflected in the interactions between the two groups and in the ways these documents describe those interactions. That many of these documents were written by men is therefore an important aspect. The rare women who traveled outside of Europe, or who were able to leave behind a record of their reactions to the Europeans who visited their peoples, are important witnesses to the process of interaction and brought their own perspective, determined to some extent by their sex, to the process. But even if the documents do not explicitly discuss women, and even if they were not written by women, they do often describe the actions by men and women that were considered appropriate, and the ways in which relationships between the sexes were supposed to be carried out. The different ways in which men and women are portrayed, the different kinds of activities they are allowed to do, and the reactions of observers to these actions are all therefore indicators of the way in which gender operates in these encounters. Gender also acted as a convenient and powerful metaphor by which Europeans and non-Europeans alike could express their own interpretation of their interactions through intimations of the masculinity or femininity of participants in the encounter and their power or lack of power. Assumptions about gender therefore provided a way in which Europeans and non-Europeans alike could describe their version of the relationship.

Finally, the documents in this volume speak about the interaction of at least two, and sometimes more, *cultures* or ways of describing and viewing the world. These could be as fundamental as language, but there was more to contacts between Europeans and non-Europeans than just trying to learn each other's languages. Europeans, whether they traveled to other parts of the world or simply speculated about them, did so using a set of assumptions, drawn from European culture, about human beings and about how they were supposed to act. The non-Europeans who swam out to meet European ships, or who were forced onto European ships to cross the Middle Passage, or who provided and carried supplies for European explorers, or who dealt with colonial administrations, also had their own, different, assumptions that guided them in these matters. In the descriptions of interaction that are given in these documents, these differing assumptions played out, as each party attempted to communicate their own thoughts and feelings about what was going on, and the other side struggled to understand them. Although these different cultures were not closed entities—Europeans learned Arabic and Swahili, and Polynesians learned English—the contacts described here reflect aspects of an ongoing process by which misunderstandings occurred because of cultural differences, and different cultures were subtly altered because of the process of contact with other cultures.

James R. Lehning
University of Utah

14

The Plantation Complex and the Slave Trade
1650–1800

TEXTS

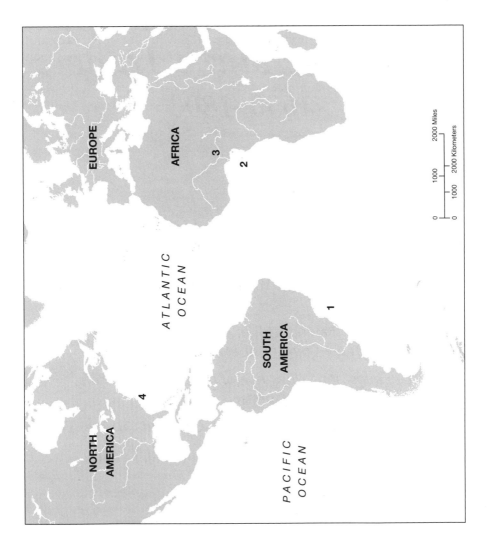

The discovery of the New World began a process that involved Europeans in important contacts with non-Europeans. Beginning almost as soon as Columbus returned to Spain, European powers established colonies throughout the Americas that provided an outlet for a wide variety of free migrants from Europe. This process of settlement meant, between 1500 and 1820, the movement of millions of people across the Atlantic. About 4 million of these came from European countries, as hidalgos, religious minorities, landless farmers, and impecunious artisans found their ways from the seacoasts of Europe across the ocean, sometimes as members of military expeditions founding settlements, at times as indentured servants bound to serve a master for several years to pay for their passage. Their arrival in the New World created constant contact between Europeans and the indigenous peoples of America. Virtually from the beginnings of European settlement, the colonists depended on Native Americans for food, advice about agriculture, and knowledge about rivers, streams, and paths through the forests of the continent. The increasing number of Europeans living in the New World opened the way for the creation of a series of economic, social, demographic, and political linkages across the Atlantic Ocean. The products of the North American and South American colonies found markets in Europe and in other colonies, and a set of trade relations developed across the Atlantic basin as Europeans increased their exploitation of the wealth of the New World. [1]

The inability of native populations or free migrants from Europe to provide an adequate labor supply for these plantations led to another form of exploitation, the import of slaves from Africa. The slave trade [2, 3, 4, 5] completed the formation of a plantation complex that involved the New World, Europe, and Africa in an intricate set of economic relationships, drawing timber, furs, and food from North America and Europe; slaves from Africa; and sugar, rum, indigo, coffee and cotton from the slave plantations of the New World tropics. Geographically, it ran from the southern part of Brazil to the Mason-Dixon line in North America. Between the fifteenth century and the nineteenth, around 10 million slaves were brought across the Atlantic to provide the labor for this complex. Several more million Africans did not survive the trip across the infamous Middle Passage, dying en route.

The slave trade to the New World was therefore not only an aspect of European contact with the Western Hemisphere, but also one of the most significant causes of contact between Europeans and Africans in the years between 1500 and 1800. Portuguese and Spanish slavers moved slaves from Senegambia, Upper Guinea, and Angola to the Caribbean Islands, Brazil, Mexico, and Peru in a trade that began in the early sixteenth century and peaked in the seventeenth century. A larger cycle began in the seventeenth century with the expansion of trade between Europe and the Americas. This cycle principally involved English, Dutch, French, and Brazilian slave traders carrying their human cargoes from western Africa (the Bight of Benin, Angola, the Bight of Biafra, and the Gold Coast) to British and French territories in the Caribbean, Bahia, Brazil, and British North America. This cycle peaked in the eighteenth century. The slave trade was abolished by Great Britain and the United States in 1808, although the end of sales and emancipation of existing slaves did not take place until the middle of the nineteenth century. By this time, the plantation complex itself was in decline, undercut by the economic and social effects of industrialization, as well as the moral reservations of a growing number of Europeans and Americans about the slave trade and slavery itself.

1. WILLIAM DAMPIER, *A VOYAGE TO NEW-HOLLAND IN THE YEAR 1699*

Captain William Dampier (1651–1715) circumnavigated the globe three times, acquiring a reputation not only as a navigator but also as a hydrographer, naturalist, author, and even pirate. Dampier went to sea as a teenager, sailing on merchant ships to Newfoundland and Java before serving in the British Navy in a war with the Dutch in the 1670s. By the end of the 1670s, he had joined in the activities of the casual buccaneers of the Caribbean. In the late 1680s, he traveled on a series of ships that took him from the coast of Sierra Leone across the Pacific, to India, and around the Cape of Good Hope to England, a voyage recounted in his *A New Voyage Round the World* published in 1697.

In 1699, he commanded the *Roebuck* on a voyage to investigate New Holland, Terra Australis, and New Guinea. Dampier's *Voyage to New Holland* (1702) recounted the events of this voyage, including his stop on his way to the Pacific at Bahia in the Portuguese colony of Brazil. His account of the port describes the comings and goings of the ships that made up the sinews of the network of trade in goods and humans that bound North and South America across the Atlantic with Africa and Europe. It also shows the importance of African slavery in the life of this colonial settlement. Dampier's third major voyage was as captain of a privateer that left England in 1703, raided the South American coast, then proceeded across the Pacific to Java, where he was seized by Dutch authorities and only managed to return to England in 1707. He made one more voyage to the New World, as pilot and advisor of a privateering expedition that sailed in 1708.

Captain Dampier's Voyages

A great many Merchants always reside at Bahia; for 'tis a Place of great Trade: I found here above 30 great Ships from Europe, with 2 of the King of Portugal's Ships of War for their Convoy; beside 2 Ships that traded to Africa only, either to Angola, Gamba, or other

Places on the Coast of Guinea; and Abundance of small Craft, that only run to and fro on this Coast, carrying Commodities from one Part of Brazil to another.

The Merchants that live here are said to be rich, and to have many Negro-Slaves in their Houses, both of Man and Women. Themselves are chiefly Portugueze, Foreigners having but little Commerce with them; yet here was one Mr. Cock an English Merchant, a very civil Gentleman and of good Repute. He had a Patent to be our English Consul, but did not Care to take upon him any publick Character, because English Ships seldom come hither, here having been none in 11 or 12 Years before this Time. Here was also a Dane, and a French Merchant or two; but all have their Effects transported to and from Europe in Portugueze Ships, none of any other Nation being admitted to trade hither. There is a Custom-house by the Sea-side, where all Goods imported or exported are entered. And to prevent Abuses there are 5 or 6 Boats that take their Turns to row about the Harbour, searching any Boats they suspect to be running of Goods.

The chief Commodities that the European Ships bring hither, are Linnen-Cloaths, both coarse and fine; some Woollens also, as Bays, Searges, Perpetuana's, &c. Hats, Stockings, both of Silk and Thread, Bisket-bread, Wheatflower, Wine (chiefly Port) Oil-Olive, Butter, Cheese, &c. and Salt-beef and Pork would there also be good Commodities. They bring hither also Iron, and all Sorts of Iron-Tools; Pewter-Vessels of all Sorts, as Dishes, Plates, Spoons, &c. Looking-glass, Beads, and other Toys; and the Ships that touch at St. Jago bring thence, as I said, Cotton-Cloath, which is afterwards sent to Angola.

The European Ships carry from hence Sugar, Tobacco, either in Roll or Snuff, never in Leaf, that I know of: These are the Staple Commodities. Besides which, here are Dye-woods, as Fustick, &c., with Woods for other Uses, as speckled Wood, Brazil, &c. They also carry home raw Hides, Tallow, Train-oil of Whales, &c. Here are also kept tame Monkeys, Parrots, Parrakites, &c. which the Seamen carry home.

The Sugar of this Country is much better than that which we bring home from our Plantations: For all the Sugar that is made here is clay'd, which makes it whiter and finer than our Muscovada, as we call our unrefin'd Sugar. Our Planters seldom refine any with Clay, unless sometimes a little to send Home as Presents for their Friends in England. Their way of doing it is by taking some of the whitest Clay and mixing it with Water, till 'tis like Cream. With this they fill up the Pans of Sugar, that are sunk 2 or 3 Inches below the Brim by the draining of the Molasses out of it: First scraping off the thin hard Crust of the Sugar that lies at the Top, and would hinder the Water of the Clay from soaking through the Sugar of the Pan. The refining is made by this Percolation. For 10 or 12 Days Time that the clayish Liquor lies soaking down the Pan, the white Water whitens the Sugar as it passes thro' it; and the gross Body of the Clay its self grows hard on the Top, and may be taken off at Pleasure; when scraping off with a Knife the very upper-part of the sugar, which will be a little sullied, that which is underneath will be white almost to the Bottom: And such as is called Brazil Sugar is thus whitened. When I was here this Sugar was sold for 50s. per 100 lb. And the Bottoms of the Pots, which is very coarse Sugar, for about 20s. per 100 lb. both Sorts being then scarce; for here was not enough to lade the Ships, and therefore some of them were to lye here till the next Season.

The European Ships commonly arrive here in February or March, and they have generally quick Passages; finding at that Time of the Year brisk Gales to bring them to the Line, little Trouble, then, in crossing it, and brisk E. N. E. Winds afterwards to bring them hither. They commonly return from hence about the latter End of May, or in June. 'Twas said when I was here that the Ships would sail hence the 20th Day of May; and therefore they were all very busy, some in taking in their Goods, others in careening and making themselves ready. The Ships that come hither usually careen at their first coming; here being a Hulk belonging to the King for that Purpose. This Hulk is under the Charge of the Superintendent I spoke of, who has a certain Sum of Money for every Ship that careens by her. He also provides Firing and other Necessaries for that Purpose: And the Ships do commonly hire of the Merchants here each 2 Cables to moor by all the Time they lye here, and so save their own Hempen Cables; for these are made of a Sort of Hair, that grows on a certain Kind of Trees, hanging down from the Top of their Bodies, and is very like the black Coyre in the East-Indies, if not the same. These Cables are strong and lasting: And so much for the European Ships.

The Ships that use the Guinea-Trade are small Vessels in comparison of the former. They carry out from hence Rum, Sugar, the Cotton-Cloaths of St. Jago, Beads, &c. and bring in Return, Gold, Ivory, and Slaves; making very good Returns.

The small Craft that belong to this Town are chiefly imployed in carrying European Goods from Bahia, the Center of the Brasilian Trade, to the other Places on this Coast; bringing back hither Sugar, Tobacco, &c. They are sailed chiefly with Negro-Slaves; and about Christmas these are mostly imployed in Whale-killing; For about that Time of the Year a Sort of Whales, as they call them, are very thick on this Coast. They come in also into the Harbours and inland Lakes, where the Seamen go out and kill them. The Fat of them is boiled to Oil; the Lean is eaten by the Slaves and poor People: And I was told by one that had frequently eaten of it, that the Flesh was very sweet and wholesome. These are said to be but small Whales; yet here are so many, and so easily killed, that they get a great deal of Money by it. Those that strike them buy their Licence for it of the King: And I was inform'd that he receives 30000 Dollars per Annum for this Fishery. All the small Vessels that use this Coasting Traffick are built here; and so are some Men of War also for the King's Service. There was one a building when I was here, a Ship of 40 or 50 Guns: And the Timber of this Country is very good and proper for this Purpose. I was told it was very strong, and more durable than any we have in Europe; and they have enough of it. As for their Ships that use the European Trade, some of them that I saw there were English built, taken from us by the French, during the late War, and sold by them to the Portugueze.

Besides Merchants and others that trade by Sea from this Port, here are other pretty wealthy Men, and several Artificers and Trades-men of most Sorts, who by Labour and Industry maintain themselves very well; especially such as can arrive at the Purchase of a Negro-Slave or two. And indeed, excepting people of the lowest Degree of all, here are scarce any but what keep Slaves in their Houses. The richer Sort, besides the Slaves of both Sexes whom they keep for servile Uses in their Houses, have Men Slaves who wait on them aboard, for State; either running by their Horse-sides when they ride out, or to carry them to and fro on their Shoulders in the Town when they make short Visits near Home. Every Gentleman or Merchant is provided with Things necessary for this Sort of Carriage. The main Thing is a pretty large Cotton Hammock of the West-India Fashion, but mostly dyed blue, with large Fringes of the same, hanging down on each Side. This is carried on the Negro's Shoulders by the help of a Bambo about 12 or 14 Foot long, to which the Hammock is hung; and a Covering comes over the Pole, hanging down on each Side like a Curtain: So that the Person so carry'd cannot be seen unless he pleases; but may either lye down, having pillows for his Head; or may sit up by being a little supported with these Pillows, and by letting both his Legs hang out over one side of the Hammock. When he hath a Mind to be seen he puts by his Curtain, and salutes every one of his Acquaintance whom he meets in the Streets; for they take a Piece of Pride in greeting one another from their Hammocks, and will hold long Conferences thus in the Street: But then their 2 Slaves who carry the Hammock have each a strong well-made Staff, with a fine Iron Fork at the upper End, and a sharp Iron below, like the Rest for a Musket, which they stick fast in the Ground, and let the Pole or Bambo of the Hammock rest upon them, till their Master's Business or the Complement is over. There is scarce a Man of any Fashion, especially a Woman, will pass the Streets but so carried in a Hammock. The Chief Mechanick Traders here, are Smiths, Hatters, Shoemakers, Tanners, Sawyers, Carpenters, Coopers, &c. Here are also Taylors, Butchers, &c. which last kill the Bullocks very dexterously, sticking them at one Blow with a sharp-pointed Knife in the Nape of the Neck, having first drawn them close to a Rail; but they dress them very slovenly. It being Lent when I came hither, there was no buying any Flesh till Easter-Eve, when a great Number of Bullocks were kill'd at once in the Slaughter-houses within the Town, Men, Women and Children flocking thither with Greater Joy to buy, and a Multitude of Dogs, almost starv'd, following them; for whom the Meat seem'd fittest, it was so lean. All these Trades-men buy Negroes, and train them up to their several Employments, which is a great Help to them; and they having so frequent Trade to Angola, and other Parts of Guinea, they have a constant Supply of Blacks both for their Plantations and Town. These Slaves are very useful in this Place for Carriage, as Porters; for as here is a great Trade by Sea, and the Landing-place is at the Foot of a Hill, too steep for drawing with Carts, so there is great need of Slaves to carry Goods up into the Town, especially for the inferiour Sort: But the Merchants have also the Convenience of a great Crane that goes with Ropes or Pullies, one End of which goes up while the other goes down. The House in which this Crane is, stands on the Brow of the Hill towards the Sea, hanging over the Precipice; and there are Planks set shelving against the Bank from thence to the Bottom, against which the Goods lean or slide as they are hoisted up or let down. The Negro-Slaves in this Town are so numerous, that they make up the greatest Part or Bulk of the Inhabitants: Every House, as I said, having some, both Men and Women, of them. Many of the Portugueze, who are Batchelors, keep of these black Women for Misses, tho' they know the Danger they are in of being poyson'd by them, if ever they give them any Occasion of Jealousy. A Gentleman of my Acquaintance, who had been familiar with his Cook-maid, lay under some such Apprehensions from her when I was there. These Slaves also of either Sex will easily be engaged to do any Sort of Mischief; even to Murder, if they are hired to do it, especially in the Night; for which Reason, I kept my Men on board as much as I could; for one of the French King's Ships being here, had several Men murther'd by them in the Night, as I was credibly inform'd.

2. ALEXANDER FALCONBRIDGE, *AN ACCOUNT OF THE SLAVE TRADE ON THE COAST OF AFRICA*

Alexander Falconbridge (?–1792) was a British surgeon who served on a number of slave ships during the 1780s on voyages from Bonny, Old and New Clabar, and Angola on the African coast to the West Indies. His experiences on these voyages formed the basis for this pamphlet, published in 1788. Although his position as surgeon on slavers allowed him to be critical of the slave trade, Falconbridge nonetheless was a participant in it, a position that affected his evaluation. His description is therefore different from that in the following selection by Olaudah Equiano.

An Account of the Slave Trade on the Coast of Africa

After permission has been obtained for *breaking trade,* as it is termed; the captains go ashore, from time to time, to examine the negroes that are exposed to sale, and to make their purchases. The unhappy wretches thus disposed of, are bought by the black traders at fairs, which are held for that purpose, at the distance of upwards of two hundred miles from the sea coast; and these fairs are said to be supplied from an interior part of the country. Many negroes, upon being questioned relative to the places of their nativity have asserted, that they have travelled during the revolution of several moons, (their usual method of calculating time) before they have reached the places where they were purchased by the black traders. At these fairs, which are held at uncertain periods, but generally every six weeks, several thousands are frequently exposed to sale, who had been collected from all parts of the country for a very considerable distance round. While I was upon the coast, during one of the voyages I made, the black traders brought down, in different canoes, from twelve to fifteen hundred negroes, which had been purchased at one fair. They consisted chiefly of men and boys, the women seldom exceeding a third of the whole number. From forty to two hundred negroes are generally purchased at a time by the black traders, according to the opulence of the buyer; and consist of those of all ages, from a month, to sixty years and upwards. Scarce any age or situation is deemed an exception, the price being proportionable. Women sometimes form a part of them, who happen to be so far advanced in their pregnancy, as to be delivered during their journey from the fairs to the coast; and I have frequently seen instances of deliveries on board ship. The slaves purchased at these fairs are only for the supply of the markets at Bonny, and Old and New Calabar.

There is great reason to believe, that most of the negroes shipped off from the coast of Africa, are *kidnapped.* But the extreme care taken by the black traders to prevent the Europeans from gaining any intelligence of their modes of proceeding; the great distance inland from whence the negroes are brought, and our ignorance of their language, (with which, very frequently, the black traders themselves are equally unacquainted) prevent our obtaining such information on this head as we could with. I have, however, by means of occasional inquiries, made through interpreters, procured some intelligence relative to the point, and such, as I think, puts the matter beyond a doubt.

From these I shall select the following striking instances:—While I was in employ on board one of the slave ships, a negroe informed me, that being one evening invited to drink with some of the black traders, upon his going away, they attempted to seize him. As he was very active, he evaded their design, and got out of their hands. He was however prevented from effecting his escape by a large dog, which laid hold of him, and compelled him to submit. These creatures are kept by many of the traders for that purpose; and being trained to the inhuman sport, they appear to be much pleased with it.

I was likewise told by a negroe woman, that as she was on her return home, one evening, from some neighbours, to whom she had been making a visit by invitation, she was kidnapped; and, notwithstanding she was big with child, sold for a slave. This transaction happened a considerable way up the country, and she had passed through the hands of several purchasers before she reached the ship. A man and his son, according to their own information, were seized by professed kidnappers, while they were planting yams, and sold for slaves. This likewise happened in the interior parts of the country, and later passing through several hands, they were purchased for the ship to which I belonged.

It frequently happens, that those who kidnap others, are themselves, in their turns, seized and sold. A negro in the West-Indies informed me, that after having been employed in kidnapping others, he had experienced this reverse. And he assured me, that it was a common incident among his countrymen.

Continual enmity is thus fostered among the negroes of Africa, and all social intercourse between them destroyed; which most assuredly would not be the case, had they not these opportunities of finding a ready sale for each other.

During my stay on the coast of Africa, I was an eye-witness of the following transaction:—A black trader invited a negroe, who resided a little way up the country, to come and see him. After the entertainment was over, the trader proposed to his guest, to treat him with a sight of one of the ships lying in the river. The unsuspicious countryman readily consented, and accompanied the trader in a canoe to the side of the ship, which he viewed with pleasure and astonishment. While he was thus employed, some black traders on board, who appeared to be in the secret, leaped into the canoe, seized the unfortunate man, and dragging him into the ship, immediately sold him.

Previous to my being in this employ, I entertained a belief, as many others have done, that the kings and principal men *breed* negroes for sale, as we do cattle. During the different time I was in the country, I took no little pains to satisfy myself in this particular; but notwithstanding I made many inquiries, I was not able to obtain the least intelligence of this being the case, which it is more than probable I should have done, had such a practice prevailed. All the information I could procure, confirms me in the belief, that to *kidnapping*, and to crimes, (and many of these fabricated as a pretext) the slave trade owes its chief support.

As soon as the wretched Africans, purchased at the fairs, fall into the hands of the black traders, they experience an earnest of those dreadful sufferings which they are doomed in future to undergo. And there is not the least room to doubt, but that even before they can reach the fairs, great numbers perish from cruel usage, want of food, travelling through inhospitable deserts, &c. They are brought from the places where they are purchased to Bonny, &c. in canoes; at the bottom of which they lie, having their hands tied with a kind of willow twigs, and a strict watch is kept over them. Their usage in other respects, during the time of the passage, which generally lasts several days, is equally cruel. Their allowance of food is so scanty, that it is barely sufficient to support nature. They are, besides, much exposed to the violent rains which frequently fall here, being covered only with mats that afford but a slight defence; and as there is usually water at the bottom of the canoes, from their leaking, they are scarcely every dry.

Nor do these unhappy beings, after they become the property of the Europeans (from whom, as a more civilized people, more humanity might naturally be expected) find their situation in the least amended. Their treatment is no less rigorous. The men negroes, on being brought aboard the ship, are immediately fastened together, two and two, by hand-cuffs on their wrists, and by irons rivetted on their legs. They are then sent down between the decks, and placed in an apartment partitioned off for that purpose. The women likewise are placed in a separate apartment between decks, but without being ironed. And an adjoining room, on the same deck, is besides appointed for the boys. Thus are they all placed in different apartments.

But at the same time, they are frequently stowed so close, as to admit of no other posture than lying on their sides. Neither will the height between decks, unless directly under the grating, permit them the indulgence of an erect posture; especially where there are platforms, which is generally the case. These platforms are a kind of shelf, about eight or nine feet in breadth, extending from the side of the ship towards the centre. They are placed nearly midway between the decks, at the distance of two or three feet from each deck. Upon these the negroes are stowed in the same manner as they are on the deck underneath.

3. THE INTERESTING NARRATIVE OF THE LIFE OF OLAUDAH EQUIANO, WRITTEN BY HIMSELF

Olaudah Equiano (1745–1797) was born a member of the Nigerian Ibo tribe in Africa. When he was eleven years old, he was kidnapped by slave traders. Sold as a slave, he was shipped across the Middle Passage to plantations in the West Indies and Virginia. After gaining his freedom in 1766, Equiano lived in England; he died there in 1797. This account of his life was written in 1788 as a part of a protest campaign in England against the slave trade. His description of his abduction and passage to the Western Hemisphere conveys the brutality and disorientation of the slave trade as few other descriptions could.

The Life of Olaudah Equiano

I hope the reader will not think I have trespassed on his patience in introducing myself to him with some account of the manners and customs of my country. They had been implanted in me with great care, and made an impression on my mind, which time could not erase, and which all the adversity and variety of fortune I have since experienced served only to rivet and record; for, whether the love of one's country be real or imaginary, or a lesson of reason, or an instinct of nature, I still look back with pleasure on the first scenes of my life, though that pleasure has been for the most part mingled with sorrow.

I have already acquainted the reader with the time and place of my birth. My father, besides many slaves, had a numerous family, of which seven lived to grow up, including myself and a sister, who was the only daughter. As I was the youngest of the sons, I became, of course, the greatest favourite with my mother, and was always with her; and she used to take particular pains to form my mind. I was trained up from my earliest years in the art of war; my daily exercise was shooting and throwing javelins; and my mother adorned me with emblems, after the manner of our greatest warriors. In this way I grew up till I was turned the age of eleven, when an end was put to my happiness in the following manner:—Generally when the grown people in the neighbourhood were gone far in the fields to labour, the children assembled together in some of the neighbours' premises to play; and commonly some of us used to get up a tree to look out for any as-

assailant, or kidnapper, that might come upon us; for they sometimes took those opportunities of our parents' absence to attack and carry off as many as they could seize. One day, as I was watching at the top of a tree in our yard, I saw one of those people come into the yard of our next neighbour but one, to kidnap, there being many stout young people in it. Immediately on this I gave the alarm of the rogue, and he was surrounded by the stoutest of them, who entangled him with cords, so that he could not escape till some of the grown people came and secured him. But alas! ere long it was my fate to be thus attacked, and to be carried off, when none of the grown people were nigh. One day, when all our people were gone out to their works as usual, and only I and my dear sister were left to mind the house, two men and a woman got over our walls, and in a moment seized us both, and, without giving us time to cry out, or make resistance, they stopped our mouths, and ran off with us into the nearest wood. Here they tied our hands, and continued to carry us as far as they could, till night came on, when we reached a small house, where the robbers halted for refreshment, and spent the night. We were then unbound, but were unable to take any food; and, being quite overpowered by fatigue and grief, our only relief was some sleep, which allayed our misfortune for a short time. The next morning we left the house, and continued travelling all the day. For a long time we had kept the woods, but at last we came into a road which I believed I knew. I had now some hopes of being delivered; for we had advanced but a little way before I discovered some people at a distance, on which I began to cry out for their assistance: but my cries had no other effect than to make them tie me faster and stop my mouth, and then they put me into a large sack. They also stopped my sister's mouth, and tied her hands; and in this manner we proceeded till we were out of the sight of these people. When we went to rest the following night they offered us some victuals; but we refused it; and the only comfort we had was in being in one another's arms all that night, and bathing each other with our tears. But alas! we were soon deprived of even the small comfort of weeping together. The next day proved a day of greater sorrow than I had yet experienced for my sister and I were then separated, while we lay clasped in each other's arms. It was in vain that we besought them not to part us; she was torn from me, and immediately carried away, while I was left in a state of distraction not to be described. I cried and grieved continually; and for several days I did not eat any thing but what they forced into my mouth. At length, after many days travelling, during which I had often changed masters, I got into the hands of a chieftain, in a very pleasant country. This man had two wives and some children, and they all used me extremely well, and did all they could to comfort me; particularly the first wife, who was something like my mother. Although I was a great many days journey from my father's house, yet these people spoke exactly the same language with us. This first master of mine, as I may call him, was a smith, and my principal employment was working his bellows, which were the same kind as I had seen in my vicinity. They were in some respects not unlike the stoves here in gentlemen's kitchens; and were covered over with leather; and in the middle of that leather a stick was fixed, and a person stood up, and worked it, in the same manner as is done to pump water out of a cask with a hand pump. I believe it was gold he worked, for it was of a lovely bright yellow colour, and was worn by the women on their wrists and ankles. . . .

The first object which saluted my eyes when I arrived on the coast was the sea, and a slave ship, which was then riding at anchor, and waiting for its cargo. These filled me with astonishment, which was soon converted into terror when I was carried on board. I was immediately handled and tossed up to see if I were found by some of the crew; and I was now persuaded that I had gotten into a world of bad spirits, and that they were going to kill me.

Their complexions too differing so much from ours, their long hair, and the language they spoke, (which was very different from any I had ever heard) united to confirm me in this belief. Indeed such were the horrors of my views and fears at the moment, that, if ten thousand worlds had been my own, I would have freely parted with them all to have exchanged my condition with that of the meanest slave in my own country. When I looked round the ship too and saw a large furnace or copper boiling, and a multitude of black people of every description chained together, every one of their countenances expressing dejection and sorrow, I no longer doubted of my fate; and, quite overpowered with horror and anguish, I fell motionless on the deck and fainted. When I recovered a little I found some black people about me, who I believed were some of those who brought me on board, and had been receiving their pay; they talked to me in order to cheer me, but all in vain. I asked them if we were not to be eaten by those white men with horrible looks, red faces, and loose hair. They told me I was not; and one of the crew brought me a small portion of spirituous liquor in a wine glass; but, being afraid of him, I would not take it out of his hand. One of the blacks therefore took it from him and gave it to me, and I took a little down my palate, which, instead of reviving me, as they thought it would, threw me into the greatest consternation at the strange feeling it produced, having never tasted any such liquor before. Soon after this the blacks who brought me on board went off, and left me abandoned to despair. I now saw myself deprived of all chance of returning to my native country, or even the least glimpse of hope of gaining the shore, which I now considered as friendly; and I even wished for my former slavery in preference to my present situation, which was filled with horrors of every kind, still heightened by my ignorance of what I was to undergo. I was not long suffered to indulge my grief; I was soon put down under the decks, and there I received such a salutation in my nostrils as I had never experienced in my life: so that, with the loathsomeness of the stench, and crying together, I became so sick and low that I was not able to eat, nor had I the least desire to taste any thing. I now wished for the last friend, death, to relieve me; but soon, to my grief, two of the white men offered me eatables; and, on my refusing to eat, one of them held me fast by the hands, and laid me across I think the windlass, and tied my feet, while the other flogged me severely. I had never experienced any thing of this kind before; and although, not being used to the water, I naturally feared that element the first time I saw it, yet nevertheless, could I have got over the nettings, I would have jumped over the side, but I could not; and, besides, the crew used to watch us very closely who were not chained down to the decks, lest we should leap into the water: and I have seen some of these poor African prisoners most severely cut for attempting to do so, and hourly whipped for not eating. This indeed was often the case with myself.

4. COMMUNICATION TO THE SOUTH CAROLINA GAZETTE, 1738

Upon arrival in the Americas, slaves from Africa were distributed through the New World as commodities in a market. Through this process, their status as objects of investment was confirmed. The following letter, written in 1738 to the *South Carolina Gazette,* suggests the dehumanizing aspects of the slave system, as the writer discusses the variations in the market for slaves.

Communication to the *South Carolina Gazette,* 1738

March 9, 1738.

Mr. Timothy, I Was in hopes that the Complaint of bad Pay and Loss on Returns made for 2 years pass by the Gentlemen of London and Bristol, who are concerned in the Negro Trade to this Province, would have prevented so great an Importation for some Years to come, and the early Advices of our Crops being lost this Year, I also imagined would have induced those Gentlemen to have sent Orders to the West Indies for the Masters adressed for this Province with such Slaves, not to proceed. But the Arrival of Capt Power with above 300 Slaves, and by him Advice that several others may be expected, make me imagine, that either the former Complaints were groundless, or, that there must be an Extravagant Profit on that Trade in this Province, by selling the Negroes at a much greater Price here than in any other Port of America. The last Reason seems to be likeliest, for I have known many Slaves bought in the Barbadoes, etc. and sent here for sale, which have been sold with good Profit.

I cannot avoid observing on this Occasion, that altho' a few Negroes annually imported into this Province might be of advantage to most People; yet such large Importations of 2600 and 2800 Negroes every Year is not only a Loss to many, but in the end may prove the Ruin of the Province, as it most certainly does that of many poor industrious Planters, who unwarily engage in buying more than they have Occasion for, or are able to pay. It is for their Sakes only, I now take the trouble of writing this, that they may not further involve themselves in utter Ruin.

Negroes may be said to be the Bait proper for catching a Carolina Planter, as certain as Beef to catch a Shark. How many under the Notion of 18 Months Credit, have been tempted to buy more Negroes than they could Possibly expect to pay in 3 Years! This is so notorious, that few Inhabitants I believe will doubt it. I have hear'd many declare their own Folly in this particular, with a Resolution never to do so again: Yet so great is the Infatuation, that the many Examples of their Neighbours Misfortunes and Danger by such Purchases do not hinder new Fools from bringing themselves into the same Difficulty.

Until about the Year 1733, the common Method of selling Negroes in this Province was, to be paid in Rice, whereby the Sellers knew to make above 10 per Cent per Annum Profits, by a Forbearance of Payment under the Title of commuting their Bonds. The Rice valued at about 37 *s.* 6 *d.* per C. and the Casks given for nothing: The Factors here were in general under no other Contract with their Employers at Home, than to remit the Rice when they had receiv'd it from the Planter. But now the Case is alter'd, the Sales and Contracts being now upon a new and quite different Footing, which I believe will in the End prove not only worse for the Merchants at Home, but also for the Factor Seller, and Planter Buyer here.

If I am rightly inform'd, the Negroes that are now sold in this Province are sent upon those Terms, *viz.* The Factors here to make good all bad Debts, to remit 2 thirds of the Value in 12 Months, the other one third in 2 Years after the Day of Sale. Now as they give Security in Great Britain to perform their Contracts, and as their further Business depends upon the doing thereof, it is no surprize to find them now more exact in requiring their Payments when it becomes due than they did 6 Years ago; and as our Currency is every Year decreasing in Value, so all others who have Remittances to make to Great Britain in Money, will be the more urgent to have their Payments.

It is so common for many Planters to buy Negroes and dry Goods for more Value than they can possibly expect to be able to pay for when due, that it may be called a general Distemper, which of late has very much encreased, by the two last bad Crops. In Case of failure of Payment they think they make full Satisfaction by giving bond payable next Year, bearing 10 per Cent Interest. This is Sufficient, I must own, to those who lend Money at Interest, or who are only concern'd in our In-land Trade; but will not answer to those who must turn the Currency into Sterling. For suppose I had a Man's Bond for 700 £ two Years ago, that Money then would have purchase 100 £ Sterling, whereas I now give 770 £ for 100 £ Sterling. Now if the Debtor pays me with 10 per Cent Interest it is 840, so that altho' he pays me at the Rate of 10 per Cent. per Annum, yet I really receive but 5 per Cent: For the 840 £. he pays me, will only purchase 110 £. Sterling, which is but 10 £. upon the 100 £. for two Years. It's worse in Rice, for two Years ago 700 £. would have bought 65 or 70 Barrels of Rice, and now it won't buy above 40 Barrels, as Rice was then 40 s. and is 71 s.

Those Reasons may be sufficient to excuse any trading Man for insisting upon punctual Payment, and also to warn those in Debt not to depend so much upon the Lenity of the Merchants in Town, besides as their is not one in 50 of those who sell Rice that will give 10 Days Credit, how can they expect the Buyers should be putt off with the Notion of paying Interest? Which it's well known will buy nothing at any Market, and Merchants can't support their Credit, or carry on Trade, without buying Produce.

My whole Design of this is only to warn the unthinking Part of our Planters against falling into the same Misfortunes next Year they have met with in this, *viz* being unable to pay their Debts. The common excuse is the Loss of Crop: But let many of those in Debt look into their Affairs, and they will find a good crop of Rice even suppos'd at 60 s. per C: not sufficient to pay all their Debts, nor will a good Crop next Year pay half the Debts now due to the trading Men in Town; and in Case a general good Crop should be made, depend upon, Rice will be under 40 s. per C.

If I may be so bold as to give my Advice in the Affair of Negroes, it would be this, that before any Planter offer to buy one more, or even to venture into a Negro Yard, he should first make up an Account of all he owes now to every Person, and then make a Calculation of what he may reasonably expect to make this Year. The most certain way to know this is, to sum up the Amounts of his last 4 Years Produce of the same Number of Hands a fourth Part of which he may expect to have this Year: For a wild Expectation of 10 Barrels per Negro only brings a Disappointment to the Owner, and in Time may prove his Ruin.

Suppose a Man has 20 Negroes, and for these 4 Years past has made in all 240 Barrels of Rice, he may expect to have 60 Barrels next Year, which at a Medium of Price will be about 700 £ Currency, now if that Person finds that he is in Debt 1000 £ or only 700 £ how can he engage for any further Payments Next Year, without exposing himself at the Mercy of his Creditors? But if the same Man finds he owes only 100 £ he may safely buy 2 Negroes and have a common Chance [to] pay [for] them besides his annual Charges. Would People take this prudent Method to think before they buy Negroes, it would in the End prove better for them. If they complain of the Merchants being pressing for Payments this Year, depend on it they will be worse next Year. Besides this Caution of those who are in Debt would make fewer Buyers and of Course cheaper Negroes, so that in Time they might be had here as cheap as in other Parts of America. But if any Person who can't pay his Debts now, encreases them by buying more Negroes, how can he desire any Person to have Patience 'till next Year? If his Slaves are then seized for Debt, who

Is to Blame? Is it not his own Act and Deed? Could he not have lived without these new Negroes? Buying the needful Apparel, Meat or Drink pleads for itself, as Mankind can't live without some Necessaries. Can any Man be certain of a better Crop next Year than he had last? If they can't they should not increase their Debts beyond absolute Necessity.

Were it possible to prevent any Negroes to be imported for 3 Years to come, I am persuaded it would be for the general Advantage of all the Inhabitants in this Province, and the only means to relieve us of the Load of Debts we are now owing to Great Britain, which I believe is equal to the Amount of 3 Years Produce.

5. SLAVE COFFLE IN AFRICA IN THE EIGHTEENTH CENTURY

The slave trade was a complicated activity that involved both Africans and Europeans. Africans remained in control of the coasts from Senegambia to the Niger, the point of interaction between European slave traders and the Africans who supplied them. Although some slaves were initially taken by Europeans on or near the coasts themselves, an organized trade soon developed. Individuals were sold into slavery either by native chiefs who wished to be rid of troublemakers, by their families, or by themselves in times of hardship. They were also kidnapped by other Africans and then sold, or had been taken as prisoners of war in domestic conflicts within West Africa. Slaves captured in the interior of West Africa were then moved to the coast in long marches that could last for weeks. In these coffles, slaves were bound hand and foot and kept together by wooden and rope braces linking one to another to make escape difficult. European traders who lived as permanent residents of the coast bought slaves when the coffles reached the ports, and kept on hand slaves to be purchased by slaving ships that set in at the port. The slaves were then placed on boats for the New World, primarily the West Indies, facing the perils of the Middle Passage and then transport from the West Indies to plantations throughout the New World.

Figure 14.1 An African slave coffle on its way to the coast. Courtesy of the National Museum of History and Technology, Smithsonian Institution.

Study Questions

1. Describe the principal features of the activity of the port of Bahia as Dampier saw them. What effects did the trade through the port have on the society of Bahia?
2. How does Alexander Falconbridge assess the consequences, for Africans and for Europeans, of the slave trade?
3. What were the effects of the enslavement of Equiano on him, other than the loss of liberty?
4. How does the author of the letter to the South Carolina Gazette approach the slave trade?
5. What impressions about the slave trade can you draw from the picture of the slave coffle?
6. What are the most important aspects of the Atlantic trading complex as portrayed in these documents?

Suggested Readings

Altman, Ida, and James Horn, eds. *"To Make America": European Emigration in the Early Modern Period*. Berkeley: University of California Press, 1991.

Bailyn, Bernard. *The Peopling of North America: An Introduction*. New York: Random House, 1986.

Curtin, Philip D. *The Rise and Fall of the Plantation Complex*. New York: Cambridge University Press, 1998.

Demos, John. *The Unredeemed Captive: A Family Story from Early America*. New York: Knopf, 1994.

Klein, Herbert S. *The Atlantic Slave Trade*. New York: Cambridge University Press, 1999.

Manning, Patrick, ed. *Slave Trades 1500–1800: Globalization of Forced Labor*. Brookfield, VT: Variorum, 1996.

McAlister, Lyle. *Spain and Portugal in the New World, 1492–1700*. Minneapolis: University of Minnesota Press, 1984.

Thornton, John. *African and Africans in the Making of the Atlantic World, 1400–1800*, 2nd ed. New York: Cambridge University Press, 1998.

White, Richard. *The Middle Ground: Indians, Empires and Republics in the Great Lakes Region, 1650–1815*. New York: Cambridge University Press, 1991.

Web Sites

1. Chronology on the History of Slavery and Racism

   http://www.innercity.org/holt/slavechron.html

2. Excerpts from Slave Narratives

   http://vi/uh/edu/pages/mintz/primary.html

3. Exploration and Settlement, 1675–1800

   http://lib.utexas.edu/Libs/PCL/Map_collection/united_states/Exploration_1675.jpg

4. The Jesuit Plantation Project

   http://www.georgetown.edu/departments/amer_studies/coverjpp.html

15

The Noble and Good Savages of the Enlightenment
1690–1792

TEXTS

For centuries Europeans had speculated about the peoples who lived outside of Europe. These speculations often revolved around the question of human nature, especially the concept of an innocent primitive, untarnished by the refinements and corruptions of civilization. The Europeans who went to the New World in the sixteenth and seventeenth centuries were also involved in a process of interpreting the supposed "primitives" that they found for their countrymen back home in Europe. The country itself was viewed as uncultivated and in a natural state, a point of origin for a history of the world. The Scottish philosopher John Locke, for example, wrote at the end of the seventeenth century that "in the beginning all the World was America." The inhabitants of the New World were viewed as innocent primitives by some, but other Europeans feared that the world outside of Europe was peopled by monstrosities, ignoble savages who would do serious harm to the physical and moral well-being of the Europeans who visited them. [1, 2, 3] The Indian Wars in New England in the seventeenth century provided many stories of barbarity, even if the experiences farther south in Pennsylvania suggested that the inhabitants were handsome, generous, and honest: true noble savages. The peoples of the Americas therefore could be seen as original humans, the stuff out of which European civilization had developed. But in their ambiguity, they posed serious problems for theories of an uninterrupted progress of the human race.

European writers who wished to reflect on European civilization through the eyes of an uncultivated visitor could also select Africans, although their color and the institution of slavery in which European civilization placed them interfered with this purpose. By the eighteenth century, Europeans viewed African society, strongly influenced by the slave trade, as unstable, marked by endemic warfare, and made up of depraved peoples whose capacity for civilization was often doubted. After the voyages of Bougainville and Cook, Pacific islanders emerged as subjects of this discussion. [4] Native Americans were also an obvious choice for such figures for much of the eighteenth century. Thus, when four Iroquois sachems from the Mohawk valley visited London in 1710, they aroused interest as curiosities themselves, but they also figured in satirical writing that attacked English religion, fashion, and politics. Implicit in these satires and discussions was the assumption that there existed a natural world in which the conventions of European civilization did not stifle individual freedom. [5]

The Enlightenment distinction between nature and civilization found expression in this contrast between European and non-European. In a number of types of discussion—scientific, philosophical, and literary—the causes and implications of the savagery of these Africans, Pacific Islanders, and Native Americans were discussed. They might be seen as representatives of an earlier stage of development. They might also be viewed as the result of degeneration from the civilization of the European world or, as in the case of Africans, from the ancient civilizations of Egypt and Carthage. Such different interpretations of the inhabitants of these newly discovered worlds would have vastly different implications for theories about the development of civilization and its problems in eighteenth-century Europe. Environment, especially climate, and isolation from the civilizations of both East and West were the most prevalent explanations given for their savagery, but it was still not clear what the meaning was for Europeans and their understanding of the world of the existence of new races living in countries about which almost nothing was known. Even without travel to other parts of the globe, therefore, Europeans in the eighteenth century found non-Europeans useful figures in literary and intellectual discussions, and speculation about the nobility or ignobility of non-Europeans proved a powerful stimulus to their own discussions of the development and character both of their own civilization and of the world in which they lived.

By the end of the eighteenth century, however, Europeans no longer needed to speculate about Caribs, Native Americans, Africans or Pacific Islanders to see possible changes in their own societies. The American and French Revolutions had provided examples of the effects of changes in society and government. [6] The new regimes of the nineteenth century came head to head with the implications of the supposed savagery of other peoples, as they faced the issue of slavery, prevalent not only in the new United States of America but also in the colonies that existed in the Caribbean and in South America. Although they might remain figures of sentiment in Romantic literature in the early nineteenth century, the rational noble savage faded from the European mind as the nineteenth century advanced, replaced by the intractable problems posed by slavery, exploration, and empire.

1. APHRA BEHN, *OROONOKO*

Aphra Behn (1640–1689?) wrote *Oroonoko* in 1688, after telling the story numerous times to friends and acquaintances. It is loosely based on her own experience in Surinam, where she traveled in 1663. Telling the story of a prince sold into slavery, the novel is the first prose work in English with a black hero. It makes significant distinctions between the inhabitants of Surinam, the Africans, and the European civilization that the character of Oroonoko aspires to adopt. Behn herself is a precursor of later women novelists such as Jane Austen, George Eliot, and the Brontë sisters. The work therefore conflicted with barriers, both in authorship and subject matter, that were present in seventeenth-century European culture.

Oroonoko; or, The History of the Royal Slave.

I do not pretend, in giving you the history of this royal slave, to entertain my reader with the adventures of a feign'd hero, whose life and fortunes fancy may manage at the poet's pleasure; nor in relating the truth, design to adorn it with any accidents, but such as arrived in earnest to him: and it shall come simply into the world, recommended by its own proper merits, and natural intrigues; there being enough of reality to support it, and to render it diverting, without the addition of invention.

I was my self an eye-witness to a great part of what you will find here set down; and what I cou'd not be witness of, I receiv'd from the mouth of the chief actor in this history, the hero himself, who gave us the whole transactions of his youth: and though I shall omit, for brevity's sake, a thousand little accidents of his life, which, however pleasant to us, where history was scarce, and adventures very rare, yet might prove tedious and heavy to my reader, in a world where he finds diversions for every minute, new and strange. But we who were perfectly charm'd with the character of this great man, were curious to gather every circumstance of his life.

The scene of the last part of his adventures lies in a colony in America, called Surinam, in the West-Indies.

But before I give you the story of this gallant slave, 'tis fit I tell you the manner of bringing them to these new colonies; those they make use of there, not being natives of the place: for those we live with in perfect amity, without daring to command 'em; but, on the contrary, caress 'em with all the brotherly and friendly affection in the world; trading with them for their fish, venison, buffalo's skins, and little rarities; as marmosets, a sort of monkey, as big as a rat or weasel, but of a marvellous and delicate shape, having face and hands like a human creature; and cousheries, a little beast in the form and fashion of a lion, as big as a kitten, but so exactly made in all parts like that noble beast, that it is it in miniature. Then for little paraketoes, great parrots, muckaws, and a thousand other birds and beasts of wonderful and surprizing forms, shapes, and colours. For skins of prodigious snakes, of which there are some threescore yards in length; as is the skin of one that may be seen at His Majesty's antiquary's; where are also some rare flies, of amazing forms and colours, presented to 'em by my self; some as big as my fist, some less; and all of various excellencies, such as art cannot imitate. Then we trade for feathers, which they order into all shapes, make themselves little short habits of 'em, and glorious wreaths for their heads, necks, arms and legs, whose tinctures are unconceivable. I had a set of these presented to me, and I gave 'em to the King's Theatre, and it was the dress of the Indian Queen, infinitely admir'd by persons of quality; and was unimitable. Besides these, a thousand little knacks, and rarities in nature; and some of art, as their baskets, weapons, aprons, etc. We dealt with 'em with beads of all colours, knives, axes, pins and needles; which they us'd only as tools to drill holes with in their ears, noses and lips, where they hang a great many little things; as long beads, bits of tin, brass or silver beat thin, and any shining trinket. The beads they weave into aprons about a quarter of an ell long, and of the same breadth; working them very prettily in flowers of several colours; which apron they wear just before 'em, as Adam and Eve did the figleaves; the men wearing a long stripe of linen, which they deal with us for. They thread these beads also on long cotton-threads, and make girdles to tie their aprons to, which come twenty times, or more, about the waste, and then cross, like a shoulder-belt, both ways, and round their necks, arms and legs. This adornment, with their long black hair, and the face painted in little specks or flowers here and there, makes 'em a wonderful figure to behold. Some of the beauties, which indeed are finely shap'd, as almost all are, and who have pretty features, are charming and novel; for they have all that is called beauty, except the colour, which is a reddish yellow; or after a new oiling, which they often use to themselves, they are of the colour of a new brick, but smooth, soft and sleek. They are extreme modest and bashful, very shy, and nice of being touch'd. And though they are all thus naked, if one lives for ever among 'em, there is not to be seen an undecent action, or glance: and being continually us'd to see one another so unadorn'd, so like our first parents before the fall, it seems as if they had no wishes, there being nothing to heighten curiosity; but all you can see, you see at once, and every moment see; and where there is no novelty, there can be no curiosity. Not but I have seen a handsome young Indian, dying for love of a very beautiful young Indian maid; but all his courtship was, to fold his arms, persue her with his eyes, and sighs were all his language: while she, as if no such lover were present, or rather as if she desired none such, carefully guarded her eyes from beholding him; and never approach'd him, but she look'd down with all the blushing modesty I have seen in the most severe and cautious of our world. And these people represented to me an absolute idea of the first state of inno-cence, before man knew how to sin: and 'tis most evident and plain, that simple nature is the most harmless, inoffensive and virtuous mistress. 'Tis she alone, if she were permitted, that better instructs the world, than all the inventions of man: religion wou'd here but de-stroy that tranquility they possess by ignorance; and laws wou'd but teach 'em to know of-fence, of which now they have no notion. They once made mourning and fasting for the death of the English Governour, who had given his hand to come on such a day to 'em, and neither came nor sent; believing, when a man's word was past, nothing but death cou'd or shou'd prevent his keeping it: and when they saw he was not dead, they ask'd him what name they had for a man who promis'd a thing he did not do? The Governour told them, such a man was a lyar, which was a word of infamy to a gentleman. Then one of 'em reply'd, Governour, you are a lyar, and guilty of that infamy. They have a native justice, which knows no fraud; and they understand no vice, or cunning, but when they are taught by the white men. They have plurality of wives; which, when they grow old, serve those that succeed 'em, who are young, but with a servitude easy and respect'd; and unless they take slaves in war, they have no other attendants.

Those on that continent where I was, had no king; but the oldest war-captain was obey'd with great resignation.

A war-captain is a man who has led them on to battle with conduct and success; of whom I shall have occasion to speak more hereafter, and of some other of their cus-toms and manners, as they fall in my way.

With these people, as I said, we live in perfect tranquility, and good understanding, as it behoves us to do; they knowing all the places where to seek the best food of the country, and the means of getting it; and for very small and unvaluable trifles, supply us with what 'tis impossible for us to get: for they do not only in the woods, and over the sevana's, in hunt-ing, supply the parts of hounds, by swiftly scouring through those almost impassable places, and by the mere activity of their feet run down the nimblest deer, and other eatable beasts; but in the water, one wou'd think they were gods of the rivers, or fellow-citizens of the deep; so rare an art they have in swimming, diving, and almost living in water; by which they command the less swift inhabitants of the floods. And then for shooting, what they cannot take, or reach with their hands, they do with arrows; and have so admirable an aim, that they will split almost an hair, and at any distance that an arrow can reach: they will shoot down oranges, and other fruit, and only touch the stalk with the dart's point, that they may not hurt the fruit. So that they being on all occasions very useful to us, we find it ab-solutely necessary to caress 'em as friends, and not to treat 'em as slaves; nor dare we do other, their numbers so far surpassing ours in that continent.

Those then whom we make use of to work in our plantations of sugar, are Negroes, black-slaves all together, who are transported thither in this manner.

Those who want slaves, make a bargain with a master, or a captain of a ship, and contract to pay him so much a-piece, a matter of twenty pound a head, for as many as he agrees for, and to pay for 'em when they shall be deliver'd on such a plantation: so that when there arrives a ship laden with slaves, they who have so contracted, go a-board, and receive their number by lot; and perhaps in one lot that may be ten, there may happen to be three or four men, the rest women and children. Or be there more or less of either sex, you are obliged to be contented with your lot.

Coramantien, a country of blacks so called, was one of those places in which they found the most advantageous trading for these slaves, and thither most of our great traders in that merchandize traffick; for that nation is very warlike and brave: and having a continual campaign, being always in hostility with one neighbouring prince or other, they had the fortune to take a great many captives: for all they took in battle were sold as slaves; at least those common men who cou'd not ransom themselves. Of these slaves so taken, the general only has all the profit; and of these generals our captains and masters of ships buy all their freights.

The King of Coramantien was himself a man of an hundred and odd years old, and had no son, tho he had many beautiful black wives: for most certainly there are beauties that can charm of that colour. In his younger years he had had many gallant men to his sons, thirteen of whom died in battle, conquering when they fell; and he had only left him for his successor, one grand-child, son to one of these dead victors, who, as soon as he could bear a bow in his hand, and a quiver at his back, was sent into the field to be train'd up by one of the oldest generals to war; where, from his natural inclination to arms, and the occasions given him, with the good conduct of the old General, he became, at the age of seventeen, one of the most expert captains, and bravest soldiers that ever saw the field of Mars: so that he was ador'd as the wonder of all that world, and the darling of the soldiers. Besides, he was adorn'd with a native beauty, so transcending all those of his gloomy race, that he struck an awe and reverence, even into those that knew not his quality; as he did into me, who beheld him with surprize and wonder, when afterwards he arrived in our world.

He had scarce arrived at his seventeenth year, when, fighting by his side, the General was kill'd with an arrow in his eye, which the Prince Oroonoko (for so was this gallant Moor call'd) very narrowly avoided; nor had he, if the General who saw the arrow shot, and perceiving it aimed at the Prince, had not bow'd his head between, on purpose to receive it in his own body, rather than it should touch that of the Prince, and so saved him.

'Twas then, afflicted as Oroonoko was, that he was proclaimed General in the old man's place: and then it was, at the finishing of that war, which had continued for two years, that the Prince came to Court, where he had hardly been a month together, from the time of his fifth year to that of seventeen; and 'twas amazing to imagine where it was he learn'd so much humanity: or, to give his accomplishments a juster name, where 'twas he got that real greatness of soul, those refined notions of true honour, that absolute generosity, and that softness that was capable of the highest passions of love and gallantry, whose objects were almost continually fighting men, or those mangled or dead, who heard no sounds but those of war and groans. Some part of it we may attribute to the care of a Frenchman of wit and learning, who finding it turn to very good account to be a sort of royal tutor to this young black, and perceiving him very ready, apt, and quick of apprehension, took a great pleasure to teach him morals, language and science; and was for it extremely belov'd and valu'd by him. Another reason was, he lov'd when he came from war, to see all the English gentlemen that traded thither; and did not only learn their language, but that of the Spaniard also, with whom he traded afterwards for slaves.

I have often seen and conversed with this great man, and been a witness to many of his mighty actions; and do assure my reader, the most illustrious Courts could not have produced a braver man, both for greatness of courage and mind, a judgment more solid, a wit more quick, and a conversation more sweet and diverting. He knew almost as much as if he had read much: he had heard of and admired the Romans: he had heard of the late civil wars in England, and the deplorable death of our great monarch; and wou'd discourse of it with all the sense and abhorrence of the injustice imaginable. He had an extreme good and graceful mien, and all the civility of a well-bred great man. He had nothing of barbarity in his nature, but in all points addressed himself as if his education had been in some European Court.

This great and just character of Oroonoko gave me an extreme curiosity to see him, especially when I knew he spoke French and English, and that I could talk with him. But though I had heard so much of him, I was as greatly surprized when I saw him, as if I had heard nothing of him; so beyond all reports I found him. He came into the room, and addressed himself to me, and some other women, with the best grace in the world. He was pretty tall, but of a shape the most exact that can be fancy'd: The most famous statuary cou'd not form the figure of a man more admirably turn'd from head to foot. His face was not of that brown rusty black which most of that nation are, but a perfect ebony, or polished jett. His eyes were the most awful that cou'd be seen, and very piercing; the white of 'em being like snow, as were his teeth. His nose was rising and Roman, instead of African and flat. His mouth the finest shaped that could be seen; far from those great turn'd lips, which are so natural to the rest of the Negroes. The whole proportion and air of his face was so nobly and exactly form'd, that bating his colour, there could be nothing in nature more beautiful, agreeable and handsome. There was no one grace wanting, that bears the standard of true beauty. His hair came down to his shoulders, by the aids of art, which was by pulling it out with a quill, and keeping it comb'd; of which he took particular care. Nor did the perfections of his mind come short of those of his person; for his discourse was admirable upon almost any subject: and whoever had heard him speak, wou'd have been convinced of their errors, that all fine wit is confined to the white men, especially to those of Christendom; and wou'd have confess'd that Oroonoko was as capable even of reigning well, and of governing as wisely, had as great a soul, as politick maxims, and was as sensible of power, as any prince civiliz'd in the most refined schools of humanity and learning, or the most illustrious Courts.

This Prince, such as I have describ'd him, whose soul and body were so admirably adorned, was (while yet he was in the Court of his grandfather, as I said) as capable of love, as 'twas possible for a brave and gallant man to be; and in saying that, I have named the highest degree of love: for sure great souls are most capable of that passion.

2. DANIEL DEFOE, *THE LIFE AND STRANGE SURPRISING ADVENTURES OF ROBINSON CRUSOE*

Daniel Defoe (1661?–1731) made his living as a merchant in London as a young man, but became increasingly active as a pamphleteer during political controversies in the 1680s and 1690s. He was imprisoned in 1703 for seditious writing, and continued his career as a political journalist after his release. In 1719, he published the first volume of *Robinson Crusoe*, a story based on the experiences of an English sailor, Alexander Selkirk, who had been shipwrecked on the island of Juan Fernandez in the South Pacific. Although much of the story concerns the survival of Crusoe, Defoe also included in his story a description of the meeting between Crusoe and a man whom Crusoe rescues from cannibals and who, renamed Friday, became his faithful companion. The story of Crusoe and Friday represents one version of contact between a civilized Englishman and a noble or good savage.

Robinson Crusoe

About a year and half after I had entertained these notions, and by long musing, had as it were resolved them all into nothing, for want of an occasion to put them in execution, I was surprised one morning early, with seeing no less than five *canoes* all on shore together on my side the island; and the people who belonged to them all landed, and out of my sight. The number of them broke all my measures, for seeing so many, and knowing that they always came four or six, or sometimes more, in a boat, I could not tell what to think of it, or how to take my measures, to attack twenty or thirty men single-handed; so I lay still in my castle, perplexed and discomforted. However, I put myself into all the same postures for an attack that I had formerly provided, and was just ready for action, if anything had presented; having waited a good while, listening to hear if they made any noise, at length, being very impatient, I set my guns at the foot of my ladder, and clambered up to the top of the hill, by my two stages as usual; standing so, however, that my head did not appear above the hill, so that they could not perceive me by any means; here I observed by the help of my perspective-glass, that they were no less than thirty in number, that they had a fire kindled, that they had had meat dressed. How they had cooked it, that I knew not, or what it was; but they were all dancing in I know not how many barbarous gestures and figures, their own way, round the fire.

While I was thus looking on them, I perceived by my perspective, two miserable wretches dragged from the boats, where it seems they were laid by, and were now brought out for the slaughter. I perceived one of them immediately fell, being knocked down, I suppose with a club or wooden sword, for that was their way, and two or three others were at work immediately, cutting him open for their cookery, while the other victim was left standing by himself, till they should be ready for him. In that very moment, this poor wretch seeing himself a little at liberty, Nature inspired him with hopes of life, and he started away from them, and ran with incredible swiftness along the sands directly towards me, I mean towards that part of the coast, where my habitation was.

I was dreadfully frighted, (that I must acknowledge) when I perceived him to run my way; and especially, when, as I thought, I saw him pursued by the whole body; and now I expected that part of my dream was coming to pass, and that he would certainly take shelter in my grove; but I could not depend by any means upon my dream for the rest of it, *viz.* that the other savages would not pursue him thither, and find him there. However, I kept my station, and my spirits began to recover, when I found that there was not above three men that followed him, and still more was I encouraged, when I found that he outstripped them exceedingly in running, and gained ground of them, so that if he could but hold it for half an hour, I saw easily he would fairly get away from them all.

There was between them and my castle, the creek which I mentioned often at the first part of my story, when I landed my cargoes out of the ship; and this, I saw plainly, he must necessarily swim over, or the poor weretch would be taken there. But when the savage escaping came thither, he made nothing of it, tho' the tide was then up, but plunging in, swam thro' in about thirty strokes or thereabouts, landed, and ran on with exceeding strength and swiftness; when the three persons came to the creek, I found that two of them could swim, but the third could not, and that standing on the other side, he looked at the other, but went no further; and soon after went softly back again, which as it happened, was very well for him in the main.

I observed, that the two who swam, were yet more than twice as long swimming over the creek, as the fellow was that fled from them. It came now very warmly upon my thoughts, and indeed irresistibly, that now was my time to get me a servant, and perhaps a companion, or assistant; and that I was called plainly by Providence to save this poor creature's life; I immediately run down the ladders with all possible expedition, fetched my two guns, for they were both but at the foot of the ladders, as I observed above; and getting up again, with the same haste, to the top of the hill, I crossed toward the sea; and having a very short cut, and all down hill, clapped myself in the way between the pursuers and the pursued; hollowing aloud to him that fled, who, looking back, was at first perhaps as much frighted at me, as at them; but I beckoned with my hand to him, to come back; and in the mean time, I slowly advanced towards the two that followed; then rushing at once upon the foremost, I knocked him down with the stock of my piece; I was loath to fire, because I would not have the rest hear; though at that distance, it would not have been easily heard, and being out of sight of the smoke too, they would not have easily known what to make of it. Having knocked this fellow down, the other who pursued with him stopped, as if he had been frighted; and I advanced apace towards him; but as I came nearer, I perceived presently, he had a bow and arrow, and was fitting it to shoot at me; so I was then necessitated to shoot at him first, which I did, and killed him at the first shoot; the poor savage who fled, but had stopped, though he saw both his enemies fallen, and killed, as he thought, yet was so frighted with the fire and noise of my piece, that he stood stock still, and neither came forward or went backward, tho' he seemed rather inclined to fly still, than to come on; I hollowed again to him, and made signs to come forward, which he easily understood, and came a little way, then stopped again, and then a little further, and stopped again, and I could then perceive that he stood trembling, as if he had been taken prisoner, and had just been to be killed, as his two enemies were; I beckoned him again to come to me, and gave him all the signs of encouragement that I could think of, and he came nearer and nearer, kneeling down every ten or twelve steps in token of acknowledgment for my saving his life. I smiled at him, and looked pleasantly, and beckoned to him to come still nearer; at length he came close to me, and then he kneeled down again, kissed the ground, and laid his head upon the ground, and taking me by the foot, set my foot upon his head; this it seems was in token of swearing to be my slave forever; I took him up, and made much of him, and encouraged him all I could. But there was more work to do yet, for I perceived the savage who I knocked down, was not killed, but stunned with the blow, and began to come to himself; so I pointed to him, and showing him the savage, that he was not dead; upon this he spoke some words to me, and though I could not understand them, yet I thought they were pleasant to hear, for they were the first sound of a man's voice, that I had heard, *my own excepted*, for above twenty-five years. But there was no time for such reflections now; the savage who was knocked down recovered himself so far, as to sit up upon the ground, and I perceived that my savage began to be afraid; but when I saw that, I presented my other piece at the man, as if I would shoot him; upon this my savage, *for so I call him now,* made a motion to me to lend him my sword, which hung naked in a belt by my side; so I did. He no sooner had it, but he runs to his enemy, and at one blow cut off his head as cleverly, no executioner in Germany could have done it sooner or better; which I thought very strange, for one who I had reason to believe never saw a sword in his life before, except their own wooden swords; however, it seems, as I learned afterwards, they make their wooden swords so sharp, so heavy, and the wood is so hard, that they will cut off heads even with them, ay, and arms, and that at one blow too; when he had done this, he comes laughing to me in sign of triumph, and brought me the sword again, and with abundance of gestures which I did not understand, laid it down, with the head of the savage that he had killed, just before me.

But that which astonished him most, was to know how I had killed the other Indian so far off; so pointing to him, he made signs to me to let him go to him; so I bade him go, as well as I could; when he came to him, he stood like one amazed, looking at him, turned him first on one side, then on t'other, looked at the wound the bullet had made, which it seems was just in his breast, where it had made a hole, and no great quantity of blood had followed, but he had bled inwardly, for he was quite dead. He took up his bow and arrows, and came back; so I turned to go away, and beckoned to him to follow me, making signs to him, that more might come after them.

Upon this he signed to me, that he should bury them with sand, that they might not be seen by the rest if they followed; and so I made signs again to him to do so; he fell to work, and in an instant he had scraped a hole in the sand, with his hands, big enough to bury the first in, and then dragged him into it, and covered him, and did so also by the other; I believe he had buried them both in a quarter of an hour; then calling him away, I carried him, not to my castle, but quite away to my cave, on the farther part of the island; so I did not let my dream come to pass in that part, *viz.* that he came into my grove for shelter.

Here I gave him bread, and a bunch of raisins to eat, and a draught of water, which I found he was indeed in great distress for, by his running; and having refreshed him, I made signs for him to go lie down and sleep; pointing to a place where I had laid a great parcel of rice-straw, and a blanket upon it, which I used to sleep upon myself sometimes; so the poor creature laid down, and went to sleep.

He was a comely handsome fellow, perfectly well made; with straight strong limbs, not too large; tall and well shaped, and, as I reckon, about twenty-six years of age. He had a very good countenance, not a fierce and surly aspect; but seemed to have something very manly in his face, and yet he had all the sweetness and softness of an European in his countenance too, especially when he smiled. His hair was long and black, not curled like wool; his forehead very high, and large, and a great vivacity and sparkling sharpness in his eyes. The colour of his skin was not quite black, but very tawny; and yet not of an ugly yellow nauseous tawny, as the Brazilians, and Virginians, and other natives of America are; but of a bright kind of a dun olive colour, that had in it something very agreeable, tho' not very easy to describe. His face was round and plump; his nose small, not flat like the negroes, a very good mouth, thin lips, and his fine teeth well set, and white as ivory. After he had slumbered, rather than slept, about half an hour, he waked again, and comes out of the cave to me; for I had been milking my goats, which I had in the enclosure just by. When he espied me, he came running to me, laying himself down again upon the ground, with all the possible signs of an humble thankful disposition, making a many antic gestures to show it. At last he lays his head flat upon the ground, close to my foot, and sets my other foot upon his head, as he had done before; and after this, made all the signs to me of subjection, servitude, and submission imaginable, to let him know, how he would serve me as long as he lived; I understood him in many things, and let him know, I was very well pleased with him; in a little time I began to speak to him, and teach him to speak to me; and first, I made him know his name should be *Friday,* which was the day I saved his life; I called him so for the memory of the time; I likewise taught him to say *Master,* and then let him know, that was to be my name; I likewise taught him to say *Yes,* and *No,* and to know the meaning of them; I gave him some milk, in an earthen pot, and let him see me drink it before him, and sop my bread in it; and I gave him a cake of bread, to do the like, which he quickly complied with, and made signs that it was very good for him.

I kept there with him all that night; but as soon as it was day, I beckoned to him to come with me, and let him know, I would give him some clothes, at which he seemed very glad, for he was stark naked. As we went by the place where he had buried the two men, he pointed exactly to the place, and shewed me the marks that he had made to find them again, making signs to me, that we should dig them up again and eat them; at this I appeared very angry, expressed my abhorrence of it, made as if I would vomit at the thoughts of it, and beckoned with my hand to him to come away, which he did immediately, with great submission. I then led him up to the top of the hill, to see if his enemies were gone; and pulling out my glass, I looked, and saw plainly the place where they had been, but no appearance of them, or of their *canoes;* so that it was plain they were gone, and had left their two comrades behind them, without any search after them.

But I was not content with this discovery; but having now more courage, and consequently more curiosity, I takes my man Friday with me, giving him the sword in his hand, with the bow and arrows at his back, which I found he could use very dexterously, making him carry one gun for me, and I two for myself, and away we marched to the place, where these creatures had been; for I had a mind now to get some fuller intelligence of them. When I came to the place, my very blood ran chill in my veins, and my heart sunk within me, at the horror of the spectacle. Indeed it was a dreadful sight, at least it was so to me, though Friday made nothing of it. The place was covered with human bones, the ground dyed with their blood, great pieces of flesh left here and there, half eaten, mangled and scorched; and in short, all the tokens of the triumphant feast they had been making there, after a victory over their enemies. I saw three skulls, five hands, and the bones of three or four legs and feet, and abundance of other parts of the bodies; and Friday, by his signs, made me understand, that they brought over four prisoners to feast upon; that three of them were eaten up, and that he, pointing to himself, was the fourth. That there had been a great battle between them and their next king, whose subjects it seems he had been one of; and that they had taken a great number of prisoners, all which were carried to several places by those that had taken them in the fight, in order to feast upon them, as was done here by these wretches upon those they brought hither.

I caused Friday to gather all the skulls, bones, flesh, and whatever remained, and lay them together on a heap, and make a great fire upon it, and burn them all to ashes. I found Friday had still a hankering stomach after some of the flesh, and was still a cannibal in his nature; but I discovered so much abhorrence at the very thoughts of it, and at the least appearance of it, that he durst not discover it; for I had by some means let him know, that I would kill him if he offered it. . . .

During the long time that Friday had now been with me, and that he began to speak to me, and understand me, I was not wanting to lay a foundation of religious

knowledge in his mind; particularly I asked him one time who made him. The poor creature did not understand me at all, but thought I had asked who was his father; but I took
it by another handle, and asked him who made the sea, the ground we walked on, and
the hills, and woods; he told me it was one old Benamuckee, that lived beyond all. He
could describe nothing of this great person, but that he was very old; much older he
said, than the sea, or the land; than the moon or the stars. I asked him then, if this old person had made all things, why did not all things worship him; he looked very grave, and
with a perfect look of innocence, said, "All things do say 'O!' to him." I asked him if the
people who die in his country went away anywhere; he said, yes, they all went to Benamuckee; then I asked him whether these they eat up went thither too; he said, "Yes."

From these things, I began to instruct him in the knowledge of the true God. I told
him that the great Maker of all things lived up there, pointing up towards Heaven. That he
governs the world by the same Power and Providence by which he had made it. That he
was omnipotent, could do everything for us, give everything to us, take everything from
us; and thus by degrees I opened his eyes. He listened with great attention, and received
with pleasure the notion of Jesus Christ being sent to redeem us, and of the manner of
making our prayers to God, and his being able to hear us, even into Heaven; he told me
one day, that if our God could hear us up beyond the sun, he must needs be a greater
God than their Benamuckee, who lived but a little way off, and yet could not hear, till
they went up to the great mountains where he dwelt, to speak to him; I asked him if ever
he went thither, to speak to him; he said, no, they never went that were young men; none
went thither but the old men, who he called their Oowocakee, that is, as I made him explain it to me, their religious, or clergy; and that they went to say O, (so he called saying
prayers) and then came back, and told them what Benamuckee said. By this I observed,
that there is priestcraft, even amongst the most blinded ignorant pagans in the world;
and the policy of making a secret religion, in order to preserve the veneration of the people to the clergy, is not only to be found in the Roman, but perhaps among all religions in
the world, even among the most brutish and barbarous savages.

I endeavoured to clear up this fraud to my man Friday, and told him, that the pre-
tence of their old men going up the mountains, to say O to their god Benamuckee, was a
cheat, and their bringing word from thence what he said, was much more so; that if they
met with any answer, or spake with any one there, it must be with an evil spirit. And then
I entered into a long discourse with him about the Devil, the original of him, his rebel-
lion against God, his enmity to man, the reason of it, his setting himself up in the dark
parts of the world to be worshipped instead of God, and as God; and the many strata-
gems he made use of to delude mankind to his ruin; how he had a secret access to our
passions, and to our affections, to adapt his snares so to our inclinations as to cause us
even to be our own tempters, and to run upon our destruction by our own choice.

3. *A VILLAGE OF THE SAVAGES OF CANADA FROM BARON DE LAHONTAN, NEW VOYAGES TO NORTH-AMERICA.*

Louis-Armand, Baron de Lohanton (1666–ca. 1715), a member of the marine corps of France, set sail at the age of seventeen for Canada as part of an
expedition intended to help control, by military force, the Iroquois who in-

habited the French colony. While in Canada, he served in the region around Quebec and Montreal and participated in several military campaigns against the Iroquois. The knowledge he acquired of native languages and diplomacy made him an invaluable officer for the officials of Canada, and he was kept in the colony for several years, carrying our assignments in the region around Lake Huron, traveling as far west as Sault Ste-Marie. By 1693 he had returned to Europe, although as an exile in Holland, England, and Germany due to conflicts with French officials in Canada and Paris. His *New Voyages to North-America,* published in 1703, was written to earn money, and was well received and widely read. The book and its illustrations became an important part of the information available to educated Europeans in the eighteenth century about the "savages" who lived in North America. Figure 15.1 presents a version of North American civilization as seen by Europeans.

4. DENIS DIDEROT, *SUPPLEMENT TO BOUGAINVILLE'S VOYAGE*

Denis Diderot (1713–1784) was one of the leading figures of the French Enlightenment, best known as coeditor, with J. Le Rond d'Alembert, of the *Encyclopédie,* a massive compilation of knowledge marked by the devotion to reason and nature characteristic of the Enlightenment. Many of the essays he wrote after 1760 were not published until after his death. One of these was the *Supplement to the Voyage of Bougainville.* Although Diderot was only speculating on the basis of Louis-Antoine de Bougainville's account of his voyage across the Pacific in 1766 to 1769, the *Supplement* illustrates both the ways philosophers discussed the relationship between civilization and the state of nature, and how discussions of non-Europeans could provide a means for criticism of European civilization.

The Adieux of the Old Man

He was the father of a numerous family. At the arrival of the Europeans, he gave them a look of disdain, without expressing either astonishment, terror, or curiosity. They approached him; he turned his back towards them, withdrawing into his hut. His silence and his concern betrayed only too well his thoughts: he lamented to himself the departed beautiful past of his country. On the departure of Bougainville, when the inhabitants gathered in a crowd on the shore, pulling at his clothes, holding his comrades in their arms, and crying, this old man stepped forward with a somber air and said:

"Cry, unhappy Tahitians! Cry; if only this was the arrival, and not the departure of these ambitious and trouble-making men; one day, you will know them better. One day, they will return, in one hand the piece of wood that you see attached to the belt of this one here, and the blade that hangs by the side of that one there, in the other, to enslave

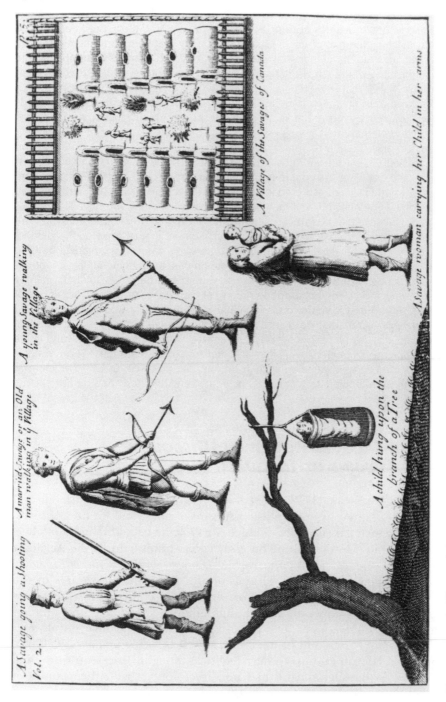

Figure 15.1 A village of the Savages of Canada. Courtyesy of MacMillan and Company.

you, to slaughter you, or to subject you to their extravagances and their vices; one day you will serve under them, as corrupt, as mean, as unhappy as them. But I console myself; I am reaching the end of my life; and the calamity that I am announcing to you, I will not see any of it. Oh Tahitians! my friends! you have had a means to escape this unhappy future; but I would rather die than give you advice. They are going away, let them live."

Then addressing himself to Bougainville, he added: "And you, chief of the brigands who obey you, quickly move your vessel from our shore: we are innocent, we are happy; and you can only harm our happiness. We follow the pure instinct of nature; and you have tried to erase its effects from our souls. Here everything is in common; and you have preached to us I do not know what distinction between 'yours' and 'mine.' Our daughters and our wives are common to us; you have shared this privilege with us; and you have lit in them unknown emotions. They have become insane in your arms; you have become ferocious in theirs. They began to hate each other; you have fought over them; and they have returned to us stained with your blood. We are free; and you have hidden in our land the basis of our future slavery. You are neither a god, nor a demon: who are you then, to make slaves? Orou! you who understands the language of these men, tell all of us, as you told me, what they wrote on this shield of metal: 'this country is ours.' This country is yours? And why? Because you set foot here? If a Tahitian one day landed on your shores, and he inscribed on one of your stones or on the bark of one of your trees: 'this country belongs to the inhabitants of Tahiti,' what would you think? You are the stronger! And what does that mean? When someone took one of the contemptible trinkets that fill your boat, you were amazed, you revenged yourself; and in the same instant you planned in your heart the theft of an entire country! You are not a slave: you would suffer death sooner than be one, and you wish us to serve you! You think then that the Tahitian does not know how to defend his liberty and die?"

5. JEAN-JACQUES ROUSSEAU, *DISCOURSE ON THE ORIGINS OF INEQUALITY*

Jean-Jacques Rousseau (1712–1778) was born in Geneva, Switzerland, and worked as an engraver's apprentice, a servant, a tutor, and eventually secretary to the French ambassador at Venice. In 1750, he gained fame in intellectual circles in France by winning an essay competition held by the Academy of Dijon. Five years later, his controversial *Discourse on the Origins of Inequality* added to this fame. Rousseau became one of the principle figures of the French Enlightenment, an associate of Diderot as a contributor to the *Encyclopédie,* the great compendium of Enlightenment knowledge and opinion published in the 1750s and 1760s. He also published two popular novels, *Julie or the New Héloise* (1760) and *Emile* (1762), as well as *The Social Contract* (1762), his principal contribution to western political thought. Rousseau's traveling was limited to Europe, and he had no direct contact with the peoples of other continents. But like many political and social commentators of his time he used the abstraction of an uncivilized man, who was for Rousseau a good, rational, and conscientious creature, as a contrast with his speculations about the corrupting effects of civilization.

Discourse on the Origin of Inequality

The Second Part

The first man who, having enclosed a piece of ground, bethought himself of saying *This is mine,* and found people simple enough to believe him, was the real founder of civil society. From how many crimes, wars and murders, from how many horrors and misfortunes might not any one have saved mankind, by pulling up the stakes, or filling up the ditch, and crying to his fellows, "Beware of listening to this impostor; you are undone if you once forget that the fruits of the earth belong to us all, and the earth itself to nobody." But there is great probability that things had then already come to such a pitch, that they could no longer continue as they were; for the idea of property depends on many prior ideas, which could only be acquired successively, and cannot have been formed all at once in the human mind. Mankind must have made very considerable progress, and acquired considerable knowledge and industry which they must also have transmitted and increased from age to age, before they arrived at this last point of the state of nature. Let us then go farther back, and endeavour to unify under a single point of view that slow succession of events and discoveries in the most natural order.

Man's first feeling was that of his own existence, and his first care that of self-preservation. The produce of the earth furnished him with all he needed, and instinct told him how to use it. Hunger and other appetites made him at various times experience various modes of existence; and among these was one which urged him to propagate his species—a blind propensity that, having nothing to do with the heart, produced a merely animal act. The want once gratified, the two sexes knew each other no more; and even the offspring was nothing to its mother, as soon as it could do without her.

Such was the condition of infant man; the life of an animal limited at first to mere sensations, and hardly profiting by the gifts nature bestowed on him, much less capable of entertaining a thought of forcing anything from her. But difficulties soon presented themselves, and it became necessary to learn how to surmount them: the height of the trees, which prevented him from gathering their fruits, the competition of other animals desirous of the same fruits, and the ferocity of those who needed them for their own preservation, all obliged him to apply himself to bodily exercises. He had to be active, swift of foot, and vigorous in fight. Natural weapons, stones and sticks, were easily found: he learnt to surmount the obstacles of nature, to contend in case of necessity with other animals, and to dispute for the means of subsistence even with other men, or to indemnify himself for what he was forced to give up to a stronger.

In proportion as the human race grew more numerous, men's cares increased. The difference of soils, climates and seasons, must have introduced some differences into their manner of living. Barren years, long and sharp winters, scorching summers which parched the fruits of the earth, must have demanded a new industry. On the seashore and the banks of rivers, they invented the hook and line, and became fishermen and eaters of fish. In the forests they made bows and arrows, and became huntsmen and warriors. In cold countries they clothed themselves with the skins of the beasts they had slain. The lightning, a volcano, or some lucky chance acquainted them with fire, a new resource against the rigours of winter: they next learned how to preserve this element, then how to reproduce it, and finally how to prepare with it the flesh of animals which before they had eaten raw.

This repeated relevance of various beings to himself, and one to another, would naturally give rise in the human mind to the perceptions of certain relations between them. Thus the relations which we denote by the terms, great, small, strong, weak, swift, slow, fearful, bold, and the like, almost insensibly compared at need, must have at length produced in him a kind of reflection, or rather a mechanical prudence, which would indicate to him the precautions most necessary to his security.

The new intelligence which resulted from this development increased his superiority over other animals, by making him sensible of it. He would now endeavour, therefore, to ensnare them, would play them a thousand tricks, and though many of them might surpass him in swiftness or in strength, would in time become the master of some and the scourge of others. Thus, the first time he looked into himself, he felt the first emotion of pride; and, at a time when he scarce knew how to distinguish the different orders of beings, by looking upon his species as of the highest order, he prepared the way for assuming pre-eminence as an individual.

Other men, it is true, were not then to him what they now are to us, and he had no greater intercourse with them than with other animals; yet they were not neglected in his observations. The conformities, which he would in time discover between them, and between himself and his female, led him to judge of others which were not then perceptible; and finding that they all behaved as he himself would have done in like circumstances, he naturally inferred that their manner of thinking and acting was altogether in conformity with his own. This important truth, once deeply impressed on his mind, must have induced him, from an intuitive feeling more certain and much more rapid than any kind of reasoning, to pursue the rules of conduct, which he had best observe towards them, for his own security and advantage.

Taught by experience that the love of well-being is the sole motive of human actions, he found himself in a position to distinguish the few cases, in which mutual interest might justify him in relying upon the assistance of his fellows; and also the still fewer cases in which a conflict of interests might give cause to suspect them. In the former case, he joined in the same herd with them, or at most in some kind of loose association, that laid no restraint on its members, and lasted no longer than the transitory occasion that formed it. In the latter case, every one sought his own private advantage, either by open force, if he thought himself strong enough, or by address and cunning, if he felt himself the weaker.

In this manner, men may have insensibly acquired some gross ideas of mutual undertakings, and of the advantages of fulfilling them: that is, just so far as their present and apparent interest was concerned: for they were perfect strangers to foresight, and were so far from troubling themselves about the distant future, that they hardly thought of the morrow. If a deer was to be taken, every one saw that, in order to succeed, he must abide faithfully by his post: but if a hare happened to come within the reach of any one of them, it is not to be doubted that he pursued it without scruple, and, having seized his prey, cared very little, if by so doing he caused his companions to miss theirs.

It is easy to understand that such intercourse would not require a language much more refined than that of rooks or monkeys, who associate together for much the same purpose. Inarticulate cries, plenty of gestures and some imitative sounds, must have been for a long time the universal language; and by the addition, in every country, of some conventional articulate sounds (of which, as I have already intimated, the first institution is not too easy to explain) particular languages were produced; but these were rude and imperfect, and nearly such as are now to be found among some savage nations.

Hurried on by the rapidity of time, by the abundance of things I have to say, and by the almost insensible progress of things in their beginnings, I pass over in an instant a multitude of ages; for the slower the events were in their succession, the more rapidly may they be described.

These first advances enabled men to make others with greater rapidity. In proportion as they grew enlightened, they grew industrious. They ceased to fall asleep under the first tree, or in the first cave that afforded them shelter; they invented several kinds of implements of hard and sharp stones, which they used to dig up the earth, and to cut wood; they then made huts out of branches, and afterwards learnt to plaster them over with mud and clay. This was the epoch of a first revolution, which established and distinguished families, and introduced a kind of property, in itself the source of a thousand quarrels and conflicts. As, however, the strongest were probably the first to build themselves huts which they felt themselves able to defend, it may be concluded that the weak found it much easier and safer to imitate, than to attempt to dislodge them: and of those who were once provided with huts, none could have any inducement to appropriate that of his neighbour; not indeed so much because it did not belong to him, as because it could be of no use, and he could not make himself master of it without exposing himself to a desperate battle with the family which occupied it.

The first expansions of the human heart were the effects of a novel situation, which united husbands and wives, fathers and children, under one roof. The habit of living together soon gave rise to the finest feelings known to humanity, conjugal love and paternal affection. Every family became a little society, the more united because liberty and reciprocal attachment were the only bonds of its union. The sexes, whose manner of life had been hitherto the same, began now to adopt different ways of living. The women became more sedentary, and accustomed themselves to mind the hut and their children, while the men went abroad in search of their common subsistence. From living a softer life, both sexes also began to lose something of their strength and ferocity: but, if individuals became to some extent less able to encounter wild beasts separately, they found it, on the other hand, easier to assemble and resist in common.

The simplicity and solitude of man's life in this new condition, the paucity of his wants, and the implements he had invented to satisfy them, left him a great deal of leisure, which he employed to furnish himself with many conveniences unknown to his fathers: and this was the first yoke he inadvertently imposed on himself, and the first source of the evils he prepared for his descendants. For, besides continuing thus to enervate both body and mind, these conveniences lost with use almost all their power to please, and even degenerated into real needs, till the want of them became far more disagreeable than the possession of them had been pleasant. Men would have been unhappy at the loss of them, though the possession did not make them happy.

We can here see a little better how the use of speech became established, and insensibly improved in each family, and we may form a conjecture also concerning the manner in which various causes may have extended and accelerated the progress of language, by making it more and more necessary. Floods or earthquakes surrounded inhabited districts with precipices or waters: revolutions of the globe tore off portions from the continent, and made them islands. It is readily seen that among men thus collected and compelled to live together, a common idiom must have arisen much more easily than among those who still wandered through the forests of the continent. Thus it is very possible that after their first essays in navigation the islanders brought over the use of speech to the continent: and it is at least very probable that communities and languages were first established in islands, and even came to perfection there before they were known on the mainland.

Everything now begins to change its aspect. Men, who have up to now been roving in the woods, by taking to a more settled manner of life, come gradually together, form separate bodies, and at length in every country arises a distinct nation, united in character and manners, not by regulations or laws, but by uniformity of life and food, and the common influence of climate. Permanent neighbourhood could not fail to produce, in time, some connection between different families. Among young people of opposite sexes, living in neighbouring huts, the transient commerce required by nature soon led, through mutual intercourse, to another kind not less agreeable, and more permanent. Men began now to take the difference between objects into account, and to make comparisons; they acquired imperceptibly the ideas of beauty and merit, which soon gave rise to feelings of preference. In consequence of seeing each other often, they could not do without seeing each other constantly. A tender and pleasant feeling insinuated itself into their souls, and the least opposition turned it into an impetuous fury: with love arose jealousy; discord triumphed, and human blood was sacrificed to the gentlest of all passions.

As ideas and feelings succeeded one another, and heart and head were brought into play, men continued to lay aside their original wildness; their private connections became every day more intimate as their limits extended. They accustomed themselves to assemble before their huts round a large tree; singing and dancing, the true offspring of love and leisure, became the amusement, or rather the occupation, of men and women thus assembled together with nothing else to do. Each one began to consider the rest, and to wish to be considered in turn; and thus a value came to be attached to public esteem. Whoever sang or danced best, whoever was the handsomest, the strongest, the most dexterous, or the most eloquent, came to be of most consideration; and this was the first step towards inequality, and at the same time towards vice. From these first distinctions arose on the one side vanity and contempt and on the other shame and envy: and the fermentation caused by these new leavens ended by producing combinations fatal to innocence and happiness.

As soon as men began to value one another, and the idea of consideration had got a footing in the mind, every one put in his claim to it, and it became impossible to refuse it to any with impunity. Hence arose the first obligations of civility even among savages; and every intended injury became an affront; because, besides the hurt which might result from it, the party injured was certain to find in it a contempt for his person, which was often more insupportable than the hurt itself.

Thus, as every man punished the contempt shown him by others, in proportion to his opinion of himself, revenge became terrible, and men bloody and cruel. This is precisely the state reached by most of the savage nations known to us: and it is for want of having made a proper distinction in our ideas, and seen how very far they already are from the state of nature, that so many writers have hastily concluded that man is naturally cruel, and requires civil institutions to make him more mild; whereas nothing is more gentle than man in his primitive state, as he is placed by nature at an equal distance from the stupidity of brutes, and the fatal ingenuity of civilised man. Equally confined by instinct and reason to the sole care of guarding himself against the mischiefs which threaten him, he is restrained by natural compassion from doing any injury to others, and is not led to do such a thing even in return for injuries received. For, according to the axiom of the wise Locke, *There can be no injury, where there is no property.*

But it must be remarked that the society thus formed, and the relations thus established among men, required of them qualities different from those which they possessed from their primitive constitution. Morality began to appear in human actions, and every one, before the institution of law, was the only judge and avenger of the injuries done him, so that the goodness which was suitable in the pure state of nature was no longer proper in the new-born state of society. Punishments had to be made more severe, as opportunities of offending became more frequent, and the dread of vengeance had to take the place of the rigour of the law. Thus, though men had become less patient, and their natural compassion had already suffered some diminution, this period of expansion of the human faculties, keeping a just mean between the indolence of the primitive state and the petulant activity of our egoism, must have been the happiest and most stable of epochs. The more we reflect on it, the more we shall find that this state was the least subject to revolutions, and altogether the very best man could experience; so that he can have departed from it only through some fatal accident, which, for the public good, should never have happened. The example of savages, most of whom have been found in this state, seems to prove that men were meant to remain in it, that it is the real youth of the world, and that all subsequent advances have been apparently so many steps towards the perfection of the individual, but in reality towards the decrepitude of the species.

So long as men remained content with their rustic huts, so long as they were satisfied with clothes made of the skins of animals and sewn together with thorns and fishbones, adorned themselves only with feathers and shells, and continued to paint their bodies different colours, to improve and beautify their bows and arrows and to make with sharp-edged stones fishing boats or clumsy musical instruments; in a word, so long as they undertook only what a single person could accomplish, and confined themselves to such arts as did not require the joint labour of several hands, they lived free, healthy, honest and happy lives, so long as their nature allowed, and as they continued to enjoy the pleasures of mutual and independent intercourse. But from the moment one man began to stand in need of the help of another; from the moment it appeared advantageous to any one man to have enough provisions for two, equality disappeared, property was introduced, work became indispensable, and vast forests became smiling fields, which man had to water with the sweat of his brow, and where slavery and misery were soon seen to germinate and grow up with the crops.

6. THE REVOLUTIONARY MOMENT

The French Revolution of 1789 brought about the possibility of realizing the ideals of the Enlightenment, as the collapse of the Old Regime monarchy brought to power in France a series of assemblies made up of men imbued with those ideals. The reconstruction of the French state and society was to occupy those assemblies for the next decade, marked by the radicalism of the Terror of 1793–1794. The overthrow of the Committee of Public Safety and its leader Maximilien Robespierre in 1794 and the coup d'état of Napoleon Bonaparte in 1799 ended the radicalism of the Revolution.

The revolutionary ideals turned out in many instances to be contradictory and difficult to implement, and nowhere was this more the case than in its ringing declarations of the liberty and equality of all men. Although certainly causing conflict within France, these ideals had a dramatic effect on French colonies in the Caribbean, where planter had quickly rallied to the Revolution in 1789 but also sought to deny free men of color equal political rights and insisted on the need to maintain slavery. The island of Saint-Domingue (Haiti) became a focal point for these conflicts in the 1790s. In January 1789, the people of color on the island petitioned the government in Paris for full rights; another petition, this one to the new National Assembly, followed in October 1789. Both petitions were eventually denied in December 1789, and a decree the following March left the question to a new Colonial Assembly in Saint-Domingue. This sparked several rebellions against the new government of the island, before the French National Assembly granted full equality to people of color in April 1792.

In the meantime, however, the black slaves on the island had revolted, and by late 1793 an army under the leadership of Toussaint L'Ouverture had gained control of the island. In February 1794, the French National Convention officially abolished slavery, bringing Toussaint into adherence to the French Republic. In 1796 he became lieutenant governor of Saint-Domingue and in 1797 commander-in-chief of French armies on the island. By October 1798, he had expelled the French military command and assumed effective control of the island. In July 1801, Toussaint proclaimed a constitution that gave him power for life, but in 1802 he was forced to surrender to the French. He was brought to France, where he died in 1803. The French restored slavery in their colonies in 1802, but in 1803 the black leaders of Haiti declared an independent republic. This confirmed the end of slavery in Haiti, but the institution was not definitively abolished in French possessions until 1848.

Decree of the National Convention of 16 Pluviôse Year II of the French Republic, one and indivisible, Which abolishes the slavery of Negroes in the Colonies.

The National Convention declares that the slavery of Negroes in all the Colonies is abolished; in consequence it decrees that all men, without distinction of color, living in the colonies, are French citizens, and enjoy all the rights assured by the constitution.

Constitution of the French Colony of Saint-Domingue of 17 August 1801 (29 Thermidor Year IX).

Title Two.

Of the Inhabitants.

    3. There cannot exist any slave on this territory; servitude here is forever abolished. All men born here live and die free and French.

    4. All men, no matter what their color, are eligible for all positions.

    5. There exist no other distinction than those of virtues and talents, and no other superiority than that which the law gives in the exercise of a public function. The law is the same for all, no matter whom it punishes or whom it protects.

Study Questions

1. What are the qualities that Aphra Behn attributes to the characters of the King of Coramantien and Oroonoko? How do they differ from the inhabitants of Surinam?
2. How would you describe the principal aspects of the relationship between Robinson Crusoe and Friday?
3. What consequences does Diderot think there will be from Bougainville's visit to Tahiti?
4. How does Rousseau describe the development of civilizations?
5. Do the two documents from the French Revolution make the same assumptions about non-Europeans as are evident in the four preceding documents?

Suggestions for Further Reading

Barker, Anthony J. *The African Link: British Attitudes to the Negro in the Era of the Atlantic Slave Trade, 1550–1807*. London: Frank Cass, 1978.

Berkhofer, Robert F. Jr. *The White Man's Indian*. New York: Random House, 1978.

Blackburn, Robin. *The Overthrow of Colonial Slavery 1776–1848*. New York: Verso, 1988.

Cranston, Maurice. *The Noble Savage: Jean-Jacques Rousseau, 1754–1762*. Chicago: University of Chicago Press, 1991.

Marshall, P. J. and Williams, Glyndwr. *The Great Map of Mankind*. London: J. M. Dent & Sons Ltd., 1982.

Meek, Ronald L. *Social Science and the Ignoble Savage*. New York: Cambridge University Press, 1976.

Web Sites

1. Denis Diderot, 1713–1784

   http://Stanley.feldberg.brandies.edu/~teuber/diderotbio.html

2. Eighteenth-Century E-Texts (Daniel Defoe)

   http://andromeda.Rutgers.edu/~jlynch/18th/d.html

3. The European Enlightenment

   http://www.wsu.edu/~dee/ENLIGHT/ENLIGHT.HTM

4. Internet Modern History Text Book: Enlightenment

   http://www.fordham/edu/halsall/mod/modsbook10.html

5. Jean-Jacques Rousseau Works on the Web

   http://www.wabash.edu/Rousseau/worksonweb.html

16

Pacific Exploration
1763–1850

TEXTS

1. *A Journal of A Voyage Round the World in His Majesty's Ship Endeavour, in the Years 1768, 1769, 1770, and 1771*

2. John Ledyard, *A Journal of Captain Cook's Last Voyage*

3. Johann Zoffany, *The Death of Captain Cook*

4. James Boswell, *Life of Johnson*

5. Charles Darwin, *Beagle Diary*

6. Herman Melville, *Omoo*

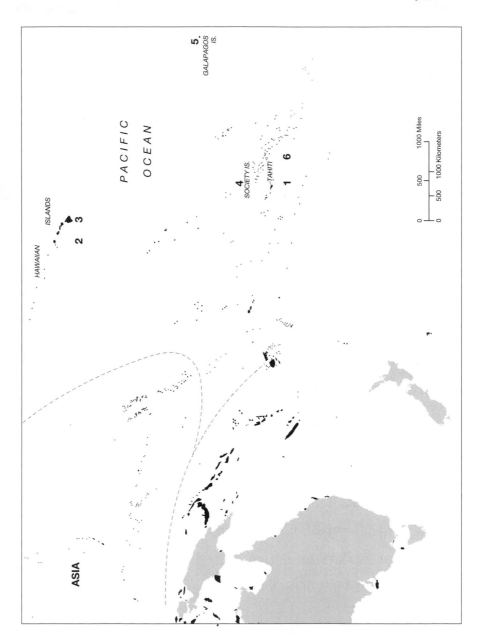

Europeans first visited the Pacific in the early sixteenth century, with the voyage of Ferdinand Magellan in 1512. Following Magellan, other explorers came to the South Sea, searching for a passage to the east. P. F. de Quiros in 1606, Jacques Le Maire in 1616, Abel Tasman in 1643, and William Dampier in 1700 extended the European presence and increased European knowledge of the area. But it was in the last third of the eighteenth century that the Pacific truly became a part of the world known by European mariners, adventurers, and governments. The end of the Seven Years' War in 1763 opened the way for exploration and discovery in the waters between the Americas and the East Indies. In 1764, an English captain, John Byron, sailed around the globe in twenty-two months, a record for circumnavigation. In 1767 and 1768, another English ship, the *Dolphin,* commanded by Samuel Wallis, sailed more slowly across the Pacific, discovering the island of Tahiti before returning to England. A second ship, the *Swallow,* captained by Philip Carteret, had been separated from Byron at Cape Horn, but also successfully crossed the Pacific, discovering Pitcairn Island. At the same time, Louis-Antoine de Bougainville, a Frenchman, also circumnavigated the globe.

Wallis, Byron, Carteret, and Bougainville were precursors of the three voyages of Captain James Cook, the best-known explorer of this era. In 1768, he left London in the *Endeavour* for the Pacific on a voyage to Tahiti for the observation of the transit of the planet Venus. [1] This first voyage also took Cook and his passengers, among whom was the famous botanist Joseph Banks, to New Zealand and to Botany Bay, near present-day Sydney, Australia. By the time they returned to England in 1771, Cook had become the symbol of European exploration of the Pacific. On his second voyage, beginning in 1772, Cook spent three years sailing in the Pacific Ocean and below the Antarctic Circle. His voyage definitively debunked the legend of a Great Southern Continent, whose existence had been hypothesized by many early geographers, and added substantially to European knowledge of significant parts of the Pacific. Finally, in 1776, Cook undertook a third voyage, on the *Resolution,* in search of a northwest passage from the North Pacific to the Atlantic Ocean. On this voyage he discovered the Hawaiian Islands, which he used as a winter base for his forays up the northwest coast of North America. Tragically, on February 14, 1779, Cook was killed by Hawaiians while repairing a damaged foremast on the Resolution. [2, 3]

Cook's voyages had made the Pacific more familiar to Europeans, contributing to their knowledge of geography, botany, and other civilizations. He provided a powerful impetus to European attempts to make sense of this new world they had found, and it became more common for Europeans to visit the Pacific. They took back to Europe people from the Pacific islands, whose presence in Europe inspired comparisons between Europeans and those from, literally, the other side of the world. [4] Whalers from London and Nantucket in Massachusetts opened up the Pacific whaling grounds, seeking oil from sperm whales as a fuel to light Europe and America. In the 1840s and 1850s, European and American navies opened up China and Japan to western trade, bringing more Europeans into the Pacific. As more and more European ships crossed the ocean and visited its islands, scientists came to examine and document the plants and animals of the new lands. [5] These ships, whatever their purposes, left behind shipwrecked sailors and deserters, who became willing or unwilling beachcombers. [6] By the early nineteenth century, the Pacific and its peoples had become firmly fixed in Europeans' visions of the world and their place in it.

1. *A Journal of A Voyage Round the World in His Majesty's Ship Endeavour, in the Years 1768, 1769, 1770, and 1771*

The first voyage of Captain James Cook to the Pacific, as a part of a European effort to observe the transit of the planet Venus close to the earth, occasioned a widespread interest by educated men and women in Europe in the Pacific islands. Several accounts, from Cook's own journal to the scientific journals of Joseph Banks, were published and contributed to this interest. Possibly authored by a midshipman on the *Endeavour*, J. M. Magra, the *Journal of a Voyage Round the World in His Majesty's Ship Endeavour, in the Years 1768, 1769, 1770 and 1771* (1771) was one of the first accounts published after the return to England of Captain James Cook's first voyage to the Pacific.

A Journal of A Voyage Round the World

Monday the 10th of April, in the morning we saw Oznabrug Island, bearing N.W. by W. half W. six leagues distant; and leaving it to the northward, at noon we discovered George's Island from the maintopmast head, and stood towards it; but having little wind, it was the 13th in the morning when we came to anchor in Port Royal bay; and immediately after the captain went on shore in the long-boat, attended by the marines, but returned again in the afternoon, having seen no person of any distinction or consideration among the natives, though he had presented a few beads and other trifles to some of them. The next morning several of the officers and gentlemen landed on the westermost part of the bay, where they were treated with great hospitality by the natives, who gave them provisions dressed in their own manner, with some pieces of cloth manufactured by themselves, and afterwards conducted them through several parts of the island.

    The third day after our arrival several chiefs of the island came on board, and brought with them a few hogs, and a small quantity of fruit. The following day we marked out a place for erecting a fortification to secure us in observing the transit of Venus, for which we were to wait; and at the same time pitched our tents, &c. on shore, planting centinels to guard our tools and utensils, who were directed to suffer none of the natives to come within certain limits; one of the marines however being careless, and willing to amuse himself with their droll gestures and attitudes, allowed several of them to approach him too nearly, who suddenly wrested the musquet out of his hands, and endeavoured to stab him with the bayonet, and afterwards escaped to the woods. One of them, however, who was the first aggressor, was shot through the head in creeping among the bushes, by a party sent in pursuit of them; two or three others were likewise wounded, as we were afterwards informed, though no intelligence could ever be procured of the musquet which they had carried off. . . .

The soil of the island, on the more elevated parts, is dry, and consists of a red loam, which is very deep; but the vallies are covered with a fertile black mould. The island is under the government of a single chief, whose authority is unlimited, and who appoints deputies that preside in different districts, to preserve good order, and collect those impositions or duties, which by long establishment have become his due. And though no particular laws have been enacted among them, yet certain penalties or punishments, from long usage and ancient custom, are annexed to certain crimes or misdemeanors. Thus, for example, those who steal clothes or arms, are commonly put to death, either by hanging or drowning in the sea; but those who steal provisions are bastinadoed. By this practice they wisely vary the punishment of the same crime, when committed from different motives; judging, perhaps, that he who steals cloth or arms, steals because he is either idle or avaricious, qualities which probably will always continue with the offender to the disturbance of society; but he who steals from hunger is impelled by one of the most importunate desires of nature, and will not offend again, unless the same impulse recurs, which it is not likely will often happen.

The natives of Otahitee are unequal in stature, some of them being six feet and three inches in height, others not more than five feet and a half; commonly however they are tall and large in size, but not strong and vigorous; their joints being more flexible than those of the most delicate European woman I have ever seen. From infancy they habituate themselves to dancing, according to their own peculiar mode, which consists of very extravagant distortions and gesticulations, together with various inflexions of their bodies and limbs, which being frequently practified, seem, like the effect of early habit in our tumblers, to be the cause of that enlarged motion in their joints, which prevents their attaining a degree of strength proportionate to their size. In sitting they commonly incline very much forward, but in walking they carry themselves very erect, even when advanced in old age.

Their complection is brown, but much lighter than that of the natives of America; some few among them appeared almost as white as Europeans, and several had red hair, though it is commonly black and strait.

The women of Otahitee have agreeable features, are well proportioned, sprightly, and lascivious; neither do they esteem continence as a virtue, since almost every one of our crew procured temporary wives among them, who were easily retained during our stay. The inhabitants intermarry with each other for life, but with this singular circumstance, that as soon as a man has taken a wife he is excluded the society of the women, and of the unmarried of his own sex, at the time of their meals, being compelled to eat with his servants. For this reason they are not solicitous to attach themselves to a single object, during the earlier part of life, but pursue incontinent gratifications where inclination leads, until a woman becomes pregnant, when the father by long established custom is compelled to marry her.

A considerable part of Otahitee is cultivated and planted with cocoa-nut trees, plaintains, and bananoes, cloth-trees, bread-trees, yams, and potatoes like those of Europe, which have however a bitterish taste. Their animal food consists of fish of various kinds, which they take in different ways, and with great dexterity; these they frequently eat raw, a practice in which some of our people imitated them, and thought it not unpalatable; they likewise feed on swine, of which they have a considerable plenty, but prefer the flesh of dogs to that of all other animals. They have also wild ducks, which differ but very little from those of Europe. They roast or rather bake their meat in a subterraneous oven, made by digging a hole in the ground and lining it with a stone bottom; in this they kindle a fire, and lay several loose stones upon it; when they are all sufficiently heated the fire and ashes are removed, and the meat being wrapped in leaves is placed in the oven, and the hot loose stones laid immediately upon it, and the whole is then covered over with earth; in this manner it is excellently dressed, retaining all its succulency: they have no salt, but instead of it use sea-water. They are immoderate eaters, and swallow large mouthfuls at once. Instead of bread they eat yams, potatoes, plantains, &c. together with a large milky farinaceous fruit, which when baked resembles bread both in texture and taste. They make a kind of paste from the pulp or white substance adhering to the inside of the cocoa-nut shell and bananas, which commonly serves them for supper and breakfast: their common drink is water and the milk or juice of cocoa-nuts. They have no kind of spiritous liquor, except that which is made from a species of pepper growing here, which they ferment in water; but this is so scarce that it is rarely drank, except by the chiefs of the country. They have none among them who pretend to any kind of medical knowledge which is not common to every body. They have indeed but few diseases, and to these they apply but a few empirical remedies, which from experience they think useful, without knowing or enquiring concerning the manner of their operation. Their instruments of music are a large drum, and a kind of flute, made from the joint of a reed, having three perforations or holes, which is blown through the nose. Their fish-hooks are of various sizes; those for taking sharks are very large, and made from heavy solid wood, of a proper figure, and pointed. They have smaller hooks, made likewise from wood, and pointed with bones, which are commonly barbed; besides these they have a variety of very small hooks, made of different circular figures, from mother of pearl. Their lines are made from the fibres of the bark of a tree, which composes almost all their cordage.

2. John Ledyard, *A Journal of Captain Cook's Last Voyage*

John Ledyard, from Groton, Connecticut, enlisted as a corporal in the Royal Marines on the *Resolution*, Captain James Cook's ship on his third voyage to the Pacific. When a split foremast forced the *Resolution* to return to Kealakekua Bay, on the island of Hawai'i, Ledyard commanded the fort on shore that protected the repair of the foremast. He did not, therefore, closely observe the events that led to the death of Cook. Nevertheless, his account provides a description of the conflicts between Cook and the islanders that culminated in the attack on Cook and his death.

A Journal of Captain Cook's Last Voyage

On the 13th at night the Discovery's large cutter which was at her usual moorings at the bower buoy was taken away.

On the 14th the captains met to consult what should be done on this alarming occasion, and the issue of their opinions was that one of the two captains should land with armed boats and a guard of marines at Kiverua, and attempt to persuade Kireeakoo who was then at his house in that town to come on board upon a visit, and that when he was on board he should be kept prisoner until his subjects should release him by a restitution of the cutter, and if it was afterwards thought proper, he or some of the family who might accompany him should be kept as perpetual hostages for the good behavior of the people, during the remaining part of our continuance at Kireekatooa, and this plan was the more approved of by Cook as he had so repeatedly on former occasions to the southward employed it with success.

Clerke was then in a deep decline in his health, and too feeble to undertake the affair though it naturally devolved upon him as a point of duty not well transferable, he therefore beged Cook to oblige him so much as to take that part of the business of the day upon himself in his stead. This Cook agreed to, but previous to his landing made some additional arrangements respecting the possible event of things, though it is certain from the appearance of the subsequent arrangements that he guarded more against the flight of Kireeaboo or those he could wish to see, than from an attack, or even much insult. The disposition of our guards when the movements began were thus: Cook in his pennace with six private marines: a corporal, serjeant and two lieutenants of marines went a head followed by the launch with other marines and seamen on one quarter, and the small cutter on the other with only the crew on board. This part of the guard rowed for Kireekakoa. Our large cutter and two boats from the Discovery had orders to proceed to the mouth of the bay, form at equal distances across, and prevent any communication by water from any other part of the island to the towns within the bay, or from them without. Cook landed at Kiverua about nine o'clock in the morning with the marines in the pennace, and went by a circuitous march to the house of Kireeaboo in order to evade the suspicion of any design. This rout led them through a considerable part of the town which discovered every symptom of mischief, though Cook blinded by some fatal cause could not perceive it, or too self-confident would not regard it.

The town was evacuated by the women and children, who had retired to the circumadjacent hills, and appeared almost destitute of men, but there were at that time 200 chiefs and more than twice that number of other men detached and secreted in different parts of the houses nearest to Kireeaboo exclusive of unknown numbers without the skirts of the town, and those that were seen were dressed many of them in black. When the guard reached Kireeaboo's house, Cook ordered the lieutenant of marines to go in and see if he was at home, and if he was to bring him out; the lieutenant went in and found the old man siting with two or three old women of distinction, and when he gave Kireeaboo to understand that Cook was without and wanted to see him he discovered the greatest marks of uneasiness, but arose and accompanied the lieutenant out, holding his hand; when he came before Cook he squated down upon his hams as a mark of humiliation, and Cook took him by the hand from the lieutenant, and conversed with him.

The appearance of our parade both by water and on shore, though conducted with the utmost silence and with as little ostentation as possible, had alarmed the towns on both

sides of the bay, but particularly Kiverua, who were in complete order for an onset otherwise it would have been a matter of surprise, that though Cook did not see 20 men in passing through the town, yet before he had conversed 10 minutes with Kireeaboo he was
surrounded by three or four hundred people, and above half of them chiefs. Cook grew un-
easy when he observed this, and was the more urgent in his persuasions with Kireeaboo to
go on board, and actually persuaded the old man to go at length, and led him within a rod
or two of the shore, but the just fears and conjectures of the chiefs at last interposed. They
held the old man back, and one of the chiefs threatened Cook when he attempted to make
them quit Kireeaboo. Some of the crowd now cried out that Cook was going to take their
king from them and kill him, and there was one in particular that advanced towards Cook
in an attitude that alarmed one of the guard who presented his bayonet and opposed him:
Acquainting Cook in the mean time of the danger of his situation, and that the Indians in a
few minutes would attack him, that he had overheard the man whom he had just stopped
from rushing in upon him say that our boats which were out in the harbour had just killed
his brother and he would be revenged. Cook attended to what this man said, and desired
him to shew him the Indian that had dared to attempt a combat with him, and as soon as
he was pointed out Cook fired at him with a blank. The Indian perceiving he received no
damage from the fire rushed from without the croud a second time, and threatened any
one that should oppose him. Cook perceiving this fired a ball, which entering the Indian's
groin he fell and was drawn off by the rest. Cook perceiving the people determined to oppose his designs, and that he should not succeed without further bloodshed ordered the
lieutenant of marines (Mr. Phillips) to withdraw his men and get them into the boats, which
were then laying ready to receive them. This was effected by the serjeant, but the instant
they began to retreat Cook was hit with a stone, and perceiving the man who hove, shot him
dead: The officer in the boats perceiving the guard retreating, and hearing this third discharge ordered the boats to fire, this occasioned the guard to face about and fire, and then
the attack became general, Cook and Mr. Phillips were together a few paces in the rear of
the guard, and perceiving a general fire without orders quitted Kireeaboo, and ran to the
shore to put a stop to it, but not being able to make themselves heard, and being close
pressed upon by the chiefs they joined the guard and fired as they retreated. Cook having
at length reached the margin of the water between the fire of the boats waved with his hat
to cease firing and come in, and while he was doing this a chief from behind stabed him
with one of our iron daggers just under the shoulder-blade, and passed quite through his
body. Cook fell with his face in the water and immediately expired. Mr. Phillips not being
able any longer to use his susee drew his sword and engaging the chief who he saw kill
Cook soon dispatched him, his guard in the mean time were all killed but two, and they had
plunged into the water and were swimming to the boats, he stood thus for some time the
butt of all their force, and being as complete in the use of his sword as he was accomplished: his noble achievements struck the barbarians with awe, but being wounded and
growing faint from loss of blood, and excessive action, he plunged into the sea with his
sword in his hand and swam to the boats, where however he was scarcely taken on board
before somebody saw one of the marines that had swam from the shore laying flat upon
the bottom. Phillips hearing this run aft, threw himself in after him and brought him up with
him to the surface of the water and both were taken in.

The boats had hitherto kept up a very hot fire, and laying off without the reach of
any weapons but stones had received no damage, and being fully at leisure to keep up
an unremitted and uniform action made great havoc among the Indians, particularly
among the chiefs who stood foremost in the crowd and were most exposed, but whether

from their bravery or ignorance of the real cause that deprived so many of them of life, they made such a stand, may be questioned since it is certain that they in general if not universally understood, heretofore that it was the fire only of our arms that destroyed them, this seems to be strengthened by the circumstance of the large thick mats they were observed to wear, which were also constantly kept wet, and furthermore the Indian that Cook fired at with a blank discovered no fear when he found his mat unburnt, saying in their language when he throwed it to the by-standers that there was no fire had touched it. This may be supposed at least to have had some influence. It is however certain whether from one or both those causes that the numbers who fell made no apparent impression on those, who survived, they were immediately taken off and had their places supplied in a constant determined succession.

Lieutenant Gore who commanded as first lieutenant under Cook in the Resolution, which lay opposite the place where this attack was made, perceiving with his glass that the guard on shore was cut off, and that Cook had fell, immediately passed a spring upon one of the cabies, and bringing the ship's starboard guns to bear, and fired two round shot over the boats into the middle of the croud and both the thunder of the cannon and the effects of the shot, opperated so powerfully, that it produced a most precipitate retreat from the shore to the town. This was done that the boats might land and secure our dead. But the lieutenant who commanded the boats did not chose to improve the hint, though the people in the boats were eager at least to get the bodies of their comrades and their lost commander, if they did no more. Mr. Phillips was so enraged at this palpable mitance of apparent pusilanimity, that the altercation he had with this other lieutenant would have ended in the immediate death of one of them had not a signal from the ship that instant hove out put an end to it by orders to return.

When the boats from the shore reached the ships the boats in the mouth of the bay also returned. The conduct of the lieutenant, who commanded the boats at the town, was an object that required an early attention, but from the situation of other matters of more immediate importance it was defered. Our mast that was repairing at Kireekakoa, and our astronomical tents were only protected by a corporal and six marines exclusive of the carpenters at work upon it, and demanded immediate protection: As soon, therefore, as the people were refreshed with some grog and reinforced they were ordered thither. In the mean time the marine who had been taken up by Mr. Phillips discovered returning life and seemed in a way to recover, and we found Mr. Phillips's wound not dangerous, though, very bad. We also observed at Kiverua that our dead were drawn of by the Indians, which was a mortifying sight, but after the boats were gone they did it in spite of our cannon, which were firing at them several minutes, but they had no sooner effected this matter than they retired to the hills to avoid our shot. The expedition to Kiverua had taken up about an hour and an half, and we lost besides Cook a corporal and three marines.

3. JOHANN ZOFFANY, *THE DEATH OF CAPTAIN COOK*

The death of Cook also became a well-known image for painters of the time. Johann Zoffany (1733–1810) was a successful painter in late-eighteenth-century England, nominated as a member of the Royal Academy in 1769. He planned to accompany Cook on his second voyage in 1772 to work with the

Figure 16.1 The Death of Captain Cook. © National Maritime Museum Picture Library, London, England.

naturalist Joseph Banks, but withdrew, like Banks, because of the failure of the Admiralty to provide an acceptable ship for the expedition. In 1783, Zoffany went to India, where he gained his fortune painting commissions for the British officers and families who had settled there. He returned to England in 1790. His *The Death of Captain Cook,* painted around 1795, was hung at the Greenwich Naval Hospital.

4. JAMES BOSWELL, *LIFE OF JOHNSON*

Omai, a native of the island of Huahine in the Society Islands, was taken to England in 1771 by Captain Tobias Furneaux of the *Adventure,* the ship that accompanied James Cook on his first voyage. Omai was lionized during the six years he spent in England, being introduced into English society, meeting King George III, having his portrait painted and dining with educated men such as Samuel Johnson, a dinner recorded by Johnson's biographer, James Boswell. He provided an example of uncivilized nature in the middle of English civilization, but Omai was not allowed to remain in Europe. On James Cook's third voyage, in 1777, Omai was returned to his native island.

Life of Johnson

On Wednesday, April 3, in the morning I found him very busy putting his books in order, and as they were generally very old ones, clouds of dust were flying around him. He had on a pair of large gloves such as hedgers use. His present appearance put me in mind of my uncle, Dr. Boswell's description of him, 'A robust genius, born to grapple with whole libraries.'

I gave him an account of a conversation which had passed between me and Captain Cook, the day before, at dinner at Sir John Pringle's; and he was much pleased with the conscientious accuracy of that celebrated circumnavigator, who set me right as to many of the exaggerated accounts given by Dr. Hawkesworth of his Voyages. I told him that while I was with the Captain, I catched the enthusiasm of curiosity and adventure, and felt a strong inclination to go with him on his next voyage. JOHNSON. 'Why, Sir, a man *does* feel so, till he considers how very little he can learn from such voyages.' BOSWELL. 'But one is carried away with the general grand and indistinct notion of A VOYAGE ROUND THE WORLD.' JOHNSON. 'Yes, Sir, but a man is to guard himself against taking a thing in general.' I said I was certain that a great part of what we are told by the travellers to the South Sea must be conjecture, because they had not enough of the language of those countries to understand so much as they have related. Objects falling under the observation of the senses might be clearly known; but every thing intellectual, every thing abstract— politicks, morals, and religion, must be darkly guessed. Dr. Johnson was of the same opinion. He upon another occasion, when a friend mentioned to him several extraordinary facts, as communicated to him by the circumnavigators, slily observed, 'Sir, I never before knew how much I was respected by these gentlemen; they told *me* none of these things.'

He had been in company with Omai, a native of one of the South Sea Islands, after he had been some time in this country. He was struck with the elegance of his behaviour, and accounted for it thus: 'Sir, he had passed his time, while in England, only in the best company; so that all that he had acquired of our manners was genteel. As a proof of this, Sir, Lord Mulgrave and he dined one day at Streatham; they sat with their backs to the light fronting me, so that I could not see distinctly; and there was so little of the savage in Omai, that I was afraid to speak to either, lest I should mistake one for the other.'

A gentleman' expressed a wish to go and live three years at Otaheité, or New-Zealand, in order to obtain a full acquaintance with people, so totally different from all that we have ever known, and be satisfied what pure nature can do for man. JOHNSON. 'What could you learn, Sir? What can savages tell, but what they themselves have seen? Of the past, or the invisible, they can tell nothing. The inhabitants of Otaheité and New-Zealand are not in a state of pure nature; for it is plain they broke off from some other people. Had they grown out of the ground, you might have judged of a state of pure nature. Fanciful people may talk of a mythology being amongst them; but it must be invention. They have once had religion, which has been gradually debased. And what account of their religion can you suppose to be learnt from savages? Only consider, Sir, our own state: our religion is in a book; we have an order of men whose duty it is to teach it; we have one day in the week set apart for it and this is in general pretty well observed: yet ask the first ten gross men you meet, and hear what they can tell their religion.'

5. CHARLES DARWIN, *BEAGLE DIARY*

Science formed an important part of the motivation for European explo- ration of the Pacific, and indeed was the principal reason for Cook's first voy- age to Tahiti, from which he participated in an effort to track the passage of the planet Venus close to the earth in 1768. The presence of Joseph Banks on the *Endeavour* indicated another important contribution of science. On this and subsequent voyages, scientists formed an important part of the ship's company, inventorying the minerals, plants, and animals they found in the Pacific. Upon their return, they presented their results in memoirs and in lec- tures to the scientific academies and institutes of Europe. Science became an integral part of the European penetration into the Pacific.

Charles Darwin (1809–1882) studied medicine at Edinburgh University and botany and geology at Cambridge University. He read and was strongly influenced by Humboldt's *Personal Narrative* (see Chapter 20), becoming en- thusiastic about natural history. Although he is best known for the theory of natural selection elaborated in his *The Origins of Species* (1859) and *The Descent of Man* (1871), at the beginning of his career as a botanist and geologist he sailed across the Pacific on the ship *Beagle*. On a voyage to extend the survey of South America and to carry out a chain of chronometric measurements around the world, the *Beagle* sailed on December 27, 1831, and returned on October 6, 1836. The voyage not only turned Darwin from an inexperienced scientist into one of great discipline, method, and knowledge, but it also raised questions in his mind about the origins of the earth and the different forms of life on it, and provided him with an empirical basis for the specula- tions set out in his later works.

Beagle Diary

October 8th.—We arrived at James Island: this island, as well as Charles Island, were long since thus named after our kings of the Stuart line. Mr. Bynoe, myself, and our servants were left here for a week, with provisions and a tent, whilst the Beagle went for water. We found here a party of Spaniards, who had been sent from Charles Island to dry fish, and to salt tortoise-meat. About six miles inland, and at the height of nearly 2000 feet, a hovel had been built in which two men lived, who were employed in catching tortoises, whilst the others were fishing on the coast. I paid this party two visits, and slept there one night. As in the other islands, the lower region was covered by nearly leafless bushes, but the trees were here of a larger growth than elsewhere, several being two feet and some even two feet nine inches in diameter. The upper region being kept damp by the clouds, supports a green and flourishing vegetation. So damp was the ground, that there were large beds of a coarse cyperus, in which great numbers of a very small water-rail lived and bred. While staying in this upper region, we lived entirely upon tortoise-meat: the breast-plate roasted (as the Gauchos do *carne con cuero*), with the flesh on it, is very good; and the young tortoises make excellent soup; but otherwise the meat to my taste is indifferent.

One day we accompanied a party of the Spaniards in their whale-boat to a salina, or lake from which salt is procured. After landing, we had a very rough walk over a rugged field of recent lava, which has almost surrounded a tuff-crater, at the bottom of which the salt-lake lies. The water is only three or four inches deep, and rests on a layer of beautifully crystallized, white salt. The lake is quite circular, and is fringed with a border of bright green succulent plants; the almost precipitous walls of the crater are clothed with wood, so that the scene was altogether both picturesque and curious. A few years since, the sailors belonging to a sealing-vessel murdered their captain in this quiet spot; and we saw his skull lying among the bushes.

During the greater part of our stay of a week, the sky was cloudless, and if the trade-wind failed for an hour, the heat became very oppressive. On two days, the thermometer within the tent stood for some hours at 93°; but in the open air, in the wind and sun, at only 85°. The sand was extremely hot; the thermometer placed in some of a brown colour immediately rose to 137°, and how much above that it would have risen, I do not know, for it was not graduated any higher. The black sand felt much hotter, so that even in thick boots it was quite disagreeable to walk over it.

The natural history of these islands is eminently curious, and well deserves attention. Most of the organic productions are aboriginal creations, found nowhere else; there is even a difference between the inhabitants of the different islands; yet all show a marked relationship with those of America, though separated from that continent by an open space of ocean, between 500 and 600 miles in width. The archipelago is a little world within itself, or rather a satellite attached to America, whence it has derived a few stray colonists, and has received the general character of its indigenous productions. Considering the small size of these islands, we feel the more astonished at the number of their aboriginal beings, and at their confined range. Seeing every height crowned with its crater, and the boundaries of most of the lava-streams still distinct, we are led to believe that within a period, geologically recent, the unbroken ocean was here spread out. Hence, both in space and time, we seem to be brought somewhat near to that great fact—that mystery of mysteries—the first appearance of new beings on this earth. . . . I have not as yet noticed by far the most remarkable feature in the natural history of this archipelago; it is, that the different islands to a considerable extent are inhabited by a different set of beings. My attention was first called to this fact by the Vice-Governor, Mr. Lawson, declaring that the tortoises differed from the different islands, and that he could with certainty tell from which island any one was brought. I did not for some time pay sufficient attention to this statement, and I had already partially mingled together the collections from two of the islands. I never dreamed that islands, about fifty or sixty miles apart, and most of them in sight of each other, formed of precisely the same rocks, placed under a quite similar climate, rising to a nearly equal height, would have been differently tenanted; but we shall soon see that this is the case. It is the fate of most voyagers, no sooner to discover what is most interesting in any locality, then they are hurried from it; but I ought, perhaps, to be thankful that I obtained sufficient materials to establish this most remarkable fact in the distribution of organic beings.

The inhabitants, as I have said, state that they can distinguish the tortoises from the different islands; and that they differ not only in size, but in other characters. Captain Porter has described those from Charles and from the nearest island to it, namely, Hood Island, as having their shells in front thick and turned up like a Spanish saddle, whilst the tortoises from James Island are rounder, blacker, and have a better taste when cooked. M. Bibron, moreover, informs me that he has seen what he considers two distinct species of tortoise from the Galapagos, but he does not know from which islands. The specimens that I brought from three islands were young ones; and probably owing to this cause, neither Mr. Gray nor myself could find in them any specific differences. I have remarked that the marine Amblyrhynchus was larger at Albermarle Island than elsewhere; and M. Bibron informs me that he has seen two distinct aquatic species of this genus; so that the different islands probably have their representative species or races of the Amblyrhynchus, as well as of the tortoise. My attention was first thoroughly aroused, by comparing together the numerous specimens, shot by myself and several other parties on board, of the mocking-thrushes, when, to my astonishment, I discovered that all those from Charles Island belonged to one species (Mimus trifasciatus); all from Albermarle Island to M. parvulus; and all from James and Chatham Islands (between which two other islands are situated, as connecting links) belonged to M. melanotis. These two latter species are closely allied, and would by some ornithologists be considered as only well-marked races or varieties; but the Mimus trifasciatus is very distinct. Unfortunately most of the specimens of the finch tribe were mingled together; but I have strong reasons to suspect that some of the species of the sub-group Geospiza are confined to separate islands. If the different islands have their representatives of Geospiza, it may help to explain the singularly large number of the species of this sub-group in this one small archipelago, and as a probable consequence of their numbers, the perfectly graduated series in the size of their beaks. Two species of the sub-group Cactornis, and two of Camarhynchus, were procured in the archipelago; and of the numerous specimens of these two sub-groups shot by four collectors at James Island, all were found to belong to one species of each; whereas the numerous specimens shot either on Chatham or Charles Island (for the two sets were mingled together) all belonged to the two other species: hence we may feel almost sure that these islands possess their representative species of these two sub-groups. In land-shells this law of distribution does not appear to hold good. In my very small collection of insects, Mr. Waterhouse remarks, that of those which were ticketed with their locality, not one was common to any two of the islands.

If we now turn to the Flora, we shall find the aboriginal plants of the different islands wonderfully different. I give all the following results on the high authority of my friend Dr. J. Hooker. I may premise that I indiscriminately collected everything in flower on the different islands, and fortunately kept my collections separate. Too much confidence, however, must not be placed in the proportional results, as the small collections brought home by some other naturalists, though in some respects confirming the results, plainly show that much remains to be done in the botany of this group: the Leguminosæ, moreover, have as yet been only approximately worked out. . . .

Hence we have the truly wonderful fact, that in James Island, of the thirty-eight Galapageian plants, or those found in no other part of the world, thirty are exclusively confined to this one island; and in Albermarle Island, of the twenty-six aboriginal Gala-pageian plants, twenty-two are confined in this one island, that is, only four are at present known to grow in the other islands of the archipelago; and so on, as shown in the above table, with the plants from Chatham and Charles Islands. This fact will, perhaps, be rendered even more striking, by giving a few illustrations:—thus, Scalesia, a remarkable arborescent genus of the Compositæ, is confined to the archipelago: it has six species; one from Chatham, one from Albemarle, one from Charles Island, two from James Island, and the sixth from one of the three latter islands, but it is not known from which: not one of these six species grows on any two islands. Again, Euophorbia, a mundane or widely distributed genus, has here eight species, of which seven are confined to the archipelago, and not one found on any two islands: Acalypha and Borreria, both mundane genera, have respectively six and seven species, none of which have the same species on two islands, with the exception of one Borreria, which does occur on two islands. The species of the Compositæ are particularly local; and Dr. Hooker has furnished me with several other most striking illustrations of the difference of the species on the different islands. He remarks that this law of distribution holds good both with those genera confined to the archipelago, and those distributed in other quarters of the world: in like manner we have seen that the different islands have their proper species of the mundane genus of tortoise, and of the widely distributed American genus of the mocking-thrush, as well as of two of the Galapageian sub-groups of finches, and almost certainly of the Galapageian genus Amblyrhynchus.

The distribution of the tenants of this archipelago would not be nearly so wonderful, if, for instance, one island had a mocking-thrush, and a second island some other quite distinct genus;—if one island had its genus of lizard, and a second island another distinct genus, or none whatever;—or if the different islands were inhabited, not by representative species of the same genera of plants, but by totally different genera, as does to a certain extent hold good; for, to give one instance, a large berry-bearing tree at James Island has no representative species in Charles Island. But it is the circumstance, that several of the islands possess their own species of the tortoise, mocking-thrush, finches, and numerous plants, these species having the same general habits, occupying analogous situations, and obviously filling the same place in the natural economy of this archipelago, that strikes me with wonder. It may be suspected that some of those representative species, at least in the case of the tortoise and of some of the birds, may hereafter prove to be only well-marked races; but this would be of equally great interest to the philosophical naturalist. I have said that most of the islands are in sight of each other: I may specify that Charles Island is fifty miles from the nearest part of Chatham Island, and thirty-three miles from the nearest part of Albermarle Island. Chatham Island is sixty miles from the nearest part of James Island, but there are two intermediate islands between them which were not visited by me. James Island is only ten miles from the nearest part of Albermarle Island, but the two points where the collections were made are thirty-two miles apart. I must repeat, that neither the nature of the soil, nor height of the land, nor the climate, nor the general character of the associated beings, and therefore their action one on another, can differ much in the different islands. If there be any sensible difference in their climates, it must be between the windward group (namely Charles and Chatham Islands), and that to leeward; but there seems to be no corresponding difference in the productions of these two halves of the archipelago.

The only light which I can throw on this remarkable difference in the inhabitants of the different islands, is, that very strong currents of the sea running in a westerly and

W.N.W. direction must separate, as far as transportal by the sea is concerned, the southern islands from the northern ones; and between these northern islands a strong N.W. current was observed, which must effectually separate James and Albemarle Islands. As the archipelago is free to a most remarkable degree from gales of wind, neither the birds, insects, nor lighter seeds, would be blown from island to island. And lastly, the profound depth of the ocean between the islands, and their apparently recent (in a geological sense) volcanic origin, render it highly unlikely that they were ever united; and this, probably, is a far more important consideration than any other, with respect to the geographical distribution of their inhabitants. Reviewing the facts here given, one is astonished at the amount of creative force, if such an expression may be used, displayed on these small, barren, and rocky islands; and still more so, at its diverse yet analogous action on points so near each other. I have said that the Galapagos Archipelago might be called a satellite attached to America, but it should rather be called a group of satellites, physically similar, organically distinct, yet intimately related to each other, and all related in a marked, though much lesser degree, to the great American continent.

6. HERMAN MELVILLE, *OMOO*

Herman Melville (1819–1891) worked as a clerk in the New York State Bank before shipping as a cabin boy on a ship bound for Liverpool, England, in 1837. In 1841 he joined the crew of the *Acushnet,* a New England whaler heading for the Southern Whale Fishery. This voyage provided him with the material for his most famous literary work, the novel *Moby Dick* (1851). But it also provided other experiences concerning not just whaling but also beachcombing in the Pacific islands. He left the *Acushnet* in the Marquesas Islands in 1842, living in the valley of Typee on that island for several months. He then joined the crew of an Australian whaler, the *Lucy Ann,* but deserted again in Tahiti. He finally returned to Boston in 1844 after enlisting in the U.S. Navy as a seaman on the frigate *United States.* He wrote about his experiences on the Marquesas and in Tahiti in the romantic narratives *Typee* (1846) and *Omoo* (1847).

Omoo

It was the earliest dawn. The morning only showed itself along the lower edge of a bank of purple clouds, pierced by the misty peaks of Tahiti. The tropical day seemed too languid to rise. Sometimes, starting fitfully, it decked the clouds with faint edgings of pink and gray, which, fading away, left all dim again. Anon, it threw out thin, pale rays, growing lighter and lighter, until at last, the golden morning sprang out of the East with a bound—darting its bright beams hither and thither, higher and higher, and sending them, broadcast, over the face of the heavens.

All balmy from the groves of Tahiti, came an indolent air, cooled by its transit over the waters; and grateful under foot was the damp and slightly yielding beach, from which the waves seemed just retired.

The doctor was in famous spirits; removing his Roora, he went splashing into the sea; and, after swimming a few yards, waded ashore, hopping, skipping, and jumping along the beach; but very careful to cut all his capers in the direction of our journey.

Say what they will of the glowing independence one feels in the saddle, give me the first morning flush of your cheery pedestrian!

Thus exhilarated, we went on, as light-hearted and care-free as we could wish.

And here I cannot refrain from lauding the very superior inducements which most intertropical countries afford, not only to mere rovers like ourselves, but to penniless people generally. In these genial regions, one's wants are naturally diminished; and those which remain are easily gratified: fuel, house-shelter, and if you please, clothing, may be entirely dispensed with.

How different, our hard northern latitudes! Alas! the lot of a "poor devil," twenty degrees north of the tropic of Cancer, is indeed pitiable.

At last, the beach contracted to hardly a yard's width, and the dense thicket almost dipped into the sea. In place of the smooth sand, too, we had sharp fragments of broken coral, which made travelling exceedingly unpleasant. "Lord! my foot!" roared the doctor, fetching it up for inspection, with a galvanic fling of the limb. A sharp splinter had thrust itself into the flesh, through a hole in his boot. My sandals were worse yet; their soles taking a sort of fossil impression of everything trod upon.

Turning round a bold sweep of the beach, we came upon a piece of fine, open ground, with a fisherman's dwelling in the distance, crowning a knoll which rolled off into the water.

The hut proved to be a low, rude erection, very recently thrown up; for the bamboos were still green as grass, and the thatching, fresh and fragrant as meadow hay. It was open upon three sides; so that, upon drawing near, the domestic arrangements within were in plain sight. No one was stirring; and nothing was to be seen but a clumsy old chest of native workmanship, a few calabashes, and bundles of tappa hanging against a post; and a heap of something, we knew not what, in a dark corner. Upon close inspection, the doctor discovered it to be a loving old couple, locked in each other's arms, and rolled together in a tappa mantle.

"Halloa! Darby!" he cried, shaking the one with a beard. But Darby heeded him not; though Joan, a wrinkled old body, started up in affright, and yelled aloud. Neither of us attempting to gag her, she presently became quiet; and after staring hard, and asking some unintelligible questions, she proceeded to rouse her still slumbering mate.

What ailed him, we could not tell; but there was no waking him. Equally in vain were all his dear spouse's cuffs, pinches, and other endearments; he lay like a log, face up, and snoring away like a cavalry trumpeter.

"Here, my good woman," said Long Ghost, "just let *me* try;" and, taking the patient right by his nose, he so lifted him bodily, into a sitting position, and held him there until his eyes opened. When this event came to pass, Darby looked round like one stupefied; and then, springing to his feet, backed away into a corner, from which place we became the objects of his earnest and respectful attention.

"Permit me, my dear Darby, to introduce to you my esteemed friend and comrade, Paul," said the doctor, gallanting me up with all the grimace and flourish imaginable.

Upon this, Darby begun to recover his faculties, and surprised us not a little, by talking a few words of English. So far as could be understood, they were expressive of his having been aware, that there were two "karhowrees" in the neighbourhood; that he was glad to see us, and would have something for us to eat in no time.

How he came by his English, was explained to us before we left. Some time previous, he had been a denizen of Papeetee, where the native language is broidered over with the most classic sailor phrases. He seemed to be quite proud of his residence there, and alluded to it in the same significant way in which a provincial informs you that in his time he has resided in the capital. The old fellow was disposed to be garrulous; but being sharp-set, we told him to get breakfast; after which we would hear his anecdotes. While employed among the calabashes, the strange, antiquated fondness between these old semi-savages was really amusing. I made no doubt that they were saying to each other, "Yes, my love"—"No, my life," just in the way that some young couples do at home.

They gave us a hearty meal; and, while we were discussing its merits, they assured us, over and over again, that they expected nothing in return for their attentions; more: we were at liberty to stay as long as we pleased, and, as long as we *did* stay, their house and everything they had, was no longer theirs, but ours; still more: they themselves were our slaves—the old lady, to a degree that was altogether superfluous. This, now, is Tahitian hospitality! Self-immolation upon one's own hearthstone for the benefit of the guest.

The Polynesians carry their hospitality to an amazing extent. Let a native of Waiurar, the westernmost part of Tahiti, make his appearance as a traveller at Partoowye, the most easterly village of Imeeo, though a perfect stranger, the inhabitants on all sides accost him at their doorways, inviting him to enter, and make himself at home. But the traveller passes on, examining every house attentively, until, at last, he pauses before one which suits him, and then exclaiming, "Ah, ena maitai" (this one will do, I think), he steps in, and makes himself perfectly at ease, flinging himself upon the mats, and very probably calling for a nice young cocoa-nut, and a piece of toasted bread-fruit, sliced thin, and done brown.

Curious to relate, however, should a stranger carrying it thus bravely, be afterward discovered to be without a house of his own, why, he may thenceforth go a-begging for his lodgings. The "karhowrees," or white men, are exceptions to this rule. Thus is it precisely as in civilised countries; where those who have houses and lands are incessantly bored to death with invitations to come and live in other people's houses, while many a poor gentleman who inks the seams of his coat, and to whom the like invitation would be really acceptable, may go and sue for it. But to the credit of the ancient Tahitians, it should here be observed, that this blemish upon their hospitality is only of recent origin, and was wholly unknown in old times. So told me Captain Bob.

In Polynesia it is esteemed a great hit, if a man succeed in marrying into a family, to which the best part of the community is related (Heaven knows it is otherwise with us). The reason is, that when he goes a-travelling, the greater number of houses are the more completely at his service.

Receiving a paternal benediction from old Darby and Joan, we continued our journey; resolved to stop at the very next place of attraction which offered.

Nor did we long stroll for it. A fine walk along a beach of shells, and we came to a spot, where with trees here and there, the land was all meadow, sloping away to the water, which stirred a sedgy growth of reeds bordering its margin. Close by was a little cove, walled in with coral, where a fleet of canoes was dancing up and down. A few paces distant, on a natural terrace overlooking the sea, were several native dwellings, newly thatched, and peeping into view out of the foliage, like summer-houses.

As we drew near, forth came a burst of voices; and presently, three gay girls, overflowing with life, health, and youth, and full of spirits and mischief. One was arrayed in a flaunting robe of calico; and her long black hair was braided behind in two immense tresses, joined together at the ends, and wreathed with the green tendrils of a vine. From her self-possessed and forward air I fancied she might be some young lady from Papeetee, on a visit to her country relations. Her companions wore mere slips of cotton cloth; their hair was dishevelled; and, though very pretty, they betrayed the reserve and embarrassment characteristic of the provinces.

The little gypsy first mentioned ran up to me with great cordiality; and giving the Tahitian salutation, opened upon me such a fire of questions, that there was no understanding, much less answering, them. But our hearty welcome to Loohooloo, as she called the hamlet, was made plain enough. Meanwhile, Doctor Long Ghost gallantly presented an arm to each of the other young ladies, which at first they knew not what to make of; but at last, taking it for some kind of a joke, accepted the civility.

The names of these three damsels were at once made known by themselves; and being so exceedingly romantic, I cannot forbear particularising them. Upon my comarade's arms, then, were hanging Night and Morning, in the persons of Farnowar, or the Day-born, and Farnoopoo, or the Night-born. She with the tresses was very appropriately styled Marhar-Rarrar, the Wakeful, or Bright-eyed.

By this time, the houses were emptied of the rest of their inmates—a few old men and women, and several strapping young fellows rubbing their eyes and yawning. All crowded round putting questions as to whence we came. Upon being informed of our acquaintance with Zeke, they were delighted; and one of them recognised the boots worn by the doctor. "Keekee (Zeke) maitai," they cried, "nuee nuee hanna hanna portarto"—(makes plenty of potatoes).

There was now a little friendly altercation as to who should have the honour of entertaining the strangers. At last, a tall old gentleman, by name Marharvai, with a bald head and white beard, took us each by the hand, and led us into his dwelling. Once inside, Marharvai, pointing about with his staff, was so obsequious in assuring us that his house was ours, that Long Ghost suggested he might as well hand over the deed.

It was drawing near noon; so after a light lunch of roasted bread-fruit, a few whiffs of a pipe, and some lively chatting, our host admonished the company to lie down, and take the everlasting siesta. We complied; and had a social nap all round.

Study Questions

1. In Ledyard's account, what was the cause of the death of Captain Cook?
2. Are there differences apparent between Ledyard's description of the death of Cook and the way this is portrayed in the painting?
3. Discuss the ways in which the Pacific islanders are portrayed in the different texts.
4. How does Melville relate to the Tahitian people he meets?
5. Both Cook's first voyage and Darwin's trip on the *Beagle* were for scientific purposes. What similarities and differences do you see in the approaches of the two expeditions?

Suggested Readings

Beaglehole, J. C. *The Exploration of the Pacific.* London: Adam & Charles Black, 1947.

Beaglehole, J. C. *The Life of Captain James Cook.* Stanford, CA: Stanford University Press, 1974.

Carter, Paul. *The Road to Botany Bay.* New York: Knopf, 1988.

Dening, Greg. *Islands and Beaches.* Chicago: Dorsey Press, 1980.

Kuykendall, Ralph S. *The Hawaiian Kingdom.* Honolulu: University of Hawaii Press, 1966.

Maude, H. E. "Beachcombers and Castaways." In *Of Islands and Men: Studies in Pacific History.* New York: Oxford University Press, 1968.

Smith, Bernard. *Imagining the Pacific in the Wake of the Cook Voyages.* New Haven: Yale University Press, 1992.

Spate, O. H. K. *Paradise Found and Lost.* Minneapolis: University of Minnesota Press, 1988.

Web Sites

1. Captain Cook Study Unit

   www.freespace.virgin.net/chris.jones

2. Captain Cook: Voyages of Discovery. Hunterian Museum, University of Glasgow

   www.gla.ac.uk/Museum/HuntMus/Cook/

3. Pacific Studies World Wide Web Virtual Library

   www.coombs.anu.edu.au/wwwvl-PacificStudies.html

17

African Exploration
1820–1885

TEXTS

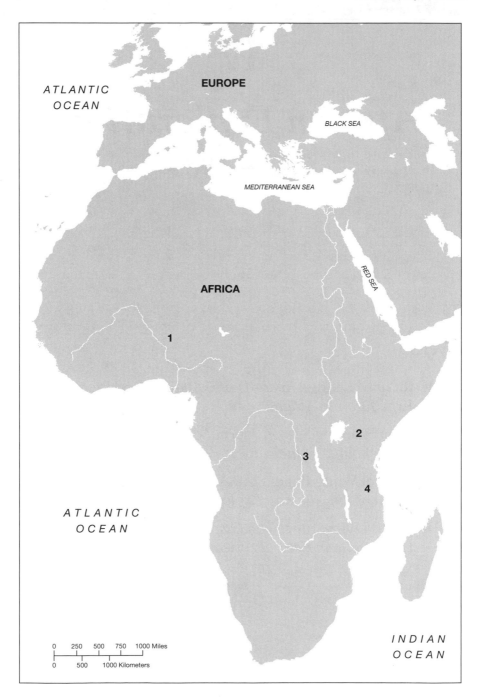

Euuropean contact with the continent of Africa had been limited to coastal settlements until the late eighteenth century. At that time some increased contact began, with one initial focus being the Nile river basin, which extended from Alexandria on the Mediterranean Sea southward, eventually splitting into two tributary streams, the Blue Nile to the east and the White Nile which originated in the Great Lakes region of the continent. Under the control of the Ottoman emperor in Constantinople, Egypt was the initial point of contact, and Cairo, 100 miles from the delta, was the focal point for trade up the Nile, to Damascus and the Red Sea to the east, and to the Fezzan in the west. The first European to venture beyond Cairo was James Bruce, an Englishman, who in 1769 tried to go up the Nile from Cairo. He found himself blocked by local warfare around Aswan, and made his way east across the desert to the Red Sea. In November 1769, he turned toward the interior, after finally extricating himself from the pirates who controlled Massawa. By mid-February 1770, he had reached Gondar, the principle city of Ethiopia, over-looking Lake Tana, the source of the Blue Nile.

Bruce returned to England, where his stories about native practices he had seen were greeted with derision and disbelief. But his works proved valuable twenty years later, in the hands of a French army which invaded Egypt in 1798 under the command of Napoleon Bonaparte. Landing at Alexandria, Napoleon easily defeated the Mameluke soldiers of the Egyptian army in July 1798, with the Battle of the Pyramids on July 21 the decisive victory. However, on August 1 the British navy defeated the French fleet in the Battle of the Nile in Abukir Bay, trapping the French army in Egypt. An expedition south to try to capture the remaining Mamelukes eventually reached Aswan, providing for the first time European documentation of the civilizations upriver. In July 1799, a Turkish invasion to regain control of Egypt led to the Battle of Abukir on July 25, 1799. This was a devastating defeat for the Turks, leading to their surrender.

The British finally forced the surrender of the French in July 1801, but themselves left soon after, leaving in Egypt a vacuum of European power, which was filled in the next decade by Muhammad Ali, a Turk who gained control in 1807 against both the Turks and the remaining Mamelukes. But the French expedition had led to significant cultural contact. A scholar, Vivant Denon, had accompanied the French expedition upriver, viewing and sketching ancient temples. There were other archaeological discoveries, such as the Rosetta Stone which was found by the French and then surrendered to the British in 1801, and eventually deciphered in the 1820s, providing key insights for European scholars into the Arabic language. The French expedition also collected many valuable artifacts, which became the basis of the Orientalist collection of the Louvre Museum in Paris.

The search for geographic knowledge, especially the sources of the Nile and the Niger rivers (initially thought to be connected to each other), motivated subsequent European visitors. Thomas Legh and the Rev. Charles

Smelt went as far as Aswan and Ibrim on the Nile in 1813. John Lewis Burck-hardt traveled in the Nile valley and Ethiopia for the African Association of England, supposedly in search of sources of the Niger; he died in 1817 during his travels. Further west, in 1825 a British expedition left the port of Bada-gry in present-day Nigeria hoping to reach by an overland route the market city of Timbuctoo in West Africa. Headed by Naval Lt. Hugh Clapperton, this expedition ended in disaster, with the deaths of the British leaders. [1] A Cornish manservant, Richard Lander, found himself in the middle of West Africa, the only European on the expedition to remain alive. He managed to reach the coast, where he survived a test by poison and returned to England safely. In 1830, Lander and his brother returned to the quest for the Niger. They floated down the river to its mouth on the Atlantic, thus determining both the course of the Niger River and that it was separate from the Nile River.

In East Africa a British military expedition established a temporary European presence in 1868, defeating Emperor Theodore of Ethiopia, a ruler who had consolidated power in East Africa but had imprisoned a number of Europeans. Having defeated Theodore, however, the British forces departed and European presence in that part of the continent again became negligible. European attention in the third quarter of the century was focused rather on the search for the final determination of the source of the White Nile in the lake region of central Africa. Two British explorers, Richard Burton and John Hanning Speke, sighted Lake Victoria on an expedition in 1857–1859, but were unable to conclusively show that it was the source of the White Nile. Speke returned with John Grant in 1860–1863, and claimed to have definitively proven Lake Victoria to be the source of the Nile. [2] On the heels of Speke and Grant, another Englishman, Samuel Baker, discovered the other source of the Nile, Lake Albert, in 1864. [3]

Burton, Speke, and Baker all attracted great public attention to themselves and to the exploration of sub-Saharan Africa. Another figure at this time was the Scottish medical missionary, David Livingstone, who in 1856, to similar acclaim, had published his own account of travels through the African continent. Livingstone returned to Africa in 1866 [4], eventually dying there in 1873. His apparent disappearance led to a relief expedition under the command of *New York Herald Tribune* reporter H. M. Stanley, who found Livingstone in 1871. Stanley himself led another expedition between 1874 and 1877, on which he circumnavigated Lake Victoria, proving that it flowed out only into the Nile. On this expedition he continued west to the Congo basin and to the Atlantic, thus connecting the two great areas of exploration that had dominated European interest for a century. Sub-Saharan Africa, the "Dark Continent," had now been crossed by European explorers. A mystery no longer, it instead became a place of opportunity for travel and political and economic domination.

1. RICHARD LANDER, RECORDS OF CAPTAIN CLAPPERTON'S LAST EXPEDITION TO AFRICA

Richard Lander was a Cornishman who had lived in the West Indies in his childhood. In 1825, he was hired as a manservant on a British expedition, led by Lieutenant Hugh Clapperton, searching for the route of the Niger and the fabled city of Timbuctoo. The expedition landed in the port of Badagry, near the current site of Lagos in Nigeria, and struck off inland. It very quickly began to exhibit one of the most important difficulties European exploration in Africa faced. Two months into the expedition, disease struck the party, rapidly killing three of the Europeans, and, as so often happened in the exploration of Africa, leaving only a skeleton of the original expedition to continue. Clapperton himself died in April 1825, leaving Lander on his own. He managed to reach Badagry in November, carrying with him Clapperton's journals. In Badagry he was accused by Portuguese slavers of being a spy, and subjected to a test by poison by the king of Badagry. Surviving this, he managed to board a British ship and return to England, producing an account of the trip that combined Clapperton's journal with his own description of events after Clapperton's death. In 1830, he returned to Africa to continue the search for the Niger, leading an expedition that included his brother John. Finding the Niger at Bussa, the closest to its mouth that any European had been to that point, they continued downstream until by October they were approaching the mouth, where they were captured by pirates and taken as slaves. Eventually ransomed, they returned to England, having finally found the route of the Niger. In 1834, on still another expedition to the Niger, Richard Lander was killed.

Records of Captain Clapperton's Last Expedition to Africa

On Saturday, the roads being rendered almost impassable, in consequence of the rains that had fallen the preceding night, it was not without experiencing considerable difficulty that we could pursue our journey. The mud and water reached, in some places, almost to the horses' shoulders; and Dawson, who was ill with ague, was unable to retain his seat on the animal's back, and fell three or four times in the mire, till he became so much exhausted by struggling to regain his seat, that, in despair, he at last flung his arms only across the horse's back; and panting with his exertions, was in this manner dragged to a considerable distance. At eleven o'clock we arrived at the village of Egbo; and after partaking of a slight refreshment, each of us being indisposed in a greater or less degree, we stretched ourselves at full length on our mats, in the hope of obtaining a little sleep. Dawson, however, was taken dreadfully ill, and his moanings of distress prevented me from closing my eyes. He pronounced the names of his wife and children, whom he had left in England, with a bitter emphasis, and reproached himself repeatedly with having deserted them, to perish miserably in a strange country. In this manner he complained till the afternoon, refusing all consolation, when he became a little more composed; and Captain Pearce fell asleep. My master had quitted the apartment just before; and the medicine-chest lying open by Dawson's side, he perceived it, and pointing to a phial, desired a black attendant to fill him a glass of its contents; which being promptly done, he eagerly swallowed it. Whilst this was going on I had fallen into a slumber; and on awaking, about a quarter of an hour afterwards, not hearing Dawson's groans, I asked how he did; but receiving no answer, I went to his bed-side, and found him a cold and stiffened corpse! The sight of so unexpected and ghastly a spectacle caused me to shudder, and I involuntarily made an exclamation of surprise and terror, that awoke Captain Pearce, who asked what was the matter. Before I had time to reply, he had raised himself on his couch, and the truth instantly bursting upon him—"What!" said he, "is Dawson dead? Well, poor fellow, *his* sufferings are over; *I* cannot long survive him;" and with a deep sigh he sunk back exhausted on his mat, without making any further remark.

On examining the bottle from which the unfortunate man had desired the liquor to be taken, I found it to be partly filled with *ether,* which he must have mistaken for something else, and which had caused his almost immediate dissolution. As soon as the natives were made acquainted with the circumstance, they set up their death-yell; and if all the fiends of darkness had joined in chorus, they could not have produced an effect more frightfully and fearfully appalling than was the sound produced in that instance. Captain Clapperton hastened to silence them, which, after some difficulty, he succeeded in doing; but the awfully terrific noise the people made, seemed to be ringing in our ears the whole of the night. As dead bodies cannot be left exposed a great while in tropical countries, Dawson was buried on the evening of his death, followed to the grave by the whole of our black attendants and myself. Captain Clapperton read the funeral service over his remains, which were then deposited in the earth, and we returned to Captain Pearce, whom we had left alone in the hut. Our party was now reduced to three whites, one of whom was dangerously ill; my master himself was in a much worse state of health than he would either acknowledge or believe; and I was but just recovering from a disease that had nearly proved fatal to me. A gloom was therefore cast upon the countenances of our little band, as we prepared to proceed, on the morning of Sunday; but Captain Pearce rallying a little, we set off in more cheerful spirits.

The appearance of the country, from Jannah to Tshow, is greatly superior to that from the coast to the former place, being clearer of wood, and in a higher state of cultivation, swelling likewise into easy and delightful undulations. Streams of water fertilize the vallies; and the hills, covered with a lively verdure, are adorned with lofty and handsome trees. The towns of the natives, from Badagry to Tshow, with a few exceptions only, like those in the island of Madagascar, are situated in the bosom of thick woods, and are entered by paths so intricate, that, like the labyrinth of Woodstock, they are known to none but the inhabitants themselves. Sometimes, however, they have only one path, which is generally defended by strong stockades or a mud wall, and sometimes by both together.

On Tuesday morning we continued our journey, with a cool strengthening breeze and a serene atmosphere, which seemed to invigorate each of us with renewed life and spirit; and, after two hours' travelling, we arrived at Engwâ. In the course of the journey, for the first time since leaving the ship, we perceived great numbers of trees, stripped of their foliage, and the grass beaten to the ground, so that, with the exception of the absence of frost and snow, the country looked like many parts of England in the month of November or December. Several of the natives in this, as in almost every other instance, either accompanied or followed us on the way, and we experienced as much civility from them as our countrymen would have bestowed upon us in our native land. They were, generally speaking, neatly dressed in cap, shirt (tobe), and trousers, and very cleanly in their personal appearance.

About eleven o'clock Captain Pearce became suddenly worse, and an hour or two afterwards was delirious. He talked much and incoherently, in detached sentences; at one time apparently conversing with his mother in the most affectionate terms, asking her questions, and answering them himself, and the next moment reverting to his own melancholy condition, and muttering something which no one could understand. In this pitiable state he remained till nine o'clock in the evening, when he fell into a stupor, from which he awoke about half an hour afterwards, and attempting to raise himself on his couch, with a faint groan, and a convulsive throe, he fell back and instantly expired.

Both Captain Clapperton and myself were deeply affected as we enveloped the lifeless body in its shroud; and a host of gloomy reflections crowded upon our minds, to see the once spirited and cheerful companion of our wanderings stretched out before us, the shadow only of a man, clothed in the mournful habiliments of death. Next morning, about eleven o'clock, the body was borne to the place of its interment, followed by my master and myself, with the messengers of the kings of Badagry and Katunga, and a great number of natives, who all behaved with the strictest decorum. As in the former instance, Captain Clapperton, although extremely unwell, in a tremulous voice and agitated manner, read the funeral service, interrupted only by his own emotion, which he found it impossible to conceal. The corpse having been consigned to the grave, it was soon closed over him for ever, and my master and myself, with heavy hearts and melancholy anticipations, returned to our cheerless habitation. The following inscription, at the desire of Captain Clapperton, I carved on a board, which was placed at the head of the pit, over which a shed was built by the natives; and a strong bamboo fence surrounded the whole:—

"Here lie the remains of Robert Pearce, Captain in the Royal Navy of England, who died 27th Dec. 1825, aged 28, much regretted by those that survive of the mission.

"H. CLAPPERTON.
"R. LANDER."

Captain Pearce had rendered himself a general favourite by his gentle and pleasing manners, and excellent natural disposition. My master was particularly attached to him, and esteemed him highly, while the natives almost adored him. His companionable qualities were great, and he displayed them to advantage in our toilsome journeyings, raising the spirits of the party by his wit and cheerfulness, and infusing his own good temper into the breasts of every one. He was besides an excellent limner and draughtsman, and possessed an aptitude for picking up the various languages of the natives, which bade fair to render him of the most essential service to the mission. No one deplored his loss, or felt the want of his pleasant society, more than myself. Just after he was taken ill, at his own request, as soon as the day's toil was over, I was constantly with him, and at night my mat was placed close to his. We used to chat for whole hours together, on different circumstances of our lives; and my little history afforded him a fund of amusement. Any thing, indeed, that promised to divert our thoughts from the calamities which threatened us, was resorted to, and every trifling incident we had each met with from our childhood repeated a thousand times over, in order to dole away the long, still, dismal hours of night, when sickness prevented either of us from closing our eyes. Throughout Captain Pearce's illness, his patience, resignation, and manly fortitude never forsook him; he was conscious that he should ultimately sink under the influence of a disorder that was visibly wasting him, and daily reducing his strength: nevertheless, this belief neither shook his firmness nor damped his spirits, and he always spoke of his anticipated dissolution with a serious calmness of manner that surprised and pleased me. None of us thought that his end was so near; we expected he would have struggled on at least a week or two longer; but the sorrowful event disappointed the hopes we had cherished, and he expired prematurely, to the infinite regret of every one.

Mr. Houtson returned on Saturday the 31st, with the afflictive intelligence of the decease of Dr. Morrison, which mournful circumstance occurred at Jannah, by a coincidence, singular in misfortune, on the same day, and as nearly as possible at the same hour as that in which Captain Pearce had breathed his last. He was decently interred by Mr. Houtson on the 28th, near to the house in which they had resided; and the ceremonies of the Church of England were performed over his remains by the same gentleman.

2. John Hanning Speke, *Journal of the Discovery of the Source of the Nile*

John Hanning Speke (1827–1864) was educated for the army and in 1844 joined a regiment of Bengal native infantry in the British colony of India. His service there provided him with the opportunity to undertake hunting and exploration expeditions in the Himalayas and Tibet. At the end of his Indian service, in 1854, he began to pursue his dream of exploring Central Equatorial Africa. He joined an expedition led by Lieutenant Richard Burton, but Speke was wounded in an attack on the expedition by Somalis and returned to England to recover. He served in the Crimean War, and at its end in 1856 received an invitation to join Burton on another African expedition, aiming to explore the territory around Lake Nyassa. Departing in December 1856, the expedition penetrated to Lake Tanganyika in spite of illness that struck both Speke and Burton. Burton's ill health gave Speke the opportunity to press on alone for Lake Victoria, which he reached in early August 1858. Speke was convinced this was the source of the Nile River, a conclusion Burton did not share. Speke returned to England ahead of Burton, announced the discovery to the Royal Geographical Society and in the press, taking credit for it himself. A second expedition, leaving England in 1860, confirmed the discovery to Speke's satisfaction, although still not to Burton's. Speke died in a hunting accident in 1864 on the eve of a public debate with Burton on the subject.

Journal of the Discovery of the Source of the Nile

23*d*. Three boats arrived, like those used on the Murchison Creek, and when I demanded the rest, as well as a decisive answer about going to Kamrasi's, the acting mkungŭ said he was afraid accidents might happen, and he would not take me. Nothing would frighten this pig-headed creature into compliance, though I told him I had arranged with the king to make the Nile the channel of communication with England. I therefore applied to him for guides to conduct me up the river, and ordered Bombay and Kasoro to obtain fresh orders from the king, as all future wazungŭ, coming to Uganda to visit or trade, would prefer the passage by the river. I shot another buck in the evening, as the Waganda loved their skins, and also a load of Guinea-fowl—three, four, and five at a shot—as Kasoro and his boys prefer them to any thing.

24*th.* The acting officer absconded, but another man came in his place, and offered to take us on the way up the river to-morrow, humbugging Kasoro into the belief that his road to the palace would branch off from the first stage, though in reality it was here. The mkungŭ's women brought pombé, and spent the day gazing at us, till, in the evening, when I took up my rifle, one ran after Bana to see him shoot, and followed like a man; but the only sport she got was on an ant-hill, where she fixed herself some time, popping into her mouth and devouring the white ants as fast as they emanated from their cells; for, disdaining does, I missed the only pongo buck I got a shot at in my anxiety to show the fair one what she came for.

Reports came to-day of new cruelties at the palace. Kasoro improved on their off-hand manslaughter by saying that two kamravionas and two sakibobos, as well as all the old wakungŭ of Sunna's time, had been executed by the orders of King Mtésa. He told us, moreover, that if Mtésa ever has a dream that his father directs him to kill any body as being dangerous to his person, the order is religiously kept. I wished to send a message to Mtésa by an officer who is starting at once to pay his respects at court; but, although he received it, and promised to deliver it, Kasoro laughed at me for expecting that one word of it would ever reach the king; for, however appropriate or important the matter might be, it was more than any body dare do to tell the king, as it would be an infringement of the rule that no one is to speak to him unless in answer to a question. My second buck of the first day was brought in by the natives, but they would not allow it to approach the hut until it had been skinned; and I found their reason to be a superstition that otherwise no others would ever be killed by the inmates of that establishment.

I marched up the left bank of the Nile, at a considerable distance from the water, to the Isamba Rapids, passing through rich jungle and plantain gardens. Nango, an old friend, and district officer of the place, first refreshed us with a dish of plaintain-squash and dried fish, with pombé. He told us he is often threatened by elephants, but he sedulously keeps them off with charms; for if they ever tasted a plaintain they would never leave the garden until they had cleared it out. He then took us to see the nearest falls of the Nile—extremely beautiful, but very confined. The water ran deep between its banks, which were covered with fine grass, soft cloudy acacias, and festoons of lilac convolvuli; while here and there, where the land had slipped above the rapids, bared places of red earth could be seen, like that of Devonshire; there, too, the waters, impeded by a natural dam, looked like a huge mill-pond, sullen and dark, in which two crocodiles, laving about, were looking out for prey. From the high banks we looked down upon a line of sloping wooded islets lying across the stream, which divide its waters, and, by interrupting them, cause at once both dam and rapids. The whole was more fairy-like, wild, and romantic than—I must confess that my thoughts took that shape—any thing I ever saw outside of a theatre. It was exactly the sort of place, in fact, where, bridged across from one side-slip to the other, on a moonlight night, brigands would assemble to enact some dreadful tragedy. Even the Wangŭana seemed spell-bound at the novel beauty of the sight, and no one thought of moving till hunger warned us night was setting in, and we better look out for lodgings.

Start again, and after drinking pombé with Nango, when we heard that three wakungŭ had been seized at Kari in consequence of the murder, the march was recommenced, but soon after stopped by the mischievous machinations of our guide, who pretended it was too late in the day to cross the jungles on ahead, either by the road to the source or the palace, and therefore would not move till the morning; then, leaving us on the pretext of business, he vanished, and was never seen again. A small black fly, with thick shoulders and bullet-head, infests the place, and torments the naked arms and legs of the people with its sharp stings to an extent that must render life miserable to them.

After a long struggling march, plodding through huge grasses and jungle, we reached a district which I can not otherwise describe than by calling it a "Church Estate." It is dedicated in some mysterious manner to Lŭbari (Almighty), and although the king appeared to have authority over some of the inhabitants of it, yet others had apparently a sacred character, exempting them from the civil power, and he had no right to dispose of the land itself. In this territory there are small villages only at every fifth mile, for there is no road, and the lands run high again, while, from want of a guide, we often lost the track. It now transpired that Budja, when he told at the palace that there was no road down the banks of the Nile, did so in consequence of his fear that if he sent my whole party here they would rob these church lands, and so bring him into a scrape with the wizards or ecclesiastical authorities. Had my party not been under control, we could not have put up here; but on my being answerable that no thefts should take place, the people kindly consented to provide us with board and lodgings, and we found them very obliging. One elderly man, half-witted—they said the king had driven his senses from him by seizing his house and family—came at once on hearing of our arrival, laughing and singing in a loose, jaunty, maniacal manner, carrying odd sticks, shells, and a bundle of mbŭgŭ rags, which he deposited before me, dancing and singing again, then retreating and bringing some more, with a few plaintains from a garden, which I was to eat, as kings lived upon flesh, and "poor Tom" wanted some, for he lived with lions and elephants in a hovel beyond the gardens, and his belly was empty. He was precisely a black specimen of the English parish idiot.

At last, with a good push for it, crossing hills and threading huge grasses, as well as extensive village plantations lately devastated by elephants—they had eaten all that was eatable, and what would not serve for food they had destroyed with their trunks, not one plantain nor one hut being left entire—we arrived at the extreme end of the journey, the farthest point ever visited by the expedition on the same parallel of latitude as King Mtésa's palace, and just forty miles east of it.

We were well rewarded; for the "stones," as the Waganda call the falls, was by far the most interesting sight I had seen in Africa. Every body ran to see them at once, though the march had been long and fatiguing, and even my sketch-block was called into play. Though beautiful, the scene was not exactly what I expected; for the broad surface of the lake was shut out from view by a spur of hill, and the falls, about 12 feet deep, and 400 to 500 feet broad, were broken by rocks. Still it was a sight that attracted one to it for hours—the roar of the waters, the thousands of passenger-fish, leaping at the falls with all their might, the Wasoga and Waganda fishermen coming out in boats and taking post on all the rocks with rod and hook, hippopotami and crocodiles lying sleepily on the water, the ferry at work above the falls, and cattle driven down to drink at the margin of the lake, made, in all, with the pretty nature of the country—small hills, grassy-topped, with trees in the folds, and gardens on the lower slopes—as interesting a picture as one could wish to see.

The expedition had now performed its functions. I saw that old Father Nile without any doubt rises in the Victoria N'yanza, and, as I had foretold, that lake is the great source of the holy river which cradled the first expounder of our religious belief. I mourned, however, when I thought how much I had lost by the delays in the journey having deprived me of the pleasure of going to look at the northeast corner of the N'yanza to see what connection there was, by the strait so often spoken of, with it and the other lake where the Waganda went to get their salt, and from which another river flowed to the north, making "Usoga an island." But I felt I ought to be content with what I had been spared to accomplish; for I had seen full half of the lake, and had information given me of the other half, by means of which I knew all about the lake, as far, at least, as the chief objects of geographical importance were concerned.

Let us now sum up the whole and see what it is worth. Comparative information assured me that there was as much water on the eastern side of the lake as there is on the western—if any thing, rather more. The most remote waters, *or top head of the Nile,* is the southern end of the lake, situated close on the third degree of south latitude, which gives to the Nile the surprising length, in direct measurement, rolling over thirty-four degrees of latitude, of above 2300 miles, or more than one eleventh of the circumference of our globe. Now from this southern point, round by the west, to where the *great* Nile stream issues, there is only one feeder of any importance, and that is the Kitangülé River: while from the southernmost point, round by the east, to the strait, there are no rivers at all of any importance; for the traveled Arabs one and all aver, that from the west of the snow-clad Kilimandjaro to the lake where it is cut by the second degree, and also the first degree of south latitude, there are salt lakes and salt plains, and the country is hilly, not unlike Unyamüézi: but they said there were no great rivers, and the country was so scantily watered, having only occasional runnels and rivulets, that they always had to make long marches in order to find water when they went on their trading journeys; and farther, those Arabs who crossed the strait when they reached Usoga, as mentioned before, during the late interregnum, crossed no river either.

3. SAMUEL WHITE BAKER, *THE ALBERT N'YANZA:* GREAT BASIN OF THE NILE AND EXPLORATIONS OF THE NILE SOURCES

Samuel Baker (1821–1893) was the son of a wealthy shipowner and bank director whose wealth made it possible for him to spend much of his life traveling around the world, accompanied by his second wife. In December 1862, Baker and his wife left Khartoum in search of Speke's expedition for the source of the Nile. He found Speke at Bunyoro, just south of Gondokoro, and after discussing the results of Speke's trip, Baker decided to attempt to complete the exploration of the River Nile. On March 14, 1864, Baker finally reached the shores of the Luta Nzigé, the western source of the Nile, which he named Lake Albert. This completed the search for the sources of the Nile, although Baker himself had not been able to follow the river all the way from Lake Albert to Gondokoro and verify that the two rivers connected.

The Albert N'Yanza

On the following morning we had the usual difficulty in collecting porters, those of the preceding day having absconded, and the others were recruited from distant villages by the native escort, who enjoyed the excuse of hunting for porters, as it gave them an opportunity of foraging throughout the neighbourhood. During this time we had to wait until the sun was high; and we thus lost the cool hours of morning and increased our fatigue. Having at length started, we arrived in the afternoon at the Kafoor river, at a bend from the south where it was necessary to cross over in our westerly course. The stream was in the centre of a marsh, and although deep, it was so covered with thickly-matted water-grass and other aquatic plants, that a natural floating-bridge was established by a carpet of weeds about two feet thick: upon this waving and unsteady surface the men ran quickly across, sinking merely to the ankles, although beneath the tough vegetation there was deep water. It was equally impossible to ride or to be carried over this treacherous surface; thus I led the way, and begged Mrs. Baker to follow me on foot as quickly as possible, precisely in my track. The river was about eighty yards wide, and I had scarcely completed a fourth of the distance and looked back to see if my wife followed close to me, when I was horrified to see her standing in one spot, and sinking gradually through the weeds, while her face was distorted and perfectly purple. Almost as soon as I perceived her, she fell, as though shot dead. In an instant I was by her side; and with the assistance of eight or ten of my men, who were fortunately close to me, I dragged her like a corpse through the yielding vegetation, and up to our waists we scrambled across to the other side, just keeping her head above the water: to have carried her would have been impossible, as we should all have sunk together through the weeds. I laid her under a tree, and bathed her head and face with water, as for the moment I thought she had fainted; but she lay perfectly insensible as though dead, with teeth and hands firmly clenched, and her eyes open, but fixed. It was a *coup de soleil.*

Many of the porters had gone on ahead with the baggage; and I started off a man in haste to recall an angarep upon which to carry her, and also for a bag with a change of clothes, as we had dragged her through the river. It was in vain that I rubbed her heart, and the black women rubbed her feet, to endeavour to restore animation. At length the litter came, and after changing her clothes, she was carried mournfully forward as a corpse. Constantly we had to halt and support her head, as a painful rattling in the throat betokened suffocation. At length we reached a village, and halted for the night.

I laid her carefully in a miserable hut, and watched beside her. I opened her clenched teeth with a small wooden wedge, and inserted a wet rag, upon which I dropped water to moisten her tongue, which was dry as fur. The unfeeling brutes that composed the native escort were yelling and dancing as though all were well; and I ordered their chief at once to return with them to Kamrasi, as I would travel with them no longer. At first they refused to return; until at length I vowed that I would fire into them should they accompany us on the following morning. Day broke, and it was a relief to have got rid of the brutal escort. They had departed, and I had now my own men, and the guides supplied by Kamrasi.

There was nothing to eat in this spot. My wife had never stirred since she fell by the *coup de soleil,* and merely respired about five times in a minute. It was impossible to remain; the people would have starved. She was laid gently upon her litter, and we started forward on our funeral course. I was ill and broken-hearted, and I followed by her side through the long day's march over wild park-lands and streams, with thick forest and deep marshy bottoms; over undulating hills, and through valleys of tall papyrus rushes, which, as we brushed through them on our melancholy way, waved over the litter like the black plumes of a hearse. We halted at a village, and again the night was passed in watching. I was wet, and coated with mud from the swampy marsh, and shivered with ague; but the cold within was greater than all. No change had taken place; she had never moved. I had plenty of fat, and I made four balls of about half a pound, each of which would burn for three hours. A piece of a broken water-jar formed a lamp, several pieces of rag serving for wicks. So in solitude the still calm night passed away as I sat by her side and watched. In the drawn and distorted features that lay before me I could hardly trace the same face that for years had been my comfort through all the difficulties and dangers of my path. Was she to die? Was so terrible a sacrifice to be the result of my selfish exile?

Again the night passed away. Once more the march. Though weak and ill, and for two nights without a moment's sleep, I felt no fatigue, but mechanically followed by the side of the litter as though in a dream. The same wild country diversified with marsh and forest. Again we halted. The night came, and I sat by her side in a miserable hut, with the feeble lamp flickering while she lay, as in death. She had never moved a muscle since she fell. My people slept. I was alone, and no sound broke the stillness of the night. The ears ached at the utter silence, till the sudden wild cry of a hyena made me shudder as the horrible thought rushed through my brain, that, should she be buried in this lonely spot, the hyena would . . . disturb her rest.

The morning was not far distant; it was past four o'clock. I had passed the night in replacing wet cloths upon her head and moistening her lips, as she lay apparently life-less on her litter. I could do nothing more; in solitude and abject misery in that dark hour, in a country of savage heathens, thousands of miles away from a Christian land, I beseeched an aid above all human, trusting alone to Him.

The morning broke; my lamp had just burnt out, and, cramped with the night's watching, I rose from my low seat, and seeing that she lay in the same unaltered state, I went to the door of the hut to breathe one gasp of the fresh morning air. I was watching the first red streak that heralded the rising sun, when I was startled by the words, "Thank God," faintly uttered behind me. Suddenly she had awoke from her torpor, and with a heart overflowing I went to her bedside. Her eyes were full of madness! She spoke, but the brain was gone!

I will not inflict a description of the terrible trial of seven days of brain fever, with its attendant horrors. The rain poured in torrents, and day after day we were forced to travel for want of provisions, not being able to remain in one position. Every now and then we shot a few guinea-fowl, but rarely; there was no game, although the country was most favourable. In the forests we procured wild honey, but the deserted villages con-tained no supplies, as we were on the frontier of Uganda, and M'tesé's people had plun-dered the district. For seven nights I had not slept, and although as weak as a reed, I had marched by the side of her litter. Nature could resist no longer. We reached a village one evening; she had been in violent convulsions successively—it was all but over. I laid her down on her litter within a hut; covered her with a Scotch plaid, and I fell upon my mat insensible, worn out with sorrow and fatigue. My men put a new handle to the pickaxe that evening, and sought for a dry spot to dig her grave!

The sun had risen when I woke. I had slept, and, horrified as the idea flashed upon me that she must be dead, and that I had not been with her, I started up. She lay upon her bed, pale as marble, and with that calm serenity that the features assume when the cares of life no longer act upon the mind, and the body rests in death. The dreadful thought bowed me down; but as I gazed upon her in fear, her chest gently heaved, not with the convulsive throbs of fever, but naturally. She was asleep; and when at a sudden noise she opened her eyes, they were calm and clear. She was saved! When not a ray of hope remained, God alone knows what helped us. The gratitude of that moment I will not attempt to describe.

The 14th March.—The sun had not risen when I was spurring my ox after the guide, who, having been promised a double handful of beads on arrival at the lake, had caught the enthusiasm of the moment. The day broke beautifully clear, and having crossed a deep valley between the hills, we toiled up the opposite slope. I hurried to the summit. The glory of our prize burst suddenly upon me! There, like a sea of quicksilver, lay far beneath the grand expanse of water—a boundless sea horizon on the south and southwest, glittering in the noon-day sun; and on the west, at fifty or sixty miles' distance, blue mountains rose from the bosom of the lake to a height of about 7,000 feet above its level.

It is impossible to describe the triumph of that moment; here was the reward for all our labour—for the years of tenacity with which we had toiled through Africa. England had won the sources of the Nile! Long before I reached this spot, I had arranged to give three cheers with all our men in English style in honour of the discovery, but now that I looked down upon the great inland sea lying nestled in the very heart of Africa, and thought how vainly mankind had sought these sources throughout so many ages, and reflected that I had been the humble instrument permitted to unravel this portion of the great mystery when so many greater than I had failed, I felt too serious to vent my feelings in vain cheers for victory, and I sincerely thanked God for having guided and supported us through all dangers to the good end. I was about 1,500 feet above the lake, and I looked down from the steep granite cliff upon those welcome waters—upon that vast reservoir which nourished Egypt and brought fertility where all was wilderness—upon that great source so long hidden from mankind; that source of bounty and of blessings to millions of human beings; and as one of the greatest objects in nature, I determined to honour it with a great name. As an imperishable memorial of one loved and mourned by our gracious Queen and deplored by every Englishman, I called this great lake "the Albert N'yanza." The Victoria and the Albert lakes are the two sources of the Nile.

4. DAVID LIVINGSTONE, *THE LAST JOURNALS OF DAVID LIVINGSTONE IN CENTRAL AFRICA*

David Livingstone (1813–1873) began working in a cotton factory in Lanarkshire, England, at the age of ten, teaching himself botany, zoology, and geology as he worked at his loom. At the age of twenty, he began to wish to become a medical missionary in China, but when in 1840 he had completed his medical training and been ordained a missionary for the nonsectarian London Missionary Society, he embarked for South Africa. He spent the next fifteen years journeying through that part of the continent. He returned to

England in 1858 and published his journals, which brought him renown in Europe and America. He returned to Africa in late 1858, beginning a journey around Lake Nyassa that ended in 1864. A final journey began in 1866. Several times rumors spread in Europe and America that he had been killed, leading to relief expeditions, the most famous of which was headed by *New York Herald Tribune* reporter William H. Stanley. Livingstone continued in search of the origins of the Nile River, but died attempting to reach the Lualaba River, which he thought must be the Upper Nile. His body was returned to England on a British warship, and he was buried in Westminster Abbey.

The Last Journals of David Livingstone in Central Africa

June 19*th*, 1866.—We passed a woman tied by the neck to a tree, and dead. The people of the country explained that she had been unable to keep up with the other slaves in a gang, and her master had determined that she should not become the property of any one else if she recovered after resting for a time. I may mention here that we saw others tied up in a similar manner, and one lying in the path shot or stabbed, for she was in a pool of blood. The explanation we got invariably was that the Arab who owned these victims was enraged at losing his money by the slaves becoming unable to march, and vented his spleen by murdering them; but I have nothing more than common report in support of attributing this enormity to the Arabs.

June 20*th*.—Having returned to Metaba, we were told by Kinazombé, the chief, that no one had grain to sell but himself. He had plenty of powder and common cloth from the Arabs, and our only chance with him was parting with our finer cloths and other things that took his fancy. He magnified the scarcity in front in order to induce us to buy all we could from him, but he gave me an ample meal of porridge and guinea-fowl before starting.

June 21*st*.—We had difficulties about carriers; but on reaching an island in the Rovuma called Chimiki, we found the people were Makoa, and more civil and willing to work than the Waiyau: we sent men back to bring up the havildar to a very civil head man called Chirikaloma.

June 22*d*.—A poor little boy with *prolapsus ani* was carried yesterday by his mother many a weary mile, lying over her right shoulder—the only position he could find ease in; an infant at the breast occupied the left arm, and on her head were carried two baskets. The mother's love was seen in binding up the part when we halted, while the coarseness of low civilization was evinced in the laugh with which some black brutes looked at the sufferer.

June 23*d*.—The country is covered with forest, much more open than farther east. We are now some eight hundred feet above the sea. The people all cultivate maize near the Rovuma, and on islands where moisture helps them; nearly all possess guns, and plenty of powder and fine beads—red ones strung on the hair, and fine blue ones in rolls on the neck, fitted tightly like soldiers' stocks. The lip-ring is universal; teeth filed to points.

June 24*th*.—Immense quantities of wood are cut down, collected in heaps, and burned to manure the land, but this does not prevent the country having an appearance of forest. Divine service at 8.30 A.M.; great numbers looking on. They have a clear idea of the Supreme Being, but do not pray to him. Cold south winds prevail; temperature, 55°. One of the mules is very ill; it was left with the havildar when we went back to Ngozo, and probably remained uncovered at night; for as soon as we saw it, illness was plainly visible. Whenever an animal has been in their power, the sepoys have abused it. It is difficult to feel charitably to fellows whose scheme seems to have been to detach the Nassick boys from me first; then, when the animals were all killed, the Johanna men; afterward they could rule me as they liked, or go back and leave me to perish; but I shall try to feel as charitably as I can in spite of it all, for the mind has a strong tendency to brood over the ills of travel. I told the havildar, when I came up to him at Metaba, what I had done, and that I was very much displeased with the sepoys for compassing my failure, if not death; an unkind word had never passed my lips to them: to this he could bear testimony. He thought that they would only be a plague and trouble to me, but he "would go on and die with me."

Stone boiling is unknown in these countries, but ovens are made in ant-hills. Holes are dug in the ground for baking the heads of large game, as the zebra, feet of elephants, humps of rhinoceros; and the production of fire by drilling between the palms of the hands is universal. It is quite common to see the sticks so used attached to the clothing or bundles in traveling; they wet the blunt end of the upright stick with the tongue, and dip it in the sand to make some particles of silica adhere before inserting it in the horizontal piece. The wood of a certain wild fig-tree is esteemed as yielding fire readily.

In wet weather they prefer to carry fire in the dried balls of elephants' dung which are met with—the male's being about eight inches in diameter, and about a foot long; they also employ the stalk of a certain plant which grows on rocky places for the same purpose.

We bought a senzé, or *Aulacaudatus Swindernianus,* which had been dried over a slow fire. This custom of drying fish, flesh, and fruits, on stages over slow fires, is practiced very generally: the use of salt for preservation is unknown. Besides stages for drying, the Makondé use them, about six feet high, for sleeping on, instead of the damp ground: a fire beneath helps to keep off the mosquitoes, and they are used by day as convenient resting-places and for observation.

Pottery seems to have been known to the Africans from the remotest times, for fragments are found everywhere, even among the oldest fossil bones in the country. Their pots for cooking, holding water and beer, are made by the women, and the form is preserved by the eye alone, for no sort of machine is ever used. A foundation or bottom is first laid, and a piece of bone or bamboo used to scrape the clay, or to smooth over the pieces which are added to increase the roundness; the vessel is then left a night: the next morning a piece is added to the rim—as the air is dry, several rounds may be added—and all is then carefully smoothed off; afterward it is thoroughly sun-dried. A light fire of dried cow-dung, or corn-stalks, or straw, and grass with twigs, is made in a hole in the ground for the final baking. Ornaments are made on these pots of black-lead, or before being hardened by the sun they are ornamented for a couple or three inches near the rim, all the tracery being in imitation of plaited basket-work.

Chirikaloma says that the surname of the Makoa, to whom he belongs, is Mirazi; others have the surname Melola or Malola—Chimposola. All had the half-moon mark when in the southeast; but now they leave it off a good deal and adopt the Waiyau marks, because of living in their country. They show no indications of being named after beasts and birds. Mirazi was an ancestor. They eat all clean animals, but refuse the hyena, leopard, or any beast that devours dead men.

June 25th.—On leaving Chirikaloma, we came on to Namalo, whose village that morning had been deserted, the people moving off in a body toward the Matambwé country, where food is more abundant. A poor little girl was left in one of the huts from being too weak to walk, probably an orphan. The Arab slave-traders flee from the path as soon as they hear of our approach. The Rovuma is from fifty-six to eighty yards wide here. No food to be had for either love or money.

Near many of the villages we observe a wand bent, and both ends inserted into the ground. A lot of medicine, usually the bark of trees, is buried beneath it. When sickness is in a village, the men proceed to the spot, wash themselves with the medicine and water, creep through beneath the bough, then bury the medicine and the evil influence together. This is also used to keep off evil spirits, wild beasts, and enemies.

Chirikaloma told us of a child in his tribe which was deformed from his birth. He had an abortive toe where his knee should have been. Some said to his mother, "Kill him;" but she replied, "How can I kill my son?" He grew up and had many fine sons and daughters, but none deformed like himself; this was told in connection with an answer to my question about the treatment of Albinoes: he said they did not kill them, but they never grew to manhood. On inquiring if he had ever heard of cannibals, or people with tails, he replied, "Yes, but we have always understood that these and other monstrosities are met with only among you sea-going people." The other monstrosities he referred to were those who are said to have eyes behind the head as well as in front. I have heard of them before, but then I was near Angola, in the west.

The rains are expected here when the Pleiades appear in the east soon after sunset; they go by the same name here as farther south: Lemila, or the "hoeings."

In the route along the Rovuma, we pass among people who are so well supplied with white calico by the slave-trade from Kilwa that it is quite a drug in the market: we can not get food for it. If we held on westward, we should cross several rivers flowing into the Rovuma from the southward, as the Zandulo, the Sanjenzé, the Lochiringo, and then, in going round the north end of Nyassa, we should pass among the Nindi, who now inhabit the parts vacated by the Mazitu, and imitate them in having shields and in marauding. An Arab party went into their country, and got out again only by paying a whole bale of calico. It would not be wise in me to venture there at present, but if we return this way we may; meanwhile we shall push on to Mataka, who is only a few days off from the middle of the Lake, and has abundance of provisions.

June 26th.—My last mule died. In coming along in the morning we were loudly accosted by a well-dressed woman who had just had a very heavy slave-taming stick put on her neck. She called in such an authoritative tone to us to witness the flagrant injustice of which she was the victim, that all the men stood still, and went to hear the case. She was a near relative of Chirikaloma, and was going up the river to her husband, when the old man (at whose house she was now a prisoner) caught her, took her servant away from her, and kept her in the degraded state we saw. The withes with which she was bound were green and sappy. The old man said in justification that she was running away from Chirikaloma, and he would be offended with him if he did not secure her.

I asked the officious old gentleman in a friendly tone what he expected to receive from Chirikaloma, and he said, "Nothing." Several slaver-looking fellows came about, and I felt sure that the woman had been seized in order to sell her to them, so I gave the captor a cloth to pay to Chirikaloma if he were offended, and told him to say that I, feeling ashamed to see one of his relatives in a slave-stick, had released her, and would take her on to her husband.

She is evidently a lady among them, having many fine beads and some strung on elephant's hair; she has a good deal of spirit too, for on being liberated she went into the old man's house and took her basket and calabash. A virago of a wife shut the door and tried to prevent her, as well as to cut off the beads from her person; but she resisted like a good one, and my men thrust the door open and let her out, but minus her slave. The other wife—for old Officious had two—joined her sister in a furious tirade of abuse, the elder holding her sides in regular fish-wife fashion, till I burst into a laugh, in which the younger wife joined. I explained to the different head men in front of this village what I had done, and sent messages to Chirikaloma explanatory of my friendly deed to his relative, so that no misconstruction should be put on my act.

We passed a slave woman shot or stabbed through the body, and lying on the path. A group of men stood about a hundred yards off on one side, and another of women on the other side, looking on; they said an Arab who passed early that morning had done it, in anger at losing the price he had given for her, because she was unable to walk any longer.

June 27th.—To-day we came upon a man dead from starvation, as he was very thin. One of our men wandered and found a number of slaves with slave-sticks on, abandoned by their master from want of food; they were too weak to be able to speak or say where they had come from; some were quite young. We crossed the Tulosi, a stream coming from south, about twenty yards wide.

At Chenjewala's the people are usually much startled when I explain that the numbers of slaves we see dead on the road have been killed partly by those who sold them; for I tell them that if they sell their fellows, they are like the man who holds the victim while the Arab performs the murder.

Chenjewala blamed Machemba, a chief above him on the Rovuma, for encouraging the slave-trade; I told him I had traveled so much among them that I knew all the excuses they could make: each head man blamed some one else.

"It would be better if you kept your people, and cultivated more largely," said I. "Oh, Machemba sends his men and robs our gardens after we have cultivated," was the reply. One man said that the Arabs who come and tempt them with fine clothes are the cause of their selling: this was childish, so I told them they would very soon have none to sell; their country was becoming jungle, and all their people who did not die in the road would be making gardens for Arabs at Kilwa and elsewhere.

June 28th.—When we got about an hour from Chenjewala's we came to a party in the act of marauding; the owners of the gardens made off for the other side of the river, and waved to us to go against the people of Machemba, but we stood on a knoll with all our goods on the ground, and waited to see how matters would turn out. Two of the marauders came to us, and said they had captured five people. I suppose they took us for Arabs, as they addressed Musa. They then took some green maize, and so did some of my people, believing that as all was going, they who were really starving might as well have a share.

I went on a little way with the two marauders, and by the foot-prints thought the whole party might amount to four or five, with guns: the gardens and huts were all deserted. A poor woman was sitting, cooking green maize, and one of the men ordered her to follow him. I said to him, "Let her alone; she is dying." "Yes," said he, "of hunger;" and went on without her.

We passed village after village, and gardens all deserted! We were now between two contending parties. We slept at one garden; and as we were told by Chenjewala's people to take what we liked, and my men had no food, we gleaned what congo-beans, bean-leaves, and sorghum stalks we could—poor fare enough, but all we could get.

June 29th.—We came on to Machemba's brother, Chimseia, who gave us food at once. The country is now covered with deeper soil, and many large acacia-trees grow in the rich loam; the holms too are large, and many islands afford convenient maize grounds. One of the Nassick lads came up and reported his bundle, containing two hundred and forty yards of calico, had been stolen; he went aside, leaving it on the path (probably fell asleep), and it was gone when he came back. I can not impress either on them or the sepoys that it is wrong to sleep on the march.

Akosakoné, whom we had liberated, now arrived at the residence of her husband, who was another brother of Machemba. She behaved like a lady all through, sleeping at a fire apart from the men. The ladies of the different villages we passed condoled with her, and she related to them the indignity that had been done to her. Besides this she did us many services: she bought food for us, because, having a good address, we saw that she could get double what any of our men could purchase for the same cloth; she spoke up for us when any injustice was attempted, and, when we were in want of carriers, volunteered to carry a bag of beads on her head. On arriving at Machemba's brother, Chimseia, she introduced me to him, and got him to be liberal to us in food on account of the service we had rendered to her. She took leave of us all with many expressions of thankfulness, and we were glad that we had not mistaken her position or lavished kindness on the undeserving.

One Johanna man was caught stealing maize, then another, after I had paid for the first. I sent a request to the chief not to make much of a grievance about it, as I was very much ashamed at my men stealing; he replied that he had liked me from the first, and I was not to fear, as whatever service he could do he would most willingly, in order to save me pain and trouble. A sepoy now came up, having given his musket to a man to carry, who therefore demanded payment. As it had become a regular nuisance for the sepoys to employ people to carry for them, telling them that I would pay, I demanded why he had promised in my name. "Oh, it was but a little way he carried the musket," said he. Chimseia warned us next morning, June 30th, against allowing any one to straggle or steal in front, for stabbing and plundering were the rule. The same sepoy who had employed a man to carry his musket now came forward, with his eyes fixed and shaking all over. This, I was to understand, meant extreme weakness; but I had accidentally noticed him walking quite smartly before this exhibition, so I ordered him to keep close to the donkey that carried the havildar's luggage, and on no account to remain behind the party. He told the havildar that he would sit down only for a little while; and, I suppose, fell asleep, for he came up to us in the evening as naked as a robin.

I saw another person bound to a tree and dead—a sad sight to see, whoever was the perpetrator. So many slave-sticks lie along our path, that I suspect the people hereabouts make a practice of liberating what slaves they can find abandoned on the march, to sell them again.

A large quantity of maize is cultivated at Chimsaka's, at whose place we this day arrived. We got a supply, but being among thieves, we thought it advisable to move on to the next place (Mtarika's). When starting, we found that fork, kettle, pot, and shot-pouch had been taken. The thieves, I observed, kept up a succession of jokes with Chuma and Wikatani, and when the latter was enjoying them, gaping to the sky, they were busy putting the things of which he had charge under their cloths! I spoke to the chief, and he got the three first articles back for me.

A great deal if not all the lawlessness of this quarter is the result of the slave-trade, for the Arabs buy whoever is brought to them; and in a country covered with forest as this is, kidnapping can be prosecuted with the greatest ease; elsewhere the people are honest and have a regard for justice.

Study Questions

1. What are the principal characteristics of Africa as described by each of these explorers?
2. In each of these accounts, the principal characters are Europeans. What non-Europeans appear in the accounts?
3. What different kinds of relationships are there between the Europeans and the non-Europeans in these accounts?
4. What evidence convinced Speke that he had discovered the source of the Nile?
5. The unusual aspect of Baker's expedition was the presence of his wife as a member of the party. From the selection given here, what effect did her presence have on the expedition?
6. How does Livingstone react to the different aspects of African society that he encounters?

Suggestions for Further Reading

Chaudhuri, Nupur, and Margaret Strobel, eds. *Western Women and Imperialism: Complicity and Resistance*. Bloomington: Indiana University Press, 1992.

Gray, Richard. *A History of the Southern Sudan, 1839–1889*. London: Oxford University Press, 1964.

Hall, Richard. *Lovers on the Nile*. London: Collins, 1980.

Hargreaves, John G. *West Africa Partitioned*. Madison: University of Wisconsin Press, 1974, 1985.

Lovell, Mary S. *A Rage to Live*. New York: W. W. Norton, 1998.

Moorehead, Alan. *The White Nile*. New York: Harper and Row, 1960.

Moorehead, Alan. *The Blue Nile*. New York: Harper and Row, 1962.

Web Sites

1. Africa, South of the Sahara; Exploration Fifteenth–Nineteenth centuries

   http://www-sul.stanford.edu/depts/ssrg/africa/history/hisexplore.html

2. The Age of Exploration

   http://www.robinsonresearch.com/AFRICA/HISTORY/exploration.htm

3. Cushing Library: Africa, Selections from the Rex B. Grey Collections

   http://library.tamu.edu/cushing/onlinex/africa

4. The "Institut d'Egypte and the *Description de l'Egypte* (The Napoleonic Invasion of Egypt)

   http://www.napoleon.org/us/us_cd/bib/articles/textes/institut.html

5. Nineteenth-Century Maps: Cairo

   http://www.ias.berkeley.edu/cmes/icmc/19th.htm

18

The Expansion of European Empires 1783–1900

TEXTS

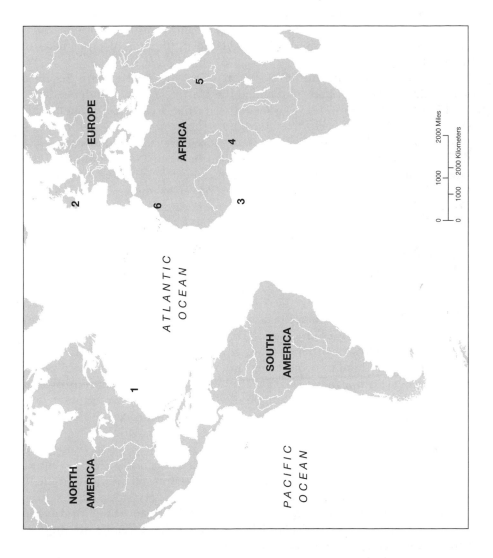

The nineteenth century saw European contact with the rest of the world increase in frequency and intensity. The gradual imposition of political control by European powers, especially Great Britain and France, over large parts of Asia and Africa, was an important aspect of this. Although most intense after 1870, when the so-called "New Imperialism" led to a European scramble for control of different parts of sub-Saharan Africa and to confrontations between European powers in Africa and Asia, it had begun much earlier, in a long phase of "informal empire" during which European merchants and governments slowly expanded their influence in other parts of the world.

For Great Britain, the development of an informal empire began at least with the Treaty of Paris that ended the War of American Independence in 1783. [1] The minister who negotiated that treaty, Lord Shelburne, sketched out in his speech defending the treaty a new vision of the British Empire, one in which economic ties were more important and less expensive than the political ties that had been broken between London and the new United States of America. [2] Following this policy, over the next half-century Great Britain used its political and military power to improve trading conditions for its citizens in Africa and Asia. In numerous places, armed intervention led to or defended commercial treaties that guaranteed British influence and favored treatment for British merchants.

In the course of the century, however, these interventions increasingly led to more active European participation in the governments of Africa and Asia. The weakness of the Ottoman Empire made its North African territories particularly vulnerable. France was first to attack this declining empire, invading Algeria in 1830, consolidating its control there in the 1840s, and incorporating the territory into France in 1871. European merchants continued to establish themselves in other parts of North Africa, bringing their governments in behind them to protect their interests and to assert national power against other European powers. In 1881, France established control over Tunisia, and in 1882, Britain and France established a protectorate over Egypt. France and Germany competed for control of Morocco, leading finally in 1912 to a French protectorate over that part of North Africa.

In West Africa one of the principal instigators of colonial control was the antislavery campaign that especially dominated British policy making towards Africa. With Great Britain's abolition of the transatlantic slave trade in 1807, European navies assumed responsibility for preventing slavers from leaving the coast of West Africa for the New World. The increased British and French presence in West Africa initially took the form of treaties of influence with coastal tribes. This could also lead to armed intervention, as the British found on the Gold Coast. [3] The weak coastal tribes there were caught between the British presence and the more powerful Asanti further inland. British intervention in 1824 began a process that would lead to further intervention and annexation in 1874. Especially after 1840, the British and French used anti-slave trade activity as a way of increasing their own influence in Senegambia and the south coast of West Africa. Beginning in 1854, French troops moved east from Senegal farther into the interior, both consolidating and extending French control in the area. Although this progressed fitfully due to stronger French focus on developments in Europe than Africa, the French advance continued into the Western Sudan over the next forty years, forming the basis for French West Africa. In the 1880s, several expeditions farther south led by Savorgnan de Brazza made France a major European power north of the Congo River, laying the groundwork, through treaties with indigenous tribes, for what would become French Equatorial Africa. [4]

South of the Congo River colonization initially took the form of a private company, the International Congo Association, created by the king of the Belgians, Leopold II. With Leopold borrowing money from the Belgian state to finance his imperial venture, the Association concluded treaties for the Association with over five hundred tribal chiefs in the early 1880s, establishing its domination over them. The expansion of Leopold's domain into the heart of the continent helped to disrupt existing European arrangements in Africa. Many European governments remained hesitant about colonization, but small groups of advocates of colonization pressed them to advance claims. Challenges to the longstanding hegemony of British interests led that country to make further claims, even to territories over which it had little if any control. This spurred on the colonial parties in France, Germany, and Portugal, and in West Africa and South Africa, one or more of these countries challenged the British presence. These new colonies were potential disrupters of the European peace, and in 1885, an international congress was held in Berlin. This meeting of the major powers turned the International Congo Association into the Congo Free State. It also set down the rules for expansion in Africa: a European power with holdings on the coast had prior rights to the back country; occupation must not be on paper only, but must consist of real occupation by administrators or troops; and each power must give proper notice to the others as to what territories it considered its own.

A wild scramble for "real occupation" began after the Berlin Congress, and by 1900, the entire continent, except for Ethiopia and Liberia, had been parceled out. [5, 6] Colonial administrations developed, building up the positions of local chiefs who signed treaties with the colonial power, and ruling indirectly through these chiefs. The African empires in 1900 consisted of two east-west belts, German and French, cut by a north-south belt, projected by the British as running from the Cape of Good Hope to Cairo. The meeting points of these belts precipitated crises in European diplomacy, notably in the Nile in 1898 in the Fashoda crisis, and from 1898 to 1902 in the Boer War. Portugal, in the meantime, held on to its older colonies in Angola, Mozambique, and Guinea (Bissau).

In Asia, Britain continued to rule one of its older colonies, India, which since 1600 had been loosely controlled through the British East India Company. A mutiny of Indian troops in 1857 led to the establishment of direct government control, making India the "jewel of the British Empire." In 1878, Victoria took the title empress of India, and after 1904, Empire Day (the Queen's birthday, May 24) became an annual, if unofficial, celebration of Britain's power, especially in India. France established an Asian colony in the 1870s, in Indochina, with the final conquest of the northern part, Tonkin, coming in 1885. Germany also laid claim to Asian territory, the Bismarck Islands, and the Netherlands continued its holdings in Indonesia. By the eve of the First World War, therefore, imperial possessions had become an important characteristic of virtually all European Great Powers, as well as several lesser powers.

1. THE SECOND BRITISH EMPIRE: *ANGLO-AMERICAN TREATY OF PEACE, 1783*

The first British Empire, in North America, peaked with the Treaty of Paris in 1763 that ended the Seven Years' War and ended the French challenge to British hegemony in North America. Only twenty years later, however, the independence of the thirteen American colonies brought that empire into eclipse. The articles of peace agreed upon between Great Britain and the United States confirmed American independence, but also began the reformulation of British imperial policy, away from the formal control that had marked its earlier empire in North America and toward policies aimed at preserving British economic advantage in areas outside of Europe.

Definitive Treaty of Peace

Concluded at Paris September 3, 1783; ratified by Congress January 14, 1784; proclaimed January 14, 1784.

In the name of the Most Holy and Undivided Trinity.

It having pleased the Divine Providence to dispose the hearts of the most serene and most potent Prince George the Third, by the Grace of God King of Great Britain, France, and Ireland, Defender of the Faith, Duke of Brunswick and Luneburg, Arch-Treasurer and Prince Elector of the Holy Roman Empire, &ca., and of the United States of America, to forget all past misunderstandings and differences that have unhappily interrupted the good correspondence and friendship which they mutually wish to restore; and to establish such a beneficial and satisfactory intercourse between the two countries, upon the ground of reciprocal advantages and mutual convenience, as may promote and secure to both perpetual peace and harmony: And having for this desirable end already laid the foundation of peace and reconciliation, by the provisional articles, signed at Paris, on the 30th of Nov'r, 1782, by the commissioners empowered on each part, which articles were agreed to be inserted in and to constitute the treaty of peace proposed to be concluded between the Crown of Great Britain and the said United States, but which treaty was not to be concluded until terms of peace should be agreed upon between Great Britain and France, and His Britannic Majesty should be ready to conclude such treaty accordingly; and the treaty between Great Britain and France having since been concluded, His Britannic Majesty and the United States of America, in order to carry into full effect the provisional articles above mentioned, according to the tenor thereof, have constituted and appointed, that is to say, His Britannic Majesty on his part, David Hartley, esqr., member of the Parliament of Great Britain; and the said United States on their part, John Adams, esqr., late a commissioner of the United States of America at the Court of Versailles, late Delegate in Congress from the State of Massachusetts, and chief justice of the said State, and Minister Plenipotentiary of the said United States to their High Mightinesses the States General of the United Netherlands; Benjamin Franklin, esq're, late Delegate in Congress from the State of Pennsylvania, president of the convention of the said State, and Minister Plenipotentiary from the United States of America at the Court of Versailles; John Jay, esq're, late president of Congress, and chief justice of the State of New York, and Minister Plenipotentiary from the said United States at the Court of Madrid, to be the Plenipotentiaries for the concluding and signing the present definitive treaty; who, after having reciprocally communicated their respective full powers, have agreed upon and confirmed the following articles:

Article I.

His Britannic Majesty acknowledges the said United States, viz. New Hampshire, Massachusetts Bay, Rhode Island, and Providence Plantations, Connecticut, New York, New Jersey, Pennsylvania, Delaware, Maryland, Virginia, North Carolina, South Carolina, and Georgia, to be free, sovereign and independent States; that he treats with them as such, and for himself, his heirs and successors, relinquishes all claims to the Government, propriety and territorial rights of the same, and every part thereof.

Article II.

And that all disputes which might arise in future, on the subject of the boundaries of the said United States may be prevented, it is hereby agreed and declared, that the following are, and shall be their boundaries, viz: From the northwest angle of Nova Scotia, viz. that angle which is formed by a line drawn due north from the source of Saint Croix River to the Highlands; along the said Highlands which divide those rivers that empty themselves into the river St. Lawrence, from those which fall into the Atlantic Ocean, to the northwesternmost head of Connecticut River; thence down along the middle of that river, to the forty-fifth degree of north latitude; from thence, by a line due west on said latitude, until it strikes the river Iroquois or Cataraquy; thence along the middle of said river into Lake Ontario, through the middle of said lake until it strikes the communication by water between that lake and Lake Erie; thence along the middle of said communication into Lake Erie, through the middle of said lake until it arrives at the water communication between that lake and Lake Huron; thence along the middle of said water communication into the Lake Huron; thence through the middle of said lake to the water communication between that lake and Lake Superior; thence through Lake Superior northward of the Isles Royal and Phelipeaux, to the Long Lake; thence through the middle of said

Long Lake, and the water communication between it and the Lake of the Woods, to the said Lake of the Woods; thence through the said lake to the most northwestern point thereof, and from thence on a due west course to the river Mississippi; thence by a line to be drawn along the middle of the said river Mississippi until it shall intersect the northernmost part of the thirty-first degree of north latitude. South, by a line to be drawn due east from the determination of the line last mentioned, in the latitude of thirty-one degrees north of the Equator, to the middle of the river Apalachicola or Catahouche; thence along the middle thereof to its junction with the Flint River; thence strait to the head of St. Mary's River; and thence down along the middle of St. Mary's River to the Atlantic Ocean. East, by a line to be drawn along the middle of the river St. Croix, from its mouth in the Bay of Fundy to its source, and from its source directly north to the aforesaid Highlands, which divide the rivers that fall into the Atlantic Ocean from those which fall into the river St. Lawrence; comprehending all islands within twenty leagues of any part of the shores of the United States, and lying between lines to be drawn due east from the points where the aforesaid boundaries between Nova Scotia on the one part, and East Florida on the other, shall respectively touch the Bay of Fundy and the Atlantic Ocean; excepting such islands as now are, or heretofore have been, within the limits of the said province of Nova Scotia.

Article III.

It is agreed that the people of the United States shall continue to enjoy unmolested the right to take fish of every kind on the Grand Bank, and on all the other banks of New-foundland; also in the Gulph of Saint Lawrence, and at all other places in the sea where the inhabitants of both countries used at any time heretofore to fish. And also that the inhabitants of the United States shall have liberty to take fish of every kind on such part of the coast of Newfoundland as British fishermen shall use (but not to dry or cure the same on that island) and also on the coasts, bays and creeks of all other of His Britannic Majesty's dominions in America; and that the American fishermen shall have liberty to dry and cure fish in any of the unsettled bays, harbours and creeks of Nova Scotia, Magdalen Islands, and Labrador, so long as the same shall remain unsettled; but so soon as the same or either of them shall be settled, it shall not be lawful for the said fishermen to dry or cure fish at such settlements, without a previous agreement for that purpose with the inhabitants, proprietors or possessors of the ground.

Article IV.

It is agreed that creditors on either side shall meet with no lawful impediment to the recovery of the full value in sterling money, of all bona fide debts heretofore contracted.

Article V.

It is agreed that the Congress shall earnestly recommend it to the legislatures of the respective States, to provide for the restitution of all estates, rights and properties which have been confiscated, belonging to real British subjects, and also of the estates, rights and properties of persons resident in districts in the possession of His Majesty's arms, and who have not borne arms against the said United States. And that persons of any other description shall have free liberty to go to any part or parts of any of the thirteen United States, and therein to remain twelve months, unmolested in their endeavours to obtain the restitution of such of their estates, rights and properties as may have been confiscated; and that Congress shall also earnestly recommend to the several States a reconsideration and revision of all acts or laws regarding the premises, so as to render the said laws or acts perfectly consistent, not only with justice and equity, but with that spirit of conciliation which, on the return of the blessings of peace, should universally prevail. And that Congress shall also earnestly recommend to the several States, that the estates, rights and properties of such last mentioned persons, shall be restored to them, they refunding to any persons who may be now in possession, the *bona fide* price (where any has been given) which such persons may have paid on purchasing any of the said lands, rights or properties, since the confiscation. And it is agreed, that all persons who have any interest in confiscated lands, either by debts, marriage settlements or otherwise, shall meet with no lawful impediment in the prosecution of their just rights.

Article VI.

That there shall be no future confiscations made, nor any prosecutions commenc'd against any person or persons for, or by reason of the part which he or they may have taken in the present war; and that no person shall, on that account, suffer any future loss or damage, either in his person, liberty or property; and that those who may be in confinement on such charges, at the time of the ratification of the treaty in America, shall be immediately set at liberty, and the prosecutions so commenced be discontinued.

Article VII.

There shall be a firm and perpetual peace between His Britannic Majesty and the said States, and between the subjects of the one and the citizens of the other, wherefore all hostilities, both by sea and land, shall from henceforth cease: All prisoners on both sides shall be set at liberty, and His Britannic Majesty shall, with all convenient speed, and without causing any destruction, or carrying away any negroes or other property of the American inhabitants, withdraw all his armies, garrisons and fleets from the said United States, and from every post, place and harbour within the same; leaving in all fortifications the American artillery that may be therein: And shall also order and cause all archives, records, deeds and papers, belonging to any of the said States, or their citizens, which, in the course of the war, may have fallen into the hands of his officers, to be forthwith restored and deliver'd to the proper States and persons to whom they belong.

Article VIII.

The navigation of the river Mississippi, from its source to the ocean, shall for ever remain free and open to the subjects of Great Britain, and the citizens of the United States.

Article IX.

In case it should so happen that any place or territory belonging to Great Britain or to the United States, should have been conquer'd by the arms of either from the other, before the arrival of the said provisional articles in America, it is agreed, that the same shall be restored without difficulty, and without requiring any compensation.

2. Lord Shelburne, *Debate in the Lords on the Preliminary Articles of Peace,* February 17, 1783

William Petty, marquis of Lansdowne, known as Lord Shelburne (1737–1805), was one of the principal architects of this new imperial vision. As a member of the House of Lords, he was an outspoken critic of the American War, condemning as early as 1775 attempts to coerce the Americans into "a blind and servile submission." When the government of Lord North fell in 1782, Shelburne became secretary of state in the new Rockingham ministry that followed, and formed his own cabinet in July of 1782 upon the death of Lord Rockingham. He directed the negotiations for an American peace which culminated in treaties with the United States on November 30, 1782, and with France and Spain on January 20, 1783. Many political figures, however, felt that Shelburne had conceded too much in the treaties, and it proved difficult to gain their ratification in parliament. In February 1783, Shelburne was forced to defend his diplomatic policies in a heated debate in the House of Lords.

Debate in the Lords on the Preliminary Articles of Peace

Let us examine them, my lords, let us take the several assertions in their turn and without wishing to intrude too much on your lordships time, I shall be pardoned for giving a distinct answer to each head of objection. Ministry, in the first place, is blamed for drawing the boundary they have done between the territories of the United States and those of our sovereign in Canada. I wish to examine every part of the treaties on the fair rule of the value of the district ceded—to examine it on the amount of the exports and imports, by which alone we could judge of its importance. The exports of this country to Canada, then, were only £140,000 and the imports were no more than £50,000. Suppose the entire fur trade sunk into the sea, where is the detriment to this country? Is £50,000 a year imported in that article any object for Great Britain to continue a war of which the people of England, by their representatives, have declared their abhorrence? Surely it is not. But much less must this appear in our sight, when I tell parliament, and the whole kingdom, that for many years past, one year with another, the preservation of this annual import of £50,000 has cost this country, on an average, £800,000. I have the vouchers in my pocket, should your lordships be inclined to examine the fact. But the trade is not given up, it is only divided, and divided for our benefit. I appeal to all men conversant with the nature of that trade, whether its best resources in Canada do not lie to the northward. What, then, is the result of this part of the treaty, so wisely, and with so much sincere love on the part of England clamoured against by noble lords? Why this. You have generously given America, with whom every call under Heaven urges you to stand on the footing of brethren, a share in a trade, the monopoly of which you sordidly preserved to yourselves, at the loss of the enormous sum of £750,000. Monopolies, some way or other, are ever justly punished. They forbid rivalry, and rivalry is of the very essence of the well-being of trade. This seems to be the æra of protestantism in trade. All Europe appear enlightened, and eager to throw off the vile shackles of oppressive ignorant monopoly; that unmanly and illiberal principle, which is at once ungenerous and deceitful. A few interested Canadian merchants might complain; for merchants would always love monopoly, without taking a moment's time to think whether it was for their interest or not. I avow that monopoly is always unwise; but if there is any nation under heaven, who ought to be the first to reject monopoly, it is the English. Situated as we are between the old world and the new, and between the southern and northern Europe, all that we ought to covet upon earth is free trade, and fair equality. With more industry, with more enterprize, with more capital than any trading nation upon earth, it ought to be our constant cry, let every market be open, let us meet our rivals fairly, and we ask no more. It is a principle on which we have had the wisdom to act with respect to our brethren of Ireland; and, if conciliation be our view, why should we not reach it out also to America? Our generosity is not much, but, little as it is, let us give it with a grace. Indeed, to speak properly, it is not generosity to them, but œconomy to ourselves; and in the boundaries which are established we have saved ourselves the immense sum of £800,000 a-year, and shewed to the Americans our sincere love and fair intentions, in dividing the little bit of trade which nature had laid at their doors; and telling them that we desired to live with them in communion of benefits, and in the sincerity of friendship.

3. "WAR WITH THE ASHANTEE," ANNUAL REGISTER 1824

British presence on the Gold Coast of Africa in the early nineteenth century was largely commercial, but also included a military presence, with forts along the coast. This brought the British into conflicts between British merchants and African tribes on and near the coast. Beginning in 1816, a series of treaties were negotiated between the British and the principal of these tribes, the Asanti. Although these treaties protected trade relations between the Asanti and the British, disputes about them arose and escalated in the early 1820s. In 1823, the capture of a British sergeant led to the outbreak of war between British and Asanti, a war known as the Mankatasa or McCarthy, after the British governor of the Gold Coast, Sir Charles McCarthy. The war dragged on until 1826, and its effect was to confirm British presence on the Gold Coast and, by giving Britain ownership of the land on which its forts stood, to consolidate and deepen British power in the region.

War with the Ashantee

The Ashantees, not withstanding their threatening movements, did not venture upon an attack. During the night they occupied Parson's-Croom, a village within one mile of the fort, and retired early on the 24th to the encampment which they had quitted two days before. From that time up to the end of the month, they contented themselves with detaching strong parties to lay waste the adjacent country, and to burn and destroy all the villages within their reach. This they were enabled to do with perfect impunity; for the whole of the garrison at Cape Coast and for both castle and town (exclusive of a very small unorganized force, on which little dependence could be placed) amounted only to 316 rank and file, many of them very young soldiers, of whom 104 were in hospital, 12 were sick in quarters, 32 were recruits, and 12 were boys.

On the 4th of July, the Thetis arrived from England with a few troops; and on the 6th, the garrison was further strengthened by a body of auxiliaries from Accra. Intelligence of these events induced the enemy to concentrate his strength, and, for that purpose, to recal the detachments which were ravaging the country and burning the villages far and wide. On the 7th, part of their army was observed from Cape Coast, defiling in great force over a hill, by several paths, towards some heights near the left of their position, where the king's tent was erected.

On the 8th, the Accra auxiliaries, who had been supplied with arms and ammunition as far as the scanty means of the settlement would permit, were, with the Cape Coast people, placed in position on a strong and commanding chain of heights (opposite to the enemy), round the town and fort. They were employed until the 11th in clearing away the bush, fortifying their posts, and watching the motions of the Ashantees, with whom there was occasionally some skirmishing, and who on their part were equally busy in cutting paths towards our posts.

On the 11th, soon after day-light, the enemy were seen descending in several masses of great strength into, and forming their line across, the valley leading to the right of our position, which was about half a mile from the town. About two in the afternoon, their advance having been fired upon by our skirmishers, a general engagement ensued, which at dusk, terminated in their being defeated at all points, and obliged to retire. Two camps on the right of their position, which they had weakened to reinforce their left, were burnt and plundered by part of the unorganized forces, who, although daily driven out of the town to their posts at the point of the bayonet, fought on this occasion for four hours with great courage. The Ashantees displayed considerable bravery, and made several gallant but ineffectual attempts to turn our right wing.

The regulars had 3 men wounded, and an officer killed. The militia 1 man killed; and 5 wounded. The unorganized armed forces 102 killed, and 440 wounded.

The Ashantee force was estimated at no less than 16,000 fighting men. Their loss in killed and wounded could not be ascertained; but their dead were very numerous on the scene of action; and the prisoners and deserters stated it to be great, and that many chiefs were killed and wounded.

On the 12th, the enemy again appeared drawn up in the valley, apparently with the design of making another attempt on our positions. In order to draw them into some movement that might expose their intentions, colonel Sutherland twice or thrice ordered a body of skirmishers to creep up and open a fire on them, and then retire. This fire was each time returned with great animation from the enemy's whole line for about half an hour, after our skirmishers had retired unobserved. As they made no demonstration of advancing, a few random shot from a field-piece were fired through the bush in the direction of their line. They then retired towards the head of the valley, where they remained on the 13th. On the following night, they retreated by the government garden, Elmina, and Fettue, towards Doonquah, which is on the direct route to Ashantee. On the 19th, they again appeared within five miles of Cape Coast: but on the 20th they withdrew.

It afterwards appeared, that the result of the action of the 11th, together with the sufferings produced by disease and want of provisions, had occasioned strong symptoms of insubordination and discontent in the Ashantee army. As early as the night of the

11th, whole bands had deserted; and though four out of six captains, who had been re-taken, had been beheaded after being tortured, while the other two remained prisoners in heavy logs, the desertion still continued; and the king found it impossible to continue the campaign, or to prolong his desultory warfare in the neighbourhood of Cape Coast.

The miseries, however, of which his presence had been the cause, did not cease with his departure. The plantations of India corn, yams, plantains, and bananas, which form the food of the natives, had been entirely destroyed, and the Fantees, who had escaped the sword, had still to dread the more lingering perils of famine. Beef was at sixteen guineas a tierce at Cape Coast, and flour or bread could scarcely be obtained at any price.

4. TREATY CONCLUDED BETWEEN ALBERT DOLISIE AND THE CHIEFS OF ALIMA, 17 OCTOBER 1884

French exploration of equatorial Africa was dominated by the expeditions led by Pierre Savorgnan de Brazza (1842–1905) between 1875 and 1885. These expeditions went through territories north of the Congo River, the boundary with the International Congo Association established by King Leopold II of Belgium. They were remarkable in that Brazza did not use force to impose European will on the Africans. Nonetheless, they provided the basis for French claims to what became the French Congo through the treaties, such as this one, that Brazza and his second-in-command, Albert Dolisie, concluded with the numerous chiefs of the tribes of the Congo basin.

Treaty Concluded between Albert Dolisie and the Chiefs of Alima

In the name of France

And in virtue of the powers that have been delegated to us by Monsieur Pierre Savorgnan de Brazza, Ship's Ensign, chevalier of the Legion of Honor, Commissioner in West Africa of the government of the French Republic,

I, Albert Dolisie, graduate of the Ecole Polytechnique, reserve officer of Naval Artillery, have concluded the following treaty with the undersigned chiefs, in their names and in those of their successors.

Article I. The chiefs Ibaka, Moulouka, Ibaka-Sili-Mokémo, Mangi son of Haka, N'Galiéné, successors of the deceased king Mokémo, the great chief of Abanho, inheritors of sovereign authority and of property rights over the territories located at the mouths of the Alima and on the two banks of this river, and exercising themselves today this same authority over these same places, and these same rights,

The chief Ibaka named above, heir by Mokémo of the sovereign rights of which Mokémo was the first inheritor, at the same time as the property rights of the lands of the deceased Mololi the great chief Abanho to which Mokémo succeeded in the exercise of all his rights, on all his territories equally located at the mouths of the river Alima,

All acting in their names and in the names of their successors, declare that they renew the conventions proclaimed the eighth of October 1880 at N'Couna between the deceased Mokémo and M. Pierre Savorgnan de Brazza, Ship's Ensign, head of the Mission of Ogooué and of the Congo,

And place all their ports under the suzerainty and the protection of France.

Article II. The chiefs Molouka and Mokélé, assisted by a notable of the region, Bamukala, undersigned current successors of the great chief Dolollé through the inheritance of Mokémo the sole owner of the soil,

Declare that they recognize the sovereignty of the chief Ibaka and accept all the engagements taken in the preceding article by Ibaka concerning the territories where they live and others of which they are the owners or the chiefs,

And subscribe without any restriction to the engagements and conditions expressed in the following articles:

Article III. France recognizes all the above-named chiefs, recognizes their rights cited above and promises to all of them aid and protection.

Article IV. The chiefs and the members of their tribes conserve all of their property and lands. They are able to rent them or sell them to Europeans of all nationalities and to receive the rents in the form and under the conditions in usage in the country.

Article V. To safeguard the interests of the members of their tribes, all sales and all rents of land must, to be valid, be made before a representative of the French government.

Article VI. Commerce will be carried out freely and on the basis of the most perfect equality between indigenous peoples and subjects of France and other countries.

The chiefs commit themselves to use all of their influence to carry out measures that will be taken after this to abolish the slave trade.

Article VII. The chiefs commit themselves never to interfere with transactions between sellers and buyers, never to intercept communications, and to use their authority only to protect commerce, develop their peoples, and facilitate the movement of goods, either through French posts or through others established in the country.

Article VIII. The chiefs cede to the government of the French Republic, in full ownership and without any payment, a plot of land of which the location and the size remain to be determined, and whether it will be on the mainland or on the islands of the Congo that are a part of their territories, to be used to establish a post.

Article IX. The present treaty, containing our signature as well as those of the undersigned chiefs, takes effect on the same day as its signing.

Made in the Village of Essoukou October 17, 1884.

The Delegate of the Commissioner of the Government
Signed: A Dolisie   Signed: N'Galiémé
Signatures of Chiefs: Ibaka +
                      Moulouka +
                      Ibaka Sili Mokémé +
                      Mangi +
                      Moboula +
                      Mokélé +
Signatures of Gamokala +
John Gomez,
Interpreting Corporal +

I undersigned, Joseph Michaud, civilian member of the West African Mission, certify that the present treaty was freely discussed with the designated chiefs and in the presence of the members of their tribes, that it was read to them, explained and commented upon, and that it was accepted by them in complete understanding of its terms.

I also certify the authenticity of the signatures of the chiefs and of Gamokala, signatures all of which were made in my sight.

Essoukou, 17 October 1884.

Signed: Michaud

Seen by: P. S. de Brazza

5. J. A. HOBSON, *IMPERIALISM: A STUDY*

John A. Hobson (1858–1940) was born into a middle-class family in the industrial city of Derby, England, the son of a newspaper publisher who was active in Liberal Party politics, and educated in local grammar schools and at Lincoln College at Oxford University. He then began a teaching career, first at Faversham and then at Exeter. In 1887, however, he moved to London, where he turned to journalism and began elaborating a critique of capitalism that supported greater state intervention in the economy. These views made him an academic outsider, but increased his focus on radical journalism. He was active in two intellectual discussion groups, the Ethical Movement and the Rainbow Circle, which included a variety of liberal and radical reformers of the prewar era as members. During the Boer War (1899–1902), he used his knowledge of South Africa, gained as a special correspondent of the *Manchester Guardian* just before the outbreak of the war, as the basis for antiwar activity. *Imperialism: A Study* (1902) was written against the background of the Boer War. During World War I, he continued to campaign for peace, and in 1924, he joined the Labour Party and acted as an economic advisor to Ramsay MacDonald's Labour government in 1929.

Imperialism: A Study

No mere array of facts and figures adduced to illustrate the economic nature of the new Imperialism will suffice to dispel the popular delusion that the use of national force to secure new markets by annexing fresh tracts of territory is a sound and a necessary policy for an advanced industrial country like Great Britain. It has indeed been proved that recent annexations of tropical countries, procured at great expense, have furnished poor and precarious markets, that our aggregate trade with our colonial possessions is virtually stationary, and that our most profitable and progressive trade is with rival industrial nations, whose territories we have no desire to annex, whose markets we cannot force, and whose active antagonism we are provoking by our expansive policy.

But these arguments are not conclusive. It is open to Imperialists to argue thus:"We must have markets for our growing manufactures, we must have new outlets for the investment of our surplus capital and for the energies of the adventurous surplus of our population: such expansion is a necessity of life to a nation with our great and growing powers of production. An ever larger share of our population is devoted to the manufactures and commerce of towns, and is thus dependent for life and work upon food and raw materials from foreign lands. In order to buy and pay for these things we must sell our goods abroad. During the first three-quarters of the century we could do so without difficulty by a natural expansion of commerce with continental nations and our colonies, all of which were far behind us in the main arts of manufacture and the carrying trades. So long as England held a virtual monopoly of the world markets for certain important classes of manufactured goods, Imperialism was unnecessary. During the last thirty years this manufacturing and trading supremacy has been greatly impaired: other nations, especially Germany, the United States, and Belgium, have advanced with great rapidity, and while they have not crushed or even stayed the increase of our external trade, their competition is making it more and more difficult to dispose of the full surplus of our manufactures at a profit. The encroachments made by these nations upon our old markets, even in our own possessions, make it most urgent that we should take energetic means to secure new markets. These new markets must lie in hitherto undeveloped countries, chiefly in the tropics, where vast populations live capable of growing economic needs which our manufacturers and merchants can supply. Our rivals are seizing and annexing territories for similar purposes, and when they have annexed them close them to our trade. The diplomacy and the arms of Great Britain must be used in order to compel the owners of the new markets to deal with us: and experience shows that the safest means of securing and developing such markets is by establishing 'protectorates' or by annexation. The present value of these markets must not be taken as a final test of the economy of such a policy; the process of educating civilised needs which we can supply is of necessity a gradual one, and the cost of such Imperialism must be regarded as a capital outlay, the fruits of which posterity will reap. The new markets may not be large, but they form serviceable outlets for the overflow of our great textile and metal industries, and, when the vast Asiatic and African populations of the interior are reached, a rapid expansion of trade may be expected to result.

"Far larger and more important is the pressure of capital for external fields of investment. Moreover, while the manufacturer and trader are well content to trade with foreign nations, the tendency for investors to work towards the political annexation of countries which contain their more speculative investments is very powerful. Of the fact of this pressure of capital there can be no question. Large savings are made which cannot find any profitable investment in this country; they must find employment elsewhere, and it is to the advantage of the nation that they should be employed as largely as possible in lands where they can be utilised in opening up markets for British trade and employment for British enterprise.

"However costly, however perilous, this process of imperial expansion may be, it is necessary to the continued existence and progress of our nation; if we abandoned it we must be content to leave the development of the world to other nations, who will everywhere cut into our trade, and even impair our means of securing the food and raw materials we require to support our population. Imperialism is thus seen to be, not a choice, but a necessity." . . .

Over-production in the sense of an excessive manufacturing plant, and surplus capital which cannot find sound investments within the country, force Great Britain, Germany, Holland, France to place larger and larger portions of their economic resources outside the area of their present political domain, and then stimulate a policy of political expansion so as to take in the new areas. The economic sources of this movement are laid bare by periodic trade-depressions due to an inability of producers to find adequate and profitable markets for what they can produce. The Majority Report of the Commission upon the Depression of Trade in 1885 put the matter in a nut-shell. "That, owing to the nature of the times, the demand for our commodities does not increase at the same rate as formerly; that our capacity for production is consequently in excess of our requirements, and could be considerably increased at short notice; that this is due partly to the competition of the capital which is being steadily accumulated in the country." The Minority Report straightly imputes the condition of affairs to "over-production." Germany is at the present time suffering severely from what is called a glut of capital and of manufacturing power: she must have new markets; her Consuls all over the world are "hustling" for trade; trading settlements are forced upon Asia Minor; in East and West Africa, in China and elsewhere the German Empire is impelled to a policy of colonisation and protectorates as outlets for German commercial energy.

Every improvement of methods of production, every concentration of ownership and control, seems to accentuate the tendency. As one nation after another enters the machine economy and adopts advanced industrial methods, it becomes more difficult for its manufacturers, merchants, and financiers to dispose profitably of their economic resources, and they are tempted more and more to use their Governments in order to secure for their particular use some distant undeveloped country by annexation and protection.

The process we may be told is inevitable, and so it seems upon a superficial inspection. Everywhere appear excessive powers of production, excessive capital in search of investment. It is admitted by all business men that the growth of the powers of production in their country exceeds the growth in consumption, that more goods can be produced than can be sold at a profit, and that more capital exists than can find remunerative investment.

It is this economic condition of affairs that forms the taproot of Imperialism. If the consuming public in this country raised its standard of consumption to keep pace with every rise of productive powers, there could be no excess of goods or capital clamorous to use Imperialism in order to find markets: foreign trade would indeed exist, but there would be no difficulty in exchanging a small surplus of our manufactures for the food and raw material we annually absorbed, and all the savings that we made could find employment, if we chose, in home industries.

There is nothing inherently irrational in such a supposition. Whatever is, or can be, produced, can be consumed, for a claim upon it, as rent, profit, or wages, forms part of the real income of some member of the community, and he can consume it, or else exchange it for some other consumable with some one else who will consume it. With everything that is produced a consuming power is born. If then there are goods which cannot get consumed, or which cannot even get produced because it is evident they cannot get consumed, and if there is a quantity of capital and labour which cannot get full employment because its products cannot get consumed, the only possible explanation of this paradox is the refusal of owners of consuming power to apply that power in effective demand for commodities. . . .

Thus we reach the conclusion that Imperialism is the endeavour of the great controllers of industry to broaden the channel for the flow of their surplus wealth by seeking foreign markets and foreign investments to take off the goods and capital they cannot sell or use at home.

The fallacy of the supposed inevitability of imperial expansion as a necessary outlet for progressive industry is now manifest. It is not industrial progress that demands the opening up of new markets and areas of investment, but mal-distribution of consuming power which prevents the absorption of commodities and capital within the country. The over-saving which is the economic root of Imperialism is found by analysis to consist of rents, monopoly profits, and other unearned or excessive elements of income, which, not being earned by labour of head or hand, have no legitimate *raison d'être*. Having no natural relation to effort of production, they impel their recipients to no corresponding satisfaction of consumption: they form a surplus wealth, which, having no proper place in the normal economy of production and consumption, tends to accumulate as excessive savings. Let any turn in the tide of politico-economic forces divert from these owners their excess of income and make it flow, either to the workers in higher wages, or to the community in taxes, so that it will be spent instead of being saved, serving in either of these ways to swell the tide of consumption—there will be no need to fight for foreign markets or foreign areas of investment.

6. V. I. LENIN, *IMPERIALISM: THE HIGHEST STAGE OF CAPITALISM*

V. I. Lenin (1870–1924) was the founder of the Bolshevik Party in Russia and leader of the Bolshevik Revolution in 1917 that established the Union of Soviet Socialist Republics. Born Vladimir Ilich Ulianov, he was the son of a bureaucrat in the czarist educational system and received a university education, gaining a law degree in 1891. The execution of his older brother, Alexander, for plotting the assassination of the czar, moved him toward radical political activity, and in 1893, he moved to Saint-Petersburg and began to help organize a Russian marxist movement that emphasized the revolutionary potential of the growing working class, rather than the peasantry that the populist movement had emphasized. Later that decade he began to publish pamphlets using marxist theory to analyze the attempt to carry out a revolution in Russia. In 1900, after being held in Siberian exile for three years, he moved to western Europe, where he remained for most of the time until 1917. There he continued both his theoretical writing and political organizing. His particular contribution to marxist thought was his insistence that leadership by intellectuals was a vital concern for the revolutionary struggle, with the party as the instrument by which the spontaneity of the working class could be disciplined. In 1903, this position led to a split between the Lenin-led Bolshevik faction of Russian marxists and their more social-democratic rivals, the Mensheviks. In 1916, he published *Imperialism: The Highest Stage of Capitalism,* which extended marxist thought to take into account the growth of European empires in the last quarter of the nineteenth century. In the spring of 1917, after the czarist government had collapsed under pressures of the war, Lenin returned to Russia, seizing power in the October 1917 Revolution and consolidating it during the following Civil War. Wounded in an assassination attempt in 1918, and the victim of two strokes in 1922, he died in 1924.

Imperialism: The Highest Stage of Capitalism

VII. Imperialism, as a Special Stage of Capitalism

We must now try to sum up, to draw together the threads of what has been said above on the subject of imperialism. Imperialism emerged as the development and direct continuation of the fundamental characteristics of capitalism in general. But capitalism only became capitalist imperialism at a definite and very high stage of its development, when certain of its fundamental characteristics began to change into their opposites, when the features of the epoch of transition from capitalism to a higher social and economic system had taken shape and revealed themselves in all spheres. Economically, the main thing in this process is the displacement of capitalist free competition by capitalist monopoly. Free competition is the basic feature of capitalism, and of commodity production generally; monopoly is the exact opposite of free competition, but we have seen the latter being transformed into monopoly before our eyes, creating large-scale industry and forcing out small industry, replacing large-scale by still larger-scale industry, and carrying concentration of production and capital to the point where out of it has grown and is growing monopoly: cartels, syndicates and trusts, and merging with them, the capital of a dozen or so banks, which manipulate thousands of millions. At the same time the monopolies, which have grown out of free competition, do not eliminate the latter, but exist above it and alongside it, and thereby give rise to a number of very acute, intense antagonisms, frictions and conflicts. Monopoly is the transition from capitalism to a higher system.

If it were necessary to give the briefest possible definition of imperialism we should have to say that imperialism is the monopoly stage of capitalism. Such a definition would include what is most important, for, on the one hand, finance capital is the bank capital of a few very big monopolist banks, merged with the capital of the monopolist associations of industrialists; and, on the other hand, the division of the world is the transition from a colonial policy which has extended without hindrance to territories unseized by any capitalist power, to a colonial policy of monopolist possession of the territory of the world, which has been completely divided up.

But very brief definitions, although convenient, for they sum up the main points, are nevertheless inadequate, since we have to deduce from them some especially important features of the phenomenon that has to be defined. And so, without forgetting the conditional and relative value of all definitions in general, which can never embrace all the concatenations of a phenomenon in its full development, we must give a definition of imperialism that will include the following five of its basic features:

(1) the concentration of production and capital has developed to such a high stage that it has created monopolies which play a decisive role in economic life; (2) the

merging of bank capital with industrial capital, and the creation, on the basis of this "finance capital", of a financial oligarchy; (3) the export of capital as distinguished from the export of commodities acquires exceptional importance; (4) the formation of international monopolist capitalist associations which share the world among themselves, and (5) the territorial division of the whole world among the biggest capitalist powers is completed. Imperialism is capitalism at that stage of development at which the dominance of monopolies and finance capital is established; in which the export of capital has acquired pronounced importance; in which the division of the world among the international trusts has begun, in which the division of all territories of the globe among the biggest capitalist powers has been completed.

We shall see later that imperialism can and must be defined differently if we bear in mind not only the basic, purely economic concepts—to which the above definition is limited—but also the historical place of this stage of capitalism in relation to capitalism in general, or the relation between imperialism and the two main trends in the working-class movement. The thing to be noted at this point is that imperialism, as interpreted above, undoubtedly represents a special stage in the development of capitalism.

X. The Place of Imperialism in History

We have seen that in its economic essence imperialism is monopoly capitalism. This in itself determines its place in history, for monopoly that grows out of the soil of free competition, and precisely out of free competition, is the transition from the capitalist system to a higher socioeconomic order. We must take special note of the four principal types of monopoly, or principal manifestations of monopoly capitalism, which are characteristic of the epoch we are examining.

Firstly, monopoly arose out of the concentration of production at a very high stage. This refers to the monopolist capitalist associations, cartels, syndicates and trusts. We have seen the important part these play in present-day economic life. At the beginning of the twentieth century, monopolies had acquired complete supremacy in the advanced countries, and although the first steps towards the formation of the cartels were taken by countries enjoying the protection of high tariffs (Germany, America), Great Britain, with her system of free trade, revealed the same basic phenomenon, only a little later, namely, the birth of monopoly out of the concentration of production.

Secondly, monopolies have stimulated the seizure of the most important sources of raw materials, especially for the basic and most highly cartelised industries in capitalist society: the coal and iron industries. The monopoly of the most important sources of raw materials has enormously increased the power of big capital, and has sharpened the antagonism between cartelised and non-cartelised industry.

Thirdly, monopoly has sprung from the banks. The banks have developed from modest middleman enterprises into the monopolists of finance capital. Some three to five of the biggest banks in each of the foremost capitalist countries have achieved the "personal link-up" between industrial and bank capital, and have concentrated in their hands the control of thousands upon thousands of millions which form the greater part of the capital and income of entire countries. A financial oligarchy, which throws a close network of dependence relationships over all the economic and political institutions of present-day bourgeois society without exception—such is the most striking manifestation of this monopoly.

Fourthly, monopoly has grown out of colonial policy. To the numerous "old" motives of colonial policy, finance capital has added the struggle for the sources of raw materials, for the export of capital, for spheres of influence, i.e., for spheres for profitable deals, concessions, monopoly profits and so on, economic territory in general. When the colonies of the European powers, for instance, comprised only one-tenth of the territory of Africa (as was the case in 1876), colonial policy was able to develop by methods other than those of monopoly—by the "free grabbing" of territories, so to speak. But when nine-tenths of Africa had been seized (by 1900), when the whole world had been divided up, there was inevitably ushered in the era of monopoly possession of colonies and, consequently, of particularly intense struggle for the division and the redivision of the world.

The extent to which monopolist capital has intensified all the contradictions of capitalism is generally known. It is sufficient to mention the high cost of living and the tyranny of the cartels. The intensification of contradictions constitutes the most powerful driving force of the transitional period of history, which began from the time of the final victory of world finance capital.

Monopolies, oligarchy, the striving for domination and not for freedom, the exploitation of an increasing number of small or weak nations by a handful of the richest or most powerful nations—all these have given birth to those distinctive characteristics of imperialism which compel us to define it as parasitic or decaying capitalism. More and more prominently there emerges, as one of the tendencies of imperialism, the creation of the "rentier state", the usurer state, in which the bourgeoisie to an ever-increasing degree lives on the proceeds of capital exports and by "clipping coupons". It would be a mistake to believe that this tendency to decay precludes the rapid growth of capitalism. It does not. In the epoch of imperialism, certain branches of industry, certain strata of the bourgeoisie and certain countries betray, to a greater or lesser degree, now one and now another of these tendencies. On the whole, capitalism is growing far more rapidly than before; but this growth is not only becoming more and more uneven in general, its unevenness also manifests itself, in particular, in the decay of the countries which are richest in capital (Britain).

In regard to the rapidity of Germany's economic development, Riesser, the author of the book on the big German banks, states: "The progress of the preceding period (1848–70), which had not been exactly slow, compares with the rapidity with which the whole of Germany's national economy, and with it German banking, progressed during this period (1870–1905) in about the same way as the speed of the mail coach in the good old days compares with the speed of the present-day automobile . . . which is whizzing past so fast that it endangers not only innocent pedestrians in its path, but also the occupants of the car." In its turn, this finance capital which has grown with such extraordinary rapidity is not unwilling, precisely because it has grown so quickly, to pass on to a more "tranquil" possession of colonies which have to be seized—and not only by peaceful methods—from richer nations. In the United States, economic development in the last decades has been even more rapid than in Germany, *and for this very reason*, the parasitic features of modern American capitalism have stood out with particular prominence. On the other hand, a comparison of, say, the republican American bourgeoisie with the monarchist Japanese or German bourgeoisie shows that the most pronounced political distinction diminishes to an extreme degree in the epoch of imperialism—not because it is unimportant in general, but because in all these cases we are talking about a bourgeoisie which has definite features of parasitism.

The receipt of high monopoly profits by the capitalists in one of the numerous branches of industry, in one of the numerous countries, etc., makes it economically possible for them to bribe certain sections of the workers, and for a time a fairly considerable minority of them, and win them to the side of the bourgeoisie of a given industry or given nation against all the others. The intensification of antagonisms between imperialist nations for the division of the world increases this urge. And so there is created that bond between imperialism and opportunism, which revealed itself first and most clearly in Great Britain, owing to the fact that certain features of imperialist development were observable there much earlier than in other countries. Some writers, L. Martov, for example, are prone to wave aside the connection between imperialism and opportunism in the working-class movement—a particularly glaring fact at the present time—by resorting to "official optimism" (à la Kautsky and Huysmans) like the following: the cause of the opponents of capitalism would be hopeless if it were progressive capitalism that led to the increase of opportunism, or, if it were the best-paid workers who were inclined towards opportunism, etc. We must have no illusions about "optimism" of this kind. It is optimism in respect of opportunism; it is optimism which serves to conceal opportunism. As a matter of fact the extraordinary rapidity and the particularly revolting character of the development of opportunism is by no means a guarantee that its victory will be durable: the rapid growth of a painful abscess on a healthy body can only cause it to burst more quickly and thus relieve the body of it. The most dangerous of all in this respect are those who do not wish to understand that the fight against imperialism is a sham and humbug unless it is inseparably bound up with the fight against opportunism.

From all that has been said in this book on the economic essence of imperialism, it follows that we must define it as capitalism in transition, or, more precisely, as moribund capitalism. It is very instructive in this respect to note that bourgeois economists, in describing modern capitalism, frequently employ catchwords and phrases like "interlocking", "absence of isolation", etc.; "in conformity with their functions and course of development", banks are "not purely private business enterprises; they are more and more outgrowing the sphere of purely private business regulation". And this very Riesser, whose words I have just quoted, declares with all seriousness that the "prophecy" of the Marxists concerning "socialisation" has "not come true"!

Study Questions

1. What were the principal characteristics of the relationship between Great Britain and the United States of America as envisaged in the Articles of Peace that ended the Revolutionary War and in Lord Shelburne's defense in Parliament of the peace treaty?
2. Both the account of the War with the Ashantee and the treaty concluded by Dolisie with the chiefs of Alima describe relationships between Europeans and the non-Europeans with whom they are either fighting or concluding treaties. What are the principal characteristics of these relationships, and how do they differ in the two situations?
3. What explanations do Hobson and Lenin provide for the nineteenth-century expansion of European empires? How do they differ from each other, and from the motivations of Shelburne, the British in the Asanti territory, and Dolisie in the Congo?

Suggestions for Further Reading

Bayly, C. A. *Imperial Meridian: The British Empire and the World 1780–1830.* New York: Longman, 1989.

Brunschwig, Henri. *French Colonialism 1871–1914: Myths and Realities.* New York: Praeger, 1964.

Curtin, Philip D. *The World and the West: The European Challenge and the Overseas Response in the Age of Empire.* New York: Cambridge University Press, 2000.

Fage, J. D., and Roland Oliver, eds. *The Cambridge History of Africa,* Vols. 5 and 6. New York: Cambridge University Press, 1976, 1985.

Fieldhouse, D. K. *Colonialism 1870–1945: An Introduction.* London: Weidenfeld and Nicolson, 1981.

Fieldhouse, D. K. *Economics and Empire 1830–1914.* London: Macmillan, 1984.

Hargreaves, John G. *West Africa Partitioned.* Madison: University of Wisconsin Press, 1974, 1985.

Kanya-Forstner, A. S. *The Conquest of the Western Sudan: A Study in French Military Imperialism.* Cambridge: Cambridge University Press, 1969.

Robinson, Ronald, and John Gallagher with Alice Denny. *Africa and the Victorians.* New York: Saint-Martin's Press, 1961.

Web Sites

1. The Age of Imperialism

   http://www.fresno.k12.ca.us/schools/s090/lloyd/imperialism.htm(?)

2. European Imperialism: The New Imperialism

   http://www.winsor.edu/library/euroimpe.htm

3. Internet Modern History Text Book: Imperialism

   http://www.fordham.edu/halsall/mod/modsbook34.html

19

Race and Science
1830–1904

TEXTS

In the eighteenth century, race was a concept that was rarely used except when employed in proslavery arguments. In the course of the nineteenth century, however, the term acquired a more precise and culturally more powerful meaning as the authority of science endorsed it as a way of classifying human beings. "Race" came to mean the idea that there were a fixed number of human types, each with its own characteristics, both physical and mental, which if mixed could, for better or for worse, be eroded. By the middle of the century, the idea of race had become so powerful that its claims to be an essential determinant of human behavior had become an important part of both scientific theory and popular discussion. [1]

Although the importance of race was a commonplace, the features of racial theories were themselves contested. [2] The principles of classification were open to debate, with an early interest in phrenology suggesting that "facial angles" and skull types were a principle of classification. [3] By the middle of the century, a "cephalic index" had been proposed by a Swedish scientist, Anders Retzius. Skin pigmentation was also given importance, if for no other reason than because of its visibility. Authorities such as Herbert Spencer called for the use of both mental and physical characteristics, whereas others adopted a philological approach.

Racial theorists also concerned themselves with the origins of the different races, a debate with strong religious overtones. Monogenists, although not necessarily arguing for the equality of the different races, claimed that all mankind was descended from a single source. Polygenists, on the other hand, instead claimed that each race had a different and independent origin. Racial theories also established a hierarchy of races and provided the basis for the dominance of one race over another. Once these hierarchical relationships had been established, the further question of the permanence or changeability of differences between races also arose. Degenerationists argued that lower races had regressed from the higher ones, and others held out hope for the progress of the lower races. In contrast to their eighteenth-century predecessors, however, nineteenth-century racial theorists were less optimistic about the prospects for improvement by racial inferiors.

The scientific work on evolution by Charles Darwin, published in *The Origin of Species* (1859) and *The Descent of Man* (1871), did not resolve these issues, but did become a fundamental point of reference for subsequent racial theorists. Social Darwinism, which emphasized the evolutionary importance of competition between races through natural selection, was able to draw on the scientific ideas of Darwin to legitimate its own views about racial difference and hierarchy. By the last third of the century, the racial views of mid-century were finding resonance in a number of different places. They were being adopted by those concerned about racial division within Europe. In England especially they contributed to debates about the relationship between the Irish and the English, whereas the unification of Germany after 1871 posed the question of the relationship between Germans and other Europeans. The increased contact between Europeans and sub-Saharan Africans, emphasized by the increase in political control that the New Imperialism brought, also drew on scientific or pseudoscientific theories of race. In domestic politics as well, eugenicists and others who were concerned with developing the abilities of elites and about the policies to be taken toward the industrial working classes used this language, often referring to workers as similar to "alien tribes." [4] The combination of the language of science with views about racial difference proved to be a powerful and long-lasting aspect of European contact with non-Europeans.

1. JOSEPH ARTHUR COMTE DE GOBINEAU, THE INEQUALITY OF HUMAN RACES

Joseph Arthur Comte de Gobineau (1816–1882) was born near Paris to a French bourgeois family that had aspirations to nobility. After attending school in Switzerland, he lived in Paris. In 1849, he became private secretary to Alexis de Tocqueville, the foreign minister of the new Second Republic. He later held a number of diplomatic posts before being forced to retire from the diplomatic service in 1877. His most important work, *The Inequality of Human Races,* was published in 1853–1855. The work reflected Gobineau's rejection of the French Revolution of 1789 and the democracy it espoused, but its significance lies in the importance he attributed to racial characteristics in explaining the rise and fall of civilizations, and in the influence of scientific theories of genetic determinism that the work employed. He also discussed the effects of hybridity, or racial mixing. Thus, he argued that although Aryans, the most superior members of the white race, were strong, intelligent, and brave, an infusion of black blood would improve their imaginations. However, for Gobineau, excessive racial mixing would lead to the eventual degeneration of civilization.

The Inequality of Human Races

If the human races were equal, the course of history would form an affecting, glorious, and magnificent picture. The races would all have been equally intelligent, with a keen eye for their true interests and the same aptitude for conquest and domination. Early in the world's history, they would have gladdened the face of the earth with a crowd of civilizations, all flourishing at the same time, and all exactly alike. At the moment when the most ancient Sanscrit peoples were founding their empire, and, by means of religion and the sword, were covering Northern India with harvests, towns, palaces, and temples; at the moment when the first Assyrian Empire was crowning the plains of the Tigris and Euphrates with its splendid buildings, and the chariots and horsemen of Nimroud were defying the four winds, we should have seen, on the African coast, among the tribes of the prognathous negroes, the rise of an enlightened and cultured social state, skilful in adapting means to ends, and in possession of great wealth and power.

The Celts, in the course of their migrations, would have carried with them to the extreme west of Europe the necessary elements of a great society, as well as some tincture of the ancient wisdom of the East; they would certainly have found, among the Iberian peoples spread over the face of Italy, in Gaul and Spain and the islands of the Mediterranean, rivals as well schooled as themselves in the early traditions, as expert as they in the arts and inventions required for civilization.

Mankind, at one with itself, would have nobly walked the earth, rich in understanding, and founding everywhere societies resembling each other. All nations would have judged their needs in the same way, asked nature for the same things, and viewed her from the same angle. A short time would have been sufficient for them to get into close contact with each other and to form the complex network of relations that is everywhere so necessary and profitable for progress.

But we know that such a picture is purely fantastic. The first peoples worthy of the name came together under the inspiration of an idea of union which the barbarians who lived more or less near them not only failed to conceive so quickly, but never conceived at all. The early peoples emigrated from their first home and came across other peoples, which they conquered; but these again neither understood nor ever adopted with any intelligence the main ideas in the civilization which had been imposed on them. Far from showing that all the tribes of mankind are intellectually alike, the nations capable of civilization have always proved the contrary, first by the absolutely different foundations on which they based their states, and secondly by the marked antipathy which they showed to each other. The force of example has never awakened any instinct, in any people, which did not spring from their own nature. Spain and the Gauls saw the Phœnicians, the Greeks, and the Carthaginians, set up flourishing towns, one after the other, on their coasts. But both Spain and the Gauls refused to copy the manners and the government of these great trading powers. When the Romans came as conquerors, they only succeeded in introducing a different spirit by filling their new dominions with Roman colonies. Thus the case of the Celts and the Iberians shows that civilization cannot be acquired without the crossing of blood.

Civilization is incommunicable, not only to savages, but also to more enlightened nations. This is shown by the efforts of French goodwill and conciliation in the ancient kingdom of Algiers at the present day, as well as by the experience of the English in India, and the Dutch in Java. There are no more striking and conclusive proofs of the unlikeness and inequality of races.

We should be wrong to conclude that the barbarism of certain tribes is so innate that no kind of culture is possible for them. Traces may be seen, among many savage peoples, of a state of things better than that obtaining now. Some tribes, otherwise sunk in brutishness, hold to traditional rules, of a curious complexity, in the matter of marriage, inheritance, and government. Their rites are unmeaning to-day, but they evidently go back to a higher order of ideas. The Red Indians are brought forward as an example; the vast deserts over which they roam are supposed to have been once the settlements of the Alleghanians. Others, such as the natives of the Marianne Islands, have methods of manufacture which they cannot have invented themselves. They hand them down, without thought, from father to son, and employ them quite mechanically.

When we see a people in a state of barbarism, we must look more closely before concluding that this has always been their condition. We must take many other facts into account, if we would avoid error.

Some peoples are caught in the sweep of a kindred race; they submit to it more or less, taking over certain customs, and following them out as far as possible. On the disappearance of the dominant race, either by expulsion, or by a complete absorption in the conquered people, the latter allows the culture, especially its root principles, to die out almost entirely, and retains only the small part it has been able to understand. Even this cannot happen except among nations related by blood. This was the attitude of the Assyrians towards the Chaldean culture, of the Syrian and Egyptian Greeks towards the Greeks of Europe, of the Iberians, Celts, and Illyrians in face of the Roman ideas. If the Cherokees, the Catawhas, the Muskhogees, the Seminoles, the Natchez, and the like, still show some traces of the Alleghanian intelligence, I cannot indeed infer that they are of pure blood, and directly descended from the originating stock—this would mean that a race that was once civilized can lose its civilization;—I merely say that if any of them derives from the ancient conquering type as its source, the stream is a muddy one, and has been mingled with many tributaries on the way. If it were otherwise, the Cherokees would never have fallen into barbarism. As for the other and less gifted tribes, they seem to represent merely the dregs of the indigenous population, which was forced by the foreign conquerors to combine together to form the basic elements of a new social state. It is not surprising that these remnants of civilization should have preserved, without understanding them, laws, rites, and customs invented by men cleverer than themselves; they never knew their meaning or theoretical principles, or regarded them as anything but objects of superstitious veneration. The same argument applies to the traces of mechanical skill found among them. The methods so admired by travellers may well have been ultimately derived from a finer race that has long disappeared. Sometimes we must look even further for their origin. Thus, the working of mines was known to the Iberians, Aquitanians, and the Bretons of the Scilly Isles; but the secret was first discovered in Upper Asia, and thence brought long ago by the ancestors of the Western peoples in the course of their migration.

The natives of the Caroline Islands are almost the most interesting in Polynesia. Their looms, their carved canoes, their taste for trade and navigation put a deep barrier between them and the other negroes. It is not hard to see how they come to have these powers. They owe them to the Malay blood in their veins; and as, at the same time, their blood is far from being pure, their racial gifts have survived only in a stunted and degraded form.

We must not therefore infer, from the traces of civilization existing among a barbarous people, that it has ever been really civilized. It has lived under the dominion of another tribe, of kindred blood, but superior to it; or perhaps, by merely living close to the other tribe, it has, feebly and humbly, imitated its customs. The savage races of to-day have always been savage, and we are right in concluding, by analogy, that they will continue to be so, until the day when they disappear.

Their disappearance is inevitable as soon as two entirely unconnected races come into active contact; and the best proof is the fate of the Polynesians and the American Indians.

The preceding argument has established the following facts:

(i) The tribes which are savage at the present day have always been so, and always will be, however high the civilizations with which they are brought into contact.

(ii) For a savage people even to go on living in the midst of civilization, the nation which created the civilization must be a nobler branch of the same race.

(iii) This is also necessary if two distinct civilizations are to affect each other to any extent, by an exchange of qualities, and give birth to other civilizations compounded from their elements. That they should ever be fused together is of course out of the question.

(iv) The civilizations that proceed from two completely foreign races can only touch on the surface. They never coalesce, and the one will always exclude the other.

The preceding paragraphs are enough to show how impossible it is that the civilizations belonging to racially distinct groups should ever be fused together. The irreconcilable antagonism between different races and cultures is clearly established by history, and such innate repulsion must imply unlikeness and inequality. If it is admitted that the European cannot hope to civilize the negro, and manages to transmit to the mulatto only a very few of his own characteristics; if the children of a mulatto and a white woman cannot really understand anything better than a hybrid culture, a little nearer than their father's to the ideas of the white race,—in that case, I am right in saying that the different races are unequal in intelligence.

I will not adopt the ridiculous method that is unhappily only too dear to our ethnologists. I will not discuss, as they do, the moral and intellectual standing of individuals taken one by one.

I need not indeed speak of morality at all, as I have already admitted the power of every human family to receive the light of Christianity in its own way. As to the question of intellectual merit, I absolutely refuse to make use of the argument, "every negro is a fool." My main reason for avoiding it is that I should have to recognize, for the sake of balance, that every European is intelligent; and heaven keep me from such a paradox!

I will not wait for the friends of equality to show me such and such passages in books written by missionaries or sea-captains, who declare that some Yolof is a fine carpenter, some Hottentot a good servant, that some Kaffir dances and plays the violin, and some Bambara knows arithmetic.

I am ready to admit without proof all the marvels of this kind that anyone can tell me, even about the most degraded savages. I have already denied that even the lowest tribes are absolutely stupid. I actually go further than my opponents, as I have no doubt that a fair number of negro chiefs are superior, in the wealth of their ideas, the synthetic power of their minds, and the strength of their capacity for action, to the level usually reached by our peasants, or even by the average specimens of our half-educated middle class. But, I say again, I do not take my stand on the narrow ground of individual capacity. It seems to me unworthy of science to cling to such futile arguments. If Mungo Park or Lander have given a certificate of intelligence to some negro, what is to prevent another traveller, who meets the same phœnix, from coming to a diametrically opposite conclusion? Let us leave these puerilities, and compare together, not men, but groups. When, as may happen some day, we have carefully investigated what the different groups can and cannot do, what is the limit of their faculties and the utmost reach of their intelligence, by what nations they have been dominated since the dawn of history—then and then only shall we have the right to consider why the higher individuals of one race are inferior to the geniuses of another. We may then go on to compare the powers of the average men belonging to these types, and to find out where these powers are equal and where one surpasses the other. But this difficult and delicate task cannot be performed until the relative position of the different races has been accurately, and to some extent mathematically, gauged. I do not even know if we shall ever get clear and undisputed results, if we shall ever be free to go beyond a mere general conclusion and come to such close grips with the minor varieties as to be able to recognize, define, and classify the lower strata and the average minds of each nation. If we can do this, we shall easily be able to show that the activity, energy, and intelligence of the least gifted individuals in the dominant races, are greater than the same qualities in the corresponding specimens produced by the other groups.

Mankind is thus divided into unlike and unequal parts, or rather into a series of categories, arranged, one above the other, according to differences of intellect.

2. MATTHEW ARNOLD, ON THE STUDY OF CELTIC LITERATURE

Matthew Arnold (1822–1888) was the son of an eminent Victorian, Dr. Thomas Arnold, headmaster of Rugby School and an influential reformer of English public schools. Matthew was educated at Rugby and then Balliol College, Oxford, eventually becoming an inspector of schools and professor of poetry at Oxford. In the 1850s and 1860s, he published numerous collections of poetry even as he was becoming a prolific literary and social critic. In a witty and learned style, he argued that both in literature and in politics England needed to develop "culture," an elite sense of the free play of critical intelligence and leisurely judgment.

Although *Culture and Anarchy* (1869) is Arnold's best-known work, his *On the Study of Celtic Literature* (1867) also deserves attention as a reflection of and a contribution to the nineteenth-century debate about race. In this essay Arnold was writing as an English literary critic but nonetheless propounded supposedly scientific views about the Celtic and Saxon origins of the English "race." His views are an indicator of the spread of scientific arguments about race into other areas of learning, and about the prestige and authority wielded by these scientific views.

On the Study of Celtic Literature

The bent of our time is towards science, towards knowing things as they are; so the Celt's claims towards having his genius and its works fairly treated, as objects of scientific investigation, the Saxon can hardly reject, when these claims are urged simply on their own merits, and are not mixed up with extraneous pretensions which jeopardise them. What the French call the *science des origines,* the science of origins—a science which is at the bottom of all real knowledge of the actual world, and which is every day growing in interest and importance—is very incomplete without a thorough critical account of the Celts and their genius, language, and literature. This science has still great progress to make, but its progress, made even within the recollection of those of us who are in middle life, has already affected our common notions about the Celtic race; and this change, too, shows how science, the knowing things as they are, may even have salutary practical consequences. I remember, when I was young, I was taught to think of Celt as separated by an impassable gulf from Teuton; my father, in particular, was never weary of contrasting them; he insisted much oftener on the separation between us and them than on the separation between us and any other race in the world; in the same way Lord Lyndhurst, in words long famous, called the Irish, "aliens in speech, in religion, in blood." This naturally created a profound sense of estrangement; it doubled the estrangement which political and religious differences already made between us and the Irish: it seemed to make this estrangement immense, incurable, fatal. It begot a strange reluctance, as any one may see by reading the preface to the great text-book for Welsh poetry, the *Myvyrian Archæology,* published at the beginning of this century, to further— nay, allow—even among quiet, peaceable people like the Welsh, the publication of the documents of their ancient literature, the monuments of the Cymric genius; such was the sense of repulsion, the sense of incompatibility, of radical antagonism, making it seem dangerous to us to let such opposites to ourselves have speech and utterance. Certainly the Jew—the Jew of ancient times, at least—then seemed a thousand degrees nearer than the Celt to us. Puritanism had so assimilated Bible ideas and phraseology; names like Ebenezer, and notions like that of hewing Agag in pieces, came so natural to us, that the sense of affinity between the Teutonic and the Hebrew nature was quite strong; a steady, middle-class Anglo-Saxon much more imagined himself Ehud's cousin than Ossian's. But meanwhile, the pregnant and striking ideas of the ethnologists about the true natural grouping of the human race, the doctrine of a great Indo-European unity, comprising Hindoos, Persians, Greeks, Latins, Celts, Teutons, Slavonians, on the one hand, and, on the other hand, of a Semitic unity, and of a Mongolian unity, separated by profound distinguishing marks from the Indo-European unity and from one another, was slowly acquiring consistency and popularising itself. So strong and real could the sense of sympathy or antipathy, grounded upon real identity or diversity in race, grow in men of culture, that we read of a genuine Teuton, Wilhelm von Humboldt, finding, even in the sphere of religion, that sphere where the might of Semitism has been so overpowering, the food which most truly suited his spirit in the productions not of the alien Semitic genius, but of the genius of Greece or India, the Teuton's born kinsfolk of the common Indo-European family. "Towards Semitism he felt himself," we read, "far less drawn;" he had the consciousness of a certain antipathy in the depths of his nature to this, and to its "absorbing, tyrannous, terrorist religion," as to the opener, more flexible Indo-European genius, this religion appeared. "The mere workings of the old man in him!" Semitism will readily reply; and though one can hardly admit this short and easy method of settling the matter, it must be owned that Humboldt's is an extreme case of Indo-Europeanism, useful as letting us see what may be the power of race and primitive constitution, but not likely, in the spiritual sphere, to have many companion cases equalling it. Still, even in this sphere, the tendency is in Humboldt's direction; the modern spirit tends more and more to establish a sense of native diversity between our European bent and the Semitic bent, and to eliminate, even in our religion, certain elements as purely and excessively Semitic, and therefore, in right, not combinable with our European nature, not assimilable by it. This tendency is now quite visible even among ourselves, and even, as I have said, within the great sphere of the Semitic genius, the sphere of religion; and for its justification this tendency appeals to science, the science of origins; it appeals to this science as teaching us which way our natural affinities and repulsions lie. It appeals to this science, and in part it comes from it; it is, in considerable part, an indirect practical result from it.

In the sphere of politics, too, there has, in the same way, appeared an indirect practical result from this science; the sense of antipathy to the Irish people, of radical estrangement from them, has visibly abated amongst all the better part of us; the remorse for past ill-treatment of them, the wish to make amends, to do them justice, to fairly unite, if possible, in one people with them, has visibly increased; hardly a book on Ireland is now published, hardly a debate on Ireland now passes in Parliament, without this appearing. Fanciful as the notion may at first seem, I am inclined to think that the march of science—science insisting that there is no such original chasm between the Celt and the Saxon as we once popularly imagined, that they are not truly, what Lord Lyndhurst called them, *aliens in blood* from us, that they are our brothers in the great Indo-European family—has had a share, an appreciable share, in producing this changed state of feeling. No doubt, the release from alarm and struggle, the sense of firm possession, solid security, and overwhelming power; no doubt these, allowing and encouraging humane feelings to spring up in us, have done much; no doubt a state of fear and danger, Ireland in hostile conflict with us, our union violently disturbed, might, while it drove back all humane feelings, make also the old sense of utter estrangement revive. Nevertheless, so long as such a malignant revolution of events does not actually come about, so long the new sense of kinship and kindliness lives, works, and gathers strength; and the longer it so lives and works, the more it makes any such malignant revolution improbable. And this new, reconciling sense has, I say, its roots in science.

However, on these indirect benefits of science we must not lay too much stress. Only this must be allowed; it is clear that there are now in operation two influences, both favourable to a more attentive and impartial study of Celtism than it has yet ever received from us. One is, the strengthening in us of the feeling of Indo-Europeanism; the other, the strengthening in us of the scientific sense generally. The first breaks down barriers between us and the Celt, relaxes the estrangement between us; the second begets the desire to know his case thoroughly, and to be just to it. This is a very different matter from the political and social Celtisation of which certain enthusiasts dream; but it is not to be despised by any one to whom the Celtic genius is dear; and it is possible, while the other is not.

3. JOHN BEDDOE, *THE RACES OF BRITAIN*

John Beddoe (1826–1911) was educated as a medical doctor at University College London and served in the Crimea during the Crimean War, helping treat casualties from that war. Upon his return he set up a medical practice in Bristol, where he lived for the rest of his life. While earning a living from his medical practice, he began the amateur studies of hair and eye color that were to form the basis for *The Races of Britain,* a work that combines the Victorian concerns with race, excellence, and science. For his work, he was well honored, becoming president of the Anthropological Society of London, a fellow of the Royal Society, and president of the Royal Anthropological Institute.

Beddoe worked at a time when scientific methods of observation and data analysis were still in their infancy, and he developed a method in which he would mark on a small, handheld card information concerning the hair and eye coloring of individuals he passed on the street. In the 1860s, he joined with Dr. Barnard Davis, the leading craniologist in the country, to undertake an enquiry into the physical characteristics of the bone structure of the human head. In *The Races of Britain,* published in 1885, Beddoe used this information as the basis for an argument relating physical characteristics, ethnic descent, and psychological characteristics that, in the guise of a careful scientific inquiry, reflects nineteenth-century European convictions about race as a fundamental human characteristic.

The Races of Britain

My first observations were vitiated by faulty classification; but I soon settled down into the system to which I have since adhered, and which recommended itself chiefly by its convenience, as it generally enabled me to locate an individual in his proper class and division on a very cursory inspection.

I acknowledge three classes of eyes, distinguished as much by shade as by colour—light, intermediate or neutral, and dark. To the first class are assigned all blue, bluish-gray and light gray eyes (cærulei, cinereo-cœrulescentes, cœsii). These correspond to the five blue types of Broca, 11, 12, 13, 14, 15, and to No. 10, his lightest green. It was perhaps a mistake to include the darkest blue (No. 11) in this category, as in an unfavourable light it is liable to be confounded with "black."

In the third class I put the so-called black eyes, and those usually called brown and dark hazel. These correspond to the deeper shades of Broca's orange, green, and violet-gray, Nos. 1, 2, 3, 6, 7, 16, 17, 18.

To the second, or neutral class, remain dark gray, brownish-gray, very light hazel or yellow, hazel-gray, formed by streaks of orange radiating into a bluish-gray field, and most shades of green, together with all the eyes of whose colour I remain uncertain after an ordinarily close inspection. These correspond pretty exactly, I believe, to 4, 5, 8, 9, 19, and 20.

Each of my three classes of eyes is sub-divided into five, in accordance with the accompanying colour of hair:

Class R includes all shades which approach more nearly to red than to brown, yellow, or flaxen.

Class F (fair) includes flaxen, yellow, golden, some of the lightest shades of our brown, and some pale auburns in which the red hue is not very conspicuous.

Class B includes numerous shades of brown, answering nearly, I believe, to the French chatain and chatain-clair, but perhaps less extensive on the dark side.

Class D corresponds nearly with the French brun, most of their brun-foncés, and the darkest chatains, and includes the remaining shades of our brown up to

Class N (niger), which includes not only the jet-black, which has retained the same colour from childhood, and is generally very coarse and hard, but also that very intense brown which occurs in people who in childhood have had dark brown (or in some cases deep red) hair, but which in the adult cannot be distinguished from coal-black, except in a very good light.

When unable to decide in which of two columns (*e.g.*, B or D) an individual ought to be inscribed, I divide him between the two, by a Solomonian judgment, and set down ½ or .5, in each of them.

When engaged in this work I set down in his proper place on my card of observation every person (with the exceptions to be mentioned presently) whom I meet, or who passes me within a short distance, say from one to three yards. As a rule, I take no note of persons who apparently belong to the upper classes, as these are more migratory and more often mixed in blood. I neglect those whom I suppose to be under age—fixing the point roughly at 18 or 20 for men, 17 or 18 for women—as well as all those whose hair has begun to grizzle. Thus I get a fairly uniform material to work upon, though doubtless the hair of most people does darken considerably between 20 and 40 or 50. In order to preserve perfect fairness, I always examine first, out of any group of persons, the one who is nearest, rather than the one to whom my attention is most drawn. Certain colours of the hair, such as red, certain shades of the eye, such as light gray, can be discerned at a very considerable distance; but I take no note of anyone who does not approach me so nearly that I can recognise the more obscure colours. Much allowance needs to be made for the varying effects of light. Direct sunlight is better avoided when possible; I always choose the shady side of a street on a sunny day. Considerable difficulties are created by the freaks of fashion. I once visited Friesland, in order to study the physical type of that region. Conceive my disappointment when I found myself surrounded by comely damsels and buxom matrons, not one of whom suffered a single yellow hair to stray beyond her lace cap or silver-gilt head-plate. When I began to work in England dark hair was in fashion among the women; and light and reddish hues were dulled with greasy unguents. In later years fair hair has been more in vogue; and golden shades, sometimes unknown to nature, are produced by art. Among men, on the other hand, the close cropping of the head, borrowed from the French, makes comparisons difficult. Fortunately, most vagaries of this kind are little prevalent in the classes among whom I seek my material.

It may be objected that there is no security that many of the persons observed may not be aliens to the place or neighbourhood wherein they are encountered. Certainly, there is no such security. But if a sufficient number of observations be secured, and the upper and other notoriously migratory classes (who are mostly easy of recognition) be excluded, the probability is immense that the great majority of the remainder have been born within a moderate radius of the centre of observation; and the majority will determine the position of the community in my chromatic scale.

A ready means of comparing the colours of two peoples or localities is found in the Index of Nigrescence. The gross index is gotten by subtracting the number of red and fair-haired persons from that of the dark-haired, together with twice the black-haired. I double the black, in order to give its proper value to the greater tendency to melanosity shown thereby; while brown (chestnut) hair is regarded as neutral, though in truth most of the persons placed in B are fair-skinned, and approach more nearly in aspect to the xanthous than to the melanous variety.

$$D + 2N - R - F = \text{index}.$$

From the gross index the net, or percentage index, is of course readily obtained.

It must not be supposed that, in devoting so much time and care to the collection of facts relating to colour, I was influenced by any excessive estimate of their importance. My chief inducement was the great abundance of the material, which, from a scientific point of view, was running to waste. The same thing might indeed be said of the heads of the British population; for they were also generally neglected by ethnologists, whatever phrenologists might be doing, the former being almost entirely absorbed in ancient craniology. But there was a very important difference between these two lines of enquiry: the one could be pursued without the concurrence of the subjects, the other could not. Had there been anything like a complete craniological record, had there even been anything approaching the amount of ancient and mediæval material that can be used in France or Switzerland, one might have neglected the heads of one's contemporaries, in consequence of the obstacle just mentioned; but in truth the record is anything but complete or satisfactory, notwithstanding the exertions of Davis and Thurnam, of Bateman, of Greenwell and Rolleston, of Daniel Wilson, James Hunt, and Pitt-Rivers. This lamentable defect arises partly from the destructive ignorance of our earlier antiquaries, who, while they carefully collected every fragment of a potsherd from the barrows they explored, utterly neglected, and exposed to decay, the often more important osseous remains. Even now "finds" frequently occur, the benefit of which is lost to anthropology, from the absence of qualified observers, and the lack of knowledge or interest in the finders and their neighbours. It is not long since there existed several mediæval ossuaries in England, systematic observations in which might have been of some value; but with the exception of those at Hythe, Rothwell, and Micheldean, they have all, I fear, been destroyed. Thus a very fine one at Ripon was destroyed, unmeasured and undescribed, by the late Dean Macneile, and another in the crypt of Tamworth was turned out to make room for a heating apparatus. These misfortunes are the more to be regretted, inasmuch as we really do not possess sufficient osseous material in our museums for determining the form and size of the skull of the modern Englishman. The few we have are in great part those of criminals, lunatics, and paupers. In this respect, owing to a prejudice, from some points of view respectable, we are behind most European nations; and when, in such works as those of Topinard and De Quatrefages, we see comparisons drawn between the ordinary skullforms of different countries, England is usually conspicuous by its absence.

On account of this dearth of material, I have measured a considerable number of living British heads, and shall make use of the results of these measurements in the present volume. As no accredited method existed when the work was begun, it was necessary to frame one. The difficulties in the way were considerable, and certainly were but partially overcome. It was necessary to avoid fatiguing or irritating the subjects; yet it was desirable to obtain as many data as possible suitable for comparison with those taken from ancient crania. With much regret I abandoned the use of Mr. Busk's excellent craniometer, and with it all radial measurements, because it sinned against the former of these requirements, and restricted myself to the use of the index callipers and graduated tape.

There are few points on the living head that are positively identifiable; and I was compelled to retain the use of some which are open to the objection of not being so. Some of the tape measures are affected by the variations in quantity and length of hair, though to a less extent than might be supposed. The following are those which I have been accustomed to take:

A. With the callipers.   (*a*) Lengths.

1. Maximum length from the glabella.

2. Length from the inion or occipital tuberosity to the most prominent part of the frontal curve.

3. Glabello-inial length.

4. Maximum length according to Barnard Davis, *i.e.*, from the ophryon, or the flat space above the glabella.

By the use of these four it is possible, in pursuance of one of Broca's suggestions, to work out the degree of prominence of the occiput, of the forehead, and of the glabella, and thus to compensate in some degree the lack of radial measurements.

5. Vertico-mental length, or maximum length of the whole head from crown to chin.

(*b*) Breadths.

6. Frontal minimum breadth, just above the brows.

7. Breadth at the stephanion, or maximum frontal. This is very uncertain; in many heads it is impossible to be sure whereabout the stephanion is.

8. Zygomatic breadth, maximum.

9. Auricular breadth, gotten, in accordance with Broca's recommendation, at the pit just in front of the helix, and above the condyle of the jaw and the root of the zygoma. This is a valuable measurement, the point being so easily identifiable. In conjunction with No. 11, it yields information as to the breadth of the base of the skull.

10. Maximum breadth, wherever found, and where found.

11. Mastoid breadth. Taken at the most prominent part of the external mastoid curve. This is very faulty, from the difficulty of fixing on the same point in different heads, the shape of the mastoid protuberances varying much.

B. With the tape.   (*e*) Circumferences.

12. Circumference in the line of length 1.

13.	do.	do.	do.	2.
14.	do.	do.	do.	3.
15.	do.	do.	do.	4.

13, 14, and 15 are of comparatively little value, seldom adding anything to the information given by 1, 2, 3, 4, 9, and 10. I often omit them.

(*c*) Arcs.

16. From the nasal notch to the inion, or occipital tuberosity.

17. From opposite the centre of one auricular meatus to that of the other, in a vertical line. This is very useful. Taken in connexion with 1 and 16, it gives a fair idea of the height of the head; but it has disadvantages, of which the chief is the uncertainty of the vertical line.

18. From the centre of one meatus to that of the other, along the superciliary ridges and the glabella. Indicates the comparative frontal and occipital development.

It is perhaps unfortunate, especially in view of the great attention now given to the facial bones, that I have seldom taken the length from the chin to the nasal notch, nor the breadth nor length of the nose. It has been my custom, however, to sketch the facial portrait by means of a few initial letters. Thus F., Sc., Pr., Br., Aq., Si., Ang. sketches a man of Fair complexion, Scutiform face, with Prominent brows, Broad cheekbones, Aquiline and Sinuous nose, and Angular chin.

I have spoken of the necessity and frequent difficulty of obtaining the consent of the owner of the head to be examined. His reluctance may sometimes be overcome by means of money, without going to the extent of the new hat always jocularly demanded in such cases. Sometimes other means have proved successful. I cannot resist detailing those by which I succeeded in obtaining a valuable series of head-measurements in Kerry. Our travelling party consisted of Dr. Barnard Davis, Dr. T. Wise, Mr. Windele, and myself. Whenever a likely little squad of natives was encountered the two archæologists got up a dispute about the relative size and shape of their own heads, which I was called in to settle with the callipers. The unsuspecting Irishmen usually entered keenly into the debate, and before the little drama had been finished were eagerly betting on the sizes of their own heads, and begging to have their wagers determined in the same manner.

4. HAVELOCK ELLIS, *A STUDY OF BRITISH GENIUS*

Havelock Ellis (1859–1939) was a critic and essayist best known for his pioneering contributions to the scientific study of human sexuality. He was educated at private schools, and at the age of sixteen traveled to Australia on a ship captained by his father. Ellis remained in Australia, teaching at an isolated school in the Australian bush, until 1879. His years in Australia convinced him of the value of the search for scientific truth, and on his return to England, he began medical studies. Although he was an uneven student, and hardly ever practiced medicine, he did gain a scientific grounding that was to serve him well in his subsequent research. In 1897, he began publication of what would become his best-known work, the controversial *Studies in the Psychology of Sex*, which was finally completed in 1928. Ellis had, however, much broader interests, publishing a number of other studies of sexuality, as well as works on topics as diverse as criminology and literature. *A Study of British Genius*, published in 1904, is indicative both of this breadth of interest and Ellis's scientific approach to the investigation of the pressing social and intellectual questions of his day.

A Study of British Genius

When we turn to the south-western focus of English genius we find ourselves among people of different mental texture, but of equal mental distinction. In positive intellectual achievement they compare with the slow and patient people of East Anglia, while as brilliant personalities they are in the very first rank. They are sailors rather than scholars, and courtiers, perhaps, rather than statesmen; they are innovators, daring free-thinkers, pioneers in the physical and intellectual worlds. Raleigh, on both sides a Devonshire man, is the complete type of these people. They are, above all, impressive personalities, aggressive, accomplished, irresistible, breaking rather than bending, without the careful foresight of the laborious and self-distrustful people of the east coast. This district alone has furnished a third of the great sailors of Britain, and the most brilliant group, with Drake and Hawkins and Gilbert as well as Raleigh. The expansive Elizabethan age gave the men of these parts their supreme chance, and they availed themselves of it to the utmost. Great Britain's most eminent soldiers have not usually been English, but one of the most famous of all, Marlborough, belongs to this region. In the arts of peace this southwestern focus shows especially well in painting. It cannot, indeed, be compared to the East Anglian focus in this respect, but Reynolds belongs to Devon, and is a typical representative of the qualities of this region on the less aggressive side, just as Raleigh is on the more militant side, both alike charming and accomplished personalities. Both in the material and spiritual worlds there is an imaginative exaltation, an element of dash and daring, in the men of this south-western district, which seems to carry them through safely. The southwestern focus is not quite so homogeneous as the eastern group. Somerset, which is the centre of the focus, seems to me to present its real and characteristic kernel, especially on the purely intellectual side. We do not find here the dashing recklessness, the somewhat piratical tendency, nor quite the same brilliant personal qualities as at the western part of the peninsula. The Somerset group of men are superficially more like those of East Anglia, but in reality with a very distinct physiognomy of their own. Like the rest of this region, Somerset is a land of great sailors, but the typical sailor hero of Somerset is Blake, and the difference between Blake and Raleigh is significant of the difference between the men of Somerset and the men of Devon. Somerset has produced the philosophers of this region, Roger Bacon, Hobbes, Locke; and in more recent days Bagehot and Huxley have been typical thinkers of the group. Hooker, the "judicious," is among the men of Devon. They are not often scholars (notwithstanding the presence of the "ever-memorable" Hales), being prone to rely much on their own native qualities. One recalls the remark of Hobbes, when charged with an indifference to books: "If I read as much as other people I should know as little as other people." While less concrete than the East Anglians, these eminent thinkers have not the abstract metaphysical tendencies of the North British philosophers; they reveal a certain practical sagacity, a determination to see things clearly, a hatred of cant and shams, a "positive" tendency, which is one of the notes of purely English thought and may be said to have its headquarters here. The representative scientific man of this region is the brilliant and versatile Thomas Young, whose luminous intelligence and marvellous intuition render him a typical example of genius in its purest form.

It is easy to define the nature of the genius of the Welsh Border. It is artistic in the widest sense, and notably poetic; there is a tendency to literary and oratorical eloquence, frequently tinged with religious or moral emotion, and among those who belong entirely to this district there are no scientific men of the first order. This region has the honour of claiming Shakespeare; and it may be pointed out that it is difficult to account for Shakespeare without assuming in him the presence of a large though not predominant Celtic element. Landor, one of the greatest of English masters of prose, comes in part within the Welsh Border, as does Fielding, while Purcell, the greatest of English musical composers, also probably belongs to this district. Sir Thomas Browne, though only a Welsh Borderer on his father's side, is very typical, and Macaulay is characteristic of the Celt as historian. The presence of Mrs. Siddons, although the genius of the Kemble family is attributed mainly to their Irish mother, helps to indicate the characteristics of this region, which although it has produced fewer great personalities than the two main foci of English genius, has certainly had its full share in some of the very greatest. The part of the Welsh Border in Darwin was small, but though he was more characteristically a son of the Anglo-Danish and East Anglian regions, it was probably not without its influence.

It has already been made clear that the county of Kent constitutes a remarkable, though small, centre of English genius. I was formerly inclined to regard this very interesting district as dependent on the important East Anglian focus. I am convinced, however, that this is a mistake. If we carefully contemplate the eminent persons produced by Kent it will be seen that they can be more easily affiliated, on the whole, to the south-western than to the East Anglian focus. Harvey, for instance, the greatest of the Kentish men, resembled the south-western people as much in intellectual temperament, as, by his short stature, dark hair and eyes, choleric constitution, he resembled them anthropologically. This seeming affinity of the genius of Kent to that of the south-western promontory, though it cannot be said to be complete identity, may perhaps be regarded as one of the numerous facts which tend to invalidate the belief, widely prevalent a few years ago under the influence of several eminent historians and ultimately resting on some rhetorical expressions of Gildas, that the Romano-British inhabitants of Kent were entirely exterminated by the Teutonic invaders.

Undoubtedly, however, the Teutonic element is considerable in all this south-eastern part of England, as far westwards as Wilts. One is indeed tempted to ask whether it may serve to explain another psychological phenomenon which is revealed by the distribution of English genius. The Jutes came to Kent; the Saxons occupied the regions to the west of Kent. This district, including (with Kent and Essex) the whole of the light-haired populations of southern England, is occupied by the counties of Sussex, Surrey, Hampshire and Berkshire. Except in so far as Surrey is suburban to London and profits by this proximity, all this region is comparatively bare of aboriginal genius. Mackintosh observed, in his notable study of the psychic characteristics of British peoples, that the unmixed English Saxon, unlike the Angle (and possibly unlike the Jute), is marked by mental mediocrity. One is tempted to ask whether this fact, if it is a fact, may be invoked to explain the result of the present inquiry as regards this region.

I do not propose to consider in detail the distribution of ability in the other parts of the British Islands, for the figures are here too small to yield reliable results. The distribution of ability in Wales, Scotland and Ireland is, however, so definitely confined to certain districts that a mere inspection of the crude figures suffices to give us for each of these countries a fairly close conception of their intellectual geography.

Study Questions

1. How does Gobineau distinguish between different races?
2. How does Arnold connect science with his views about the Celts?
3. What is the basis for Beddoe's distinctions between races?
4. What implications does Ellis draw from the racial distinctions he sees in Great Britain?
5. All these studies in some way present evidence in support of their contentions about race. Which of them seem to you most convincing? Why? Which seem least convincing? Why?

Suggestions for Further Reading

Chamberlin, J. Edwards, and Sander L. Gilman, eds. *Degeneration*. New York: Columbia University Press, 1985.

Glass, Bentley, Owsei Temkin, and William L. Straus Jr., eds. *Forerunners of Darwin, 1745–1859*. Baltimore, MD: The Johns Hopkins University Press, 1959.

Kiernan, V. G. *The Lords of Human Kind: Black Man, Yellow Man, and White Man in an Age of Empire*. Boston: Little, Brown and Company, 1969.

Stoler, Ann Laura, and Frederick Cooper, eds. *Tensions of Empire*. Berkeley: University of California Press, 1997.

Young, Robert M. *Darwin's Metaphor*. New York: Cambridge University Press, 1985.

Web Sites

1. John Beddoe: from *The Races of Britain*

   http://www.people.virginia.edu/~dnp5c/Victorian/racesbrit.html

2. Herbert Spencer: Social Darwinism

   http://www.fordham.edu/halsall/mod/spencer-darwin.html

20

Orientalism and Orientalist Art: Learning about the East 1784–1887

TEXTS

The part of the world known to Europeans as the Orient (India, the lands of North Africa and the Ottoman Empire, Turkey and Asia Minor, Egypt and Syria) held a position of great significance for them, as the birthplace of European civilization and religion, and as a location for early attempts at political domination. Beginning in the late eighteenth century, Orientalism, the scholarly study of those areas, became a significant activity in Western Europe. European scholars began to develop the tools for learning the Persian and Arabic languages and literatures. [1] This European interest was related to growing European control over these parts of the world, and it generated controversies among the elites of North Africa, the Middle East, and South Asia. [2] By the early nineteenth century, the archaeology, culture, and politics of the region had become objects of close attention by Europeans. [3, 4] Orientalist studies also became fundamental to the training of generations of colonial administrators.

The Orient was also at this time a place in which Europeans could reflect upon their own civilization by comparing it with those that they found there, and the possibilities of travel to the region made it a likely destination for wealthy European travelers. The increased contact between Europe and the East that began with the Napoleonic campaign in Egypt continued in the course of the nineteenth century, as trade increased, European states increased their political control over the region, and steamships and railroads made it easier for Europeans to visit. For creative artists in particular, it was a source of subject matter that could be treated without reference to the restrictive rules of classicism that dominated European art in the eighteenth and early nineteenth centuries. A subject drawn from this part of the world, therefore, provided an opportunity to allow the imagination full flight, a possibility that meshed well with the attempts of Romanticism to give primary importance to the imagination. The apparent strength of Oriental passions, the cruelty of its rulers, and especially the inaccessibility of Oriental women, veiled and in harems, provided powerful inspiration for casual tourists as well as poets and painters from Europe. Poets such as Chateaubriand and Gérard de Nerval made tours of the region and utilized its images in their works. Beginning with paintings by Baron Gros (French, 1771–1835) of the Napoleonic campaign in Egypt, and continuing through poems of Lord Byron and Victor Hugo, Orientalism in the creative arts reached its full flowering with the paintings of Eugene Delacroix in the 1820s and 1830s. [5] By the middle of the century, it had become easier for European painters to visit North Africa and the Near East, and an Orientalist school of painting existed. In the last third of the century, Orientalist images were immensely popular: paintings commanded high prices and critical acclaim, and copies and variants of Orientalist paintings became commonplace. [6]

Although Orientalist art began as a process of cataloging the topography of places and the customs of people unfamiliar to the West, its subject matter presented challenges to the European practice of painting. In contrast to the relatively cluttered landscape of Europe, which provided anchors for painters' compositions, the emptiness of the desert led to new compositional techniques. All visitors to the region were struck by the brilliance of the North African and Middle Eastern light, contrasting so sharply with the darkness of northern European painting and challenging the palette that European painters brought to their Orientalist paintings. Especially after the middle of the nineteenth century, the realist aesthetic becoming prevalent among European painters challenged Orientalist painters to represent the external world truthfully, leading to a meticulousness about detail that convinced many viewers that they were seeing the results of objective observation. But inevitably even the most realist of Orientalist painters emphasized some aspects of their subject and ignored others. Few if any paintings portrayed the poverty and disease many visitors saw, and although harems fascinated westerners, there was little reflection upon or portrayal of the implications of these for the women who lived in them.

1. SIR WILLIAM JONES, *PREFACE* TO *GRAMMAR* OF THE *PERSIAN LANGUAGE*

Sir William Jones (1746–1794) was a pioneer in England in the study of Asia, and especially Asian languages. He arrived in Calcutta in 1784 and was one of the principal figures in the founding of the Asiatick Society, an organization devoted to the study of Asian language and literature. He had already published a *Grammar of the Persian Language* in 1771 that not only provided the means for Englishmen to learn Persian, but also spelled out the Orientalist viewpoint that Asian languages had characteristics matching, if not exceeding, those of classical Latin and Greek, and that learning them opened up an impressive literature to Europeans. At a time when educational authorities in India, the Committee of Public Instruction, and the government were engaged in a debate concerning the utility of instruction in these languages for the Indian elite, Jones was a principal figure on the Orientalist side that sought to continue government support for this instruction. Although unsuccessful, the admiration that Jones and others expressed for classical Indian literature provided the basis for the nineteenth-century revival of Hinduism among English-educated Indians. This selection, from the *Preface* to his *Grammar of the Persian Language,* expresses Jones's appreciation of Persian and his reasons for desiring its continued study. It also indicates the ambivalent relationship that members of the imperial culture could have toward the native culture.

Preface *to* Grammar of the Persian Languages

The Persian language is rich, melodious, and elegant; it has been spoken for many ages by the greatest princes in the politest courts of Asia; and a number of admirable works have been written in it by historians, philosophers, and poets, who found it capable of expressing with equal advantage the most beautiful and the most elevated sentiments.

It must seem strange, therefore, that the study of this language should be so little cultivated at a time when a taste for general and diffusive learning seems universally to prevail; and that the fine productions of a celebrated nation should remain in manuscript upon the shelves of our publick libraries, without a single admirer who might open their treasures to his countrymen, and display their beauties to the light, but if we consider the subject with a proper attention, we shall discover a variety of causes which have concurred to obstruct the progress of Eastern literature.

Some men never heard of the Asiatick writings, and others will not be convinced that there is any thing valuable in them; some pretend to be busy, and others are really idle; some detest the Persians, because they believe in Mahomed, and others despise their language, because they do not understand it: we all love to excuse, or to conceal, our ignorance, and are seldom willing to allow any excellence beyond the limits of our own attainments: like the savages, who thought that the sun rose and set for them alone, and could not imagine that the waves, which surrounded their island, left coral and pearls upon any other shore.

Another obvious reason for the neglect of the Persian language is the great scarcity of books, which are necessary to be read before it can be perfectly learned: the greater part of them are preserved in the different museums and libraries of Europe, where they are shewn more as objects of curiosity than as sources of information; and are admired, like the characters on a Chinese screen, more for their gay colours than for their meaning.

Thus, while the excellent writings of Greece and Rome are studied by every man of a liberal education, and diffuse a general refinement through our part of the world, the works of the Persians, a nation equally distinguished in ancient history, are either wholly unknown to us, or considered as entirely destitute of taste and invention.

But if this branch of literature has met with so many obstructions from the ignorant, it has, certainly, been checked in its progress by the learned themselves; most of whom have confined their study to the minute researches of verbal criticism; like men who discover a precious mine, but instead of searching for the rich ore, or for gems, amuse themselves with collecting smooth pebbles and pieces of crystal. Others mistook reading for learning, which ought to be carefully distinguished by every man of sense, and were satisfied with running over a great number of manuscripts in a superficial manner, without condescending to be stopped by their difficulty, or to dwell upon their beauty and elegance. The rest have left nothing more behind them than grammars and dictionaries; and though they deserve the praises due to unwearied pains and industry, yet they would, perhaps, have gained a more shining reputation, if they had contributed to beautify and enlighten the vast temple of learning, instead of spending their lives in adorning only its porticos and avenues.

There is nothing which has tended more to bring polite letters into discredit, than the total insensibility of commentators and cricticks to the beauties of the authors whom they profess to illustrate: few of them seem to have received the smallest pleasure from the most elegant compositions, unless they found some mistake of a transcriber to be corrected, or some established reading to be changed, some obscure expression to be explained, or some clear passage to be made obscure by their notes.

It is a circumstance equally unfortunate, that men of the most refined taste and the brightest parts are apt to look upon a close application to the study of languages as inconsistent with their spirit and genius: so that the state of letters seems to be divided into two classes, men of learning who have no taste, and men of taste who have no learning.

M. de Voltaire, who excels all writers of his age and country in the elegance of his style, and the wonderful variety of his talents, acknowledges the beauty of the Persian images and sentiments, and has verified a very fine passage from Sadi, whom he compares to Petrarch: if that extraordinary man had added a knowledge of the Asiatick languages to his other acquisitions, we should by this time have seen the poems and histories of Persia in an European dress, and any other recommendation of them would have been unnecessary.

But there is yet another cause which has operated more strongly than any before mentioned towards preventing the rise of oriental literature; I mean the small encouragement which the princes and nobles of Europe have given to men of letters. It is an indisputable truth, that learning will always flourish most where the amplest rewards are proposed to the industry of the learned; and that the most shining periods in the annals of literature are the reigns of wife and liberal princes, who know that fine writers are the oracles of the world, from whose testimony every king, statesman, and hero must expect the censure or approbation of posterity. In the old states of Greece the highest honours were given to poets, philosophers, and orators; and a single city (as an eminent writer observes) in the memory of one man, produced more numerous and splendid monuments of human genius than most other nations have afforded in a course of ages.

The liberality of the Ptolemies in Egypt drew a number of learned men and poets to their court, whose works remain to the present age the models of taste and elegance; and the writers, whom Augustus protected, brought their composition to a degree of perfection, which the language of mortals cannot surpass. Whilst all the nations of Europe were covered with the deepest shade of ignorance, the Califs in Asia encouraged the Mahomedans to improve their talents, and cultivate the fine arts; and even the Turkish Sultan, who drove the Greeks from Constantinople, was a patron of literary merit, and was himself an elegant poet. The illustrious family of Medici invited to Florence the learned men whom the Turks had driven from their country, and a general light succeeded the gloom which ignorance and superstition had spread through the western world. But that light has not continued to shine with equal splendour; and though some slight efforts have been made to restore it, yet it seems to have been gradually decaying for the last century: it grows very faint in Italy; it seems wholly extinguished in France; and whatever sparks of it remain in other countries are confined to the closets of humble and modest men, and are not general enough to have their proper influence.

2. RAMMOHUN ROY, *LETTER ON EDUCATION*

Ambivalence about the study of South Asian culture existed on the other side of the colonial relationship, among those Indians who were forced to come to terms with British control of their country. This was expressed in 1835 by a leader of the Hindu community, Rammohun Roy, who argued against the reestablishment of a college of Sanskrit studies in Bengal. Roy had himself funded several schools that emphasized the study of English language and literature, and was convinced that this study was vital for the young men of Bengal so that they could gain the most modern European education and become assimilated into British culture. His letter therefore provided valuable arguments on the Committee of Public Instruction against Orientalists who, like Jones a generation earlier, had emphasized exposure to Hindu literature for the Indian elite.

A Letter on English Education

To His Excellency the Right Honourable Lord Amherst, Governor-General in Council.

My Lord,

Humbly reluctant as the natives of India are to obtrude upon the notice of Government the sentiments they entertain on any public measure, there are circumstances when silence would be carrying this respectful feeling to culpable excess. The present rulers of India, coming from a distance of many thousand miles to govern a people whose language, literature, manners, customs, and ideas, are almost entirely new and strange to them, cannot easily become so intimately acquainted with their real circumstances as the natives of the country are themselves. We should therefore be guilty of a gross dereliction of duty to ourselves and afford our rulers just grounds of complaint at our apathy, did we omit on occasions of importance like the present, to supply them with such accurate information as might enable them to devise and adopt measures calculated to be beneficial to the country, and thus second by our local knowledge and experience their declared benevolent intentions for its improvement.

The establishment of a new Sanscrit School in Calcutta evinces the laudable desire of Government to improve the natives of India by education,—a blessing for which they must ever be grateful, and every well-wisher of the human race must be desirous that the efforts made to promote it, should be guided by the most enlightened principles, so that the stream of intelligence may flow in the most useful channels.

When this seminary of learning was proposed, we understood that the Government in England had ordered a considerable sum of money to be annually devoted to the instruction of its Indian subjects. We were filled with sanguine hopes that this sum would be laid out in employing European gentlemen of talent and education to instruct the natives of India in Mathematics, Natural Philosophy, Chemistry, Anatomy, and other useful sciences, which the natives of Europe have carried to a degree of perfection that has raised them above the inhabitants of other parts of the world.

While we looked forward with pleasing hope to the dawn of knowledge, thus promised to the rising generation, our hearts were filled with mingled feelings of delight and gratitude, we already offered up thanks to Providence of inspiring the most generous and enlightened nations of the West with the glorious ambition of planting in Asia the arts and sciences of Modern Europe.

We find that the Government are establishing a Sanscrit school under Hindu Pandits to impart such knowledge as is already current in India. This seminary (similar in character to those which existed in Europe before the time of Lord Bacon) can only be expected to load the minds of youth with grammatical niceties and metaphysical distinctions of little or no practical use to the possessors or to society. The pupils will there acquire what was known two thousand years ago with the addition of vain and empty subtleties since then produced by speculative men, such as is already commonly taught in all parts of India.

The Sanscrit language, so difficult that almost a life time is necessary for its acquisition, is well known to have been for ages a lamentable check to the diffusion of knowledge, and the learning concealed under this almost impervious veil, is far from sufficient to reward the labour of acquiring it. But if it were thought necessary to perpetuate this language for the sake of the portion of valuable information it contains, this might be much more easily accomplished by other means than the establishment of a new Sanscrit College; for there have been always and are now numerous professors of Sanscrit in the different parts of the country engaged in teaching this language, as well as the other branches of literature which are to be the object of the new seminary. Therefore their more diligent cultivation, if desirable, would be effectually promoted, by holding out premiums and granting certain allowances to their most eminent professors, who have already undertaken on their own account to teach them, and would by such rewards be stimulated to still greater exertion.

From these considerations, as the sum set apart for the instruction of the natives of India was intended by the Government in England for the improvement of its Indian subjects, I beg leave to state, with due deference to your Lordship's exalted situation, that if the plan now adopted be followed, it will completely defeat the object proposed, since no improvement can be expected from inducing young men to consume a dozen years of the most valuable period of their lives, in acquiring the niceties of Vyakaran or Sanskrit Grammar, for instance, in learning to discuss such points as the following: *khada,* signifying to eat, *khadati* he or she or it eats, query, whether does *khadati* taken as a whole convey the meaning he, she or it eats, or are separate parts of this meaning conveyed by distinctions of the words, as if in the English language it were asked how much meaning is there in the *eat* and how much in the *s,* and is the whole meaning of the word conveyed by these two portions of it distinctly or by them taken jointly?

Neither can much improvement arise from such speculations as the following which are the themes suggested by the Vedanta,—in what manner is the soul absorbed in the Deity? What relation does it bear to the Divine Essence? Nor will youths be fitted to be better members of society by the Vedantic doctrines which teach them to believe, that all visible things have no real existence, that as father brother, &c., have no actual entity, they consequently deserve no real affection, and therefore the sooner we escape from them and leave the world the better.

Again, no essential benefit can be derived by the student of the *Mimansa* from knowing what it is that makes the killer of a goat sinless by pronouncing certain passages of the Vedanta and what is the real nature and operative influence of passages of the Vedas, &c.

The student of the Nyaya Sastra cannot be said to have improved his mind after he has learned from it into how many ideal classes the objects in the universe are divided and what speculative relation, the soul bears to the body, the body to the soul, the eye to the ear, &c.

In order to enable your Lordship to appreciate the utility of encouraging such imaginary learning as above characterized, I beg your Lordship will be pleased to compare the state of science and literature in Europe before the time of Lord Bacon with the progress of knowledge made since he wrote.

If it had been intended to keep the British nation in ignorance of real knowledge, the Baconian philosophy would not have been allowed to displace the system of the schoolmen which was the best calculated to perpetuate ignorance. In the same manner the Sanscrit system of education would be the best calculated to keep this country in darkness, if such had been the policy of the British legislature. But as the improvement of the native population is the object of the Government, it will consequently promote a more liberal and enlightened system of instruction, embracing Mathematics, Natural Philosophy, Chemistry, Anatomy, with other useful sciences, which may be accomplished with the sums proposed by employing a few gentlemen of talent and learning educated in Europe and providing a College furnished with necessary books, instruments, and other apparatus.

In presenting this subject to your Lordship, I conceive myself discharging a solemn duty which I owe to my countrymen, and also to that enlightened sovereign and legislature which have extended their benevolent care to this distant land, actuated by a desire to improve the inhabitants, and therefore humbly trust you will excuse the liberty I have taken in thus expressing my sentiments to your Lordship.

I have the honour, &c.,

RAMMOHUN ROY.

3. FRANÇOIS-RENÉ, VICOMTE DE CHATEAUBRIAND, TRAVELS FROM PARIS TO JERUSALEM, AND FROM JERUSALEM TO PARIS

The vicomte de Chauteaubriand (1768–1848) was both a major figure in French literary romanticism and an important political leader during the Restoration of the Bourbon kings of France from 1815 to 1830. The youngest son of a Breton noble, he was commissioned in the French army and was presented at the court of Louis XVI in 1787. During the Revolution of the 1790s, he was initially torn between his family's royalist sympathies and his own attraction to the political ideas of the philosophers of the Enlightenment. During the most radical phrases of the Revolution, he first fought on the side of the emigres against the Revolutionary government, then went into exile in England.

During his time in exile, Chateaubriand became more interested in Christianity, and his *Le Génie du christianisme* (1802) marked his conversion to a natural religious sentiment and his rejection of the religious doctrines of the Enlightenment. He served briefly under Napoleon as French ambassador to the papacy, but spent much of this time traveling in Greece, the Near East, and Spain, providing him with material for later fiction, as well as for the *Travels from Paris to Jerusalem, and from Jerusalem to Paris*, published in 1812. His writings helped revolutionize French letters, epitomizing the emphasis on color and exoticism that marked the Romantic movement, and he was elected to the Académie Française in 1811.

The fall of Napoleon in 1814 led to a revival in Chateaubriand's political fortunes. Under the restored Bourbon Louis XVIII, he was minister to the king, a peer of France, ambassador to Berlin and London, and minister of foreign affairs. His star waned after the accession to the throne of Charles X, and the last two decades of his life were spent in retirement. His posthumously published *Mémoires d'Outre-tombe* (1848–1850) allowed him to present his own life against the background of the transition from the Old Regime to the modern nineteenth century.

Travels from Paris to Jerusalem, and from Jerusalem to Paris

We passed through the canal of Menouf, which prevented me from seeing the fine wood of palm-trees on the great western branch; but the Arabs then infested the west bank of that branch which borders on the Libyan Desert. On leaving the canal of Menouf, and continuing to ascend the river, we perceived on our left the ridge of Mount Mokattam, and on our right the high sandy downs of Libya. In the intermediate space between these two chains of mountains, we soon descried the tops of the Pyramids, from which we were yet upwards of ten leagues distant. During the remainder of our voyage, which took us near eight hours, I remained upon deck, to contemplate these tombs; which seemed to increase in magnitude and height as we approached. The Nile, which then resembled a little sea; the mixture of the sands of the desert, and the freshest verdure; the palm-trees, the sycamores, the domes, the mosques, and the minarets of Cairo; the distant pyramids of Sakkarah, from which the river seemed to issue as from its immense reservoirs, altogether formed a scene to which the world cannot produce a parallel. "But in spite of all the efforts of men," says Bossuet, "their insignificance is invariably apparent; these pyramids were tombs!—nay, more; the kings by whom they were erected had not the satisfaction of being interred in them, and consequently did not enjoy their sepulchre."

I confess, however, that at the first sight of the Pyramids, the only sentiment I felt was admiration. Philosophy, I know, can sigh or smile at the reflection, that the most stupendous monument ever erected by the hand of man is a tomb: but why should we behold in the pyramid of Cheops nothing but a heap of stones and a skeleton? It was not from a sense of his nothingness that man reared such a sepulchre, but from the instinct of his immortality: this sepulchre is not the boundary which marks the termination of the career of a day, but the entrance of a life without end; 'tis an everlasting gate erected on the confines of eternity. "All these people" (of Egypt), says Diordorus Siculus, "considering the duration of life as a very short period, and of little importance, are on the other hand extremely solicitous about that long memory which virtue leaves behind it. For this reason, they give to the habitations of the living the name of inns, where they sojourn only for a short time; but that of eternal abodes to the tombs of the dead, which they are never more to quit. Accordingly, the kings have manifested a certain indifference in regard to the construction of their palaces, and bestowed all their attention on that of their tombs."

It is insisted, at the present day, that all monuments had a physical utility, and it is not considered that there is for nations a moral utility of a much higher order, which was studied by the legislators of antiquity. Is, then, nothing to be learned from the sight of a tomb? If any lesson is taught by it, why should we complain that a king resolved to render that lesson perpetual? Majestic monuments constitute an essential part of the glory of every human society. Unless we maintain that it is a matter of indifference whether a nation leaves behind it a name or no name in history, we cannot condemn those structures which extend the memory of a people beyond its own existence, and make it contemporary with the future generations that fix their residence in its forsaken fields. Of what consequence is it, then, whether these edifices were amphitheatres or sepulchres? Every thing is a tomb with a nation that no longer exists. When man is gone, the monuments of his life are still more vain than those of his death: his mausoleum is at least serviceable to his ashes; but do his palaces retain any particle of his pleasures?

Most certainly, if we would be strict, a little grove is sufficient for all, and six feet of ground, as Mathew Molé observes, will always do justice to the greatest man in the world: God may be adored under a tree, as beneath the dome of St. Peter's; and a man may live in a cottage as well as in the Louvre. The error of this mode of reasoning consists in transferring one order of things into another. Besides, a nation is not more happy when it lives in ignorance of the arts, than when it leaves behind striking evidences of its genius. People have ceased to believe in the existence of those communities of shepherds who pass their days in innocence, and beguile the delicious hours with rambling in the recesses of forests. Full well we know that these honest pastors make war upon each other, that they may feast upon the sheep of their neighbours. Their bowers are neither shaded with vines, nor embalmed with the perfume of flowers; you are suffocated in their habitation with the smoke, and stifled with the stench of milk. In poetry, and in philosophy, a petty, half-barbarous tribe may enjoy every earthly blessing; but merciless history subjects them to the same calamities as the rest of mankind. Are they who so loudly exclaim against glory—are they, I would ask, totally regardless of renown? For my part, so far from considering the monarch who erected the great Pyramid as a madman, I look upon him to have been a sovereign of a magnanimous disposition. The idea of vanquishing time by a tomb, of surviving generations, manners, laws, and ages, by a coffin, could not have sprung from a vulgar mind. If this be pride, it is at least a grand pride. Such a vanity as that which produced the great Pyramid, that has withstood the ravages of three or four thousand years, must certainly, in the end, be accounted as something.

For the rest, these Pyramids reminded me of less pompous monuments, though they were likewise sepulchres: I mean those edifices of turf, which cover the remains of the Indians on the banks of the Ohio. When I visited these, I was in a very different state of mind from that in which I contemplated the mausoleums of the Pharaohs: I was then beginning my journey, and now I am finishing it. The world, at these two periods of my life, wore to me precisely the appearance of the two deserts in which I have seen these two species of tombs; a smiling wilderness, and barren sands.

4. EDWARD WILLIAM LANE, AN ACCOUNT OF THE MANNERS AND CUSTOMS OF THE MODERN EGYPTIANS, WRITTEN IN EGYPT DURING THE YEARS 1833, 1834, AND 1835

Edward William Lane (1801–1876) received a grammar school education and planned a university education, but instead trained as an engraver in London. Poor health led him to abandon that trade, and in July 1825, he sailed to Alexandria, Egypt, hoping to further his interest in the Near East and possibly gain a post as British consul there. He joined a group of English scholars inventorying ancient Egyptian monuments, learned Arabic, and adopted native dress. Although he spent much of his time on this trip in Cairo, he also journeyed up the Nile. The result of this first trip to Egypt was a manuscript, never published, entitled a "Description of Egypt." But a proposal to publish the chapters dealing with the modern inhabitants of Cairo led Lane to return to Egypt to gather more information. During this trip he lived, as much as possible, the life of an Egyptian man of learning in Cairo, adopting the common Orientalist position of trying to become a part of Near Eastern society and culture. The resulting book, *An Account of the Manners and Customs of the Modern Egyptians, Written in Egypt during the Years 1833, 1834, and 1835*, was an immediate success in Great Britain and Europe when it was published in 1836, and was reprinted and reedited numerous times. He later translated the *Thousand and One Nights* (1838–1840) and *Selections from the Kur-an* (1843). Recognized as the chief of Arabic scholars in the West, he undertook the preparation of a thesaurus of the Arabic language, a task that occupied the rest of his life.

An Account of the Manners and Customs of the Modern Egyptians

Egypt has long been celebrated for its public dancing-girls; the most famous of whom are of a distinct tribe, called "Ghawázee." A female of this tribe is called "Gházeeyeh;" and a man, "Gházee;" but the plural Ghawázee is generally understood as applying to the females. The error into which most travellers in Egypt have fallen, or confounding the common dancing-girls of this country with the 'A'l'mehs, who are female singers, has already been exposed. The Ghawázee perform, unveiled, in the public streets, even to amuse the rabble. Their dancing has little of elegance. They commence with a degree of decorum; but soon, by more animated looks, by a more rapid collision of their castanets of brass, and by increased energy in every motion, they exhibit a spectacle exactly agreeing with the descriptions which Martial and Juvenal have given of the performances of the female dancers of Gades. The dress in which they generally thus exhibit in public is similar to that which is worn by women of the middle classes in Egypt in private; that is, in the hareem; consisting of a yelek, or an 'anter´ee, and the shintiyán, &c., of handsome materials. They also wear various ornaments: their eyes are bordered with the kohl (or black collyrium); and the tips of their fingers, the palms of their hands, and their toes and other parts of their feet, are usually stained with the red dye of the henna, according to the general custom of the middle and higher classes of Egyptian women. In general, they are accompanied by musicians (mostly of the same tribe), whose instruments are the kemengeh, or the rebáb, and the tár; or the darabukkeh and zummárah or the zemr: the tár is usually in the hands of an old woman.

The Ghawázee often perform in the court of a house, or in the street, before the door, on certain occasions of festivity in the hareem; as, for instance, on the occasion of a marriage, or the birth of a child. They are never admitted into a respectable hareem; but are not unfrequently hired to entertain a party of men in the house of some rake. In this case, as might be expected, their performances are yet more lascivious than those which I have already mentioned. Some of them, when they exhibit before a private party of men, wear nothing but the shintiyán (or trousers) and a tób (or very full shirt or gown) of semitransparent, coloured gauze, open nearly half-way down the front. To extinguish the least spark of modesty which they may yet sometimes affect to retain, they are plentifully supplied with brandy or some other intoxicating liquor. The scenes which ensue cannot be described.

I need scarcely add, that these women are the most abandoned of the courtesans of Egypt. Many of them are extremely handsome; and most of them are richly dressed. Upon the whole, I think they are the finest women in Egypt. Many of them have slightly aquiline noses: but in most respects, they resemble the rest of the females of this country. Women, as well as men, take delight in witnessing their performances; but many persons among the higher classes, and the more religious, disapprove of them.

The Ghawázee being distinguished, in general, by a cast of countenance differing, though slightly, from the rest of the Egyptians, we can hardly doubt that they are, as themselves assert, a distinct race. Their origin, however, is involved in much uncertainty. They call themselves "Barámikeh," or "Barmek'ees;" and boast that they are descended from the famous family of that name who were the objects of the favour, and afterwards of the capricious tyranny, of Hároon Er-Rasheed, and of whom we read in several of the tales of "The Thousand and One Nights:" but, as a friend of mine lately observed to me, they probably have no more right to call themselves "Barámikeh" than because they resemble that family in liberality, though it is liberality of a different kind. In many of the tombs of the ancient Egyptians, we find representations of females dancing at private entertainments, to the sounds of various instruments, in a manner similar to the modern Ghawázee, but even more licentious; one or more of these performers being generally depicted in a state of perfect nudity, though in the presence of men and women of high stations. This mode of dancing we find, from the monuments here alluded to, most of which bear the names of kings, which prove their age, to have been common in Egypt in very remote times; even before the Exodus of the Israelites. It is probable, therefore, that it has continued without interruption; and perhaps the modern Ghawázee are descended from the class of female dancers who amused the Egyptians in the times of the early Pharaohs. From the similarity of the Spanish fandango to the dances of the Ghawázee, we might infer that it was introduced into Spain by the Arab conquerors of that country, were we not informed that the Gaditanæ, or females of Gades (now called Cadiz), were famous for such performances in the times of the early Roman Emperors. However, though it hence appears that the licentious mode of dancing here described has so long been practised in Spain, it is not improbable that it was originally introduced into Gades from the East, perhaps by the Phœnicians.

The Ghawázee mostly keep themselves distinct from other classes, abstaining from marriages with any but persons of their own tribe; but sometimes a Gházeeyeh makes a vow of repentance, and marries a respectable Arab; who is not generally considered as disgraced by such a connexion. All of them are brought up for the venal profession; but not all as dancers; and most of them marry; though they never do this until they have commenced their career of venality. The husband is subject to the wife: he performs for her the offices of a servant and procurer; and generally, if she be a dancer, he is also her musician: but a few of the men earn their subsistence as blacksmiths or tinkers. Most of the Gházeeyehs welcome the lowest peasant, if he can pay even a very trifling sum. Though some of them are possessed of considerable wealth, costly ornaments, &c., many of their customs are similar to those of the people whom we call "gipsies," and who are supposed, by some, to be of Egyptian origin. It is remarkable that the gipsies in Egypt often pretend to be descended from a branch of the same family to whom the Ghawázee refer their origin; but their claim is still less to be regarded than that of the latter, because they do not unanimously agree on this point. I shall have occasion to speak of them more particularly in the next chapter. The ordinary language of the Ghawázee is the same as that of the rest of the Egyptians; but they sometimes make use of a number of words peculiar to themselves, in order to render their speech unintelligible to strangers. They are, professedly, of the Muslim faith; and often some of them accompany the Egyptian caravan of pilgrims to Mekkeh. There are many of them in almost every large town in Egypt, inhabiting a distinct portion of the quarter allotted to public women in general. Their ordinary habitations are low huts, or temporary sheds, or tents; for they often move from one town to another: but some of them settle themselves in large houses; and many possess black female slaves (by whose prostitution they increase their property), and camels, asses, cows, &c., in which they trade. They attend the camps, and all the great religious and other festivals; of which they are, to many persons, the chief attractions. Numerous tents of Gházeeyehs are seen on these occasions. Some of these women add, to their other allurements, the art of singing; and equal the ordinary 'Awálim. Those of the lower class dress in the same manner as other low prostitutes. Some of them wear a gauze tób, over another shirt, with the shintiyán, and a crape or muslin ṭarḥah; and in general they deck themselves with a profusion of ornaments, as necklaces, bracelets, anklets, a row of gold coins over the forehead, and sometimes a nose-ring. All of them adorn themselves with the kohl and ḥenna. There are some other dancing-girls and courtesans who call themselves Ghawázee, but who do not really belong to that tribe.

Many of the people of Cairo, affecting, or persuading themselves, to consider that there is nothing improper in the dancing of the Ghawázee but the fact of its being performed by females, who ought not thus to expose themselves, employ men to dance in the same manner; but the number of these male performers, who are mostly young men, and who are called "Khäwals", is very small. They are Muslims, and natives of Egypt. As they personate women, their dances are exactly of the same description as those of the Ghawázee; and are, in like manner, accompanied by the sounds of castanets: but, as if to prevent their being thought to be really females, their dress is suited to their unnatural profession; being partly male, and partly female: it chiefly consists of a tight vest, a girdle, and a kind of petticoat. Their general appearance, however, is more feminine than masculine: they suffer the hair of the head to grow long, and generally braid it, in the manner of the women: the hair on the face, when it begins to grow, they pluck out; and they imitate the women also in applying kohl and ḥenna to their eyes and hands. In the streets, when not engaged in dancing, they often even veil their faces; not from shame, but merely to affect the manners of women. They are often employed, in preference to the Ghawázee, to dance before a house, or in its court, on the occasion of a marriage-fête, or the birth of a child, or a circumcision; and frequently perform at public festivals.

There is, in Cairo, another class of male dancers, young men and boys, whose performances, dress, and general appearance are almost exactly similar to those of the Khäwals; but who are distinguished by a different appellation, which is "Gink;" a term that is Turkish, and has a vulgar signification which aptly expresses their character. They are generally Jews, Armenians, Greeks, and Turks.

5. EUGÈNE DELACROIX, *ALGERIAN WOMEN IN THEIR HAREM*

Eugène Delacroix (1798–1863) was the leading figure of the French Romantic school of painting. He displayed his first canvas at the annual Salon in 1822 with a controversial painting entitled *The Bark of Dante*, showing the emotional turbulence of form and color that marked his work throughout his career. He made his only visit to North Africa in 1832, spending six months traveling in the entourage of a French nobleman, the count de Mornay. In spite of this brief direct encounter, however, his experience with North Africa provided him with important themes for a succession of paintings.

Perhaps his most famous painting is *The Death of Sardanapalus* (1827), based on a poem by the British romantic Lord Byron and recounting a legend from the fourth century B.C. A violent collection of colors, the scene as painted by Delacroix suggests the languid and irrational characterizations that marked western versions of the East, as well as the use of sexual metaphors to convey violent domination and exploitation. In *The Fanatics of Tangier* (1838), Delacroix approached North African civilization from a different perspective, using as his subject the actions of a Sufi brotherhood (the `Isawiyyah sufi brotherhood), whose ceremonies involved strenuous jumping and leaping to the accompaniment of music. The painting contrasts the threatening mysticism and religious beliefs of the fanatics with the calm of the Arab chieftain in the right-hand section of the painting and with the other Arabs watching from the balconies. The larger contrast is between the irrationality of the Arab fanatics and the rationality of European civilization. *Algerian Women in Their Harem* (1834), shown here, is Delacroix's version of another common theme in Western versions of the Orient, the position of women in Islamic society in general, and the harem in particular. Western commentators often described Islamic society as barbaric because of its marginalization and exploitation of women, and the harem was seen as the most obvious symbol of this. Delacroix may have himself been able to visit a harem in Algiers, an exceptional event for European men.

Figure 20.1 Eugene Delacroix (French, 1798–1863), "Algerian Women in their Harem," 1834. Oil on canvas, 71 × 90 ¼ in (180 x 229 cm). Musee Nationaux, Paris.

6. JEAN-LÉON GÉRÔME, *THE CARPET MERCHANT*

Jean-Léon Gérôme (1824–1904) made his Salon debut in 1847, beginning a successful career painting portraits for Parisian society figures and large state commissions. He first visited Egypt in 1856, and made numerous trips thereafter to the Near East, Constantinople, and Asia Minor. A professor at the Ecole des Beaux-Arts in Paris, he was one of the most influential painters of his generation.

Gérôme's Orientalist works portrayed many different aspects of Eastern society and culture. In *Prayer in the Mosque of `Amr* (ca. 1872), he uses as his subject the Islamic religion, showing the interior of the oldest mosque on the continent of Africa, in the city of Cairo. In *Harem in the Kiosk* (ca. 1875–1880) Gérôme takes up the pervasive Western theme of women and the harem. *The Carpet Merchant* (ca. 1887), reproduced here, also takes a stereotyped view of the East, showing a merchant in Cairo that he visited with his friends Richard Lenoir, Edmond About, and Frédéric Masson in 1868. The architecture and lighting of the courtyard in which the merchant conducts his business form an important part of the scene, counterpointed by the piles of rugs in the foreground and the donkey on the right. The varied clientele shows a range of social levels, although Gérôme did not include any Europeans by placing himself and his friends offstage, viewing, but not participating, in the exotic scene.

Figure 20.2 Jean-Léon Gérôme (French 1824–1904), "The Carpet Merchant," 1887. The William Hood Dunwoody Fund. The Minneapolis Institute of Arts.

Study Questions

1. What advantages does Jones see in the study of the Persian language?
2. Why does Roy think the British should teach South Asians Western subjects rather than supporting a Sanscrit school?
3. How does seeing the pyramids affect Chateaubriand?
4. How are the public dancers that Lane describes treated in Egyptian society?
5. What are the principal features of Eastern society portrayed in the paintings by Delacroix and Gérôme? How similar or different are these from the features noted by Jones, Chateaubriand, and Lane?

Suggestions for Further Reading

Daniel, Norman. *Islam and the West: The Making of an Image.* Oxford: Oneworld, 1992.

Jullian, Philippe. *The Orientalists.* Oxford: Phaidon, 1977.

Nochlin, Linda. "The Imaginary Orient." *Art in America* 71 (1983): 119–131, 186–191.

Painter, G. *Chateaubriand: A Biography.* New York: Knopf, 1978.

Said, Edward. *Orientalism.* New York: Random House, 1979.

Said, Edward. *Culture and Imperialism.* New York: Alfred A. Knopf, 1993.

Stevens, Mary Anne, ed. *The Orientalists: Delacroix to Matisse.* London: Royal Academy of Arts, 1984.

Thornton, Lynne, ed. *The Orientalists: Painter-Travellers 1828–1908.* Paris: ACR Edition Internationale, 1983.

Web Sites

1. Frederick Goodall

   http://www.thecolors.com/artclassic/frederick_goodall.html

2. Market Day Outside the Walls of Tangiers, Morocco (on Louis Comfort Tiffany and his paintings)

   http://nmaa-ryder.si.edu/journal/seitchek4.html

3. Orient: *The Violating Gaze* (The French Orientalist Paintings)

   http://home.uchicago.edu/~mahmed/Or_art.html

21

Travel
1799–1900

TEXTS

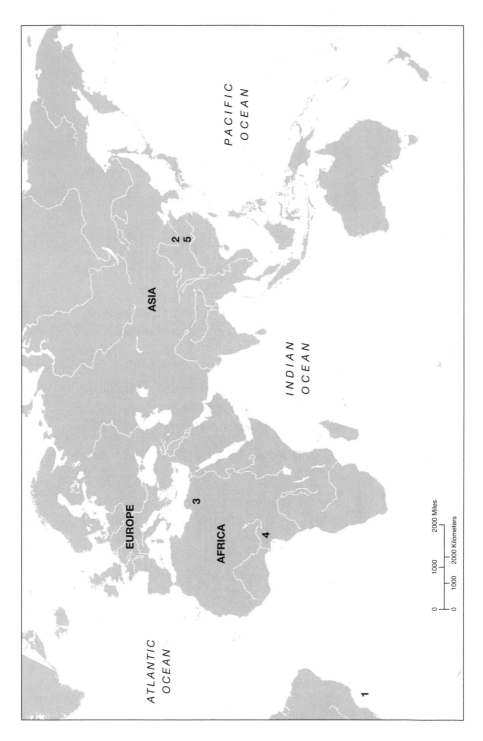

Even if Europeans like Rousseau and Diderot spoke about non-Europeans without ever having left Europe, men like James Cook, Richard Lander, and John Speke were travelers of the first order. But especially in the nineteenth century travel itself became an increasingly distinct form of contact, with characteristics and viewpoints that distinguished it from the exploration that preceded it and the tourism that marked the twentieth century. New means of travel, such as the steamship and the railroad, made travel easier, and the labor that Cook went through to get to Australia in the late eighteenth century was dramatically reduced for nineteenth-century voyagers. North Africa became a day's sail from southern France and Italy; the Middle East was only a little longer. The opening of the Suez Canal in 1869 cut travel times between Great Britain and its most important colony, making "A Passage to India" a more common part of Britons' experiences.

Travel to Asia, Africa, and South America nevertheless remained a major task in the nineteenth century: The Baedeker guides and Thomas Cook tours that would provide step-by-step instructions for travel were still in the future. As the following accounts show, the places that had previously been the province of daring explorers were now open to other Europeans, but their trips involved their own sets of paraphernalia. [1] European travelers did not travel alone, even if their accounts often make it sound as if they did. They were accompanied by servants, some of whom originated not in Europe but in other parts of the world. They also required assistance from the societies they visited, which were asked or required to provide supplies, lodging, porters, oarsmen, and translators, as well as the military and diplomatic protection needed by those who followed in the explorers' footsteps. [2] The experience of having "been explored" made indigenous societies more prepared to received later travelers, and they remained a vital, if often unacknowledged, part of any traveler's trip.

The accounts published by nineteenth-century travelers were one of the ways in which European knowledge and perceptions of the rest of the world and the peoples who lived there were mediated. Because travel is dislocating and decentering, these travelers approached and wrote about the rest of the world from the perspectives of their own European cultures even as they placed themselves physically and mentally outside of that culture. [3] Europe provided the models, language, and standards by which other parts of the world were judged and described; those other parts of the world allowed a reflection back on Europe, often in self-satisfied judgment of European superiority, but at times with recognition of both European failings and the European contribution to the problems seen in other lands.

In the course of the nineteenth century, the writings produced by European travelers slowly acquired a distinctive quality. Although the work of Alexander von Humboldt and Aimé Bonpland has been viewed as a precursor of many different forms of writing about other parts of the world, such as geography, geology, and ethnography, the later examples in this section were involved increasingly in distinguishing their accounts from other forms of writing about travel. [4] They were not fictional, although there was often controversy about the validity of their observations. They were not as superficial as tourist accounts, such as the guidebooks that began telling travelers what foreign places were worth seeing. They were also different from ethnographic writing, a social science with increasingly strident claims to scientific knowledge, especially after the 1880s. [5] Travelers, rather, had their own perspective: they claimed to experience the world with open eyes and open minds, appreciating the "true" character of what they visited, and their bestselling accounts interpreted to their European readers the foreign societies and peoples they had visited.

1. ALEXANDER VON HUMBOLDT AND AIMÉ BONPLAND, *PERSONAL NARRATIVE OF TRAVELS TO THE EQUINOCTIAL REGIONS OF AMERICA DURING THE YEARS 1799–1804*

Alexander von Humboldt (1769–1859) was the son of a Prussian army officer. After training at the Universities of Frankfurt an der Oder and Gottingen, and the School of Mines at Freiburg, he became an inspector of mines in the Prussian civil service. His interest in geography was inspired by Johan Georg Forster, who had sailed on Cook's second voyage. In 1790, Humboldt traveled to England with Forster, and in 1799, a substantial inheritance allowed him to leave his Prussian post and undertake, with the botanist Aimé Bonpland, a five-year voyage of exploration in Mexico and South America (1814–1819). After his return, he published the following account of this trip, displaying a wide interest in geography, geology, geophysics, and the economic and political conditions of the peoples he encountered. He also attempted to construct a rational description of the universe, an important corrective to the tendency of geographers to collect miscellaneous observations. He later became scientific adviser to the king of Prussia and continued to carry out scientific research, contributing to the discovery of the magnetic pole in 1838. His attempt to document different vegetation in different climates makes him the founder of both plant geography and climatology.

Personal Narrative of Travels to the Equinoctial Regions of America During the Years 1799–1804

Night had set in when we crossed for the last time the bed of the Orinoco. We purposed to rest near the little fort San Rafael, and on the following morning at daybreak to set out on our journey through the plains of Venezuela. Nearly six weeks had elapsed since our arrival at Angostura; and we earnestly wished to reach the coast, with the view of finding, at Cumana, or at Nueva Barcelona, a vessel in which we might embark for the island of Cuba, thence to proceed to Mexico. After the suffering to which we had been exposed during several months, whilst sailing in small boats on rivers infested by mosquitos, the idea of a sea-voyage was not without its charms. We had no idea of ever again returning to South America. Sacrificing the Andes of Peru to the Archipelago of the Philippines, (of which so little is known,) we adhered to our old plan of remaining a year in New Spain, then proceeding in a galleon from Acapulco to Manilla, and returning to Europe by way of Bassora and Aleppo. We imagined that, when we had once left the Spanish possessions in America, the fall of that ministry which had procured for us so many advantages, could not be prejudicial to the execution of our enterprise.

Our mules were in waiting for us on the left bank of the Orinoco. The collection of plants, and the different geological series, which we had brought from the Esmeralda and Rio Negro, had greatly augmented our baggage; and, as it would have been dangerous to lose sight of our herbals, we expected to make a very slow journey across the Llanos. The heat was excessive, owing to the reverberation of the soil, which was almost everywhere destitute of vegetation; yet the centigrade thermometer during the day (in the shade) was only from thirty to thirty-four degrees, and during the night, from twenty-seven to twenty-eight degrees. Here, therefore, as almost everywhere within the tropics, it was less the absolute degree of heat, than its duration, that affected our sensations. We spent thirteen days in crossing the plains, resting a little in the Caribbee (Caraibes) missions, and in the little town of Pao. The eastern part of the Llanos, through which we passed, between Angostura and Nueva Barcelona, presents the same wild aspect as the western part, through which we had passed from the valleys of Aragua to San Fernando de Apure. In the season of drought, (which is here called summer,) though the sun is in the southern hemisphere, the breeze is felt with greater force in the Llanos of Cumana, than in those of Caracas; because those vast plains, like the cultivated fields of Lombardy, form an inland basin, open to the east, and closed on the north, south, and west, by high chains of primitive mountains. Unfortunately, we could not avail ourselves of this refreshing breeze, of which the Llaneros, or the inhabitants of the plains, speak with rapture. It was now the rainy season north of the equator; and though it did not rain in the plains, the change in the declination of the sun had for some time caused the action of the polar currents to cease. In the equatorial regions, where the traveller may direct his course by observing the direction of the clouds, and where the oscillations of the mercury in the barometer indicate the hour almost as well as a clock, everything is subject to a regular and uniform rule. The cessation of the breezes, the setting-in of the rainy season, and the frequency of electric explosions, are phenomena which are found to be connected together by immutable laws.

On entering the Llanos of Nueva Barcelona, we met with a Frenchman, at whose house we passed the first night, and who received us with the kindest hospitality. He was a native of Lyons, and he had left his country at a very early age. He appeared extremely indifferent to all that was passing beyond the Atlantic, or, as they say here, disdainfully enough, when speaking of Europe, "on the other side of the great pool" (al otro lado del charco). Our host was employed in joining large pieces of wood by means of a kind of glue called *guayca*. This substance, which is used by the carpenters of Angostura, resembles the best animal glue. It is found perfectly prepared between the bark and the alburnum of a creeper of the family of the Combretaceæ. It probably resembles in its chemical properties birdlime, the vegetable principle obtained from the berries of the mistletoe, and the internal bark of the holly. An astonishing abundance of this glutinous matter issues from the twining branches of the *vejuco de guayca* when they are cut. Thus, we find within the tropics a substance in a state of purity, and deposited in peculiar organs, which in the temperate zone can be procured only by artificial means.

We did not arrive until the third day at the Caribbee missions of Cari. We observed that the ground was less cracked by the drought in this country than in the Llanos of Calabozo. Some showers had revived the vegetation. Small gramina, and especially those herbaceous sensitive-plants so useful in fattening half-wild cattle, formed a thick turf. At great distances one from another, there arose a few fan-palms (Corypha tectorum), rhopalas (chaparro), and malpighios with coriaceous and glossy leaves. The humid spots are recognized at a distance by groups of mauritia, which are the sago-trees of those countries. Near the coast this palm-tree constitutes the whole wealth of the Guaraon Indians; and it is somewhat remarkable that we also found it one hundred and sixty leagues farther south, in the midst of the forests of the Upper Orinoco, in the savannahs that surround the granitic peak of Duida. It was loaded at this season with enormous clusters of red fruit, resembling fir-cones. Our monkeys were extremely fond of this fruit, which has the taste of an over-ripe apple. The monkeys were placed with our baggage on the backs of the mules, and they made great efforts to reach the clusters that hung over their heads. The plain was undulating from the effects of the mirage; and when, after travelling for an hour, we reached the trunks of the palm-trees, which appeared like masts in the horizon, we observed with astonishment how many things are connected with the existence of a single plant. The winds, losing their velocity when in contact with the foliage and the branches, accumulate sand around the trunk. The smell of the fruit, and the brightness of the verdure, attract from afar the birds of passage, which love to perch on the slender, arrow-like branches of the palm-tree. A soft murmuring is heard around; and overpowered by the heat, and accustomed to the melancholy silence of the plains, the traveller imagines he enjoys some degree of coolness on hearing the slightest sound of the foliage. If we examine the soil on the side opposite to the wind, we find it remains humid long after the rainy season. Insects and worms, everywhere else so rare in the Llanos, here assemble and multiply. This one solitary and often stunted tree, which would not claim the notice of the traveller amid the forests of the Orinoco, spreads life around it in the desert.

On the 13th of July we arrived at the village of Cari, the first of the Caribbee missions that are under the Observantin monks of the college of Piritu. We lodged as usual at the convent, that is, with the clergyman. Our host could scarcely comprehend "how natives of the north of Europe could arrive at his dwelling from the frontiers of Brazil by the Rio Negro, and not by way of the coast of Cumana." He behaved to us in the most affable manner, at the same time manifesting that somewhat importunate curiosity which the appearance of a stranger, not a Spaniard, always excites in South America. He expressed his belief that the minerals we had collected must contain gold; and that the plants, dried with so much care, must be medicinal. Here, as in many parts of Europe, the sciences are thought worthy to occupy the mind only so far as they confer some immediate and practical benefit on society.

We found more than five hundred Caribs in the village of Cari; and saw many others in the surrounding missions. It is curious to observe this nomade people, recently attached to the soil, and differing from all the other Indians in their physical and intellectual powers. They are a very tall race of men, their height being from five feet six inches, to five feet ten inches. According to a practice common in America, the women are more sparingly clothed than the men. The former wear only the *guajuco,* or *perizoma,* in the form of a band. The men have the lower part of the body wrapped in a piece of blue cloth, so dark as to be almost black. This drapery is so ample, that, on the lowering of the temperature towards evening, the Caribs throw it over their shoulders. Their bodies tinged with *onoto,* their tall figures, of a reddish copper-colour, and their picturesque drapery, when seen from a distance, relieved against the sky as a background, resemble antique statues of bronze. The men cut their hair in a very peculiar manner, very much in the style of the monks. A part of the forehead is shaved, which makes it appear extremely high, and a circular tuft of hair is left near the crown of the head. This resemblance between the Caribs and the monks is not the result of mission life. It is not caused, as had been erroneously supposed, by the desire of the natives to imitate their masters, the Franciscan monks. The tribes that have preserved their wild independence, between the sources of the Carony and the Rio Branco, are distinguished by the same *cerquillo de frailes,* which the early Spanish historians at the time of the discovery of America attributed to the nations of the Carib race. All the men of this race whom we saw either during our voyage on the Lower Orinoco, or in the missions of Piritu, differ from the other Indians not only in the tallness of their stature, but also in the regularity of their features. Their noses are smaller, and less flattened; the cheek-bones are not so high; and their physiognomy has less of the Mongol character. Their eyes, which are darker than those of the other hordes of Guiana, denote intelligence, and it may even be said, the habit of reflection. The Caribs have a gravity of manner, and a certain look of sadness which is observable among most of the primitive inhabitants of the New World. The expression of severity in their features is heightened by the practice of dyeing their eyebrows with the juice of *caruto:* they also lengthen their eyebrows, thereby giving them the appearance of being joined together; and they often mark their faces all over with black spots to give themselves a more fierce appearance. The Carib women are less robust and good-looking than the men. On them devolves almost the whole burden of domestic work, as well as much of the out-door labour. They asked us eagerly for pins, which they stuck under their lower lip, making the head of the pin penetrate deeply into the skin. The young girls are painted red, and are almost naked. Among the different nations of the old and the new worlds, the idea of nudity is altogether relative. A woman in some parts of Asia is not permitted to show the tips of her fingers; while an Indian of the Carib race is far from considering herself unclothed if she wear round her waist a *guajuco* two inches broad. Even this band is regarded as less essential than the pigment which covers the skin. To go out of the hut without being painted, would be to transgress all the rules of Carib decency.

The Indians of the missions of Piritu especially attracted our attention, because they belong to a nation which, by its daring, its warlike enterprises, and its mercantile spirit, has exercised great influence over the vast country extending from the equator towards the northern coast. Everywhere on the Orinoco we beheld traces of the hostile incursions of the Caribs: incursions which heretofore extended from the sources of the Carony and the Erevato as far as the banks of the Ventuari, the Atacavi, and the Rio Negro. The Carib language is consequently the most general in this part of the world; it has even passed (like the language of the Lenni-Lenapes, or Algonkins, and the Natchez or Muskoghees, on the west of the Alleghany mountains) to tribes which have not a common origin.

2. EVARISTE-RÉGIS HUC, *A JOURNEY THROUGH THE CHINESE EMPIRE*

The early modern attention to spreading different forms of Christianity through missionary activity continued in the nineteenth century as Europeans went to different parts of the world as missionaries. Joseph Gabet (1808–1853) and Régis Evariste Huc (1813–1860) were born in France and trained as Roman Catholic priests in that country. Both entered the order of Saint-Lazare, which maintained a mission in China at the border with Mongolia. Gabet arrived in China in 1835, and in 1836 journeyed to the Lazarist mission in Mongolia. Huc arrived in 1841, joining the Mongolian mission in 1843 under the supervision of Gabet. In 1844, the two priests began a journey to Lhasa, returning to Macao in 1846. Gabet returned to Europe in 1846, and was sent on another mission, this time to Brazil, where he died in 1853. Huc remained in Macao until 1848, finishing the manuscript of the account of their travels. He returned to Northern China in 1848, but ill health forced him to return to France in 1852. The following year, he decided to leave the Lazarists and their missionary task. In 1854 he published an additional, more detailed account of his trip through China with Gabet, called *The Chinese Empire*. He remained a parish priest in France until his death in 1860.

A Journey Through the Chinese Empire

On leaving Tien-men, where we passed a pleasant day, there was appointed to accompany us as escort to the following stage a young military Mandarin, whose manners and gossip amused us much. His little, pale, lively face, with a touch of sarcasm in it, excited interest and curiosity; although a soldier, he had more brains than most of the men of letters, and no one was more convinced of this than himself. As he spoke not only with ease but with elegance, he was not backward in the use of his tongue; he discussed every thing that came into his head with decision and authority, interlarding his long harangues with pleasantries and witticisms not wanting in smartness. Above all, he boasted of a long residence at Canton, and of some small displays of prowess against the English, as well as of having studied the manners and customs of foreign nations, and of being thus fitted to appreciate and judge definitively every subject on the face of the earth.

　　When we halted for our mid-day meal, he began to tease the Mandarins of our escort most pitilessly. He talked of Sse-tchouen as of a foreign country, a mere savage region. He asked them whether civilization had begun to creep into the mountains yet. "You are not from the Thibet frontier," said he; "it is easy to perceive in your accent, manners, and appearance, that you live very near a race of savages, and this is certainly the first time you have traveled. Every thing surprises you—that is always the way with people who never stir from the place they are born in;" and he went on to point out to them many contrasts between their customs and those of Hou-pé.

To tell the truth, our Sse-tchouenites had found themselves sadly out of their element since they had left their province. They were ignorant of the manners of the country we were traversing; they were laughed at, insulted, and, above all, fleeced.

One day, for example, some soldiers of the escort had seated themselves for a few minutes before a shop. When they rose to depart, a clerk of the establishment came and demanded, with much gravity, two sapecks apiece for having rested before his door. The soldiers looked at him in amazement; but the malicious clerk held out his hand with the air of a man who has no suspicion that his demand can possibly be objected to. The poor travelers, attacked in their tenderest point—the pocket—ventured to say that they did not understand the demand. "That is very strange!" cried the clerk; and, summoning his neighbors around, "Look here! these men fancy they can sit before my shop for nothing! Where can they come from, I wonder, to be ignorant of the commonest customs!"

The neighbors exclaimed, laughed loudly, and marveled at people who were simple enough to imagine they could sit down for nothing. The soldiers, ashamed of being taken for uncivilized creatures, paid the two sapecks, saying, to excuse themselves, that such was not the custom in Sse-tchouen. They had not gone far however when some officious shop-keepers ran to tell them, as a consolation, that they were very silly to let themselves be taken in so easily.

These scenes were of daily occurrence while we were traveling through Hou-pé, and indeed we natives of the West found ourselves more at home throughout China than the inhabitants of other provinces who were unused to traveling.

Very false ideas are entertained in Europe concerning China and the Chinese. It is spoken of as an empire of remarkable and imposing unity, as a perfectly homogeneous nation, so that to know one Chinese is to know them all; and after passing some time in a Chinese town, you are capable of describing life throughout this vast country. This is far from being the case, though no doubt there are certain characteristics to be found throughout, which constitute the Chinese type.

These characteristics are remarkable in the face, the language, the manners, the ideas, and certain national prejudices; but they are distinguished by such varieties of shade, such well-defined differences, that it is easy to tell whether you are dealing with the men of the north, south, east, or west. In passing from one province to another, you become aware of these modifications; the language changes by degrees till it is no longer intelligible; the dress alters in form so much that you can distinguish a citizen of Canton from one of Pekin by it alone. Each province has customs peculiarly its own, even in important matters, in the imposition of taxes, the nature of contracts, and the construction of houses. There exist also particular privileges and laws which the government dare not abolish, and which the functionaries are forced to respect; there reign every where rights of established custom which destroy that civil and administrative unity that Europeans have been pleased to attribute to this colossal empire.

As much difference might be pointed out between the eighteen provinces as between the various states of Europe: a Chinese who passes from one to the other finds himself in a strange country, amidst a people whose habits are unknown to him, where every one is struck with the peculiarity of his face, language, and manners. There is nothing surprising in this when it is considered that the Chinese empire is composed of a number of kingdoms, often separated under the dominion of various princes, and ruled by distinct legislation. These nations, though more than once united, have never com-

bined so closely but that an observing eye could detect the different elements compos-
ing the vast whole.

Hence it follows that a sojourn in Macao or the factories of Canton does not render a man competent to judge of the Chinese nation. Even a missionary, who has resided
many years in the bosom of a Christian community, will no doubt be perfectly acquainted with the district that has been the theatre of his zealous labors; but if he under-
takes to extend his observations, and believes that the ways of the converts around him
are those of the whole empire, he deceives himself, and misleads the public opinion of
Europe. It may be imagined, therefore, how difficult it is to form a just estimate of the Chinese character and country from the writings of travelers who have paid a passing visit
to those ports open to Europeans. These writers are undoubtedly gifted with intellect
and a fertile imagination; they choose their language, and turn their sentences with an
enviable skill; when reading their books you never doubt their good faith for a moment;
there is only one thing wanting—that they should have seen the country and the nation
of which they speak.

Let us suppose that a citizen of the Celestial Empire, wishing to become acquainted with that mysterious Europe whose products he has so often admired, makes
up his mind to visit the extraordinary people of whom he has no knowledge beyond a
vague notion of their geographical position. He embarks, and, after traversing the ocean
till he is sick of seeing nothing but sea and sky, he reaches the port of Havre. Unfortunately he does not know a word of French, and is obliged to call to his assistance some
porter who has picked up, somehow or other, a little Chinese; he adorns him with the
title of interpreter or *toun-sse,* and gets on with him as best he can, eking out his words
with abundance of pantomimic gestures.

Furnished with this guide, he traverses the streets of Havre from morning till night,
disposed to make an astonishing discovery at every step, in order that he may have the
pleasure of regaling his fellow-countrymen with his wonderful adventures on his return
home. He enters every shop, is enraptured with all he sees, and buys the most extraordinary things, paying, of course, two or three times what they are worth, because there is an
understanding between his interpreter and the shopman to get as much as possible out
of the barbarian.

Of course our Chinese is a philosopher and a moralist, and therefore takes a great
many notes: he devotes the evening to this important labor, to which he calls in the aid
of his guide. He always has a long series of questions ready for him, but is a little embarrassed because he can neither make his own questions quite intelligible, nor understand
very clearly the answers returned. Nevertheless, after making the effort of coming to the
West, it is absolutely necessary to acquire a mass of information, and enlighten China on
the condition of Europe. What would people say if he had nothing to tell them after his
long journey? He writes, therefore, sometimes according to the information of a porter
whom he does not understand, sometimes at the dictation of his own suggestive imagination.

After a few months past thus in Havre, our traveler returns to his native country,
well disposed to yield to the entreaties of his friends not to deprive the public of the useful and previous information he has collected concerning an unknown country.

No doubt this Chinese will have seen many things he did not expect; and if he be
at all well informed, might prepare a very interesting article on Havre for the Pekin
Gazette. But if, not content with that, he takes up his too ready pen to compose a disserta-
tion on France, the form of its government, the character of its senate and legislature, its

iiiagistracy and army, science, arts, industry, and commerce, not to speak of the various kingdoms of Europe, which he will liken to France, we must suspect that his narrative, however picturesque and well written, will contain a mass of errors. His "Travels in Europe," as he will no doubt call his book, can not fail to convey to his countrymen very false ideas regarding the nations of the West.

Many works on China published in Europe have been written in the manner I have described, and after perusing them it is difficult to imagine China such as she really is. The China described is a work of imagination, a country which has no existence, and setting aside the great mistake regarding the unity of the Chinese empire, there are many others which we will venture to point out.

3. Richard Francis Burton, *Personal Narrative* *of a Pilgrimage to Al-Madinah and Meccah*

Richard Francis Burton (1821–1890) was an officer in the Indian Army, an expert in Orientalist studies, and an explorer. He showed his facility with languages as a youth, learning half a dozen languages and dialects, and he added languages throughout his life. He studied for a year at Trinity College, Oxford, and in 1842, he became a cadet in the Indian Army. He served in India for about seven years, although he remained on the rolls of the Indian Army until 1861. While in India he continued his study of Oriental languages as well as Islamic culture.

Upon his return to England in 1849, he quickly published a number of works of scholarship on Islam and India, and made plans for travel in the Middle East. He gained the support of the Royal Geographical Society for an expedition that would traverse the Arabian peninsula, but was forced to scale back his plans when the directors of the East India Company refused to give him three years' leave for the project. Instead, in 1853 he began a daring attempt to penetrate to the heart of Islam, the sacred city of Mecca. Disguised as an Indian-born Afghan, he traveled to Egypt and then joined pilgrims heading to Mecca. Braving both detection by his fellow pilgrims as well as the hazards of the road, he successfully reached Mecca and followed the rituals of Islamic pilgrims. His account of this was published in 1855 in his *Personal Narrative of a Pilgrimage to Al-Madinah and Meccah.*

His trip to Mecca was only one of the many travels Burton undertook in his life. He had traveled around India while on army duty there, and after his return from Mecca, he visited Somaliland on an expedition with John Hanning Speke that hoped to discover the source of the Nile. This expedition ended in disaster when the party was attacked by Somalis, seriously wounding both Burton and Speke. In 1856, however, the two undertook a second expedition up the Nile. His well-publicized disagreement with Speke on the sources of the Nile made it difficult for Burton to gain further support for his exploration projects, however, and he thereafter traveled on his own initiative. He visited the American west, West Africa, South America, and Syria. He held a number of posts as British consul, ending his career as consul in Trieste. In the last years of his life, he devoted himself to scholarship, producing translations of Oriental texts, most notably an edition of *The Arabian Nights*. Although a difficult and unconventional man, Burton was both a talented student of Oriental languages and Islamic culture, as well as a daring traveler.

Personal Narrative of a Pilgrimage to Al-Madinah and Meccah

There at last it lay, the bourn of my long and weary Pilgrimage, realising the plans and hopes of many and many a year. The mirage medium of Fancy invested the huge catafalque and its gloomy pall with peculiar charms. There were no giant fragments of hoar antiquity as in Egypt, no remains of graceful and harmonious beauty as in Greece and Italy, no barbarous gorgeousness as in the buildings of India; yet the view was strange, unique—and how few have looked upon the celebrated shrine! I may truly say that, of all the worshippers who clung weeping to the curtain, or who pressed their beating hearts to the stone, none felt for the moment a deeper emotion than did the Haji from the far-north. It was as if the poetical legends of the Arab spoke truth, and that the waving wings of angels, not the sweet breeze of morning, were agitating and swelling the black covering of the shrine. But, to confess humbling truth, theirs was the high feeling of religious enthusiasm, mine was the ecstasy of gratified pride.

Few Moslems contemplate for the first time the Ka'abah, without fear and awe: there is a popular jest against new comers, that they generally inquire the direction of prayer. This being the Kiblah, or fronting place, Moslems pray all around it; a circumstance which of course cannot take place in any spot of Al-Islam but the Harim. The boy Mohammed, therefore, left me for a few minutes to myself; but presently he warned me that it was time to begin. Advancing, we entered through the Bab Benu Shaybah, the "Gate of the Sons of the Shaybah" (old woman). There we raised our hands, repeated the Labbayk, the Takbir, and Tahlil; after which we uttered certain supplications, and drew our hands down our faces. Then we proceeded to the Shafe'is' place of worship—the open pavement between the Makam Ibrahim and the well Zemzem—where we performed the usual two-bow prayer in honour of the Mosque. This was followed by a cup of holy water and a present to the Sakkas, or carriers, who for the consideration distributed, in my name, a large earthen vaseful to poor pilgrims. . . .

Then commenced the ceremony of *Tawáf*, or circumambulation, our route being the *Mataf*—the low oval of polished granite immediately surrounding the Ka'abah. I repeated, after my Mutawwif, or cicerone, "In the Name of Allah, and Allah is omnipotent! I purpose to circuit seven circuits unto Almighty Allah, glorified and exalted!" This is technically called the Niyat (intention) of Tawaf. Then we began the prayer, "O Allah (I do this), in Thy Belief, and in Verification of Thy Book, and in Faithfulness to Thy Covenant, and in Perseverance of the Example of the Apostle Mohammed—may Allah bless Him and preserve!" till we reached the place Al-Multazem, between the corner of the Black Stone and the Ka'abah door. Here we ejaculated, "O Allah, Thou hast Rights, so pardon my transgressing them." Opposite the door we repeated, "O Allah, verily the House is Thy House, and the Sanctuary Thy Sanctuary, and the Safeguard Thy Safeguard, and this is the Place of him who flies to Thee from (hell) Fire!" At the little building called Makam Ibrahim we said, "O Allah, verily this is the Place of Abraham, who took Refuge with and fled to Thee from the Fire!— O deny my Flesh and Blood, my Skin and Bones to the (eternal) Flames!" As we paced slowly round the north or Irak corner of the Ka'abah we exclaimed, "O Allah, verily I take Refuge with Thee from Polytheism, and Disobedience, and Hypocrisy, and evil Conversation, and evil Thoughts concerning Family, and Property, and Progeny!" When fronting the Mizab, or spout, we repeated the words, " O Allah, verily I beg of Thee Faith which shall not decline, and a Certainty which shall not perish, and the good Aid of Thy Prophet Mohammed—may Allah bless Him and preserve! O Allah, shadow me in Thy Shadow on that Day when there is no Shade but Thy Shadow, and cause me to drink from the Cup of Thine Apostle Mohammed—may Allah bless Him and preserve!—that pleasant Draught after which is no Thrist to all Eternity, O Lord of Honour and Glory!" Turning the west corner, or the Rukn al-Shami, we exclaimed, "O Allah, make it an acceptable Pilgrimage, and a Forgiveness of Sins, and a laudable Endeavour, and a pleasant Action (in Thy sight), and a store which perisheth not, O Thou Glorious! O Thou Pardoner!" This was repeated thrice, till we arrived at the Yamani, or south corner, where, the crowd being less importunate, we touched the wall with the right hand, after the example of the Prophet, and kissed the finger-tips. Finally, between the south angle and that of the Black Stone, where our circuit would be completed, we said, "O Allah, verily I take Refuge with Thee from Infidelity, and I take Refuge with Thee from Want, and from the Tortures of the Tomb, and from the Troubles of Life and Death. And I fly to Thee from Ignominy in this World and the next, and I implore Thy Pardon for the Present and for the Future. O Lord, grant to me in this Life Prosperity, and in the next Life Prosperity, and save me from the Punishment of Fire."

Thus finished a Shaut, or single course round the house. Of these we performed the first three at the pace called Harwalah, very similar to the French *pas gymnastique*, or Tarammul, that is to say, "moving the shoulders as if walking in sand." The four latter are performed in Ta'ammul, slowly and leisurely; the reverse of the Sai, or running. These seven Ashwat, or courses, are called collectively one Usbu. The Moslem origin of this custom is too well known to require mention. After each Taufah or circuit, we, being unable to kiss or even to touch the Black Stone, fronted towards it, raised our hands to our ears, exclaimed, "In the Name of Allah, and Allah is omnipotent!" kissed our fingers, and resumed the ceremony of circumambulation, as before, with "Allah, in Thy Belief," &c.

At the conclusion of the Tawaf it was deemed advisable to attempt to kiss the stone. For a time I stood looking in despair at the swarming crowd of Badawi and other pilgrims that besieged it. But the boy Mohammed was equal to the occasion. During our circuit he had displayed a fiery zeal against heresy and schism, by foully abusing every Persian in his path; and the inopportune introduction of hard words into his prayers made the latter a strange patchwork; as "Ave Maria purissima,—arrah, don't ye be letting the pig at the pot,—sanctissima," and so forth. He might, for instance, be repeating "And I take Refuge with Thee from Ignominy in this World," when "O thou rejected one, son of the rejected!" would be the interpolation addressed to some long-bearded Khorasani,— "And in that to come"—"O hog and brother of a hoggess!" And so he continued till I wondered that none dared to turn and rend him. After vainly addressing the pilgrims, of whom nothing could be seen but a mosaic of occiputs and shoulder-blades, the boy Mohammed collected about half a dozen stalwart Meccans, with whose assistance, by sheer strength, we wedged our way into the thin and light-legged crowd. The Badawin turned round upon us like wild-cats, but they had no daggers. The season being autumn, they had not swelled themselves with milk for six months; and they had become such living mummies, that I could have managed single-handed half a dozen of them. After thus reaching the stone, despite popular indignation testified by impatient shouts, we monopolised the use of it for at least ten minutes. Whilst kissing it and rubbing hands and fore-head upon it I narrowly observed it, and came away persuaded that it is an aërolite. It is curious that almost all travellers agree upon one point, namely, that the stone is volcanic. Ali Bey calls it "mineralogically" a "block of volcanic basalt, whose circumference is sprinkled with little crystals, pointed and straw-like, with rhombs of tile-red feldspath upon a dark background, like velvet or charcoal, except one of its protuberances, which is reddish." Burckhardt thought it was "a lava containing several small extraneous parti-cles of a whitish and of a yellowish substance."

Having kissed the stone we fought our way through the crowd to the place called Al-Multazem. Here we pressed our stomachs, chests, and right cheeks to the Ka'abah, raising our arms high above our heads and exclaiming, "O Allah! O Lord of the Ancient House, free my Neck from Hell-fire, and preserve me from every ill Deed, and make me contented with that daily bread which Thou hast given to me, and bless me in all Thou hast granted!" Then came the Istighfar, or begging of pardon; "I beg Pardon of Allah the most high, who, there is no other God but He, the Living, the Eternal, and unto Him I re-pent myself!" After which we blessed the Prophet, and then asked for ourselves all that our souls most desired.

After embracing the Multazem, we repaired to the Shafe'is' place of prayer near the Makam Ibrahim, and there recited two prostrations, technically called *Sunnat al-Tawaf,* or the (Apostle's) practice of circumambulation. The chapter repeated in the first was "Say thou, O Infidels": in the second, "Say thou He is the one God." We then went to the door of the building in which is Zemzem: there I was condemned to another nauseous draught, and was deluged with two or three skinfuls of water dashed over my head *en douche.* This ablution causes sins to fall from the spirit like dust. During the potation we prayed, "O Allah, verily I beg of Thee plentiful daily Bread, and profitable Learning, and the healing of every Disease!" Then we returned towards the Black Stone, stood far away opposite, because un-able to touch it, ejaculated the Takbir, the Tahlil, and the Hamdilah; and thoroughly worn out with scorched feet and a burning head,—both extremities, it must be remembered, were bare, and various delays had detained us till ten A.M.,—I left the Mosque.

The boy Mohammed had miscalculated the amount of lodging in his mother's house. She, being a widow and a lone woman, had made over for the season all the apartments to her brother, a lean old Meccan, of true ancient type, vulture-faced, kite-clawed, with a laugh like a hyena, and a mere shell of body. He regarded me with no favouring eye when I insisted as a guest upon having some place of retirement; but he promised that, after our return from Arafat, a little store-room should be cleared out for me. With that I was obliged to be content, and to pass that day in the common male drawingroom of the house, a vestibule on the ground floor, called in Egypt a *Takhta-bush.* Entering, to the left was a large Mastabah, or platform, and at the bottom a second, of smaller dimensions and foully dirty. Behind this was a dark and unclean store-room containing the Hajis' baggage. Opposite the Mastabah was a firepan for pipes and coffee, superintended by a family of lean Indians; and by the side a doorless passage led to a bathing-room and staircase.

I had scarcely composed myself upon the carpeted Mastabah, when the remain-der was suddenly invaded by the Turkish, or rather Slavo-Turk, pilgrims inhabiting the house, and a host of their visitors. They were large, hairy men, with gruff voices and square figures; they did not take the least notice of me, although feeling the intrusion, I stretched out my legs with a provoking *nonchalance.* At last one of them addressed me in Turkish, to which I replied by shaking my head. His question being interpreted to me in Arabic, I drawled out, "My native place is the land of Khorasan." This provoked a stern and stony stare from the Turks, and an "ugh!" which said plainly enough, "Then you are a pestilent heretic." I surveyed them with a self-satisfied simper, stretched my legs a trifle farther, and conversed with my water-pipe. Presently, when they all departed for a time, the boy Mohammed raised, by request, my green box of medicines, and deposited it upon the Mastabah; thus defining, as it were, a line of demarcation, and asserting my privilege to it before the Turks. Most of these men were of one party, headed by a colonel of Nizam, whom they called a Bey. My acquaintance with them began roughly enough, but afterwards, with some exceptions, who were gruff as an English butcher when accosted by a lean foreigner, they proved to be kind-hearted and not unsociable men. It often happens to the traveller, as the charming Mrs. Malaprop observes, to find intercourse all the better by beginning with a little aversion.

4. MARY KINGSLEY, *TRAVELS IN WEST AFRICA*

For her first thirty years, Mary Kingsley (1862–1900) lived a life typical of Victorian women within a family in which her mother was often ill, her brother had personal difficulties, and her father, a student of foreign civilizations, frequently traveled to the Pacific and North America. After her father's death, she undertook to complement his fieldwork by traveling in Africa. Between 1893 and 1895, she took two trips to West Africa which combined travel, ethnographic fieldwork, and scientific discovery. Her background led her to invoke in her writings the authority of these different kinds of inquiry, although she herself was self-taught in ethnography and science. Her first trip took her through the Congo Free State, across the Congo River into French territory, and then back to the English possession Old Calabar, collecting natural history specimens and learning to deal with the traders that she found to be the best representatives of colonialism in West Africa. Her second voyage, which began in 1894, formed the basis for *Travels in West Africa*. On this trip she traveled through the French Congo, up the Ogowé River, across to the Rembwé River, and then down that river and back to England. Although hoping to return to Africa, she volunteered for duty as a nurse in South Africa during the Boer War, and died of enteric fever while there.

Travels in West Africa

Lembarene Island is the largest of the islands on the Ogowé. It is some fifteen miles long, east and west, and a mile to a mile and a half wide. It is hilly and rocky, uniformly clad with forest, and several little permanent streams run from it on both sides into the Ogowé. It is situated 130 miles from the sea, at the point, just below the entrance of the N'guni, where the Ogowé commences to divide up into that network of channels by which, like all great West African rivers save the Congo, it chooses to enter the ocean. The island, as we mainlanders at Kangwe used to call it, was a great haunt of mine, particularly after I came down from Talagouga and saw fit to regard myself as competent to control a canoe. I do not mean that I was cut off from it before; for M. Jacot and M. Haug were always willing to send me across in a big canoe, with the mission boys to paddle, and the boys were always ready to come because it meant "dash," and the dissipation of going to what was the local equivalent of Paris; but there was always plenty of work for them on the station, and so I did not like taking them away. Therefore when I could get there alone I went more frequently.

From Andande, the beach of Kangwe, the breadth of the arm of the Ogowé to the nearest village on the island, was about that of the Thames at Blackwall. One half of the way was slack water, the other half was broadside on to a stiff current. Now my pet canoe at Andande was about six feet long, pointed at both ends, flat bottomed, so that it floated on the top of the water; its freeboard was, when nothing was in it, some three inches, and the poor thing had seen trouble in its time, for it had a hole you could put your hand in at one end; so in order to navigate it successfully, you had to squat in the other, which immersed that to the water level but safely elevated the damaged end in the air. Of course you had to stop in your end firmly, because if you went forward the hole went down into the water, and the water went into the hole, and forthwith you foundered with all hands—*i.e.,* you and the paddle and the calabash baler. This craft also had a strong weather helm, owing to a warp in the tree of which it had been made. I learnt all these things one afternoon, paddling round the sandbank; and the next afternoon, feeling confident in the merits of my vessel, I started for the island, and I actually got there, and associated with the natives, but feeling my arms were permanently worn out by paddling against the current, I availed myself of the offer of a gentleman to paddle me back in his canoe. He introduced himself as Samuel, and volunteered the statement that he was "a very good man." We duly settled ourselves in the canoe, he occupying the bow, I sitting in the middle, and a Mrs. Samuel sitting in the stern. Mrs. Samuel was a powerful, pretty lady, and a conscientious and continuous paddler. Mr. S. was none of these things, but an ex-Bible reader, with an amazing knowledge of English, which he spoke in a quaint, falsetto, far-away sort of voice, and that man's besetting sin was curiosity. "You be Christian, ma?" said he. I asked him if he had ever met a white man who was not? "Yes, ma," says Samuel. I said "You must have been associating with people whom you ought not to know." Samuel fortunately not having a repartee for this, paddled on with his long paddle for a few seconds. "Where be your husband, ma?" was the next conversational bomb he hurled at me. "I no got one," I answer. "No got," says Samuel, paralysed with astonishment; and as Mrs. S., who did not know English, gave one of her vigorous drives with her paddle at this moment, Samuel as near as possible got jerked head first into the Ogowé, and we took on board about two bucketfuls of water. He recovered himself, however and returned to his charge. "No got one, ma?" "No," say I furiously. "Do you get much rubber round here?" "I no be trade man," says Samuel, refusing to fall into my trap for changing conversation. "Why you no got one?" The remainder of the conversation is unreportable, but he landed me at Andande all right, and got his dollar.

The next voyage I made, which was on the next day, I decided to go by myself to the factory, which is on the other side of the island, and did so. I got some goods to buy fish with, and heard from Mr. Cockshut that the poor boy-agent at Osoamokita, had committed suicide. It was a grievous thing. He was, as I have said, a bright, intelligent young Frenchman; but living in the isolation, surrounded by savage, tiresome tribes, the strain of his responsibility had been too much for him. He had had a good deal of fever, and the very kindly head agent for Woermann's had sent Dr. Pélessier to see if he had not better be invalided home; but he told the Doctor he was much better, and as he had no one at home to go to he begged him not to send him, and the Doctor, to his subsequent regret, gave in. No one knows, who has not been to visit Africa, how terrible is the life of a white man in one of these out-of-the-way factories, with no white society, and with nothing to look at, day out and day in, but the one set of objects—the forest, the river, and the beach, which in a place like Osoamokita you cannot leave for months at a time, and of which you soon know every plank and stone. I felt utterly wretched as I started home again to come up to the end of the island, and go round it and down to Andande; and paddled on for some little time, before I noticed that I was making absolutely no progress. I redoubled my exertions, and crept slowly up to some rocks projecting above the water; but pass them I could not, as the main current of the Ogowé flew in hollow swirls round them against my canoe. Several passing canoefuls of natives gave me good advice in Igalwa; but facts were facts, and the Ogowé was too strong for me. After about twenty minutes an old Fan gentleman came down river in a canoe and gave me good advice in Fan, and I got him to take me in tow—that is to say, he got into my canoe and I held on to his and we went back down river. I then saw his intention was to take me across to that disreputable village, half Fan, half Bakele, which is situated on the main bank of the river opposite the island; this I disapproved of, because I had heard that some Senegal soldiers who had gone over there, had been stripped of every rag they had on, and maltreated; besides, it was growing very late, and I wanted to get home to dinner. I communicated my feelings to my pilot, who did not seem to understand at first, so I feared I should have to knock them into him with the paddle; but at last he understood I wanted to be landed on the island and duly landed me, when he seemed much surprised at the reward I gave him in pocket-handkerchiefs. Then I got a powerful young Igalwa dandy to paddle me home.

I did not go to the island next day, but down below Fula, watching the fish playing in the clear water, and the lizards and birds on the rocky high banks; but on my next journey round to the factories I got into another and a worse disaster. I went off there early one morning; and thinking the only trouble lay in getting back up the Ogowé, and having developed a theory that this might be minimised by keeping very close to the island bank, I never gave a thought to dangers attributive to going down river; so, having by now acquired pace, my canoe shot out beyond the end rocks of the island into the main stream. It took me a second to realise what had happened, and another to find out I could not get the canoe out of the current without upsetting it, and that I could not force her back up the current, so there was nothing for it but to keep her head straight now she had bolted. A group of native ladies, who had followed my proceedings with much interest, shouted observations which I believe to have been "Come back, come back; you'll be drowned." "Good-bye, Susannah, don't you weep for me," I courteously retorted, and flew past them and the factory beaches and things in general, keenly watching for my chance to run my canoe up a siding, as it were, off the current main line. I got it at last—a projecting spit of land from the island with rocks projecting out of the water in front of it bothered the current, and after a wild turn round or so, and a near call from my terrified canoe trying to climb up a rock, I got into slack water and took a pause in life's pleasures for a few minutes. Knowing I must be near the end of the island, I went on pretty close to the bank, finally got round into the Kangwe branch of the Ogowé by a connecting creek, and after an hour's steady paddling I fell in with three big canoes going up river; they took me home as far as Fula, whence a short paddle landed me at Andande only slightly late for supper, convinced that it was almost as safe and far more amusing to be born lucky than wise.

Now I have described my circumnavigation of the island, I will proceed to describe its inhabitants. The up-river end of Lembarene Island is the most inhabited. A path round the upper part of the island passes through a succession of Igalwa villages and by the Roman Catholic missionary station. The slave villages belonging to these Igalwas are away down the north face of the island, opposite the Fan town of Fula, which I have mentioned. It strikes me as remarkable that the Igalwa, like the Dualla of Cameroons, have their slaves in separate villages; but this is the case, though I do not know the reason of it. These Igalwa slaves cultivate the plantations, and bring up the vegetables and fruit to their owners' villages, and do the housework daily.

The interior of the island is composed of high, rocky, heavily forested hills, with here and there a stream, and here and there a swamp; the higher land is towards the up-river end; down river there is a lower strip of land with hillocks. This is, I fancy, formed by deposits of sand, &c., catching in among the rocks, and connecting what was at one time several isolated islands. There are no big game or gorillas on the island, but it has a peculiar and awful house ant, much smaller than the driver ant, but with a venomous, bad bite; its only good point is that its chief food is the white ants, which are therefore kept in abeyance on Lembarene Island, although flourishing destructively on the mainland banks of the river in this locality. I was never tired of going and watching those Igalwa villagers, nor were, I think, the Igalwa villagers ever tired of observing me. Although the physical conditions of life were practically identical with those of the mainland, the way in which the Igalwas dealt with them, i.e., the culture, was distinct from the culture of the mainland Fans.

The Igalwas are a tribe very nearly akin, if not ethnically identical with, the M'pongwe, and the culture of these two tribes is on a level with the highest native African culture. African culture, I may remark, varies just the same as European in this, that there is as much difference in the manners of life between, say, an Igalwa and a Bubi of Fernando Po, as there is between a Londoner and a Laplander.

I inquired carefully, in the interests of ethnology, as to what methods of courting were in vogue previously. They said people married each other because they loved each other. I think other ethnologists will follow this inquiry up, for we may here find a real golden age, which in other races of humanity lies away in the mists of the ages behind the kitchen middens and the Cambrian rocks. My own opinion in this matter is that the earlier courting methods of the Igalwa involved a certain amount of effort on the man's part, a thing abhorrent to an Igalwa. It necessitated his dressing himself up, and likely enough fighting that impudent scoundrel who was engaged in courting her too; and above all serenading her at night on the native harp, with its strings made from the tendrils of a certain orchid, or on the marimba, amongst crowds of mosquitoes. Any institution that involved being out at night amongst crowds of those Lembarene mosquitoes would have to disappear, let that institution be what it might.

5. ISABELLA BIRD, *THE YANGTZE VALLEY AND BEYOND*

Isabella Bird Bishop (1831–1904) was born in Yorkshire, England, into a family that was both prosperous and religious. She was related to the antislavery campaigner William Wilberforce, and her aunt had been a missionary in India. After the death of her parents, Isabella began to travel, with her health as the usual reason. In 1872, she left England for a trip that took her to Australia, New Zealand, Hawaii, and the Rocky Mountains of the United States. Convinced of women's "civilizing mission," she was careful to avoid what she thought of as an offensive "masculinity," keeping women's dress and being careful to ride sidesaddle when she was in towns. In 1881, she married, but her husband died in 1885, and after a religious conversion, she left in 1889 to visit missions in the Far East. During the 1890s, she traveled in India, Turkey, Persia, Korea, Japan, and China. In 1903, while preparing for another trip to China, she fell ill, and died in October 1904.

The Yangtze Valley and Beyond

My acquaintance with the opium poppy began in the month of February on the journey from Wan Hsien to Paoning Fu. It is a very handsome plant. It is expensive to grow. It has to be attended to eight times, and needs heavy manuring. It is exposed to so many risks before the juice is secured that the growth is much of a speculation, and many Chinese regard it as being as risky as gambling. Besides its cultivation for sale, on a majority of farms it is grown for home use, as tobacco is, for smoking. It is a winter crop, and is succeeded by rice, maize, cotton, beans, etc. Certain crops can be planted between the rows of the poppies. Much oil, bearing a high price, is made from the seed. The lower leaves, which are abundant, are used in some quarters to feed pigs, and also as a vegetable. They were served up to me as such twice, and tasted like spinach. In some places the heavy stalks are dug into the ground; in others they are used as fuel, and after serving this purpose their ashes provide lye for the indigo dyers. It appears from much concurrent testimony, that in spite of heavy manuring the crop exhausts the ground.

The area devoted to the poppy in SZE CHUAN is enormous and owing to the high price of the drug and its easy transport its culture is encroaching on the rice and arable lands. The consequences of the extension of its cultivation are serious. It is admitted by the natives of SZE CHUAN that one great reason of the deficient food supply which led to the famine and distress in the eastern part of the province in 1897, was the giving of so much ground to the poppy that there was no longer a margin left on which to feed the population in years of a poor harvest.

I shall not touch on the history of the growth and use of opium in China. The authorities evidently regarded the introduction of both as a grave peril, and they were prohibited under Imperial decrees. I learn on what I regard as very reliable authority, that sixty years ago, when Cantonese brought opium cough pills into KWEICHOW and YUNNAN, and the consumers found themselves unable to give up the medicine, that the authorities were most active in suppressing its use, and even inflicted the punishment of death on many of the refractory in YUNNAN. It was then and later smuggled about the country in coffins!

Now, on many of the SZE CHUAN roads opium houses are as common as gin shops in our London slums. I learned from Chinese sources that in several of the large cities of the province eighty per cent. of the men and forty per cent. of the women are opium smokers; but this must not be understood to mean that they are opium "wrecks," for there is a vast amount of "moderate" opium smoking in China. In my boat on the Yangtze fourteen out of sixteen very poor trackers smoked opium, and among my chair and baggage coolies it was rare to find one who did not smoke, and who did not collapse about the same hour daily with the so-called unbearable craving.

The stern of my boat was a downright opium den at night, with fourteen ragged men curled up on their quilts, with their opium lamps beside them, in the height of sensuous felicity, dreaming such Elysian dreams as never visit the toiling day of a Chinese coolie, and incapable of rousing themselves to meet an emergency until the effect of the pipe passed off. Farther astern still, the *lao-pan* and his shrieking virago of a wife lay in the same blissful case, the toothless, mummied face of the *lao-pan,* expressive in the daytime of nothing but fiendish greed, with its muscles relaxed, and its deep, hard lines smoothed out. Some of these men, whose thin, worn, cotton rags were ill-fitted to meet the cold, sold most of them at Wan, rather than undergo what appeared to be literally the *agonies* of abstinence. On my inland journey I heard incidentally of many men who had sold both wives and children in order to obtain the drug, and at Paoning Fu of a man and his wife who, having previously parted with house, furniture, and all they had, to gratify their craving, at the time of my visit sold their only child, a nice girl of fourteen, educated in the Mission School, to some brutal Kansuh fur traders, who were returning home. It is quite usual when a man desires a house and land which are the property of an opium smoker, for him to wait with true Chinese patience for one, two, or three years, certain that the owner will sooner or later part with it for an old song to satisfy his opium craving when he has sold all else. It is common for the Chinese to say, "If you want to be revenged on your enemy you need not strike him, or go to law with him—you have only to entice him into smoking opium."

The Chinese condemn all but most moderate opium smoking and gambling as twin vices, and not a voice is raised in defence of either of them, even by the smokers themselves. The opium habit is regarded as a disease, for the cure of which many smokers voluntarily place themselves in opium refuges at some expense, and at a great cost of suffering, and in the market towns, thronged with native traders, there is to be seen on many stalls among innumerable native drugs and commodities, a package labelled "Remedy for Foreign Smoke," "foreign smoke" being the usual name for opium in Western China. I was impressed with the existence of a curious sort of conscience, if it can be called such, among the devotees of opium, which leads them to consider themselves as moral criminals. The Chinese generally believe that if a man takes to the opium habit, it will be to the impoverishment and ruin of his family, and that it will prevent him from fulfilling one of the first of Confucian obligations, the support of his parents in their old age. The consensus of opinion among smokers and non-smokers, as to the crime of opium smoking and its woeful results, leads me to believe that it brings about the impoverishment and ruin of families to an enormous extent. Chinese said several times to me that the reason the Japanese beat them was that they were more vigorous men, owing to the rigid exclusion of opium from Japan.

In May I saw the crop harvested. Women and children are the chief operators. In the morning longitudinal incisions are made in the seed vessel, the juice exudes, and by the evening is hard enough to be scraped into cups, after which it turns black, and after a few days' exposure is ready for packing. Heavy rain or a strong west wind during this process is very injurious. Maize, tobacco, and cotton have been previously planted, and make a good appearance as soon as the poppy stalks have been cleared away.

Eight years ago it was rather exceptional for women and children to smoke, but the Chinese estimate that in SZE CHUAN and other opium-producing regions from forty to sixty per cent. are now smokers. Where opium is not grown the habit is chiefly confined to the cities, but it is rapidly spreading.

Its existence is obvious among the lower classes from the exceeding poverty which it entails. Millions of the working classes earn barely enough to provide them with what, even to their limited notions, are the necessaries of life, and the money spent on opium is withdrawn from these. Hence the confirmed opium smoker among the poor is apt to look half starved and ragged. Still I am bound to say that I did not encounter any of those awful specimens of physical wreckage that I saw some years ago in the Malay States from the same cause.

Among the well-to-do and well-nourished classes the evils of opium are doubtless more moral than physical; among the masses both evils are combined. The lower orders of officials and "yamen runners," with their unlimited leisure, are generally smokers. Among my official escorts in SZE CHUAN, numbering in all 143 men, all but two were devotees of opium, and I was constantly delayed and inconvenienced by it. My coolies frequently broke down under the craving, and that at times as inconvenient to themselves as to me. In two towns I had to wait two hours to get my passport copied because the writers at the yamen were in the blissful haziness produced by the pipe.

So far as I have seen, the passionate craving for the drug, called by the Chinese the "Yin," (which appears to be the coming on of severe depression after the stimulant of the pipe has passed off), involves great suffering, and total abstinence, whether voluntary or enforced, produces an anguish which the enfeebled will of the immoderate smoker is powerless to contend with. The craving grows, till at the end of eighteen months from the commencement of the habit, or even less, the smoker, unless he can gratify it, becomes unable to do his work.

He feels disinclined to move, miserable all over, especially at the stomach and between the shoulders, his joints and bones ache badly, he perspires freely, he trembles with a sense of weakness, and if he cannot get the drug, he believes that he will die. I cannot learn how soon a man comes to consider himself a victim of the habit. Those who place themselves in opium refuges with the hope of cure, endure agonies which they describe to be "as if wolves were gnawing at their vitals," and would, if permitted, tear off their skin to relieve the severe internal suffering.

On my SZE CHUAN journey we were benighted on a desolate hillside, and had to spend the night in the entrance to a coal-pit, cold, wet, and badly fed. My coolies had relied on being able to buy opium, and though they were comparatively moderate smokers, they suffered so much that some of them were rolling on the ground in their pain. Dr. Main, of Hangchow, thinks that very few can be cured in opium refuges, which they enter for twenty-one days, for the debility, stomachic disorder, and depression which follow the disuse of the drug are so great, that six months of tonics and good feeling would be necessary to set them on their feet again. On the contrary, the poor wretch, low in purse, depressed, feeble, trembling, leaves the shelter of the refuge to be tempted at once to a smoke by old associates, while in cities like Hangchow and Fuchow from eight hundred to a thousand registered opium shops display their seductions, and he turns aside to the only physical and mental comfort that he knows.

I have little doubt that in the early months of the habit there is a widespread desire to abandon it. Opium refuges, in spite of the fair payment which is asked for, are always crowded. The shops and markets abound in native and foreign remedies for "foreign smoke." The native cures all contain opium, chiefly in the form of ashes, and the foreign, which are white, contain morphia. The attempts at self-cure number tens of thousands, and are very piteous, but in many cases it is merely the exchange of the opium habit for the morphia habit, and at this time morphia lozenges are making great headway in China, as an easy and unsuspected means, specially in traveling, of obtaining the sensations which have become essential to existence. The importation of morphia into China is now enormous—135,283 ounces in 1898. It is sold everywhere, and in the great west, as well as nearer the seaboard, shops are opened which sell a few articles as a blind, for the lucrative sale of the much-prized morphia pill or lozenge. Among the native cures which I have heard of the only one which seems at all efficacious is the so-called "Tea Extract," *Scutellaria vicidula*. The *Jsai li* sect, which makes abstinence from opium one of its tenets, uses this cure invariably, but the ordinary smoker is unwilling to face the severe suffering which it entails.

Smokers, I have learned, may be divided into three classes: first, the upper class, not driven by failure of means or sense of duty to abandon an indulgence which they can well afford, and which they do not enjoy to excess; second, the respectable class of small merchants, innkeepers, shopkeepers, business men, and the like, who find their families pinched and themselves losing caste by reason of their habit; third, the class—which the Chinese estimate to consist of forty per cent. of the whole in the cities, and twenty per cent. in the country—which has drifted beyond hope, and is continually re-cruited from those above it. In this are found thieves, beggars, actors, the infamous, the lost and submerged, the men who have sold lands, houses, wives, and children, and live for opium only, much as the most degraded of our dipsomaniacs live for spirits.

Besides these, there are many who are not obliged to have recourse to selling and pawning to get along, but who curtail such things as the education of their children, and flowers for their wives' heads, and who, from having eaten meat twice daily, eat it only once, or substitute for it a purely vegetable diet, which must contain much honey and sugar to relieve the heat and dryness of the mouth which the pipe produces. Then there are large numbers of smokers who have barely enough to feed themselves upon, who must eat in order to work, and who have not one *cash* left for opium. These borrow right and left, and part with all they can pledge for anything, borrowing every year from fresh lenders, and paying back a fraction of the old debts till they can borrow no longer, and drop into the submerged class aforesaid. Among these are seen the ragged, mummied wretches, who *kotow* to former acquaintances, and beg from them the ashes of their opium pipes, even drinking these with hot water to satisfy the craving.

Rich smokers smoke what is known as "Canton opium," the import from India, which they compare to a coal fire, and the native drug to a wood one. But the manufac-ture of the latter is improving rapidly; and as it is increasingly used to mix with the In-dian, a generation is growing up in the upper class which knows only the mixed drug, and apparently only the old, rich smokers use pure Indian opium, the consumption of which has fallen off enormously, though in 1898 the value of the Indian import was £4,388,385.

The mysteries of the preparation and the varieties of the product baffle the non-smoker. Both Chinese and Indian opium are now largely prepared with the ashes of the drug already once smoked, much of it flowing, only imperfectly burned, into the receiver of the pipe. In the strongest prepared opium, four ounces of ashes of the first degree are added to every ten of crude opium. Ashes of the second and even the third burning are also used. Many of the poorer classes have to content themselves with a smoke of opium ashes only, and the lowest of all users of the drug have to satisfy themselves with eating or drinking the ashes of the third burning.

There is a class which can afford to buy the pure drug, but which finds that it does not satisfy the craving, but this is merged in a far larger one of old and inveterate rich smokers of one tael's weight per day, who smoke not even the very best prepared Indian drug, for their craving needs far stronger stimulation, but ashes of the first degree. Such men give the prepared extract, weight for weight, value for value, for the ashes, and contract with opium shops to be supplied with all their ashes of the first burning. For the rich, inveterate smoker an ounce of prepared extract is mixed with six ounces of ashes of the first degree. This habit has in Chinese a specific bad name.

Pure opium appears to be seldom sold, as it fails to satisfy the craving of the practised smoker. It is not only that ashes are mixed with the fresh drug, but that they are re-boiled, and after being made up with treacle to the proper consistence are resmoked, and their ashes are then eaten by the poorest class.

Morphia, the active principle of opium, not being consumed in the smoke owing to its lack of volatility, the eating of the ashes, which contain seven per cent. and upwards of it, has a very serious effect. The fact that opium is smoked three times makes it impossible to estimate either the quantity consumed or the amount spent on the indulgence, but these are, of course, greatly in excess of that indicated by any possible returns.

Among the adjuncts of opium smoking used by rich smokers is what is called "water tobacco," supposed erroneously to be all washed in the water of the Yellow river. It is retailed in thin cakes of a brick-red colour, and is said to be mixed with arsenic, and that its excessive use, with or without opium, is dangerous to health. This tobacco is invariably smoked in "water pipes" by the upper classes in SZE CHUAN.

In the chapter on the Hangchow Hospital I have mentioned the impetus given to suicide by the painlessness of death by opium, and will not refer to it again. In this chapter I have only touched upon such mysteries and results of opium smoking as I have seen in my limited experience, or have heard of directly from Chinese through my interpreters, or facts stated in a careful paper, *The Use of Opium,* by Dr. Dudgeon, of Peking. Except for the quotation of a remark of Dr. Main, of Hangchow, on opium refuges, I have not obtained any of my material from missionaries.

From all that I have seen and heard among the Chinese themselves, I have come to believe that even moderate opium smoking involves enormous risks, and that excessive smoking brings in its train commercial, industrial, and moral ruin and physical deterioration, and this on a scale so large as to threaten the national well-being and the physical future of the race.

The most common reasons which the Chinese give for contracting the habit are pain, love of pleasure, sociability, and the want of occupation. They say that a moderate use of the pipe "advances the transaction of business, stimulates the bargaining instinct, facilitates the striking of bargains, and enables men to talk about secret and important matters which without it they would lack courage to speak of."

It is strangely true that in this industrial nation there are hundreds of thousands of people with little or nothing to do. There are the wives of the wealthy, retired, and expectant mandarins, leisured men of various classes, *literati* waiting for employment, the great army of priests and monks, and the hangers-on of *yamens,* besides which there are Government officials whose duties occupy them only one day in a month. These remarks apply chiefly to urban populations.

Outside of commercial pursuits an overpowering shadow of dulness rests on Chinese as upon much of Oriental life. The lack of an enlightened native press, and of anything deserving the name of contemporary literature; the grooviness of thought and action; the trammels of a rigid etiquette; the absence of athletics, and even of ordinary exercise; the paucity of recreations, other than the play and the restaurants, which are oftimes associated with opium shops and vicious resorts; and the fact that the learned having committed the classics to memory, by which they have rendered themselves eligible for office, have no farther motive for study—all make the blissful dreams and the oblivion of the opium pipe greatly to be desired.

It is obvious that opium has come to "stay." So lately as 1859, in Sze Chuan, which now exports opium annually to the value of nearly £2,000,000, the penalty for growing it was death, in spite of which the white poppy fields were seen in conspicuous places along the Great River; and in 1868 an Imperial edict against its cultivation was supplemented by a proclaimation to the same effect by the Viceroy of the province, and both have remained dead letters.

At all times the beautiful *Papaver somniferum* has been regarded as the enemy of China. There are no apologists for the use of opium except among foreigners. The smokers themselves are ashamed of their slavery. All alike condemn it, and regard opium as a curse as well as a vice, and from all which came under my own observation in fifteen months, I fully agree with them.

Study Questions

1. What different kinds of information did Humboldt gather as he traveled?
2. Why does Bird devote a chapter to discussing the use of opium in China?
3. In what ways do Islamic culture and his own culture as an Englishman affect Burton in his visit to Mecca?
4. What impact does the fact that Mary Kingsley and Isabella Bird were women have on their travels and the ways they were received by people they met?
5. What criteria do each of these travelers use to distinguish between their own cultures and the ones that they are visiting?

Suggestions for Further Reading

Birkett, Dea. *Spinsters Abroad: Victorian Lady Explorers.* Oxford: Basil Blackwell, 1898.

Buzard, James. *The Beaten Track.* Oxford: Oxford University Press, 1993.

Middleton, Dorothy. *Victorian Lady Travellers.* New York: E. P. Dutton, 1965.

Mills, Sara. *Discourse of Difference: An Analysis of Women's Travel Writing and Colonialism.* New York: Routledge, 1991.

Pratt, Mary Louise. *Imperial Eyes: Travel Writing and Transculturation.* New York: Routledge, 1992.

Web Sites

1. Collected Travel Writings of Isabella Bird

   http://www.ganesha-publishing.com/bird_intro.htm

2. Discovers' Web

   http://www.win.tue.nl/~engels/discovery

3. Women's Travel Writing: 1830–1930

   http://erc.lib.umn.edu:80/dynaweb/travel

22

Fictional Representations of Non-Europeans 1862–1924

TEXTS

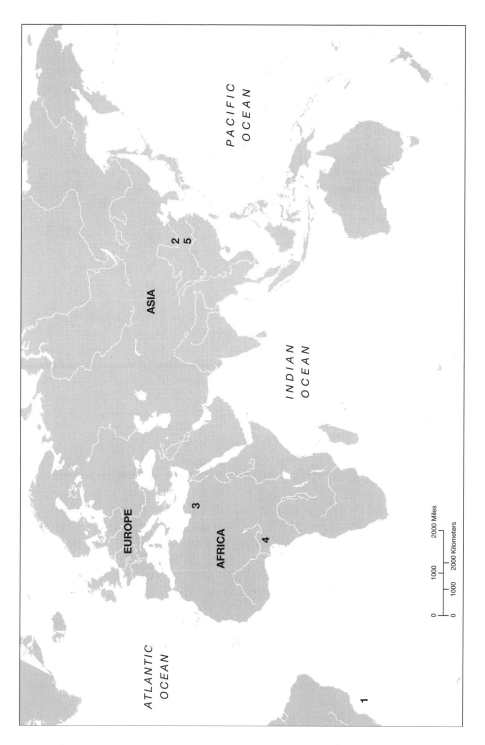

Even as European merchants and armies extended European control over other parts of the world during the nineteenth century, European culture was creating texts that demonstrated and contributed to that control. Colonialist fiction, which expressed imperialist ideas of European superiority and hegemony, became a staple of European literature during the century. This fiction offered its readers ways of thinking about exploration, conquest, and colonization. Borrowing from travelers' books and published accounts of exploration, as well as the personal experiences of its authors, this literature interpreted the empires to those who never left the imperial center. Using figurative language and fictional plots and characters, novels, poetry, and operettas about the non-European world organized the spatial, political, economic and social relationships between Europe and the rest of the world. Colonialist novels spoke about wealth that was often located in the colonies. The commercial relations that they described were often between the imperial center and the colonial periphery. Products and commodities in these works came from the colonies. They created visions of the peoples who lived in the non-European parts of the world, and by contrast also told Europeans what it meant to be a European in an imperial age.

Colonialist fiction also dealt in exoticism, the strangeness of the colonial world when seen from the imperial center. [1, 2] The colonies were places outside of European civilization, in which their stunning difference from Europe allowed a departure from the standards of behavior required in Europe. Colonialist authors were therefore able to write their fantasies on the colonial world. [3] It was a world that Europeans controlled, and in which they could escape from the strictures of European civilization. In some novels, the colonies were places that characters could go to begin anew, escaping from the restrictions of metropolitan society or overcoming the disasters of their own lives there. [4] These fantasies also often involved the conscious breaking of European taboos about sexual behavior, class, and race. [5] There was, therefore, the fascinating possibility of pleasure and escape in the colonialist novel, but it was also potentially dangerous. The violation of civilized rules could lead to terrible consequences for the individual who did so, expressed in the form of social unacceptability, moral degradation, or physical or mental illness. It could also have social consequences: the disruption of normal social relations that the colonies made possible could undercut the stability of metropolitan society in general.

These characteristics of colonialist fiction should not mask changes they expressed over time, from the height of imperial expansion in the last decades of the nineteenth century [6] through growing controversies about imperial control that surfaced after the turn of the century. Gilbert and Sullivan operettas, the boys' tales of G. A. Henty, and the romantic novels of Gustave Flaubert and Pierre Loti expressed the self-confidence of the early decades of imperial expansion, the sense of the superiority of European civilization, and the moral rectitude of European power throughout the world.

But as time passed and the contradictions of empire became more apparent, colonialist fiction reflected and portrayed the weakening of that self-confidence. Joseph Conrad's fiction precociously expressed the ambivalent relationship between European civilization and the impenetrable jungle. And, after the First World War, E. M. Forster's account of the destabilizing effects of colonialism on European norms of gender and race took forms that were inconceivable a generation earlier.

1. GUSTAVE FLAUBERT, *SALAMMBÔ*

Gustave Flaubert (1821–1880) is one of the most significant French novelists of the nineteenth century. His novels *Madame Bovary* (1857) and *Sentimental Education* (1869) represented a high point of the realist movement in fiction, the attempt to reproduce the material world in literature. As with many other writers of his time, he found inspiration in the Middle East and North Africa, covering the usual route from Greece east to Turkey, Lebanon, and Egypt, then west through Tunis and back to France through Spain between 1849 and 1851. The effect of this on Flaubert's work was different than that of earlier authors. Although Orientalist images are found throughout his writings, and *Salammbô* (1862) and *Hérodias* (1877) are more directly concerned with Orientalist topics, it is largely background in his works, a source not only of heightened sensuality but also of the bizarre and the perverse. He therefore did not achieve, nor did he particularly attempt, the fusion with the Orient that was a part of earlier, more Romanticist, versions of Orientalism.

Salammbô

Across the waves the rising moon struck a shaft of light and over the city hung vast shadows, interspersed with luminous glints of brilliant whiteness—the pole of a chariot in a courtyard, some vagrant rag of linen, the angle of a wall, or the glitter of a gold necklace on the bosom of a god. On the roofs of the temples the glass globes glittered like enormous diamonds: but half defined ruins, heaps of black earth, and gardens, made more sombre masses in the general obscurity.

At the foot of Malqua, fishermen's nets extended from house to house, like gigantic bats with outspread wings. The creaking of the hydraulic wheels that forced the water to the upper stories of the palaces had ceased. In the centre of the terraces camels tranquilly reposed, lying on their bellies after the manner of ostriches. The porters slept in the streets at the thresholds of the mansions. The colossi cast long shadows over the deserted squares. In the distance, the smoke of a sacrifice still burning escaped through the bronze tiles; and a heavy breeze brought the odour of aromatic perfumes and the scent of the sea, mingled with exhalations from the sun-heated walls.

Around Carthage the motionless waters gleamed resplendent, as the rising moon spread her light, at the same time, over the gulf, enclosed by mountains and over the lake of Tunis, where upon the banks of sand flamingoes formed long, rose-coloured lines; and farther on below the catacombs the large salt lagoon shimmered like a lake of burnished silver. The blue dome of heaven on the one side sank into the horizon down to the powdered plains, and on the other side faded away into the sea-mists; and on the summit of the Acropolis, the pyramidal cypresses bordering the temple of Eschmoûn swayed, murmuring like the swell of the waves that beat slowly along the mole at the foot of the ramparts.

Salammbô ascended to the upper terrace of her palace, supported by a slave, who carried an iron plate filled with burning charcoal.

In the centre of the terrace was a small ivory couch covered with lynx-skins, upon which were pillows made out of the feathers of the prophetic parrots—birds consecrated to the gods—and at the four corners were long cassolettes, filled with spikenard, incense, cinnamon, and myrrh. The slave lit the perfumes.

Salammbô contemplated the polar star, then slowly saluting the four quarters of the heavens knelt on the ground amid the azure powder strewn with gold stars, in imitation of the firmament. Then she pressed her elbows close against her sides, extending her forearms perfectly straight, with hands open, her head turned upward and back under the full rays of the moon, reciting:

"O RABETNA! BAALET! TANIT!" Her tones continued plaintively, as if she called some one: "ANAITIS! ASTARTE! DERCETO! ASTORETH! MYLITTA! ATHARA! ELISSA! TIRATHA! . . . By the hidden symbols . . . by the resounding timbrels . . . by the furrows of the earth . . . by the eternal silence . . . by the everlasting fruitfulness. . . . Ruler of the shadowy sea, and of the azure shore, O Queen of the humid world, all hail!"

She swayed her entire body two or three times, then threw herself face downward, with outstretched arms, flat in the dust.

Her slave lifted her up quickly, for it was appointed that after such rites some one should always lift the suppliant from her prostration, as a sign that the service was acceptable in the sight of the gods; Salammbô's nurse never failed in this pious duty. This slave had been brought, when but a child, to Carthage by some merchants of Dara-Getulia, but after her emancipation she had no wish to leave her many masters; as a proof of her willing servitude, according to a recognised custom, in her right ear a large hole was pierced. She wore a many-coloured striped skirt fitting tightly about her hips, falling straight down to her ankles, between which as she walked two tin rings struck against one another; her flat face was as yellow as her tunic; very long silver pins made a halo at the back of her head, and in one nostril was inserted a coral stud. She now stood beside the couch with eyes downcast, more erect than a Hermes.

Salammbô walked to the edge of the terrace; her eyes swept for an instant over the horizon, then she lowered her gaze to the sleeping city. She heaved a sigh from the depths of her bosom, causing her long white simarre to undulate from end to end as it hung unconfined either by girdle or agrafe. Her curved sandals with turned-up toes were hidden beneath a mass of emeralds: her hair was carelessly caught up in a net of purple silk.

She raised her head to contemplate the moon—mingling with her words the fragments of hymns as she murmured:

"How lightly dost thou turn, supported by the impalpable ether! It is luminous about thee, and the movement of thy changes distributes the winds and the fruitful dews; as thou waxest and wanest, the eyes of cats elongate or shorten, and the spots of the leopard are changed. Women scream thy name in the pangs of childbirth! Thou increasest the shell-fish! Thou causest the wind to ferment! Thou putrefiest the dead! Thou shapest the pearls at the bottom of the seas; and all germs, O goddess! are quickened in the profound obscurity of thy humidity! When thou comest forth a calmness spreadeth over the earth; the flowers close; the waves are lulled; wearied men sleep with their faces upturned toward thee; and the entire earth, with its oceans and its mountains, is reflected in thy face, as in a mirror. Thou art white, sweet, lustrous, gentle, immaculate, purifying, serene!"

The crescent moon was just then over the Hot-Springs Mountain; below it in the notch of the two summits on the opposite side of the gulf, appeared a little star, encircled by a pale light. Salammbó continued:

"But thou art a terrible mistress! . . . Likewise produced by thee are monsters, frightful phantoms, and awful dreams; thine eyes devour the stones of the edifices, and during the periods of thy rejuvenescence the sacred apes fall ill. Whither goest thou then? Why continually changest thou thy forms? Sometimes narrow and curved, thou glidest through space as a mastless galley, and again, in the midst of stars thou resemblest a shepherd guarding his flock; anon shining and round, thou grazest the summit of the mounts like a chariot wheel!

"O Tanit, dost thou not love me? I have gazed on thee so often! But, no, thou proceedest in thine azure, whilst I remain on the motionless earth? . . .

"Taanach, take your nebal and play softly on the silver string, for my heart is sad."

The slave lifted a sort of ebony harp, taller than herself, of a triangular shape like a delta, and placing the point in a crystal globe began to play with both hands.

Sounds followed low, precipitous tones, like the buzzing of bees, and growing more and more sonorous, were wafted into the night, and mingled with the lament of the waves and the rustling of the large trees on the summit of the Acropolis.

"Hush!" cried Salammbô.

"What is it, mistress? If a breeze but blow, or a cloud pass, thou art vexed and disturbed."

"I know not," she replied.

"You have exhausted yourself by praying too long," urged the slave.

"Oh! Taanach! I would dissolve myself in prayer like a flower in wine!"

"Perhaps it is the scent of the perfumes?"

"No!" said Salammbô. "The spirit of the gods dwells in sweet odours."

Then the slave talked to her of her father. It was believed that he had gone into the Amber country beyond the pillars of Melkarth.

"But mistress, if he should not return," she said, "you must choose, as was his will, a husband from among the sons of the Elders; and your unrest will vanish in the embrace of your husband."

"Why?" asked the young girl. All the sons of the Elders she had ever seen horrified her with their wild beast laughter, and their coarse limbs.

"Taanach, sometimes a feeling emanates from the innermost depths of my being, like hot flushes, heavier than the vapours arising from a volcano—voices call to me; a fiery globe rises up in my breast; it suffocates me. I seem to be about to die, when something sweet flows from my brow, extending to my very feet—thrills through every atom of my being—it is a caress which envelopes me—I feel myself crushed as if a god spread himself over and upon me. Oh! I long to lose myself in the night mists—in the ripples of the fountains, in the sap of the trees to leave my body to be but a breath of air—a ray of light, and glide through space unto thee, O Mother!"

She raised her arms to their full height, bending her body backward, pale and delicate in her white robe, as the moon; then in her ecstacy she fell panting on her ivory couch. Taanach placed around her mistress's neck a collar of amber and dolphins' teeth to banish these terrors. Salammbô said, in a voice almost inaudible, "go and bring Schahabarim here to me."

Salammbô's father had not wished that she should enter the college of priestesses, nor even that she should know aught concerning the popular Tanit. He intended her for some alliance which would serve his political aims: so that Salammbô lived alone in her palace, her mother having been dead for years. She had grown up amid abstinences, fasts, and purifications, and was always surrounded by exquisite and solemn things—her body saturated with perfumes—her soul filled with prayers. She had not tasted wine, or eaten meat, or touched an unclean animal, or put her foot in the house of death.

She was ignorant of obscene images; for each god was manifested in many different forms, and the various rites, often most contradictory, all demonstrated the same principles; and Salammbô had been taught to adore the goddess in her sidereal representation.

An influence had descended from the moon upon this maiden, for whenever the planet waned Salammbô became feeble, languishing all day, only reviving at night; during an eclipse she had nearly died.

But the jealous Rabetna revenged herself on this chaste maiden, withheld from immolation; obsessing her with allurements all the stronger because they were vague, the outgrowth of faith, strengthened by imagination.

The daughter of Hamilucar was constantly troubled about Tanit. She had learned the goddess's adventures, her journeys, and all her names, which she repeated, without their having any distinct significance for her. In order to penetrate the profundities of her dogma, she longed to know, in the most secret places of the temple, the ancient idol, with the magnificent veil, wherein rested the destiny of Carthage. The idea of a deity was not clearly revealed by her representation, and to possess or even behold her image was to share a part of her power, and in some measure to dominate her.

Salammbô turned as she recognised the tinkling of the gold bells that Schahabarim wore at the hem of his robe.

He ascended the stairs, and pausing as he reached the threshold of the terrace, folded his arms. His sunken eyes burned like lamps in a sepulchre; his long, thin body glided along in its linen robe, which was weighted by bells alternating with emerald balls about his heels. His limbs were feeble, his head oblique, his chin peaked, his skin was cold to the touch, and his yellow face, covered with deeply furrowed wrinkles, seemed as if contracted in a yearning, in an eternal chagrin.

This man was the high priest of Tanit, and he had educated Salammbô.

"Speak!" said he. "What do you wish?"

"I hoped—you almost promised me— . . ." she stammered, half fearing; then suddenly continued: "Why do you despise me? What have I neglected in the rites? You are my teacher, and you have said to me that no person is more learned than I in the mysteries of the goddess; but there are some of which you have not yet told me; is not this true, O father?"

Schahabarim remembering the orders of Hamilcar concerning his daughter's education, responded: "No! I have nothing more to teach you."

"A spirit," she resumed, "urges me to this adoration. I have climbed the steps of Eschmoûn—god of the planets and intelligences; I have slept under the golden olive tree of Melkarth—patron of all Tyrian colonies; I have opened the gates of Baal-Khamoûn—medium of light and fertilisation; I have made sacrifices to the subterranean Kabiri—to the gods of the winds, the rivers, the woods, and the mountains—but they all are too distant, too high, too insensible—you understand? But Tanit mingles in my life, she fills my soul, and I tremble with internal dartings, as if she struggled to escape the confines of my body. I feel I am about to hear her voice, behold her face; a brightness dazzles me, then I fall back again into the shadows."

Schahabarim was silent. She implored him with beseeching glances. At length he made a sign to dismiss the slave, who was not of Canaanite race. Taanach disappeared, and the priest raised one arm in the air, and began:

"Before the gods, only darkness existed, and a breath stirred, heavy and indistinct, like the consciousness of a man in a dream: it contracted itself, creating Desire and Vapour; from Desire and Vapour proceeded primitive Matter. This was a water, black, icy, profound, containing insensible monsters, incoherent parts of forms to be born, such as are painted on the walls of the sanctuaries. Then Matter condensed and became an egg. The egg broke: one half formed the earth, the other half the firmament. The sun, moon, winds, and clouds appeared, and at a crash of thunder the sentient animals awoke. Then Eschmoûn unrolled himself in the starry sphere! Khamoûn shone brilliantly in the sun; Melkarth with his arms pushed him beyond Gades; the Kabiri descended into the volcanoes; and Rabetna, like one who nourishes, leaned over the world, pouring forth her light like milk, and her night like a mantle."

"And then?" she inquired—for the priest had related the secrets of origins, to distract her by the highest, the most abstract forms; but the desire of the maiden was rekindled at his last words, and Schahabarim, half consenting, resumed:

"She inspires and governs the loves of men."

"The loves of men!" repeated Salammbô, dreamily.

"She is the soul of Carthage," continued the priest. "Although her influence reaches over all, it is here she dwells, beneath the *Sacred Veil.*"

"O father!" exclaimed Salammbô, "I shall see her, shall I not? You will take me to her? For a long time I have hesitated: now the desire to see her form devours me. Pity me; comfort me! Let us go to the temple!"

He repulsed her by a vehement gesture, full of pride.

"Never! Do you not know that to look upon her is death? The hermaphrodite Baals unveil only to us; men that we are in comprehension and women in weakness. Your desire is sacrilege. Be satisfied with the knowledge that is already yours."

She fell upon her knees, placing two fingers against her ease in sign of repentance; sobbing, crushed by the priest's words, at the same time indignant with him—filled equally with fear and humiliation.

Schahabarim remained standing, more insensible than the stones of the terrace. He looked down upon her quivering at his feet, and it afforded him a measure of delight to see her thus suffering for his divinity whom he, himself, could wholly embrace.

Already the birds sang, and a cold wind blew, and little clouds fluttered across the pale sky. Suddenly the priest perceived on the horizon behind Tunis what at first appeared to be a light mist floating over the ground; then it formed a vast curtain of grey dust spreading perpendicularly, and through the whirling mass, the heads of dromedaries, and the flash of lances and bucklers could be seen. It was the Barbarian army advancing on Carthage.

2. PIERRE LOTI, *AZIYADÉ*

Pierre Loti is the pen name adopted by Julien Viaud (1850–1923), a French naval officer who was one of the most popular novelists of late nineteenth-century France. An older brother who died while returning from service as a surgeon in the French colony of Indochina sparked Viaud's interest in the colonies and other places he read about in missionary and colonial magazines. In 1867, he entered the Ecole Navale, the French training school for naval officers, and spent the next forty-three years serving as an officer in the French navy. In 1872 he began publishing stories and travelogues based on his experiences in the navy, and in 1879, *Aziyadé*, his first novel, set in Istanbul, was published. Much of Loti's work is at least partially autobiographical, involving the development of the characters and the exotic settings in which he placed his stories. He usually wrote in the first person (Loti is the name of the narrator in one of his first novels, *The Marriage of Loti*), and his discussions of European diplomacy and of colonialism itself are therefore usually brief. He often uses female characters as the contact between the narrator and the indigenous cultures in the exotic settings for his novels, but the similarities between the plots of his different works tends to eliminate the differences between those indigenous cultures. He was elected to the Académie Française, France's highest literary honor, in 1891.

Aziyadé

Two hours after sunset, one last, solitary caïque, coming from Azar-Kapu, drew towards the jetty. Samuel was at the oars. On the cushions in the stern reclined a veiled form. I saw that it was she! When the boat came alongside, the square surrounding the mosque was deserted and the night had turned cold. Without a word I seized her hand and ran with her to the house, giving no thought to poor Samuel, who was left outside.

When at last the impossible dream had come true, and she was there in the room I had prepared for her, alone with me, behind the ironbound doors, all I could do was to throw myself at her feet and clasp her knees. I realised how desperately I had longed for her. I was drowned in ecstasy.

And then I heard her voice. For the first time she spoke and I could understand—rapture hitherto unknown! But I myself could not utter one syllable of all the Turkish I had learnt for her sake; I could only stammer in English, as before, incoherent words I did not understand myself.

"*Severim seni*, Loti," she said. (Loti, I love you, I love you.)

Aziyadé was not the first to murmur these never-dying words to me. But never before had the exquisite music of love been wafted to my ears in the Turkish language. Delicious, half-forgotten music, can it be that I hear it again, gushing with such passion from the pure depths of a woman's heart, with such enchantment that I seem never before to have listened to it, that it thrills my disillusioned soul with the music of the spheres.

I lifted her in my arms, and held her so that the lamplight fell upon her face and I could gaze at her.

"Speak again," I said, like Romeo. "Speak again."

I murmured in her ear many things that I felt she could not but understand. My powers of speech had returned and with them my Turkish, and I asked her question after question, imploring her to answer. But she only gazed at me in ecstasy. I saw that she had no idea of what I was saying, and that my voice fell upon deaf ears.

"Aziyadé," I cried, "don't you hear me?"

"No," she replied.

Then in her grave voice, she uttered these sweet, wild words: "*Senin laf yemek isterim!*" ("I wish I could devour the speech of your lips, Loti, and the sound of your voice.")

III

Eyoub, December 1876.

Aziyadé seldom speaks, and, though she often smiles, she never laughs. Her step is without sound; her movements are supple, sinuous, unhurried and inaudible.

This is a true picture of that mysterious little creature, who almost always slips away at dawn, to return at nightfall, the hour of phantoms and genii.

There is a dreamlike quality about her and she seems to cast a radiance withersoever she goes. You look to see an aureole floating above that serious and childlike countenance. Nor do you look in vain, when the light catches these ethereal, rebellious, little curls, that cluster so deliciously about her cheeks and forehead. She thinks them unbecoming, and spends an hour every morning in unsuccessful efforts to plaster them down. This labour and the business of tinting her nails a brilliant orange are her two principal occupations. She is idle, like all women brought up in Turkey. But she can do embroidery, make rose-water and write her name. She scrawls it all over the walls, as solemnly as if it were a matter of vital importance, and she sharpens all my pencils for the task.

Aziyadé conveys her thoughts to me not so much with her lips as with her eyes. Their expression has extraordinary variety and eloquence. She is so expert in this language of the eyes, that she might use the spoken word less than she does or even dispense with it entirely. Sometimes she replies with a slave or two from a Turkish song. This trick of quotation, which would be tiresome in a European woman, has on Aziyadé's lips a curious Oriental charm. Her voice, though very young and fresh, is grave and its tones are always low pitched, while the Turkish aspirates lend it at times a certain huskiness.

This girl of eighteen or nineteen is capable of forming, on a sudden impulse, some desperate resolve, and of carrying it through in defiance of everything, even death itself.

IV

In the early days at Salonica, when I used to risk both Samuel's life and my own for the sake of one short hour with her, I had nursed this insane dream: to live with her in some remote corner of the East, where my poor Samuel could join us. This dream of mine, so contrary to all Mussulman ideas, so utterly impossible from every point of view, has come true in almost every detail.

Constantinople is the only place where such a scheme could have been attempted. It is a genuine wilderness of men, of which Paris was once the prototype, an aggregate of several large towns, where every man can lead his own life without interference, and assume as many different characters as he pleases—Loti, Arif and Marketo.

Blow, blow, thou winter wind! Let the squalls of December shake the bars on doors and windows.

Safe behind our massive iron bolts, with a whole arsenal of loaded guns to protect us, and yet more secure in the inviolable sanctuary of a Turkish dwelling—warming ourselves at the copper brazier—is it not well with us, my Aziyadé, in this home of ours?

XIV

"What do you do with yourself at home?" I asked Aziyadé. "How do you get through the long days in the harem?"

"It's very dull," she replied. "I just think of you, Loti, and look at your portrait, and play with the lock of your hair and all the little odds and ends of yours which I carry off to keep me company."

To own someone's portrait and a lock of his hair seemed to Aziyadé a very strange business indeed—something that she would never have dreamt of but for me, and contrary to all her Mussulman ideas. It was an innovation of the giaour, which had for her a fascination not unmingled with awe. She must indeed have loved me to let me cut off a long tress of her hair. She shuddered to think that she might suddenly die, before it had grown again, and she appear in the next world with a great lock shorn clean off by an infidel.

"But, Aziyadé," I pressed her, "before I came to Turkey, how did you pass the time?"

"In those days, Loti, I was hardly more than a child. The first time I saw you, I had spent but ten moons in Abeddin's harem and had not yet wearied of it. I stayed in my room, sitting on my divan, smoking cigarettes or hashish, or playing cards with Emineh, my maid, or listening to the queer stories about the black men's country that Kadija tells so well.

"Fenzile-hanum taught me to embroider, and we had visits to exchange with ladies in other harems. We had our duty to our master, and there was the carriage to take us for drives. Each wife is entitled to it in turn, but we all prefer to go out together and take our airings in company.

"On the whole we get on very well. Fenzile-hanum is very fond of me. She is the oldest and most important lady in the harem. Besmé is quick-tempered and sometimes flies into a rage. But it is easy to soothe her down and she soon gets over it. Ayesha is the most spiteful of the four, but she has to keep in with us and to hide her claws, because she is also far the naughtiest. Once she actually let her lover into her room."

It had long been a dream of mine, to slip, just once, into Aziyadé's room, to form an idea of the surroundings in which my darling spent her days. We had often discussed this scheme and Fenzile-hanum had actually been consulted. But we never carried it out. The more I know of Turkish customs, the more I realise how rash it would have been.

"Our harem," Aziyadé concluded, "is generally considered a model one, because we bear with one another, and keep on such good terms."

"A pretty sort of model!" I remarked."Are there many like it in Stamboul?"

It was through the fair Ayesha-*hanum* that the contagion first crept in. In two years it has spread so rapidly, that the old gentleman's house is now a mere hotbed of intrigue, with all the servants corrupted. The great cage, despite its stout bars, is like a huge conjuring box, full of secret doors and back staircases. The captive birds can leave it with impunity, and fly off in every direction under the sun.

3. WILLIAM S. GILBERT, *THE MIKADO*

William S. Gilbert (1836–1911) was one of the most accomplished dramatists for the London stage in the second half of the nineteenth century. Beginning in 1875, he and Arthur Sullivan (1842–1900) produced a series of light operas that enjoyed great popular success in both London and New York. *The Mikado,* which premiered in 1885, ran for two years in London, had over five thousand performances in America, and was the most popular of Gilbert and Sullivan's works. This story of two Japanese lovers and their dealings with the authorities uses the foreign setting as a part of its comedy, drawing attention away from the threats to the story's hero and heroine.

The Mikado

Ko. This is simply appalling! I, who allowed myself to be respited at the last moment, simply in order to benefit my native town, am now required to die within a month, and that by a man whom I have loaded with honours! Is this public gratitude? Is this—[*Enter* NANKI-POO *with a rope in his hands.*] Go away, sir! how dare you? Am I never to be permitted to soliloquize?

Nank. Oh, go on—don't mind me.

Ko. What are you going to do with that rope?

Nank. I am about to terminate an unendurable existence.

Ko. Terminate your existence? Oh, nonsense! What for?

Nank. Because you are going to marry the girl I adore.

Ko. Nonsense, sir. I won't permit it. I am a humane man, and if you attempt anything of the kind I shall order your instant arrest. Come, sir, desist at once, or I summon my guard.

Nank. That's absurd. If you attempt to raise an alarm, I instantly perform the Happy Despatch with this dagger.

Ko. No, no, don't do that. This is horrible! [*Suddenly.*] Why, you cold-blooded scoundrel, are you aware that, in taking your life, you are committing a crime which—which—which is—Oh!

Nank. What's the matter?

Ko. Is it *absolutely certain* that you are resolved to die?

Nank. Absolutely!

Ko. Will *nothing* shake your resolution?

Nank. Nothing.

Ko. Threats, entreaties, prayers—all useless?

Nank. All! My mind is made up.

Ko. Then, if you really mean what you say, and if you are absolutely resolved to die, and if nothing whatever will shake your determination—don't spoil yourself by committing suicide, but be beheaded handsomely at the hands of the Public Executioner.

Nank. I don't see how that would benefit me.

Ko. You don't? Observe: you'll have a month to live, and you'll live like a fighting cock at my expense. When the day comes there'll be a grand public ceremonial—you'll be the central figure—no one will attempt to deprive you of that distinction. There'll be a procession—bands—dead march—bells tolling—all the girls in tears—Yum-Yum distracted—then, when it's all over, general rejoicings, and a display of fireworks in the evening. *You* won't see them, but they'll be there all the same.

Nank. Do you think Yum-Yum would really be distracted at my death?

Ko. I am convinced of it. Bless you, she's the most tender-hearted little creature alive.

Nank. I should be sorry to cause her pain. Perhaps, after all, if I were to withdraw from Japan, and travel in Europe for a couple of years, I might contrive to forget her.

Ko. Oh, I don't think you could forget Yum-Yum so easily, and, after all, what is more miserable than a love-blighted life?

Nank. True.

Ko. Life without Yum-Yum—why it seems absurd!

Nank. And yet there are a good many people in the world who have to endure it.

Ko. Poor devils, yes! You are quite right not to be of their number.

Nank. [*Suddenly.*] I *won't* be of their number!

Ko. Noble fellow!

Nank. I'll tell you how we'll manage it. Let me marry Yum-Yum to-morrow, and in a month you may behead me.

Ko. No, no. I draw the line at Yum-Yum.

Nank. Very good. If you can draw the line, so can I.

      [*Preparing rope.*

Ko. Stop, stop—listen one moment—be reasonable. How can I consent to your marrying Yum-Yum if I'm going to marry her myself?

Nank. My good friend, she'll be a widow in a month, and you can marry her then.

Ko. That's true, of course. I quite see that, but, dear me, my position during the next month will be most unpleasant—most unpleasant!

Nank. Not half so unpleasant as my position at the end of it.

Ko. But—dear me—well—I agree—after all, it's only putting off my wedding for a month. But you won't prejudice her against me, will you? You see I've educated her to be my wife; she's been taught to regard me as a wise and good man. Now I shouldn't like her views on that point disturbed.

Nank. Trust me, she shall never learn the truth from me.

Ko. [*Presenting him.*] 'Tis Nanki-Poo!

All. Hail, Nanki-Poo!

Ko. I think he'll do?

All. Yes, yes, he'll do!

Ko. He yields his life if I'll Yum-Yum surrender;

Now I adore that girl with passion tender,

And could not yield her with a ready will,

Or her allot,

If I did not

Adore myself with passion tenderer still!
All. Ah, yes!
He loves himself with passion tenderer still!
Ko. [To NANKI-POO.] Take her—she's yours!
                    Enter YUM-YUM, PEEP-BO, *and* PITTI-SING
Nank, and Yum. Oh, rapture!

Act II

SCENE—Ko-Ko's *Garden*

Yum-Yum *discovered seated at her bridal toilet, surrounded by maidens who are dressing her hair and painting her face and lips, as she judges of the effect in a mirror.*
Yum. [*Looking at herself in glass.*] Yes, I am indeed beautiful! Sometimes I sit and wonder, in my artless Japanese way, why it is that I am so much more attractive than anybody else in the whole world? Can this be vanity? No! Nature is lovely and rejoices in her loveliness. I am a child of Nature, and take after my mother.
Yum. Yes, everything seems to smile upon me. I am to be married to-day to the man I love best, and I believe I am the very happiest girl in Japan!
Peep. The happiest girl indeed, for she is indeed to be envied who has attained happiness in all but perfection.
Yum. In "all but" perfection?
Peep. Well, dear, it can't be denied that the fact that your husband is to be beheaded in a month is, in its way, a drawback.
Pitti. I don't know about that. It all depends!
Peep. At all events, *he* will find it a drawback.
Pitti. Not necessarily. Bless you, it all depends!
Yum. [*In tears.*] I think it very indelicate of you to refer to such a subject on such a day. If my married happiness is to be—to be—
Peep. Cut short.
Yum. Well, cut short—in a month, can't you let me forget it?
                    [*Weeping.*

                    Enter NANKI-POO *followed by* PISH-TUSH
Nank. Yum-Yum in tears—and on her wedding-morn!
Yum. [*Sobbing.*] They're been reminding me that in a month you're to be beheaded!
                    [*Bursts into tears.*
Pitti. Yes, we've been reminding her that you're to be beheaded!
                    [*Bursts into tears.*
Peep. It's quite true, you know, you *are* to be beheaded!
                    [*Bursts into tears.*
Nank. [*Aside.*] Humph! How some bridegrooms would be depressed by this sort of thing! [*Aloud.*] A month? Well, what's a month? Bah! These divisions of time are purely arbitrary. Who says twenty-four hours make a day?
Pitti. There's a popular impression to that effect.
Nank. Then we'll efface it. We'll call each second a minute—each minute an hour—each hour a day—and each day a year. At that rate we've about thirty years of married happiness before us!

Peep. And at that rate, this interview has already lasted four hours and three quarters!
[*Exit* Peep-Bo.

Yum. [*Still sobbing.*] Yes. How time flies when one is thoroughly enjoying oneself!

Nank. That's the way to look at it! Don't let's be downhearted! There's a silver lining to every cloud.

Yum. Certainly. Let's—let's be perfectly happy! [*Almost in tears.*

Pish. By all means. Let's—let's thoroughly enjoy ourselves.

Pitti. It's—it's absurd to cry!   [*Trying to force a laugh.*

Yum. Quite ridiculous!   [*Trying to laugh.*
[*All break into a forced and melancholy laugh.*

Enter Ko-Ko—Nanki-Poo *releases* Yum-Yum

Ko. Go on—don't mind me.

Nank. I'm afraid we're distressing you.

Ko. Never mind, I must get used to it. Only please do it by degrees. Begin by putting your arm round her waist. [Nanki-Poo *does so.*] There; let me get used to that first.

Yum. Oh, wouldn't you like to retire? It must pain you to see us so affectionate together!

Ko. No, I must learn to bear it! Now oblige me by allowing her head to rest on your shoulder. [*He does so*—Ko-Ko *much affected.*] I am much obliged to you. Now—kiss her! [*He does so*—Ko-Ko *writhes with anguish.*] Thank you—it's simple torture!

Yum. Come, come, bear up. After all, it's only for a month.

Ko. No. It's no use deluding oneself with false hopes.

Nank.⎱ What do you mean?
Yum. ⎰

Ko. [*To* Yum-Yum.] My child—my poor child. [*Aside.*] How shall I break it to her? [*Aloud.*] My little bride that was to have been—

Yum. [*Delighted.*] *Was* to have been!

Ko. Yes, you never can be mine!

Yum. [*In ecstasy.*] What!!!

Ko. I've just ascertained that, by the Milkado's law, when a married man is beheaded his wife is buried alive.

Nank.⎱ Buried alive!
Yum. ⎰

Ko. Buried alive. It's a most unpleasant death.

Nank. But whom did you get that from?

Ko. Oh, from Pooh-Bah. He's my solicitor.

Yum. But he may be mistaken!

Ko. So I thought, so I consulted the Attorney-General, the Lord Chief Justice, the Master of the Rolls, the Judge Ordinary, and the Lord Chancellor. They're all of the same opinion. Never knew such unanimity on a point of law in my life!

Nank. But stop a bit! This law has never been put in force?

Ko. Not yet. You see, flirting is the only crime punishable with decapitation, and married men never flirt.

Nank. Of course they don't. I quite forgot that! Well, I suppose I may take it that my dream of happiness is at an end!

Yum. Darling—I don't want to appear selfish, and I love you with all my heart—I don't suppose I shall ever love anybody else half as much—but when I agreed to marry you—my own—I had no idea—pet—that I should have to be buried alive in a month!

Nank. Nor I! It's the very first I've heard of it!
Yum. It—it makes a difference, don't it?
Nank. It *does* make a difference, of course!
Yum. You see—burial alive—it's such a stuffy death! You see my difficulty, don't you?
Nank. Yes, and I see my own. If I insist on your carrying out your promise, I doom you to a hideous death; if I release you, you marry Ko-Ko at once!

Trio

Yum.

> Here's a how-de-do!
> If I marry you,
> When your time has come to perish,
> Then the maiden whom you cherish
> Must be slaughtered too!
> Here's a how-de-do!

Nank.

> Here's a pretty mess!
> In a month, or less,
> I must die without a wedding!
> Let the bitter tears I'm shedding
> Witness my distress.
> Here's a pretty mess!

Ko.

> Here's a state of things!
> To her life she clings!
> Matrimonial devotion
> Doesn't seem to suit her notion—
> Burial it brings!
> Here's a state of things!

Ensemble

Yum-Yum and Nanki-Poo.	*Ko-Ko.*
With a passion that's intense	With a passion that's intense
I worship and adore,	You worship and adore,
But the laws of common sense	But the laws of common sense
We oughtn't to ignore.	You oughtn't to ignore.
If what he says is true,	If what I say is true,
It is death to marry you!	It is death to marry you!
Here's a pretty state of things!	Here's a pretty state of things!
Here's a pretty how-de-do!	Here's a pretty how-de-do!
	[*Exit* YUM-YUM.

Ko. [*Going up to* NANKI-POO.] My poor boy, I'm really very sorry for you.
Nank. Thanks, old fellow. I'm sure you are.
Ko. You see I'm quite helpless.
Nank. I quite see that.
Ko. I can't conceive any thing more distressing than to have one's marriage broken off at the last moment. But you sha'n't be disappointed of a wedding—you shall come to mine.
Nank. It's awfully kind of you, but that's impossible.

Ko. Why so?

Nank. To-day I die.

Ko. What do you mean?

Nank. I can't live without Yum-Yum. This afternoon I perform the Happy Despatch.

Ko. No, no—pardon me—I can't allow that.

Nank. Why not?

Ko. Why, hang it all, you're under contract to die by the hand of the Public Executioner in a month's time! If you kill yourself, what's to become of me? Why, I shall have to be executed in your place!

Nank. It would certainly seem so!

Enter POOH-BAH

Ko. Now then, Lord Mayor, what is it?

Pooh. The Mikado and his suite are approaching the city, and will be here in ten minutes.

Ko. The Mikado! He's coming to see whether his orders have been carried out! [*To* NANKI-POO.] Now look here, you know—this is getting serious—a bargain's a bargain, and you really mustn't frustrate the ends of justice by committing suicide. As a man of honour and a gentleman, you are bound to die ignominiously by the hands of the Public Executioner.

Nank. Very well, then—behead me.

Ko. What, now?

Nank. Certainly; at once.

Ko. My good sir, I don't go about prepared to execute gentlemen at a moment's notice. Why, I never even killed a blue-bottle!

Pooh. Still, as Lord High Executioner,——

Ko. My good sir, as Lord High Executioner I've got to behead him in a month. I'm not ready yet. I don't know how it's done. I'm going to take lessons. I mean to begin with a guinea pig, and work my way through the animal kingdom till I come to a second trombone. Why, you don't suppose that, as a humane man, I'd have accepted the post of Lord High Executioner if I hadn't thought the duties were purely nominal? I *can't* kill you—I can't kill anything!   [*Weeps.*

Nank. Come, my poor fellow, we all have unpleasant duties to discharge at times; after all, what is it? If I don't mind, why should you? Remember, sooner or later it must be done.

Ko. [*Springing up suddenly.*] *Must it?* I'm not so sure about that!

Nank. What do you mean?

Ko. Why should I kill you when making an affidavit that you've been executed will do just as well? Here are plenty of witnesses—the Lord Chief Justice and Lord High Admiral, Commander-in-Chief, Secretary of State for the Home Department, First Lord of the Treasury, and Chief Commissioner of Police. They'll all swear to it—won't you? [*To* POOH-BAH.]

Pooh. Am I to understand that all of us high Officers of State are required to perjure ourselves to ensure your safety?

Ko. Why not? You'll be grossly insulted, as usual.

Ko. It will be a ready-money transaction.

Pooh. [*Aside.*] Well, it will be a useful discipline. [*Aloud.*] Very good. Choose your fiction, and I'll endorse it! [*Aside.*] Ha! ha! Family Pride, how do you like *that,* my buck?

Nank. But I tell you that life without Yum-Yum—

Ko. Oh, Yum-Yum, Yum-Yum! Bother Yum-Yum! Here, Commissionaire [*to* POOH-BAH], go and fetch Yum-Yum. [*Exit* POOH-BAH.] Take Yum-Yum and marry Yum-Yum, only go away and never come back again. [*Enter* POOH-BAH *with* YUM-YUM *and* PITTI-SING.] Here she is. Yum-Yum, are you particularly busy?
Yum. Not particularly.
Ko. You've five minutes to spare?
Yum. Yes.
Ko. Then go along with his Grace the Archbishop of Titipu; he'll marry you at once.
Yum. But if I'm to be buried alive?
Ko. Now don't ask any questions, but do as I tell you, and Nanki-Poo will explain all.
Nank. But one moment—
Ko. Not for worlds. Here comes the Mikado, no doubt to ascertain whether I've obeyed his decree, and if he finds you alive, I shall have the greatest difficulty in persuading him that I've beheaded you. [*Exeunt* NANKI-POO *and* YUM-YUM, *followed by* POOH-BAH.] Close thing that, for here he comes!

4. JOSEPH CONRAD, *HEART OF DARKNESS*

Joseph Conrad (1857–1924) was born in the Ukraine of Polish parents. He was fascinated by the sea, and in 1874, he joined the crew of a French vessel in Marseilles. For the next twenty years, he worked as a seaman on a variety of boats, traveling to the Caribbean, Asia, and the South Pacific. In 1890, he captained an African river steamer that sailed up the Congo River, although his command was cut short by malaria and dysentery. This trip allowed him to see the region that would become the setting for *Heart of Darkness,* and also encouraged a lifelong revulsion to European colonial empires because of the exploitation he saw in the Belgian Congo. He became a British subject in 1886, and settled in England in 1896. This ended his life at sea and allowed him to begin a second career as a writer. His years as a sailor provided him with material for most of his novels and short stories. "Heart of Darkness," published in 1899 in *Blackwood's Magazine,* is one of his best-known short stories.

Heart of Darkness

"Two pilgrims were quarrelling in hurried whispers as to which bank. 'Left.' 'No, no; how can you? Right, right, of course.' 'It is very serious,' said the manager's voice behind me; 'I would be desolated if anything should happen to Mr. Kurtz before we came up.' I looked at him, and had not the slightest doubt he was sincere. He was just the kind of man who would wish to preserve appearances. That was his restraint. But when he muttered something about going on at once, I did not even take the trouble to answer him. I knew, and he knew, that it was impossible. Were we to let go our hold of the bottom, we would be absolutely in the air—in space. We wouldn't be able to tell where we were going to—

whether up or down stream, or across—till we fetched against one bank or the other,—and then we wouldn't know at first which it was. Of course I made no move. I had no mind for a smash-up. You couldn't imagine a more deadly place for a shipwreck. Whether drowned at once or not, we were sure to perish speedily in one way or another. 'I authorize you to take all the risks,' he said, after a short silence. 'I refuse to take any,' I said, shortly; which was just the answer he expected, though its tone might have surprised him. 'Well, I must defer to your judgment. You are captain,' he said, with marked civility. I turned my shoulder to him in sign of my appreciation, and looked into the fog. How long would it last? It was the most hopeless look-out. The approach to this Kurtz grubbing for ivory in the wretched bush was beset by as many dangers as though he had been an enchanted princess sleeping in a fabulous castle. 'Will they attack, do you think?' asked the manager, in a confidential tone.

"I did not think they would attack, for several obvious reasons. The thick fog was one. If they left the bank in their canoes they would get lost in it, as we would be if we attempted to move. Still, I had also judged the jungle of both banks quite impenetrable—and yet eyes were in it, eyes that had seen us. The river-side bushes were certainly very thick; but the undergrowth behind was evidently penetrable. However, during the short lift I had seen no canoes anywhere in the reach—certainly not abreast of the steamer. But what made the idea of attack inconceivable to me was the nature of the noise—of the cries we had heard. They had not the fierce character boding immediate hostile intention. Unexpected, wild, and violent as they had been, they had given me an irresistible impression of sorrow. The glimpse of the steamboat had for some reason filled those savages with unrestrained grief. The danger, if any, I expounded, was from our proximity to a great human passion let loose. Even extreme grief may ultimately vent itself in violence—but more generally takes the form of apathy. . . .

"You should have seen the pilgrims stare! They had no heart to grin, or even to revile me: but I believe they thought me gone mad—with fright, maybe. I delivered a regular lecture. My dear boys, it was no good bothering. Keep a look-out? Well, you may guess I watched the fog for the signs of lifting as a cat watches a mouse; but for anything else our eyes were of no more use to us than if we had been buried miles deep in a heap of cotton-wool. It felt like it, too—choking, warm, stifling. Besides, all I said, though it sounded extravagant, was absolutely true to fact. What we afterwards allude to as an attack was really an attempt at repulse. The action was very far from being aggressive—it was not even defensive, in the usual sense: it was undertaken under the stress of desperation, and in its essence was purely protective.

"It developed itself, I should say, two hours after the fog lifted, and its commencement was at a spot, roughly speaking, about a mile and a half below Kurtz's station. We had just floundered and flopped round a bend, when I saw an islet, a mere grassy hummock of bright green, in the middle of the stream. It was the only thing of the kind; but as we opened the reach more, I perceived it was the head of a long sandbank, or rather of a chain of shallow patches stretching down the middle of the river. They were discoloured, just awash, and the whole lot was seen just under the water, exactly as a man's backbone is seen running down the middle of his back under the skin. Now, as far as I did see, I could go to the right or to the left of this. I didn't know either channel, of course. The banks looked pretty well alike, the depth appeared the same; but as I had been informed the station was on the west side, I naturally headed for the western passage.

"No sooner had we fairly entered it than I became aware it was much narrower than I had supposed. To the left of us there was the long unintererupted shoal, and to the right a high, steep bank heavily overgrown with bushes. Above the bush the trees stood in serried ranks. The twigs overhung the current thickly, and from distance to distance a large limb of some tree projected rigidly over the stream. It was then well on in the afternoon, the face of the forest was gloomy, and a broad strip of shadow had already fallen on the water. In this shadow we steamed up—very slowly, as you may imagine. I sheered her well inshore—the water being deepest near the bank, as the sounding-pole informed me.

"One of my hungry and forbearing friends was sounding in the bows just below me. This steamboat was exactly like a decked scow. On the deck, there were two little teak-wood houses, with doors and windows. The boiler was in the fore-end, and the machinery right astern. Over the whole there was a light roof, supported on stanchions. The funnel projected through that roof, and in front of the funnel a small cabin built of light planks served for a pilot-house. It contained a couch, two camp-stools, a loaded Martini-Henry learning in one corner, a tiny table, and the steering-wheel. It had a wide door in front and a broad shutter at each side. All these were always thrown open, of course. I spent my days perched up there on the extreme fore-end of that roof, before the door. At night I slept, or tried to, on the couch. An athletic black belonging to some coast tribe, and educated by my poor predecessor, was the helmsman. He sported a pair of brass earrings, wore a blue cloth wrapper from the waist to the ankles, and thought all the world of himself. He was the most unstable kind of fool I had ever seen. He steered with no end of a swagger while you were by; but if he lost sight of you, he became instantly the prey of an abject funk, and would let that cripple of a steamboat get the upper hand of him in a minute.

"I was looking down at the sounding-pole, and feeling much annoyed to see at each try a little more of it stick out of that river, when I saw my poleman give up the business suddenly, and stretch himself flat on the deck, without even taking the trouble to haul his pole in. He kept hold on it though, and it trailed in the water. At the same time the fireman, whom I could also see below me, sat down abruptly before his furnace and ducked his head. I was amazed. Then I had to look at the river mighty quick, because there was a snag in the fairway. Sticks, little sticks, were flying about—thick: they were whizzing before my nose, dropping below me, striking behind me against my pilot-house. All this time the river, the shore, the woods, were very quiet—perfectly quiet. I could only hear the heavy splashing thump of the stern-wheel and the patter of these things. We cleared the snag clumsily. Arrows, by Jove! We were being shot at! I stepped in quickly to close the shutter on the land-side. That fool-helmsman, his hands on the spokes, was lifting his knees high, stamping his feet, champing his mouth, like a reined-in horse. Confound him! And we were staggering within ten feet of the bank. I had to lean right out to swing the heavy shutter, and I saw a face amongst the leaves on the level with my own, looking at me very fierce and steady; and then suddenly, as though a veil had been removed from my eyes, I made out, deep in the tangled gloom, naked breasts, arms, legs, glaring eyes,—the bush was swarming with human limbs in movement, glistening, of bronze colour. The twigs shook, swayed, and rustled, the arrows flew out of them, and then the shutter came to. 'Steer her straight,' I said to the helmsman. He held his head rigid, face forward; but his eyes rolled, he kept on lifting and setting down his feet gently, his mouth foamed a little. 'Keep quiet!' I said in a fury. I might just as well have ordered a tree not to sway in the wind. I darted out. Below me there was a great scuffle of feet on the iron deck; confused exclamations; a voice screamed, 'Can you turn back?' I caught sight of a V-shaped ripple on the water ahead. What? Another snag! A fusillade burst out under my feet. The pilgrims had opened with their Winchesters, and were simply squirting lead into that bush. A deuce of a lot of smoke came up and drove slowly forward. I swore at it. Now I couldn't see the ripple or the snag either. I stood in the doorway, peering, and the arrows came in swarms. They might have been poisoned, but they looked as though they wouldn't kill a cat. The bush began to howl. Our wood-cutters raised a warlike whoop; the report of a rifle just at my back deafened me. I glanced over my shoulder, and the pilot-house was yet full of noise and smoke when I made a dash at the wheel. The fool-nigger had dropped everything, to throw the shutter open and let off that Martini-Henry. He stood before the wide opening, glaring, and I yelled at him to come back, while I straightened the sudden twist out of that steamboat. There was no room to turn even if I had wanted to, the snag was somewhere very near ahead in that confounded smoke, there was no time to lose, so I just crowded her into the bank—right into the bank, where I knew the water was deep.

"We tore slowly along the overhanging bushes in a whirl of broken twigs and flying leaves. The fusillade below stopped short, as I had foreseen it would when the squirts got empty. I threw my head back to a glinting whizz that traversed the pilot-house, in at one shutter-hole and out at the other. Looking past that mad helmsman, who was shaking the empty rifle and yelling at the shore, I saw vague forms of men running bent double, leaping, gliding, distinct, incomplete, evanescent. Something big appeared in the air before the shutter, the rifle went overboard, and the man stepped back swiftly, looked at me over his shoulder in an extraordinary, profound, familiar manner, and fell upon my feet. The side of his head hit the wheel twice, and the end of what appeared a long cane clattered round and knocked over a little camp-stool. It looked as though after wrenching that thing from somebody ashore he had lost his balance in the effort. The thin smoke had blown away, we were clear of the snag, and looking ahead I could see that in another hundred yards or so I would be free to sheer off, away from the bank; but my feet felt so very warm and wet that I had to look down. The man had rolled on his back and stared straight up at me; both his hands clutched that cane. It was the shaft of a spear that, either thrown or lunged through the opening, had caught him in the side just below the ribs; the blade had gone in out of sight, after making a frightful gash; my shoes were full; a pool of blood lay very still, gleaming dark-red under the wheel; his eyes shone with an amazing lustre. The fusillade burst out again. He looked at me anxiously, gripping the spear like something precious, with an air of being afraid I would try to take it away from him. I had to make an effort to free my eyes from his gaze and attend to the steering. With one hand I felt above my head for the line of the steam whistle, and jerked out screech after screech hurriedly. The tumult of angry and warlike yells was checked instantly, and then from the depths of the woods went out such a tremulous and prolonged wail of mournful fear and utter despair as may be imagined to follow the flight of the last hope from the earth. There was a great commotion in the bush; the shower of arrows stopped, a few dropping shots rang out sharply—then silence, in which the languid beat of the stern-wheel came plainly to my ears. I put the helm hard a-starboard at the moment when the pilgrim in pink pyjamas, very hot and agitated, appeared in the doorway. 'The manager sends me—' he began in an official tone, and stopped short. 'Good God!, he said, glaring at the wounded man.

"We two whites stood over him, and his lustrous and inquiring glance enveloped us both. I declare it looked as though he would presently put to us some question in an understandable language; but he died without uttering a sound, without moving a limb, without twitching a muscle. Only in the very last moment, as though in response to some sign we could not see, to some whisper we could not hear, he frowned heavily, and that frown gave to his black death-mask an inconceivably sombre, brooding, and menacing expression. The lustre of inquiring glance faded swiftly into vacant glassiness. 'Can you steer?' I asked the agent eagerly. He looked very dubious; but I made a grab at his arm, and he understood at once I meant him to steer whether or no. To tell you the truth, I was morbidly anxious to change my shoes and socks. 'He is dead,' murmured the fellow, immensely impressed. 'No doubt about it,' said I, tugging like mad at the shoe-laces. 'And by the way, I suppose Mr. Kurtz is dead as well by this time.'"

5. E. M. FORSTER, *A PASSAGE TO INDIA*

Edward Morgan Forster (1879–1970) was educated in English public school and at King's College at Cambridge University, where he met and became friendly with the group of writers who would become known as the Bloomsbury Group. By 1910, he had established himself as a significant literary figure, publishing the well-received *A Room with a View* and *Howard's End*. He visited India for the first time in 1912–1913, traveling with the Indian Muslim patriot Syed Ross Masood, for whom he had been a tutor years earlier. In 1921–1922, he returned to India, working as secretary to the maharajah of the state of Dewas Senior. *A Passage to India* was published to widespread acclaim in 1924. It proved to be Forster's last novel: for the rest of his life, he devoted himself to short fiction and literary criticism.

A Passage to India

"To work, Mary, to work," cried the Collector, touching his wife on the shoulder with a switch.

Mrs. Turton got up awkwardly. "What do you want one to do? Oh, those purdah women! I never thought any would come. Oh dear!"

A little group of Indian ladies had been gathering in a third quarter of the grounds, near a rustic summer-house in which the more timid of them had already taken refuge. The rest stood with their backs to the company and their faces pressed into a bank of shrubs. At a little distance stood their male relatives, watching the venture. The sight was significant: an island bared by the turning tide, and bound to grow.

"I consider they ought to come over to me."

"Come along, Mary, get it over."

"I refuse to shake hands with any of the men, unless it has to be the Nawab Bahadur."

"Whom have we so far?" He glanced along the line. "H'm! h'm! much as one expected. We know why he's here, I think—over that contract, and he wants to get the right side of me for Mohurram, and he's the astrologer who wants to dodge the municipal building regulations, and he's that Parsi, and he's—Hullo! there he goes—smash into our hollyhocks. Pulled the left rein when he meant the right. All as usual."

"They ought never to have been allowed to drive in; it's so bad for them," said Mrs. Turton, who had at last begun her progress to the summer-house, accompanied by Mrs. Moore, Miss Quested, and a terrier. "Why they come at all I don't know. They hate it as much as we do. Talk to Mrs. McBryde. Her husband made her give purdah parties until she struck."

"This isn't a purdah party," corrected Miss Quested.

"Oh, really," was the haughty rejoinder.

"Do kindly tell us who these ladies are," asked Mrs. Moore.

"You're superior to them, anyway. Don't forget that. You're superior to everyone in India except one or two of the Ranis, and they're on an equality."

Advancing, she shook hands with the group and said a few words of welcome in Urdu. She had learnt the lingo, but only to speak to her servants, so she knew none of the politer forms and of the verbs only the imperative mood. As soon as her speech was over, she enquired of her companions, "Is that what you wanted?"

"Please tell these ladies that I wish we could speak their language, but we have only just come to their country."

"Perhaps we speak yours a little," one of the ladies said.

"Why, fancy, she understands!" said Mrs. Turton.

"Eastbourne, Piccadilly, High Park Corner," said another of the ladies.

"Oh yes, they're English-speaking."

"But now we can talk: how delightful!" cried Adela, her face lighting up.

"She knows Paris also," called one of the onlookers.

"They pass Paris on the way, no doubt," said Mrs. Turton, as if she was describing the movements of migratory birds. Her manner had grown more distant since she had discovered that some of the group was Westernized, and might apply her own standards to her.

"The shorter lady, she is my wife, she is Mrs. Bhattacharya," the onlooker explained. "The taller lady, she is my sister, she is Mrs. Das."

The shorter and the taller ladies both adjusted their saris, and smiled. There was a curious uncertainty about their gestures, as if they sought for a new formula which neither East nor West could provide. When Mrs. Bhattacharya's husband spoke, she turned away from him, but she did not mind seeing the other men. Indeed all the ladies were uncertain, cowering, recovering, giggling, making tiny gestures of atonement or despair at all that was said, and alternately fondling the terrier or shrinking from him. Miss Quested now had her desired opportunity; friendly Indians were before her, and she tried to make them talk, but she failed, she strove in vain against the echoing walls of their civility. Whatever she said produced a murmur of deprecation, varying into a murmur of concern when she dropped her pocket-handkerchief. She tried doing nothing, to see what that produced, and they too did nothing. Mrs. Moore was equally unsuccessful. Mrs. Turton waited for them with a detached expression; she had known what nonsense it all was from the first.

When they took their leave, Mrs. Moore had an impulse, and said to Mrs. Bhattacharya, whose face she liked, "I wonder whether you would allow us to call on you some day."

"When?" she replied, inclining charmingly.

"Whenever is convenient."

"All days are convenient."

"Thursday . . ."

"Most certainly."

"We shall enjoy it greatly, it would be a real pleasure. What about the time?"

"All hours."

"Tell us which you would prefer. We're quite strangers to your country; we don't know when you have visitors," said Miss Quested.

Mrs. Bhattacharya seemed not to know either. Her gesture implied that she had known, since Thursdays began, that English ladies would come to see her on one of them, and so always stayed in. Everything pleased her, nothing surprised. She added, "We leave for Calcutta to-day."

"Oh, do you?" said Adela, not at first seeing the implication. Then she cried, "Oh, but if you do we shall find you gone."

Mrs. Bhattacharya did not dispute it. But her husband called from the distance, "Yes, yes, you come to us Thursday."

"But you'll be in Calcutta."

"No, no, we shall not." He said something swiftly to his wife in Bengali. "We expect you Thursday."

"Thursday . . ." the woman echoed.

"You can't have done such a dreadful thing as to put off going for our sake?" exclaimed Mrs. Moore.

"No, of course not, we are not such people." He was laughing.

"I believe that you have. Oh, please—it distresses me beyond words."

Everyone was laughing now, but with no suggestion that they had blundered. A shapeless discussion occurred, during which Mrs. Turton retired, smiling to herself. The upshot was that they were to come Thursday, but early in the morning, so as to wreck the Bhattacharya plans as little as possible, and Mr. Bhattacharya would send his carriage to fetch them, with servants to point out the way. Did he know where they lived? Yes, of course he knew, he knew everything; and he laughed again. They left among a flutter of compliments and smiles, and three ladies, who had hitherto taken no part in the reception, suddenly shot out of the summer-house like exquisitely coloured swallows, and salaamed them.

Meanwhile the Collector had been going his rounds. He made pleasant remarks and a few jokes, which were applauded lustily, but he knew something to the discredit of nearly every one of his guests, and was consequently perfunctory. When they had not cheated, it was bhang, women, or worse, and even the desirables wanted to get something out of him. He believed that a "Bridge Party" did good rather than harm, or he would not have given one, but he was under no illusions, and at the proper moment he retired to the English side of the lawn. The impressions he left behind him were various. Many of the guests, especially the humbler and less Anglicized, were genuinely grateful. To be addressed by so high an official was a permanent asset. They did not mind how long they stood, or how little happened, and when seven o'clock struck, they had to be turned out. Others were grateful with more intelligence. The Nawab Bahadur, indifferent for himself and for the distinction with which he was greeted, was moved by the mere kindness that must have prompted the invitation. He knew the difficulties. Hamidullah also thought that the Collector had played up well. But others, such as Mahmoud Ali, were cynical; they were firmly convinced that Turton had been made to give the party by his official superiors and was all the time consumed with impotent rage, and they infected some who were inclined to a healthier view. Yet even Mahmoud Ali was glad he had come. Shrines are fascinating, especially when rarely opened, and it amused him to note the ritual of the English club, and to caricature it afterwards to his friends.

After Mr. Turton, the official who did his duty best was Mr. Fielding, the Principal of the little Government College. He knew little of the district and less against the inhabitants, so he was in a less cynical state of mind. Athletic and cheerful, he romped about, making numerous mistakes which the parents of his pupils tried to cover up, for he was popular among them. When the moment for refreshments came, he did not move back to the English side, but burnt his mouth with gram. He talked to anyone and he ate anything. Amid much that was alien, he learnt that the two new ladies from England had been a great success, and that their politeness in wishing to be Mrs. Bhattacharya's guests had pleased not only her but all Indians who heard of it. It pleased Mr. Fielding also. He scarcely knew the two new ladies, still he decided to tell them what pleasure they had given by their friendliness.

He found the younger of them alone. She was looking through a nick in the cactus hedge at the distant Marabar Hills, which had crept near, as was their custom at sunset; if the sunset had lasted long enough, they would have reached the town, but it was swift, being tropical. He gave her his information, and she was so much pleased and thanked him so heartily that he asked her and the other lady to tea.

"I'd like to come very much indeed, and so would Mrs. Moore, I know."

"I'm rather a hermit, you know."

"Much the best thing to be in this place."

"Owing to my work and so on, I don't get up much to the club."

"I know, I know, and we never get down from it. I envy you being with Indians."

"Do you care to meet one or two?"

"Very, very much indeed; it's what I long for. This party to-day makes me so angry and miserable. I think my countrymen out here must be mad. Fancy inviting guests and not treating them properly! You and Mr. Turton and perhaps Mr. McBryde are the only people who showed any common politeness. The rest make me perfectly ashamed, and it's got worse and worse."

It had. The Englishmen had intended to play up better, but had been prevented from doing so by their women folk, whom they had to attend, provide with tea, advise about dogs, etc. When tennis began, the barrier grew impenetrable. It had been hoped to have some sets between East and West, but this was forgotten, and the courts were monopolized by the usual club couples. Fielding resented it too, but did not say so to the girl, for he found something theoretical in her outburst. Did she care about Indian music? he enquired; there was an old professor down at the College, who sang.

"Oh, just what we wanted to hear. And do you know Doctor Aziz?"

"I know all about him. I don't know him. Would you like him asked too?"

"Mrs. Moore says he is so nice."

"Very well, Miss Quested. Will Thursday suit you?"

"Indeed it will, and that morning we go to this Indian lady's. All the nice things are coming Thursday."

"I won't ask the City magistrate to bring you. I know he'll be busy at that time."

"Yes, Ronny is always hard-worked," she replied, contemplating the hills. How lovely they suddenly were! But she couldn't touch them. In front, like a shutter, fell a vision of her married life. She and Ronny would look into the club like this every evening, then drive home to dress; they would see the Lesleys and the Callendars and the Turtons and the Burtons, and invite them and be invited by them, while the true India slid by unnoticed. Colour would remain—the pageant of birds in the early morning, brown bodies, white turbans, idols whose flesh was scarlet or blue—and movement would remain as long as there were crowds in the bazaar and bathers in the tanks. Perched up on the seat of a dogcart, she would see them. But the force that lies behind colour and movement would escape her even more effectually than it did now. She would see India always as a frieze, never as a spirit, and she assumed that it was a spirit of which Mrs. Moore had had a glimpse.

6. CLIVE LEADING THE STORMING PARTY AT DEVIKOTA IN G. A. HENTY, WITH CLIVE IN INDIA

George Alfred Henty (1832–1902), whose own life almost coincided with the reign of Queen Victoria, was an embodiment of and contributor to the Victorian imperial ideal. He covered the Crimean War early in his career as a journalist. Later, he wrote numerous books for children expressing his firm belief in British imperialism. Historical and contemporary incidents from the British Empire were the settings for tales of adventure, daring, and heroism. His books were instrumental in establishing juvenile literature as a genre of literature, and his works were among the most popular of this type. He therefore contributed to communicating to hundreds of thousands of Victorian children his vision of the ideals of the British Empire.

Figure 22.1 Clive Leading the Storming Party at Devikota. Courtesy of Blackie & Son.

Study Questions

1. What effect do Flaubert's assumptions about differences between men and women have on his depiction of Salammbô?
2. How does Loti describe the personality of Aziyadé?
3. What is the view of the Japanese that Gilbert presents in this excerpt?
4. What is the effect of traveling up the river on the narrator of *Heart of Darkness*?
5. How would you describe the relationship between Mrs. Moore and Mrs. Bhattacharya in *A Passage to India*? In what way is this relationship the result of their both being women? In what way is it affected by one of them being English and the other Indian?
6. What does the illustration suggest about the role of Clive in India?

Suggestions for Further Reading

Ashley, Leonard. *George Alfred Henty and the Victorian Mind.* San Francisco, CA: International Scholars Publications, 1999.

Batchelor, John. *The Life of Joseph Conrad.* Cambridge, MA: Blackwell, 1994.

Blanch, Lesley. *Pierre Loti: The Legendary Romantic.* San Diego, CA: Harcourt Brace Jovanovich, 1983.

Hargreaves, Alec G. *The Colonial Experience in French Fiction.* London: MacMillan Press Ltd., 1981.

Lee, Robert F. *Conrad's Colonialism.* The Hague: Mouton, 1969.

Said, Edward W. *Culture and Imperialism.* New York: Random House, 1993.

Shahane, Vasant Anant. *E. M. Forster: A Study in Double Vision.* New Delhi: Arnold-Heinemann Publishers, 1975.

Stedman, Jane W. *W. S. Gilbert: A Classic Victorian and His Theatre.* New York: Oxford University Press, 1996.

Web Sites

1. Joseph Conrad (1857–1924)

   http://www.lang.nagoya-u.ac.jp/~matsuoka/Conrad.html

2. Edward Morgan Forster (1879–1970)

   http://www.kirjasto.sci.fi/forster.htm

3. The Fourteen Gilbert and Sullivan Operas

   http:diamond/idbsu.edu/gas/#sullivan

4. The Novels of Pierre Loti

   http:www.personal.kent.edu/~rberrong/loti.htm

23

Anthropology and Ethnography
1871–1922

TEXT

1. E. B. Tylor, *Primitive Culture*

2. *Intichiuma Ceremony of Water Totem* from Baldwin Spencer and F. J. Gillen, *The Native Tribes of Central Australia*

3. Franz Boas, *The Mind of Primitive Man*

4. Emile Durkheim, *The Elementary Forms of the Religious Life*

5. Bronsilaw Malinowski, *Argonauts of the Western Pacific*

6. Bronsilaw Malinowski, *A Diary in the Strict Sense of the Term, 1914–15*

Europeans in the early nineteenth century continued, as during the Enlightenment, to speak about the "progress of civilization," and contrasts with non-European "savages" played a part in this discussion as a contrast to civilization itself. By 1850, however, the cultural history of the German Romantic Johann Gottfried Herder, the positive philosophy of the French sociologist Auguste Comte, and English utilitarian reflections on the French and Industrial Revolutions had created significant cracks in the universalist Enlightenment vision of mankind. These contributed to the development of the generally evolutionist approach taken in European debates about the origins of mankind and about race that became prominent around midcentury through the writings of Arthur de Gobineau and others. The work on evolution of Herbert Spencer, Francis Galton, and Charles Darwin gave a strongly scientific caste to these discussions about human civilization.

These had a great influence on the development in the late nineteenth century of a social science, anthropology, which claimed to be able to speak authoritatively about non-Europeans and their relationship to Europeans. Early anthropological work had joined in the Enlightenment project of speculative grand theories about the human race and its development. By the 1860s, however, it was moving toward a more empirical "science of man," but one that was increasingly marked by an evolutionary approach. This evolutionary approach was based on a number of interrelated assumptions: the psychic unity of mankind that posited the rationality of all humans; uniform stages of development that related civilizations to each other; a doctrine that emphasized the survival of customs from one stage of cultural development to another; and a comparative method that aimed at classification of data in a scientific fashion. Using what materials were at hand, such as literary texts and travel accounts, John Lubbock, John McLennan, and especially E. B. Tylor, and his successor, James Frazer, wrote highly respected accounts of the mechanisms by which civilizations had progressed over time. [1]

The increased professionalism of anthropology made it a strong voice in describing the relationships between Europeans and non-Europeans, especially those living in the parts of Asia, Africa, and Australia that were coming under formal European empire. The tension in late-nineteenth-century anthropology between empiricism and the social evolutionary approach brought about the decline of this evolutionary approach. Beginning just before the turn of the century and gaining strength in the aftermath of the First World War, a "revolution in anthropology" occurred that made fieldwork, the immersion of the anthropologist in a foreign culture, the central methodology of the discipline. [2] Missionary anthropologists such as Lorimer Fison in Fiji and Robert Hendry Codrington in Melanesia began in the 1880s and 1890s to produce field enthnographic accounts that increasingly provided the basis for anthropological theorizing. In the 1890s, Franz Boas began his career as a new type of anthropologist—often trained as a physical scientist (in Boas's case physics) and involved directly in the collection and theoretical evaluation of ethnographic evidence. [3] The most notable event in this development was the Cambridge Anthropological Expedition to the Torres Straits led by Alfred Cort Haddon in 1898–1899. By the turn of the century, Tylor was complaining that it was virtually impossible to keep up on the new information becoming available on other cultures. Not only was it becoming impossible for an anthropologist to claim authority without having done fieldwork, but also the information being generated in this way led men such as Andrew Lang to attack the evolutionary framework in which Tylor and Frazer had discussed subjects such as animism, totemism, and religion.

Assumptions of similar mental structures for both the subjects of ethnography and the Europeans who undertook those studies were reconsidered in the early twentieth century in France, where social science was strongly influenced by Emile Durkheim [4] and his student, Marcel Mauss. In the period between the world wars, the strongest statement on this subject came from Lucien Lévy-Bruhl, who argued that "primitives" were "prelogical" with a mental structure different from that of civilized men. But beginning in the 1930s, and becoming dominant after the second World War, the structuralist anthropology of Claude Lévi-Strauss revived the argument for a single mental structure common to all humans. Lévi-Strauss's career and work indicate both the continued attraction of a scientific inquiry into other cultures and the European desire for an all-encompassing theory of mankind, European and non-European.

By the First World War, both anthropological method and theory were also developing toward more empirical study of non-European cultures. The anthropologist who confirmed the central role of fieldwork in this form in the discipline, and whose work pointed toward dehistoricized functionalism rather than evolutionism or diffusionism, was Bronislaw Malinowski, whose work on the Trobriand Islands provided the model for twentieth-century anthropological fieldwork. Malinowski laid down, in the first chapter of his *Argonauts of the Western Pacific,* the methodological rules for the new anthropology, summarizing the practices that had been developing slowly since the turn of the century. But, as Malinowski's own diaries reveal, maintaining this methodological position proved difficult, as his own European culture intervened in his relations with the Trobrianders. [5, 6] At the same time as Malinowski, another British anthropologist, A. R. Radcliffe-Brown, who was strongly influenced by the French sociologist Emile Durkheim, was also moving away from evolutionist theory by arguing that the important question about any social phenomena was its function in a society that tended to remain in equilibrium—the basis of structuralist-functionalism in twentieth-century social science.

1. E. B. Tylor, *Primitive Culture*

Edward Burnett Tylor (1832–1917) was born to a prosperous Quaker family in England. His Quaker beliefs made it impossible to pass the religious tests of English universities at the time, however, and his advanced education came only at a school maintained by the Society of Friends. On a trip to Cuba in 1856, he met and began to work with Henry Christy, a businessman who had taken up archaeology and ethnography. In the course of studies of antiquity in Mexico, he noticed the survival of ancient customs into civilized societies and became convinced of the fundamental similarity of human minds. This led him to develop his interest in the development of society, and he began to pursue the foundation of a science of culture. The publication of his account of the Mexican expedition in 1861, and *Researches in the Early History of Mankind* in 1865, established him as a leading figure in the developing discipline of anthropology. At a time when discoveries in geology, archaeology, and biology were establishing the idea of evolution, Tylor became one of the principal exponents of the school of evolutionary anthropology. Although he denied being influenced by Darwin, and he was not an uncritical, unilinear evolutionist, he did argue for a progressive theory of cultural development. Although he was not in general a field researcher during his long career, Tylor did develop rules for evaluating the numerous and varied accounts of non-Western cultures that he employed. *Primitive Culture,* published in 1871, demonstrated, according to Tylor, the primacy of Primitive Man in the chronological development of culture.

Primitive Culture

In taking up the problem of the development of culture as a branch of ethnological research, a first proceeding is to obtain a means of measurement. Seeking something like a definite line along which to reckon progression and retrogression in civilization, we may apparently find it best in the classification of real tribes and nations, past and present. Civilization actually existing among mankind in different grades, we are enabled to estimate and compare it by positive examples. The educated world of Europe and America practically settles a standard by simply placing its own nations at one end of the social series and savage tribes at the other, arranging the rest of mankind between these limits according as they correspond more closely to savage or to cultured life. The principal criteria of classification are the absence or presence, high or low development, of the industrial arts, especially metal-working, manufacture of implements and vessels, agriculture, architecture, &c., the extent of scientific knowledge, the definiteness of moral principles, the condition of religious belief and ceremony, the degree of social and political organization, and so forth. Thus, on the definite basis of compared facts, ethnographers are able to set up at least a rough scale of civilization. Few would dispute that the following races are arranged rightly in order of culture:—Australian, Tahitian, Aztec, Chinese, Italian. By treating the development of civilization on this plain ethnographic basis, many difficulties may be avoided which have embarrassed its discussion. This may be seen by a glance at the relation which theoretical principles of civilization bear to the transitions to be observed as matter of fact between the extremes of savage and cultured life.

From an ideal point of view, civilization may be looked upon as the general improvement of mankind by higher organization of the individual and of society, to the end of promoting at once man's goodness, power, and happiness. This theoretical civilization does in no small measure correspond with actual civilization, as traced by comparing savagery with barbarism, and barbarism with modern educated life. So far as we take into account only material and intellectual culture, this is especially true. Acquaintance with the physical laws of the world, and the accompanying power of adapting nature to man's own ends, are, on the whole, lowest among savages, mean among barbarians, and highest among modern educated nations. Thus a transition from the savage state to our own would be, practically, that very progress of art and knowledge which is one main element in the development of culture.

But even those students who hold most strongly that the general course of civilization, as measured along the scale of races from savages to ourselves, is progress towards the benefit of mankind, must admit many and manifold exceptions. Industrial and intellectual culture by no means advances uniformly in all its branches, and in fact excellence in various of its details is often obtained under conditions which keep back culture as a whole. It is true that these exceptions seldom swamp the general rule; and the Englishman, admitting that he does not climb trees like the wild Australian, nor track game like the savage of the Brazilian forest, nor compete with the ancient Etruscan and the modern Chinese in delicacy of goldsmith's work and ivory carving, nor reach the classic Greek level of oratory and sculpture, may yet claim for himself a general condition above any of these races. But there actually have to be taken into account developments of science and art which tend directly against culture. To have learnt to give poison secretly and effectually, to have raised a corrupt literature to pestilent perfection, to have organized a successful scheme to arrest free enquiry and proscribe free expression, are works of knowledge and skill whose progress toward their goal has hardly conduced to the general good. Thus, even in comparing mental and artistic culture among several peoples, the balance of good and ill is not quite easy to strike.

If not only knowledge and art, but at the same time moral and political excellence, be taken into consideration, it becomes yet harder to reckon on an ideal scale the advance or decline from stage to stage of culture. In fact, a combined intellectual and moral measure of human condition is an instrument which no student has as yet learnt properly to handle. Even granting that intellectual, moral, and political life may, on a broad view, be seen to progress together, it is obvious that they are far from advancing with equal steps. It may be taken as man's rule of duty in the world, that he shall strive to know as well as he can find out, and to do as well as he knows how. But the parting asunder of these two great principles, that separation of intelligence from virtue which accounts for so much of the wrong-doing of mankind, is continually seen to happen in the great movements of civilization. As one conspicuous instance of what all history stands to prove, if we study the early ages of Christianity, we may see men with minds pervaded by the new religion of duty, holiness, and love, yet at the same time actually falling away in intellectual life, thus at once vigorously grasping one half of civilization, and contemptuously casting off the other. Whether in high ranges or in low of human life, it may be seen that advance of culture seldom results at once in unmixed good. Courage, honesty, generosity, are virtues which may suffer, at least for a time, by the development of a sense of value of life and property. The savage who adopts something of foreign civilization too often loses his ruder virtues without gaining an equivalent. The white invader or colonist, though representing on the whole a higher moral standard than the savage he improves or destroys, often represents his standard very ill, and at best can hardly claim to substitute a life stronger, nobler, and purer at every point than that which he supersedes. The onward movement from barbarism has dropped behind it more than one quality of barbaric character, which cultured modern men look back on with regret, and will even strive to regain by futile attempts to stop the course of history, and restore the past in the midst of the present. So it is with social institutions. The slavery recognized by savage and barbarous races is preferable in kind to that which existed for centuries in late European colonies. The relation of the sexes among many savage tribes is more healthy than among the richer classes of the Mahommedan world. As a supreme authority of government, the savage councils of chiefs and elders compare favourably with the unbridled despotism under which so many cultured races have groaned. The Creek Indians, asked concerning their religion, replied that where agreement was not to be had, it was best to "let every man paddle his canoe his own way:" and after long ages of theological strife and persecution, the modern world seems coming to think these savages not far wrong.

Among accounts of savage life, it is not, indeed, uncommon to find details of admirable moral and social excellence. To take one prominent instance, Lieut. Bruijn Kops and Mr. Wallace have described, among the rude Papuans of the Eastern Archipelago, a habitual truthfulness, rightfulness, and kindliness which it would be hard to match in the general moral life of Persia or India, to say nothing of many a civilized European district. Such tribes may count as the "blameless Ethiopians" of the modern world, and from them an important lesson may be learnt. Ethnographers who seek in modern savages types of the remotely ancient human race at large, are bound by such examples to consider the rude life of primæval man under favourable conditions to have been, in its measure, a good and happy life. On the other hand, the pictures drawn by some travellers of savagery as a kind of paradisaical state may be taken too exclusively from the bright side. It is remarked as to these very Papuans, that Europeans whose intercourse with them has been hostile become so impressed with the wild-beast-like cunning of their attacks, as hardly to believe in their having feelings in common with civilized men. Our Polar explorers may well speak in kindly terms of the industry, the honesty, the cheerful considerate politeness of the Esquimaux; but it must be remembered that these rude people are on their best behaviour with foreigners, and that their character is apt to be foul and brutal where they have nothing to expect or fear. The Caribs are described as a cheerful, modest, courteous race, and so honest among themselves that if they missed anything out of a house they said quite naturally, "There has been a Christian here." Yet the malignant ferocity with which these estimable people tortured their prisoners of war with knife and fire-brand and red pepper, and then cooked and ate them in solemn debauch, gave fair reason for the name of Carib (Cannibal) to become the generic name of man-eaters in European languages. So when we read descriptions of the hospitality, the gentleness, the bravery, the deep religious feeling of the North American Indians, we admit their claims to our sincere admiration; but we must not forget that they were hospitable literally to a fault, that their gentleness would pass with a flash of anger into frenzy, that their bravery was stained with cruel and treacherous malignity, that their religion expressed itself in absurd belief and useless ceremony. The ideal savage of the 18th century might be held up as a living reproof to vicious and frivolous London; but in sober fact, a Londoner who should attempt to lead the atrocious life which the real savage may lead with impunity and even respect, would be a criminal only allowed to follow his savage models during his short intervals out of gaol. Savage moral standards are real enough, but they are far looser and weaker than ours. We may, I think, apply the

often-repeated comparison of savages to children as fairly to their moral as to their intellectual condition. The better savage social life seems in but unstable equilibrium, liable
to be easily upset by a touch of distress, temptation, or violence, and then it becomes the
worse savage life, which we know by so many dismal and hideous examples. Altogether,
it may be admitted that some rude tribes lead a life to be envied by some barbarous
races, and even by the outcasts of higher nations. But that any known savage tribe would
not be improved by judicious civilization, is a proposition which no moralist would dare
to make; while the general tenour of the evidence goes far to justify the view that on the
whole the civilized man is not only wiser and more capable than the savage, but also
better and happier, and that the barbarian stands between.

It might, perhaps, seem practicable to compare the whole average of the civilization of two peoples, or of the same people in different ages, by reckoning each, item by
item, to a sort of sum-total, and striking a balance between them, much as an appraiser
compares the value of two stocks of merchandise, differ as they may both in quantity
and quality. But the few remarks here made will have shown how loose must be the
working-out of these rough-and-ready estimates of culture. In fact, much of the labour
spent in investigating the progress and decline of civilization has been mis-spent, in pre-
mature attempts to treat that as a whole which is as yet only susceptible of divided study.
The present comparatively narrow argument on the development of culture at any rate
avoids this greatest perplexity. It takes cognizance principally of knowledge, art, and custom, and indeed only very partial cognizance within this field, the vast range of physical,
political, social, and ethical considerations being left all but untouched. Its standard of
reckoning progress and decline is not that of ideal good and evil, but of movement
along a measured line from grade to grade of actual savagery, barbarism, and civilization. The thesis which I venture to sustain, within limits, is simply this, the savage state in
some measure represents an early condition of mankind, out of which the higher culture
has gradually been developed or evolved, by processes still in regular operation as of
old, the result showing that, on the whole, progress has far prevailed over relapse.

2. *Intichiuma Ceremony of Water Totem* from *Baldwin Spencer and F. J. Gillen, The Native Tribes of Central Australia*

Walter Baldwin Spencer (1860–1929) was trained as a biologist, but attended
E. B. Tylor's lectures at Oxford and became fascinated by the developing science of ethnography. In 1886, he become professor of biology at the University of Melbourne in Australia, where he was able to continue to explore this
interest even as he developed the botany and zoology programs there. In
1894, he was appointed as expedition zoologist on a scientific expedition that
traveled into the central Australian desert, near the town of Alice Springs.
Frank Gillen, the station manager of the transcontinental telegraph station in
Alice Springs, helped Spencer through his contacts with the Arunta aborig-
ines who lived in that part of the continent.

Figure 23.1. Intichiuma Ceremony of Water Totem. Courtesy of A. C. McClurg & Co.

In 1896, Gillen was able to arrange with the Arunta to hold a great ceremony known as Engwiera (engwura) at Alice Springs, and for three months he and Spencer lived in the midst of the ceremonies, an unprecedent ethnographic opportunity. The resulting book, *The Native Tribes of Central Australia* (1899), although it remained linked to the evolutionary views of Tylor and Frazer, emphasized the role of the results of fieldwork more than had the works of Spencer and Gillen's "armchair" predecessors. A significant part of the work consists of photographs such as this one taken by Spencer and Gillen of the ceremonies and their participants.

3. FRANZ BOAS, *THE MIND OF PRIMITIVE MAN*

Franz Boas (1858–1942) was born in Germany and completed a doctorate in physics at the University of Kiel in 1881. A few years later, he joined a geographic study of Baffin Land, but his work on that expedition also included ethnographic investigations of the Eskimos who lived in the region. This led him to shift his emphasis to anthropology, and after studying anthropometry, he began his career working among the Indians who lived on the Northwest Coast of British Columbia, a location he would return to many times for field-work in the course of his career. In 1887, he moved from Germany to New York, and in 1896 joined the faculty of Columbia University, where he remained until 1936. One of the most important figures in founding the discipline of anthropology in American universities, he trained numerous students who helped develop a particularly American form of anthropology, which was strongly influenced by Boas's views. In particular, he disagreed with the evolutionary approach current in British anthropology around the turn of the century, and argued instead that neither race, physical type, nor geographic conditions determine human cultures. Establishing the complexity and independence of human cultures led Boas to discount the unilinear theories of progression from one level of civilization to another that marked evolutionary anthropology, as well as to argue that learning and habit are the foundation of human behavior, not instinct or heredity.

The Mind of Primitive Man

Very few travellers understand the language of the people they visit; and how is it possible to judge a tribe solely by the descriptions of interpreters, or by observations of disconnected actions the incentive of which remains unknown? But even when the language of the people in known to the visitor, he is generally an unappreciative listener to their tales. The missionary has his strong bias against the religious ideas and customs of primitive people, and the trader has no interest in their beliefs and in their barbarous arts. The observers who seriously tried to enter into the inner life of a people, the Cushings, Callaways, and Greys, are few in number, and may be counted on one's fingers. Nevertheless the bulk of the argument is always based on the statements of hasty and superficial observers.

Numerous attempts have been made to describe the peculiar psychological characteristics of primitive man. Among these I would mention those of Klemm, Carus, De Gobineau, Nott and Gliddon, Waitz, Spencer, and Tylor. Their investigations are of merit as descriptions of the characteristics of primitive people, but we cannot claim for any of them that they describe the psychological characters of races independent of their social surroundings. Klemm and Wuttke designate the civilized races as active, all others as passive, and assume that all elements and beginnings of civilization found among primitive people—in America or on the islands of the Pacific Ocean—were due to an early contact with civilization. Carus divides mankind into "peoples of the day, night and dawn." De Gobineau calls the yellow race the male element, the black race the female element, and calls only the whites the noble and gifted race. Nott and Gliddon ascribe animal instincts only to the lower races, while they declare that the white race has a higher instinct which incites and directs its development.

The belief in the higher hereditary powers of the white race has gained a new life with the modern doctrine of the prerogatives of the master-mind, which have found their boldest expression in Nietzsche's writings.

All such views are generalizations which either do not sufficiently take into account the social conditions of races, and thus confound cause and effect, or were dictated by scientific or humanitarian bias, by the desire to justify the institution of slavery, or to give the greatest freedom to the most highly gifted.

Tylor and Spencer, who give an ingenious analysis of the mental life of primitive man, do not assume that these are racial characteristics, although the evolutionary standpoint of Spencer's work often seems to convey this impression.

Quite distinct from these is Waitz's point of view. He says, "According to the current opinion the stage of culture of a people or of an individual is largely or exclusively a product of his faculty. We maintain that the reverse is at least just as true. The faculty of man does not designate anything but how much and what he is able to achieve in the immediate future and depends upon the stages of culture through which he has passed and the one he has reached."

The views of the investigators show that in the domain of psychology a confusion prevails still greater than in anatomy, as to the characteristics of primitive races, and that no clear distinction is drawn between the racial and the social problem. In other words, the evidence is based partly on the supposed mental characteristics of races, no matter what their stage of culture; partly on those of tribes and peoples on different levels of civilization, no matter whether they belong to the same race or to distinct races. Still these two problems are entirely distinct. The former is a problem of heredity; the latter, a problem of environment.

Thus we recognize that there are two possible explanations of the different manifestations of the mind of man. It may be that the minds of different races show differences of organization; that is to say, the laws of mental activity may not be the same for all minds. But it may also be that the organization of mind is practically identical among all races of man; that mental activity follows the same laws everywhere, but that its manifestations depend upon the character of individual experience that is subjected to the action of these laws.

It is quite evident that the activities of the human mind depend upon these two elements. The organization of the mind may be defined as the group of laws which determine the modes of thought and of action, irrespective of the subject-matter of mental activity. Subject to such laws are the manner of discrimination between perceptions, the manner in which perceptions associate themselves with previous perceptions, the manner in which a stimulus leads to action, and the emotions produced by stimuli. These laws determine to a great extent the manifestations of the mind. In these we recognize hereditary causes.

But, on the other hand, the influence of individual experience can easily be shown to be very great. The bulk of the experience of man is gained from oft-repeated impressions. It is one of the fundamental laws of psychology that the repetition of mental processes increases the facility with which these processes are performed, and decreases the degree of consciousness that accompanies them. This law expresses the well-known phenomena of habit. When a certain perception is frequently associated with another previous perception, the one will habitually call forth the other. When a certain stimulus frequently results in a certain action, it will tend to call forth habitually the same action. If a stimulus has often produced a certain emotion, it will tend to reproduce it every time. These belong to the group of environmental causes.

The explanation of the activity of the mind of man, therefore, requires the discussion of two distinct problems. The first bears upon the question of unity or diversity of organization of the mind, while the second bears upon the diversity produced by the variety of contents of the mind as found in the various social and geographical environments. The task of the investigator consists largely in separating these two causes, and in attributing to each its proper share in the development of the peculiarities of the mind.

We will first devote our attention to the question, Do differences exist in the organization of the human mind? Since Waitz's thorough discussion of the question of the unity of the human species, there can be no doubt that in the main the mental characteristics of man are the same all over the world; but the question remains open, whether there is a sufficient difference in grade to allow us to assume that the present races of man may be considered as standing on different stages of the evolutionary series, whether we are justified in ascribing to civilized man a higher place in organization than to primitive man.

The chief difficulty encountered in the solution of this problem has been pointed out before. It is the uncertainty as to which of the characteristics of primitive man are causes of the low stage of culture, and which are caused by it; or which of the psychological characteristics are hereditary, and would not be wiped out by the effects of civilization. The fundamental difficulty of collecting satisfactory observations lies in the fact that no large groups of primitive man are brought nowadays into conditions of real equality with whites. The gap between our society and theirs always remains open, and for this reason their minds cannot be expected to work in the same manner as ours. The same phenomenon which led us to the conclusion that primitive races of our times are not given an opportunity to develop their abilities, prevents us from judging their innate faculty.

4. EMILE DURKHEIM, *THE ELEMENTARY FORMS OF THE RELIGIOUS LIFE*

Emile Durkheim (1858–1917) was born in a village in Lorraine in eastern France. While studying for the rabbinate, he became interested in a teaching career and in 1879 entered the Ecole Normale Supérieure in Paris, the elite French training school for university teachers. While at the Ecole Normale, he was influenced by the classicist Fustel de Coulanges, who taught him the importance of religious sentiments in social institutions.

After graduating from the Ecole Normale, Durkheim taught philosophy in several provincial schools. In 1885, he studied psychology in Germany, and upon his return he was appointed lecturer at the University of Bordeaux. In 1896, this position was raised to the level of professor of sociology, the first such position in a French university. In 1902, Durkheim was named professor of sociology at the Sorbonne in Paris, where he remained until his death fifteen years later.

The general thrust of Durkheim's scholarship was to overcome the existing emphasis on individualism in social theory, a legacy of the eighteenth-century Enlightenment. He published several studies that investigated the ways in which individuals achieve consensus, the necessary condition of social existence. His doctoral thesis, *The Division of Labor in Society* (1893), distinguished between forms of solidarity in societies of differing levels, and he saw increasing differences between individuals as characteristic of the organic solidarity of modern European society. However, he realized that there had to be some beliefs in common for any society to function. He later published a work on *The Rules of Sociological Method* (1895) and an empirical study of *Suicide* (1897).

Durkheim's interest in collective beliefs led him to study *The Elementary Forms of Religious Life* (1912), a work in which he argued that religion expressed the basic categories of the human mind. Although he considered religion a social matter, depending on communal participation, his work touched on a fundamental question of anthropological inquiry, human nature. His work contributed to the growing interest in culture that anthropology expressed, and laid the groundwork for later French anthropologists such as Claude Lévi-Strauss, who after the Second World War argued that all humans, whether civilized Europeans or "savage" non-Europeans, shared the same mental structures.

The Elementary Forms of Religious Life

But our study is not of interest merely for the science of religion. In fact, every religion has one side by which it overlaps the circle of properly religious ideas, and there, the study of religious phenomena gives a means of renewing the problems which, up to the present, have only been discussed among philosophers.

For a long time it has been known that the first systems of representations with which men have pictured to themselves the world and themselves were of religious origin. There is no religion that is not a cosmology at the same time that it is a speculation upon divine things. If philosophy and the sciences were born of religion, it is because religion began by taking the place of the sciences and philosophy. But it has been less frequently noticed that religion has not confined itself to enriching the human intellect, formed beforehand, with a certain number of ideas; it has contributed to forming the intellect itself. Men owe to it not only a good part of the substance of their knowledge, but also the form in which this knowledge has been elaborated.

At the roots of all our judgments there are a certain number of essential ideas which dominate all our intellectual life; they are what philosophers since Aristotle have called the categories of the understanding: ideas of time, space, class, number, cause, substance, personality, etc. They correspond to the most universal properties of things. They are like the solid frame which encloses all thought; this does not seem to be able to liberate itself from them without destroying itself, for it seems that we cannot think of objects that are not in time and space, which have no number, etc. Other ideas are contingent and unsteady; we can conceive of their being unknown to a man, a society or an epoch; but these others appear to be nearly inseparable from the normal working of the intellect. They are like the framework of the intelligence. Now when primitive religious beliefs are systematically analysed, the principal categories are naturally found. They are born in religion and of religion; they are a product of religious thought. This is a statement that we are going to have occasion to make many times in the course of this work.

This remark has some interest of itself already; but here is what gives it its real importance.

The general conclusion of the book which the reader has before him is that religion is something eminently social. Religious representations are collective representations which express collective realities; the rites are a manner of acting which take rise in the midst of the assembled groups and which are destined to excite, maintain or recreate certain mental states in these groups. So if the categories are of religious origin, they ought to participate in this nature common to all religious facts; they too should be social affairs and the product of collective thought. At least—for in the actual condition of our knowledge of these matters, one should be careful to avoid all radical and exclusive statements—it is allowable to suppose that they are rich in social elements.

Even at present, these can be imperfectly seen in some of them. For example, try to represent what the notion of time would be without the processes by which we divide it, measure it or express it with objective signs, a time which is not a succession of years, months, weeks, days and hours! This is something nearly unthinkable. We cannot conceive of time, except on condition of distinguishing its different moments. Now what is the origin of this differentiation? Undoubtedly, the states of consciousness which we have already experienced can be reproduced in us in the same order in which they passed in the first place; thus portions of our past become present again, though being clearly distinguished from the present. But howsoever important this distinction may be for our private experience, it is far from being enough to constitute the notion or category of time. This does not consist merely in a commemoration, either partial or integral, of our past life. It is an abstract and impersonal frame which surrounds, not only our individual existence, but that of all humanity. It is like an endless chart, where all duration is spread out before the mind, and upon which all possible events can be located in relation to fixed and determined guide lines. It is not *my time* that is thus arranged; it is time in general, such as it is objectively thought of by everybody in a single civilization. That alone is enough to give us a hint that such an arrangement ought to be collective. And in reality, observation proves that these indispensable guide lines, in relation to which all things are temporally located, are taken from social life. The divisions into days, weeks, months, years, etc., correspond to the periodical recurrence of rites, feasts, and public ceremonies. A calendar expresses the rhythm of the collective activities, while at the same time its function is to assure their regularity.

It is the same thing with space. As Hamelin has shown, space is not the vague and undetermined medium which Kant imagined; if purely and absolutely homogeneous, it would be of no use, and could not be grasped by the mind. Spatial representation consists essentially in a primary co-ordination of the data of sensuous experience. But this co-ordination would be impossible if the parts of space were qualitatively equivalent and if they were really interchangeable. To dispose things spatially there must be a possibility of placing them differently, of putting some at the right, others at the left, these above, those below, at the north of or at the south of, east or west of, etc., etc., just as to dispose states of consciousness temporally there must be a possibility of localizing them at determined dates. That is to say that space could not be what it is if it were not, like time, divided and differentiated. But whence come these divisions which are so essential? By themselves, there are neither right nor left, up nor down, north nor south, etc. All these distinctions evidently come from the fact that different sympathetic values have been attributed to various regions. Since all the men of a single civilization represent space in the same way, it is clearly necessary that these sympathetic values, and the distinctions which depend upon them, should be equally universal, and that almost necessarily implies that they be of social origin.

Besides that, there are cases where this social character is made manifest. There are societies in Australia and North America where space is conceived in the form of an immense circle, because the camp has a circular form; and this spatial circle is divided up exactly like the tribal circle, and is in its image. There are as many regions distinguished as there are clans in the tribe, and it is the place occupied by the clans inside the encampment which has determined the orientation of these regions. Each region is defined by the totem of the clan to which it is assigned. Among the Zuñi, for example, the pueblo contains seven quarters; each of these is a group of clans which has had a unity: in all probability it was originally a single clan which was later subdivided. Now their space also contains seven quarters, and each of these seven quarters of the world is in intimate connection with a quarter of the pueblo, that is to say with a group of clans. "Thus," says Cushing, "one division is thought to be in relation with the north, another represents the west, another the south," etc. Each quarter of the pueblo has its characteristic colour, which symbolizes it; each region has its colour, which is exactly the same as that of the corresponding quarter. In the course of history the number of fundamental clans has varied; the number of the fundamental regions of space has varied with them. Thus the social organization has been the model for the spatial organization and a reproduction of it. It is thus even up to the distinction between right and left which, far from being inherent in the nature of man in general, is very probably the product of representations which are religious and therefore collective.

Analogous proofs will be found presently in regard to the ideas of class, force, personality and efficacy. It is even possible to ask if the idea of contradiction does not also depend upon social conditions. What makes one tend to believe this is that the empire which the idea has exercised over human thought has varied with times and societies. To-day the principle of identity dominates scientific thought; but there are vast systems of representations which have played a considerable role in the history of ideas where it has frequently been set aside: these are the mythologies, from the grossest up to the most reasonable. There, we are continually coming upon beings which have the most contradictory attributes simultaneously, who are at the same time one and many, material and spiritual, who can divide themselves up indefinitely without losing anything of their constitution; in mythology it is an axiom that the part is worth the whole. These variations through which the rules which seem to govern our present logic have passed prove that, far from being engraven through all eternity upon the mental constitution of men, they depend, at least in part, upon factors that are historical and consequently social. We do not know exactly what they are, but we may presume that they exist.

5. BRONISLAW MALINOWSKI, *ARGONAUTS* OF THE *WESTERN PACIFIC*

Bronislaw Malinowski (1884–1942) was born in a Polish territory of the Austro-Hungarian Empire, and educated in physics and mathematics at the Jagellonian University in Cracow. Reading Sir James Frazer's *The Golden*

Bough led him to an interest in anthropology, which he studied at the University of Leipzig in Germany and at the London School of Economics in Great Britain. He became a reader in anthropology at the University of London in 1924, and then assumed its first chair in 1927. He trained and directed the fieldwork of a generation of social anthropologists, standing as the founder of modern anthropology, a discipline in which participant-observer fieldwork replaced speculation as the basis for general conclusions about human society.

Malinowski's emphasis on fieldwork derived from his own research, carried out in the Pacific during the First World War. As an Austrian subject, he was interned in Australia when the war broke out, and he used the time to investigate several indigenous societies on that continent. The most famous of these research projects, involving two trips to the Trobriand Islands (1915–1916 and 1917–1918) formed the basis for his most famous work, *Argonauts of the Western Pacific,* published in 1922. This book was an ambitious attempt to describe in its totality the culture of the Trobrianders.

Argonauts of the Western Pacific

On the third day, as I was sitting and taking notes in the afternoon, word ran all round the villages that the Dobuan canoes had been sighted. And indeed, as I hastened towards the shore, there could be seen, far away, like small petals floating on the horizon, the sails of the advancing fleet. I jumped at once into a canoe, and was punted along towards the promontory of Kaykuyawa, about a mile to the South of Sinaketa. There, one after the other, the Dobuan canoes were arriving, dropping their sails and undoing the mast as they moored, until the whole fleet, numbering now over eighty canoes, were assembled before me. From each a few men waded ashore, returning with big bunches of leaves. I saw them wash and smear themselves and perform the successive stages of native, festive adornment. Each article was medicated by some man or another in the canoe before it was used or put on. The most carefully handled articles of ornamentation were the ineffective looking, dried up herbs, taken out of their little receptacles, where they had remained since they had been becharmed in Dobu, and now stuck into the armlets. The whole thing went on quickly, almost feverishly, making more the impression of a piece of technical business being expeditiously performed, than of a solemn and elaborate ceremony taking place. But the ceremonial element was soon to show itself.

After the preparations were finished, the whole fleet formed itself into a compact body, not quite regular, but with a certain order, about four or five canoes being in a row, and one row behind the other. In this formation they punted along over the Lagoon, too shallow for paddling, towards the beach of Sinaketa. When they were within about ten minutes of the shore, all the conch shells began to be sounded, and the murmur of recited magic rose from the canoes. I could not come sufficiently near the canoes, for reason of etiquette, to be able to see the exact arrangement of the reciters, but I was told that it was the same as that observed by the Trobrianders, on their approach to Dobu, described in Chapter XIII. The general effect was powerful, when this wonderfully painted and fully decorated fleet was gliding swiftly over the green waters of the Lagoon towards the palm grove above the sand beach, at that moment thick with expectant natives. But I imagine that the arrival of a Trobriand fleet in Dobu must be considerably more effective even than that. The much more picturesque landscape, the ceremonial paddling with the leaf-shaped oars over the deep water, the higher sense of danger and tension, than that which the Dobuans feel, when coming to visit the meek Trobrianders, all this must make it even more dramatic and impressive than the scene I have just described.

Within some twenty metres from the shore, the canoes formed themselves into a double row, the canoe of the *toli'uvalaku* on the left flank of the first row. Kauyaporu, as soon as all the craft were in position, rose in his canoe, and in a loud voice, addressed in Dobuan those standing on the shore. His words, preserved in the memory of his hearers, were transmitted to me that same evening in their Kiriwinian equivalent. He spoke:

> "Who will be first in the Kula? The people of Vakuta or yourselves? I deem you will have the lead! Bring armshells, one basketful, two baskets; catch pigs; pluck coco-nuts; pluck betel-nut! For this is my *uvalaku*. By and by, thou, Kouta'uya, wilt make an *uvalaku,* and we shall give thee then plenty of *vaygu'a!*"

So spoke Kauyaporu, addressing his main partner, Kouta'uya, the second chief of Sinaketa. He did not address To'udawada, the most important chief, because he was not his main partner.

As soon as the speech was finished, Kouta'uya waded through the water from the beach, carrying a pair of armshells in each hand. Behind him came a small boy, the youngest son, blowing a conch shell. He was followed again by two men, who between them had a stick resting on their shoulders, on which several pairs of *mwali* (armshells) were displayed. This procession waded towards the canoe of Kauyaporu, whom Kouta'uya addressed in these words, throwing the armshells on the platform of the canoe:

> "This is a *vaga* (opening gift)! In due time, I shall make a *uvalaku* to Dobu; thou shalt return to me a big *soulava* (necklace) as *kuda* (equivalent gift) for this. Plenty more armshells thou wilt receive now. There are plenty of armshells in Sinaketa. We know there were plenty of armshells in Vakuta. By and by thou and thy *usagelu* come ashore, I shall catch a pig. I shall give you plenty of food, coco-nuts, betel-nut, sugar cane, bananas!"

As soon as he was back on the shore, his wife, the eldest one, with a *peta* basket on her head, containing a pair of armshells, went into the water and carried it to Kauyaporu's canoe, the boy with the conch shell following her also. After that, conch shells were blown on all sides on the shore, and single men or groups detached themselves from the rest, and waded towards the canoes. The *mwali* were carried with ceremony on sticks or in outstretched arm. But the grossly exaggerated way of putting one pair of armshells into a basket which was big enough to hold some four score, was only done by the chief's wife. All this lasted for perhaps half-an-hour, while the setting sun poured down its glowing light on the painted canoes, the yellow beach, and the lively bronze forms moving upon it. Then, in a few moments the Dobuan canoes were partly beached, partly moored, whilst their crews spread over the seven villages of Sinaketa. Large groups could be seen sitting on platforms chewing betel nut and conversing in Dobuan with their hosts.

For three days, the Dobuans remained in Sinaketa. Every now and then, blasts of conch shell announced that a Kula transaction had taken place, that is, that a pair of armshells had been handed over to one of the visitors. Swarms of people from the other districts had assembled in Sinaketa; every day, natives from the inland villages of Southern Boyowa crowded into their capital, whilst people from Kuboma, Luba, and Kiriwina, that is, the Central and Northern districts, were camping in their relatives' houses, in yam stores and under provisional shelters. Reckoning that the number of the visitors, that is, the Dobuans, the Amphlettans and the Vakutans, who had joined them on their way, amounted to some eight hundred; that the Sinaketans numbered about five hundred people, and that some twelve hundred had come from the other villages, it will be seen that the crowd in and about Sinaketa was considerable, numbering over two thousand.

The Trobriand natives, of course, looked after their own provisions. The Dobuans had also brought a considerable amount of food with them, and would receive some additional vegetables and pigs' flesh from their hosts, while they acquired fish from some of the other villages of Boyowa. As a matter of fact, stingaree shark and some other fish are the only articles for which the Dobuans barter on their own account. The rest of the trade, in the same way as is done in Dobu by the Sinaketans, must be done with the community who receive visitors, that is, with Sinaketa. The Sinaketans buy from the manufacturing districts of Boyowa the same industrial products that they take with them to Dobu, that is baskets, lime pots, lime spatulæ, etc. Then they sell these to the Dobuans in just the same manner and with the same profit as was described in Chapter XV. As has been said there also, a man of Sinaketa would never trade with his partner, but with some other Dobuan. Between the partners, only presents are exchanged. The gift offered by the Dobuans to the Sinaketans is called *vata'i,* and it differs only in name and not in its economic or sociological nature from the *pari* gift offered by the Boyowans to their overseas partners. The *talo'i,* or farewell gift offered to them is as a rule more substantial than the *vata'i.*

The Dobuans, during their stay in Sinaketa, lived on the beach or in their canoes. Skilfully rigged up with canopies of golden mats covering parts of the craft, their painted hulls glowing in the sun against the green water, some of the canoes presented the spectacle of some gorgeously fantastic pleasure boat. The natives waded about amongst them, making the Lagoon lively with movement, talk and laughter. Groups camped on the sea shore, boiling food in the large clay pots, smoking and chewing betel-nut. Big parties of Trobrianders walked among them, discreetly but curiously watching them. Women were not very conspicuous in the whole proceedings, nor did I hear any scandal about intrigues, although such may have taken place.

III

On the fourth day, conch shells were blown again in the morning, though on the last of the three days their sounds had almost died out. These were the signs of the departure. Food and small presents were brought to the canoes as *talo'i,* and a few *mwali* were given at the last, for which the conch shells were blown. Without any ceremony or farewell speeches, the Dobuan canoes sailed away, one after the other.

6. Bronislaw Malinowski, *A Diary in the Strict Sense of the Term,* 1914–15

Although the methods he pioneered came to dominate anthropological study in the middle of the twentieth century, the publication of Malinowski's diary in 1967 cast doubt on the basis of his conclusions. This contributed to growing concerns among anthropologists in the second half of the twentieth century about the ability of western anthropologists to truly understand non-western cultures. The following excerpt is from his field notes for the same event as described in the previous selection from *Argonauts of the Western Pacific*.

A Diary in the Strict Sense of the Term

4.5. Friday. In the morning, wrote a few letters and had breakfast with George. Around 12 I went over to Kunubanukwa. After lunch went to the village, ate *paku,* talked with the boys, when the Dobu arrived. I hurried out (and in my hurry didn't take *extra* rolls of film!). Impressions from *kula* (once again feeling of ethnographic joy!). Sitting in To-vasana's boat I looked at the *kula* ceremonies. Raffael watched from the shore. Sinaketa almost like a summer resort with all these *gumanuma* people.—I was engrossed—as an ethnographer—in all the goings-on. At the same time, Friday and Saturday morning I thought of the letters I had to write. Also Raf., whom I like very much and who creates the social atmosphere, is a factor in my "orientation." In the evening I went to see them, and was received hospitably; they asked me to come every evening. Came back very tired; didn't feel up to writing letter to N.S.

4.6. Saturday. In the morning read and wrote letters to N. S., fairly optimistically, though optimism in this matter is a flimsy illusion. Geo. A. left under my nose. We sent a canoe after the "Kayona" with Raffael. Then went to take pictures, and lounged among them. In the evening talked with a fellow from Domdom.

4.7. Sunday. *My birthday.* Again worked with camera; by sunset I was simply exhausted. Evening at Raf.'s; discussion, first on physics; theory of origin of man and totemism in Tro-briands.—It is remarkable how intercourse with whites (sympathetic ones, like the Raf-faels) makes it impossible for me to write the diary. I fall, confused, into [the way of] life there. Everything is in the shadow; my thoughts are no longer characteristic in them-selves, and they take on value *qua* conversation with Raf. And so, on Sunday morning I fumbled around, didn't leave for To'udawada until 10; then photographed a few boats—and in this way passed the time until 12 (made drawings of *lagim* and *tabuyo,* which is very tiring). Then lunch. Around 4 again took pictures on the shore and a few from a boat. Inspected boats. In the evening so tired I almost fainted. Sat with George on the ve-randa. Arrived fairly late at Raffael's.

4.8. In the morning, without my knowledge, the boats of the Dobuans left. Worked at home with a few fellows on the *kula* question. Then, at lunch time, read Stead. Thought of E. R. M. *by flashes.* (Wondering about political problems in Austr. and Poland; found an item about *poor Tommy* in newspapers; looking at Raf. and his wife, at the naughty cari-catures in *Vie Parisienne*—she is the only woman for me, more and more often.) Then, around 4 I worked again; at 5 I went to the village and saw Toula, who was doing *kula.* Then Raffael. Talk about atoms, about electricity, the existence of the soul, competition; with Auerbach leafed through *Vie Parisienne;* he told me anecdote about Lourdes, etc. At night, in bed, I thought very intensely about E. R. M.

Study Questions

1. What factors lead to the development of culture for Tylor?
2. Discuss the differences between Tylor and Boas in their views of non-Europeans.
3. What are the most important aspects you notice about the men in the photo of the Intichiuma ceremony?
4. How does Durkheim describe the relationship between religion and human nature?
5. What differences can you see in the two accounts by Malinowski of the visit of the Dobuan canoes?
6. Discuss the different ways in which each of these authors describes the relationship between their own civilization and that of the rest of the world.

Suggestions for Further Reading

Clifford, James. *The Predicament of Culture*. Cambridge: Harvard University Press, 1988.
Kardiner, Abram, and Edward Preble. *They Studied Man*. Cleveland, OH: World Publishing Company, 1961.
Stocking, George. *Victorian Anthropology*. New York: Free Press, 1987.
Stocking, George. *After Tylor: British Social Anthropology, 1888–1951*. Madison: University of Wisconsin Press, 1995.

Web Sites

1. Anthropological Texts and Indigenous Standpoints

   http://www.ion.unisa.edu.au/conf/virtualconf/weaving/papers/Nakata_papR.html

2. Anthropoligical Theories

   http://www.as.ua.edu/ant/Faculty/murphy/evol.htm

3. Emile Durkheim: His Life and Work (1858–1917)

   http://www.lang.uiuc.edu/durkheim/Biography.html

4. Alfred Cort Haddon

   http://sites.netscape.net/jeremyhodes/Hadin.htm

5. The Place of the 1898 Cambridge Anthropological Expedition to the Torres Straits in the History of British Social Anthropology

   http://www.human-nature.com/science-as-culture/hart.html

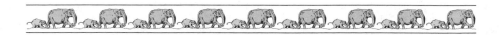

24

Independence Movements 1945–1965

TEXTS

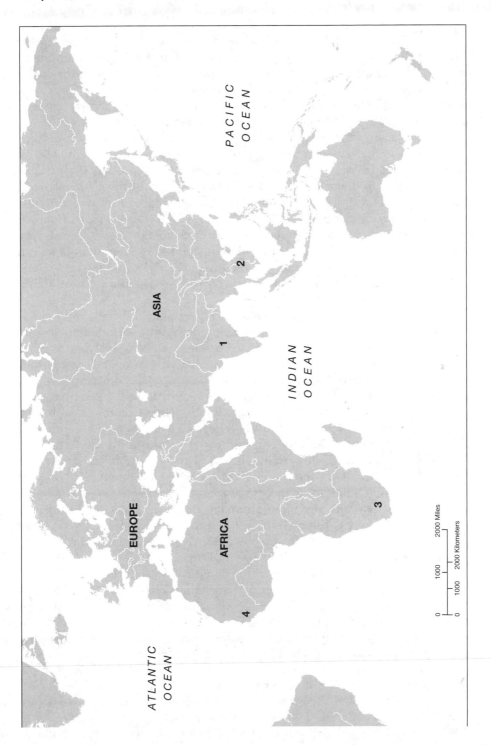

The Second World War proved unsettling to European empires, and was the preface to a dramatic development in the postwar period: the end of European empires. Between 1945 and 1965, all but the Portuguese Empire was lost by the European colonial powers, and that was to follow in the 1970s. This development was a result of the interaction of several factors. First, there was a growing nationalism—a European sentiment—among native elites in the colonies. These elites often provided the leadership for independence movements against the imperial powers. Second, the postwar era was marked by an international situation in which the two superpowers, the United States and the Soviet Union, encouraged independence and pressed the colonial powers to give up their colonies. The United States, the ally of the principal imperial powers, argued that colonialism was a thing of the past, and that attempts—such as the French Algerian War (1954–1962)—to maintain it took scarce resources away from the true threat to European security, the Cold War and the USSR. The Soviet Union tended to support indigenous groups in the colonies demanding independence, and communism became the ideology for numerous nationalist movements against western "bourgeois, capitalist" colonizers.

The two principal European imperial powers, Great Britain and France, had differing views well before 1945 of the relationship of the empire to the metropole and of the ultimate goal of European empire. In Great Britain, this notion became bound up with the idea of Commonwealth. The British white-settler colonies—Canada, New Zealand, Australia, South Africa—had received dominion status before World War I, and the assumption was that nonwhite colonies would eventually follow. In the Commonwealth, the Crown continued to act as constitutional head of each individual dominion; the parliaments obtained sovereignty and equal status with the parliament in Westminster, and the British right of veto over dominion legislation was dropped. The Ottowa Conference in 1932 moved the Commonwealth toward economic unity, as it became a free trade zone.

For Great Britain, the most traumatic instance of decolonization occurred in India, long considered the jewel of the British empire. Even before the Second World War, there had been pressure on the British goverment to grant some kind of autonomy to its Indian Empire. The two principal movements demanding this change in status dated from around the turn of the twentieth century and reflected the sharp religious division of India between Muslim and Hindu. The Indian National Congress, a Hindu organization founded in 1885, gave birth to a Congress political party committed to Hindu participation in Indian affairs. [1] The second movement, the All-India Muslim League, was founded in 1906 and represented the Muslim religionists of India.

During World War II, India was brought into the war on the British side by the decree of the British governor, a move that angered the leaders of both the Congress and the Muslim League because they had not been consulted. After the war, the labour government in Great Britain, elected in 1945, adopted a policy that favored Indian independence. With difficulty in agreeing on the terms of independence, the Indian army showing signs of dissolution, and a worsening British economic situation, on February 20, 1947, the prime minister, Clement Attlee, announced that India would be turned over to Indian control by June 1948. The major difficulty was working out some reconciliation of Hindu and Muslim interests; this proved impossible, and, finally, on August 14–15, 1947, India and Pakistan gained independence as members of the Commonwealth.

For France, the empire had been aimed not at the loosening of political ties that Britain saw in the Commonwealth, but in assimilation and association, creating a "Greater France" of 100 million Frenchmen. The French, therefore, did not envisage independence as the end of the empire; rather, in their eyes, this would mean the assimilation and association of the overseas territories into France, culturally and politically. It proved difficult, however, to maintain colonial relationships in the postwar world. Immediately after the end of the war, France attempted to reassert its control over its colonies in Indochina. However, in the eastern part, Vietnam, it was opposed by a nationalist movement, the Vietminh. The leader of this movement was Ho Chi Minh, a French-educated leader, one of the founders of the Vietnamese Communist Party, who found support from the Soviet Union for his plans for an independent Vietnam. Ho had been pressing the French government for increased Vietnamese autonomy since the 1930s, but the failure of the government in Paris to agree to this led in 1946 to the outbreak of a long war of independence. [2] The Vietnam War was one of the first examples of what came to be called a People's War, a guerrilla struggle that the French army, used to conventional warfare, found impossible to win. The climax of the war came in 1954, with the fall of a major French fortress in the north, Dien Bien Phu. The French government then began negotiations in earnest, leading to an agreement in Geneva that envisaged Vietnamese independence and reunification by 1956, and effectively ended French control over Indochina.

The problems groups in Britain and France had with the process of decolonization became very evident in 1956, with the Suez crisis. The United States had promised financial support for a major project planned by the government of Egypt, that is, the Aswan dam of the Nile, which would provide irrigation for cotton growing in the Nile valley. The U.S. secretary of state, John Foster Dulles, however, became concerned with the growing Soviet influence in Egypt, and refused aid for the dam project. In response, the president of Egypt, Gamal Abdul Nasser, nationalized the Suez Canal from the company that owned it, primarily a French-British company, twelve years ahead of schedule. Israel, with the covert diplomatic support of France and Britain, launched an attack on Egypt, toward the canal. Britain and France landed a military expedition, nominally to protect the canal. Virtually unanimous international opposition to this invasion led to its disastrous end. It was a classic imperial policy in an age of decolonization, and indicated how isolated British and French imperialism had become.

In Great Britain the experience of Suez and the coming to power of the postwar generation, especially Conservative Prime Minister Harold MacMillan, led to a rapid movement toward greater autonomy and ultimately independence for virtually all its colonies. The marking point of this is a speech given by MacMillan in Capetown, South Africa, on February 3, 1960, famous as "The winds of change" speech. [3] Over the next two years, MacMillan's government either granted or laid the basis for the independence or autonomy in the Commonwealth of virtually all of Britain's colonies.

In France, however, the inevitability of decolonization remained unappreciated by many even after the Suez Crisis. France continued to fight against the independence of Algeria. This war led to the collapse of the French Republic in 1958, the return to power of the hero of the French Resistance during World War II, Charles de Gaulle, and, in 1962, Algerian independence. The difficulties France had in letting go of its colonies were matched in some instances by the attempts of many leaders from France's colonies to find ways of reconciling their growing sense of their local identity with their participation in Francophone culture. The former colonies also faced problems in developing stable political systems after independence, a process complicated by their attempts to adapt European ideas such as democracy and socialism to their own situations. [4]

With the end of the Algerian War, European colonies had virtually disappeared, with only the Portuguese colonies in Africa, and a few vestiges such as the Falkland Islands remaining. In the early 1970s, that Portuguese Empire disappeared, as revolts in Angola, Guinea (Bissau), and Mozambique led to an army revolt in Portugal itself and withdrawal from these colonies. From a continent politically, culturally, and economically dominating much of the rest of the world, Europe had become a small place attempting to reconstruct its influence in the rest of the world on a different basis.

1. MOHANDAS K. GANDHI, *HIND SWARAJ*

Mohandas K. Gandhi (1869–1948) was born in the princedom of Porbandar, India, into the *Vaisya* or merchant caste, to a family that had furnished prime ministers of different Indian states for three generations. He studied law in England, becoming a barrister in 1891. While practicing law in Natal and Johannesburg, he began to agitate against South African discrimination against Indians. Increasingly, while living in South Africa, he saw a simple peasant life as his ideal, and Western civilization as evil. His emphasis on *Satyagraha* (nonviolent noncooperation) led to his imprisonment several times for leading civil disobedience campaigns against the British government in South Africa. However, he saw the British Empire as a positive force overall, and with the outbreak of World War I, he, like most Indian nationalists, urged Indians to serve Britain in the war. He hoped that participation in the war would bring dominion status to India, but he was disappointed. After the war he became a leader of the Indian National Congress, a Hindu organization that pressed the British for some form of Home Rule. By 1929, in the face of British intransigence, this had become a demand for complete independence, a goal not achieved until 1947. Gandhi was assassinated in 1948 by the editor of an extremist Hindu newspaper.

Hind Swaraj

READER: Is there any historical evidence as to the success of what you have called soul-force or truth-force? No instance seems to have happened of any nation having risen through soul-force. I still think that the evil-doers will not cease doing evil without physical punishment.

EDITOR: The poet Tulsidas has said: "Of religion, pity, or love, is the root, as egotism of the body. Therefore, we should not abandon pity so long as we are alive." This appears to me to be a scientific truth. I believe in it as much as I believe in two and two being four. The force of love is the same as the force of the soul or truth. We have evidence of its working at every step. The universe would disappear without the existence of that force. But you ask for historical evidence. It is, therefore, necessary to know what history means. The Gujarati equivalent means: "It so happened." If that is the meaning of history, it is possible to give copious evidence. But, if it means the doings of kings and emperors, there can be no evidence of soul-force or passive resistance in such history. You cannot expect silver ore in a tin mine. History, as we know it, is a record of the wars of the world, and so there is a proverb among Englishmen that a nation which has no history, that is, no wars, is a happy nation. How kings played, how they became enemies of one another, how they murdered one another, is found accurately recorded in history, and if this were all that had happened in the world, it would have been ended long ago. If the story of the universe had commenced with wars, not a man would have been found alive today. Those people who have been warred against have disappeared as, for instance, the natives of Australia of whom hardly a man was left alive by the intruders. Mark, please, that these natives did not use soul-force in self-defence, and it does not require much foresight to know that the Australians will share the same fate as their victims. "Those that take the sword shall perish by the sword." With us the proverb is that professional swimmers will find a watery grave.

The fact that there are so many men still alive in the world shows that it is based not on the force of arms but on the force of truth or love. Therefore, the greatest and most unimpeachable evidence of the success of this force is to be found in the fact that, in spite of the wars of the world, it still lives on.

Thousands, indeed tens of thousands, depend for their existence on a very active working of this force. Little quarrels of millions of families in their daily lives disappear before the exercise of this force. Hundreds of nations live in peace. History does not and cannot take note of this fact. History is really a record of every interruption of the even working of the force of love or of the soul. Two brothers quarrel; one of them repents and re-awakens the love that was lying dormant in him; the two again begin to live in peace; nobody takes note of this. But if the two brothers, through the intervention of solicitors or some other reason take up arms or go to law—which is another form of the exhibition of brute force,—their doings would be immediately noticed in the Press, they would be the talk of their neighbours and would probably go down to history. And what is true of families and communities is true of nations. There is no reason to believe that there is one law for families and another for nations. History, then, is a record of an interruption of the course of nature. Soul-force, being natural, is not noted in history.

READER: According to what you say, it is plain that instances of this kind of passive resistance are not to be found in history. It is necessary to understand this passive resistance more fully. It will be better, therefore, if you enlarge upon it.

EDITOR: Passive resistance is a method of securing rights by personal suffering; it is the reverse of resistance by arms. When I refuse to do a thing that is repugnant to my conscience, I use soul-force. For instance, the Government of the day has passed a law which is applicable to me. I do not like it. If by using violence I forced the Government to repeal the law, I am employing what may be termed bodyforce. If I do not obey the law and accept the penalty for its breach, I use soul-force. It involves sacrifice of self.

Everybody admits that sacrifice of self is infinitely superior to sacrifice of others. Moreover, if this kind of force is used in a cause that is unjust, only the person using it suffers. He does not make others suffer for his mistakes. Men have before now done many things which were subsequently found to have been wrong. No man can claim that he is absolutely in the right or that a particular thing is wrong because he thinks so, but it is wrong for him so long as that is his deliberate judgment. It is therefore meet that he should not do that which he knows to be wrong, and suffer the consequence whatever it may be. This is the key to the use of soul-force.

READER: You would then disregard laws—this is rank disloyalty. We have always been considered a law-abiding nation. You seem to be going even beyond the extremists. They say that we must obey the laws that have been passed, but that if the laws be bad, we must drive out the law-givers even by force.

EDITOR: Whether I go beyond them or whether I do not is a matter of no consequence to either of us. We simply want to find out what is right and to act accordingly. The real meaning of the statement that we are a law-abiding nation is that we are passive resisters. When we do not like certain laws, we do not break the heads of law-givers but we suffer and do not submit to the laws. That we should obey laws whether good or bad is a new-fangled notion. There was no such thing in former days. The people disregarded those laws they did not like and suffered the penalties for their breach. It is contrary to our manhood if we obey laws repugnant to our conscience. Such teaching is opposed to religion and means slavery. If the Government were to ask us to go about without any clothing, should we do so? If I were a passive resister, I would say to them that I would have nothing to do with their law. But we have so forgotten ourselves and become so compliant that we do not mind any degrading law.

A man who has realized his manhood, who fears only God, will fear no one else. Man-made laws are not necessarily binding on him. Even the Government does not expect any such thing from us. They do not say: "You must do such and such a thing," but they say: "If you do not do it, we will punish you." We are sunk so low that we fancy that it is our duty and our religion to do what the law lays down. If man will only realize that it is unmanly to obey laws that are unjust, no man's tyranny will enslave him. This is the key to self-rule or home rule.

It is a superstition and ungodly thing to believe that an act of a majority binds a minority. Many examples can be given in which acts of majorities will be found to have been wrong and those of minorities to have been right. All reforms owe their origin to the initiation of minorities in opposition to majorities. If among a band of robbers a knowledge of robbing is obligatory, is a pious man to accept the obligation? So long as the superstition that men should obey unjust laws exists, so long will their slavery exist. And a passive resister alone can remove such a superstition.

To use brute-force, to use gunpowder, is contrary to passive resistance, for it means that we want our opponent to do by force that which we desire but he does not. And if such a use of force is justifiable, surely he is entitled to do likewise by us. And so we should never come to an agreement. We may simply fancy, like the blind horse moving in a circle round a mill, that we are making progress. Those who believe that they are not bound to obey laws which are repugnant to their conscience have only the remedy of passive resistance open to them. Any other must lead to disaster.

READER: From what you say I deduce that passive resistance is a splendid weapon of the weak, but that when they are strong they may take up arms.

EDITOR: This is gross ignorance. Passive resistance, that is, soul-force, is matchless. It is superior to the force of arms. How, then, can it be considered only a weapon of the weak? Physical-force men are strangers to the courage that is requisite in a passive resister. Do you believe that a coward can ever disobey a law that he dislikes? Extremists are considered to be advocates of brute force. Why do they, then, talk about obeying laws? I do not blame them. They can say nothing else. When they succeed in driving out the English and they themselves become governors, they will want you and me to obey their laws. And that is a fitting thing for their constitution. But a passive resister will say he will not obey a law that is against his conscience, even though he may be blown to pieces at the mouth of a cannon.

What do you think? Wherein is courage required—in blowing others to pieces from behind a cannon, or with a smiling face to approach a cannon and be blown to pieces? Who is the true warrior—he who keeps death always as a bosom-friend, or he who controls the death of others? Believe me that a man devoid of courage and manhood can never be a passive resister.

This, however, I will admit: that even a man weak in body is capable of offering this resistance. One man can offer it just as well as millions. Both men and women can indulge in it. It does not require the training of an army; it needs no jiu-jitsu. Control over the mind is alone necessary, and when that is attained, man is free like the king of the forest and his very glance withers the enemy.

Passive resistance is an all-sided sword, it can be used anyhow; it blesses him who uses it and him against whom it is used. Without drawing a drop of blood it produces far-reaching results. It never rusts and cannot be stolen. Competition between passive resisters does not exhaust. The sword of passive resistance does not require a scabbard. It is strange indeed that you should consider such a weapon to be a weapon merely of the weak.

READER: You have said that passive resistance is a speciality of India. Have cannons never been used in India?

EDITOR: Evidently, in your opinion, India means its few princes. To me it means its teeming millions on whom depends the existence of its princes and our own.

Kings will always use their kingly weapons. To use force is bred in them. They want to command, but those who have to obey commands do not want guns: and these are in a majority throughout the world. They have to learn either body-force or soul-force. Where they learn the former, both the rulers and the ruled become like so many madmen; but where they learn soul-force, the commands of the rulers do not go beyond the point of their swords, for true men disregard unjust commands. Peasants have never been subdued by the sword, and never will be. They do not know the use of the sword, and they are not frightened by the use of it by others. That nation is great which rests its head upon death as its pillow. Those who defy death are free from all fear. For those who are labouring under the delusive charms of brute-force, this picture is not overdrawn. The fact is that, in India, the nation at large has generally used passive resistance in all departments of life. We cease to co-operate with our rulers when they displease us. This is passive resistance.

I remember an instance when, in a small principality, the villagers were offended by some command issued by the prince. The former immediately began vacating the village. The prince became nervous, apologized to his subjects and withdrew his command. Many such instances can be found in India. Real Home Rule is possible only where passive resistance is the guiding force of the people. Any other rule is foreign rule.

READER: Then you will say that it is not at all necessary for us to train the body?

EDITOR: I will certainly not say any such thing. It is difficult to become a passive resister unless the body is trained. As a rule, the mind, residing in a body that has become weakened by pampering, is also weak, and where there is no strength of mind there can be no strength of soul. We shall have to improve our physique by getting rid of infant marriages and luxurious living. If I were to ask a man with a shattered body to face a cannon's mouth, I should make a laughing-stock of myself.

READER: From what you say, then, it would appear that it is not a small thing to become a passive resister, and, if that is so, I should like you to explain how a man may become one.

EDITOR: To become a passive resister is easy enough but it is also equally difficult. I have known a lad of fourteen years become a passive resister; I have known also sick people do likewise; and I have also known physically strong and otherwise happy people unable to take up passive resistance. After a great deal of experience it seems to me that those who want to become passive resisters for the service of the country have to observe perfect chastity, adopt poverty, follow truth, and cultivate fearlessness.

Chastity is one of the greatest disciplines without which the mind cannot attain requisite firmness. A man who is unchaste loses stamina, becomes emasculated and cowardly. He whose mind is given over to animal passions is not capable of any great effort. This can be proved by innumerable instances. What, then, is a married person to do is the question that arises naturally; and yet it need not. When a husband and wife gratify the passions, it is no less an animal indulgence on that account. Such an indulgence, except for perpetuating the race, is strictly prohibited. But a passive resister has to avoid even that very limited indulgence because he can have no desire for progeny. A married man, therefore, can observe perfect chastity. This subject is not capable of being treated at greater length. Several questions arise: How is one to carry one's wife with one, what are her rights, and other similar questions. Yet those who wish to take part in a great work are bound to solve these puzzles.

Just as there is necessity for chastity, so is there for poverty. Pecuniary ambition and passive resistance cannot well go together. Those who have money are not expected to throw it away, but they *are* expected to be indifferent about it. They must be prepared to lose every penny rather than give up passive resistance.

Passive resistance has been described in the course of our discussion as truth-force. Truth, therefore, has necessarily to be followed and that at any cost. In this connection, academic questions such as whether a man may not lie in order to save a life, etc., arise, but these questions occur only to those who wish to justify lying. Those who want to follow truth every time are not placed in such a quandary; and if they are, they are still saved from a false position.

Passive resistance cannot proceed a step without fearlessness. Those alone can follow the path of passive resistance who are free from fear, whether as to their possessions, false honour, the relatives, the government, bodily injuries or death.

These observations are not to be abandoned in the belief that they are difficult. Nature has implanted in the human breast ability to cope with any difficulty or suffering that may come to man unprovoked. These qualities are worth having, even for those who do not wish to serve the country. Let there be no mistake, as those who want to train themselves in the use of arms are also obliged to have these qualities more or less. Everybody does not become a warrior for the wish. A would-be warrior will have to observe chastity and to be satisfied with poverty as his lot. A warrior without fearlessness cannot be conceived of. It may be thought that he would not need to be exactly truthful, but that quality follows real fearlessness. When a man abandons truth, he does so owing to fear in some shape or form. The above four attributes, then, need not frighten anyone. It may be as well here to note that a physical-force man has to have many other useless qualities which a passive resister never needs. And you will find that whatever extra effort a swordsman needs is due to lack of fearlessness. If he is an embodiment of the latter, the sword will drop from his hand that very moment. He does not need its support. One who is free from hatred requires no sword. A man with a stick suddenly came face to face with a lion and instinctively raised his weapon in self-defence. The man saw that he had only prated about fearlessness when there was none in him. That moment he dropped the stick and found himself free from all fear.

2. Ho Chi Minh, *Declaration of Independence of the Democratic Republic of Vietnam*

Ho Chi Minh (1890–1969) was born Nguyen That Thanh in central Vietnam, into a family that was active in opposition to French colonial control of the country. By working as a mess boy on a French liner, he was able to go to France, where he continued to work as a seaman. He settled in Paris in 1917, working as a cook, gardener, and photo retoucher, while also organizing the Vietnamese living in France into a movement in support of Vietnamese independence. The indifference toward colonies of the Western powers at the Paris peace conference at the end of World War I led him toward sympathy with the Soviet Union, and in 1920 he joined the newly formed French Communist Party. In 1930, he founded the Indochinese Communist Party, and in 1936 became its head. In 1941, he entered Vietnam and founded the Viet Minh, an organization coordinating nationalist activities for independence. At the end of World War II, the Viet Minh took control of Vietnam, and on September 2, 1945, Ho proclaimed Vietnamese independence and the foundation of a Democratic Republic of Vietnam. He was unable, however, to obtain Allied recognition, and when the French broke agreements they had made, war broke out between the Viet Minh and the French in December 1946. This war ended in the French defeat in 1954, and when the Geneva agreements ending it collapsed, another war began with the United States. Ho died in 1969 while peace talks with the United States that would eventually provide for Vietnamese independence were underway in Paris.

Declaration of Independence of the Democratic Republic of Vietnam

"We hold truths that all men are created equal, that they are endowed by their Creator with certain unalienable Rights, among these are Life, Liberty and the pursuit of Happiness."

This immortal statement is extracted from the Declaration of Independence of the United States of America in 1776. Understood in the broader sense, this means: "All peoples on the earth are born equal; every person has the right to live to be happy and free."

The Declaration of Human and Civic Rights proclaimed by the French Revolution in 1791 likewise propounds: "Every man is born equal and enjoys free and equal rights."

These are undeniable truths.

Yet, during and throughout the last eighty years, the French imperialists, abusing the principles of "Freedom, equality and fraternity," have violated the integrity of our ancestral land and oppressed our countrymen. Their deeds run counter to the ideals of humanity and justice.

In the political field, they have denied us every freedom. They have enforced upon us inhuman laws. They have set up three different political regimes in Northern, Central and Southern Viet Nam (Tonkin, Annam, and Cochinchina) in an attempt to disrupt our national, historical and ethnical unity.

They have built more prisons than schools. They have callously ill-treated our fellow-compatriots. They have drowned our revolutions in blood.

They have sought to stifle public opinion and pursued a policy of obscurantism on the largest scale; they have forced upon us alcohol and opium in order to weaken our race.

In the economic field, they have shamelessly exploited our people, driven them into the worst misery and mercilessly plundered our country.

They have ruthlessly appropriated our rice fields, mines, forests and raw materials. They have arrogated to themselves the privilege of issuing banknotes, and monopolised all our external commerce. They have imposed hundreds of unjustifiable taxes, and reduced our countrymen, especially the peasants and petty tradesmen, to extreme poverty.

They have prevented the development of native capital enterprises; they have exploited our workers in the most barbarous manner.

In the autumn of 1940, when the Japanese fascists, in order to fight the Allies, invaded Indochina and set up new bases of war, the French imperialists surrendered on bended knees and handed over our country to the invaders.

Subsequently, under the joint French and Japanese yoke, our people were literally bled white. The consequences were dire in the extreme. From Quang Tri up to the North, two millions of our countrymen died from starvation during the first months of this year.

On March 9th, 1945, the Japanese disarmed the French troops. Again the French either fled or surrendered unconditionally. Thus, in no way have they proved capable of "protecting" us; on the contrary, within five years they have twice sold our country to the Japanese.

Before March 9th, many a time did the Viet Minh League invite the French to join in the fight against the Japanese. Instead of accepting this offer, the French, on the contrary, let loose a wild reign of terror with rigour worse than ever before against Viet Minh's partisans. They even slaughtered a great number of our "*condamnes politiques*" imprisoned at Yen Bay and Cao Bang.

Despite all that, our countrymen went on maintaining, vis-a-vis the French, a humane and even indulgent attitude. After the events of March 9th, the Viet Minh League helped many French to cross the borders, rescued others from Japanese prisons and, in general, protected the lives and properties of all the French in their territory.

In fact, since the autumn of 1940, our country ceased to be a French colony and became a Japanese possession.

After the Japanese surrender, our people, as a whole, rose up and proclaimed their sovereignty and founded the Democratic Republic of Viet Nam.

The truth is that we have wrung back our independence from Japanese hands and not from the French.

The French fled, the Japanese surrendered. Emperor Bao Dai abdicated, our people smashed the yoke pressed hard upon us for nearly one hundred years, and finally made our Viet Nam an independent country. Our people at the same time overthrew the monarchical regime established tens of centuries ago, and founded the Republic.

For these reasons, we, the members of the Provisional Government representing the entire people of Viet Nam, declare that we shall from now on have no more connections with imperialist France; we consider null and void all the treaties France has signed concerning Viet Nam, and we hereby cancel all the privileges that the French arrogated to themselves on our territory.

The Vietnamese people, animated by the same common resolve, are determined to fight to the death against all attempts at aggression by the French imperialists.

We are convinced that the Allies who have recognized the principles of equality of peoples at the Conferences of Teheran and San Francisco cannot but recognize the Independence of Viet Nam.

A people which has so stubbornly opposed the French domination for more than 80 years, a people who, during these last years, so doggedly ranged itself and fought on the Allied side against Fascism, such a people has the right to be free, such a people must be independent.

For these reasons, we, the members of the Provisional Government of the Democratic Republic of Viet Nam, solemnly declare to the world:

"Viet Nam has the right to be free and independent and, in fact, has become free and independent. The people of Viet Nam decide to mobilise all their spiritual and material forces and to sacrifice their lives and property in order to safeguard their right of Liberty and Independence."

3. HAROLD MACMILLAN, *THE WINDS OF CHANGE*

Harold MacMillan (1894–1986) was prime minister of Great Britain from 1957 to 1963 as the leader of the Conservative Party, the peak of a parliamentary career that began in 1924. He succeeded Anthony Eden as prime minister following the British disaster in the Suez crisis, when Great Britain and France attempted to reassert control over the Suez Canal through a military invasion of Egypt. He benefited politically from the rising prosperity of the late 1950s, winning a strong majority on his own in elections in 1959. From this position of political strength, MacMillan began a second phase of British decolonization that either ended or negotiated the terms for the end of British control over much of its remaining empire. In 1960, in Cape Town, South Africa, he spoke to the white-settler dominated South African parliament, condemning the system of apartheid, or legal separation of the races, that supported white dominance in that country, and warning that the days of empire in Africa were coming to an end.

The Winds of Change

It is a great privilege to be invited to address the members of both Houses of Parliament in the Union of South Africa. It is a unique privilege to do so in 1960, just half a century after the Parliament of the Union came to birth. I am most grateful to you all for giving me this opportunity, and I am especially grateful to your Prime Minister who invited me to visit this country and arranged for me to address you here today. My tour of Africa—parts of Africa—the first ever made by a British Prime Minister in office, is now, alas, nearing its end, but it is fitting that it should culminate in the Union Parliament here in Cape Town, in this historic city so long Europe's gateway to the Indian Ocean, and to the East.

As in all the other countries that I have visited, my stay has been all too short. I wish it had been possible for me to spend a longer time here, to see more of your beautiful country and to get to know more of your people, but in the past week I have travelled many hundreds of miles and met many people in all walks of life. I have been able to get at least some idea of the great beauty of your countryside, with its farms and its forests, mountains and rivers, and the clear skies and wide horizons of the veldt. I have also seen some of your great and thriving cities, and I am most grateful to your Government for all the trouble they have taken in making the arrangements which have enabled me to see so much in so short a time. Some of the younger members of my staff have told me that it has been a heavy programme, but I can assure you that my wife and I have enjoyed every moment of it. Moreover, we have been deeply moved by the warmth of our welcome. Wherever we have been, in town or in country, we have been received in a spirit of friendship and affection which has warmed our hearts, and we value this the more because we know it is an expression of your goodwill, not just to ourselves but to all the people of Britain.

It is, as I have said, a special privilege for me to be here in 1960 when you are celebrating what I might call the golden wedding of the Union. At such a time it is natural and right that you should pause to take stock of your position, to look back at what you have achieved, to look forward to what lies ahead.

In the fifty years of their nationhood the people of South Africa have built a strong economy founded upon a healthy agriculture and thriving and resilient industries. During my visit I have been able to see something of your mining industry, on which the prosperity of the country is so firmly based. I have seen your Iron and Steel Corporation and visited your Council of Scientific and Industrial Research at Pretoria. These two bodies, in their different ways, are symbols of a lively, forward-looking and expanding economy. I have seen the great city of Durban, with its wonderful port, and the skyscrapers of

Johannesburg, standing where seventy years ago there was nothing but the open veldt. I have seen, too, the fine cities of Pretoria and Bloemfontein. This afternoon I hope to see something of your wine-growing industry, which so far I have only admired as a consumer.

No one could fail to be impressed with the immense material progress which has been achieved. That all this has been accomplished in so short a time is a striking testimony to the skill, energy and initiative of your people. We in Britain are proud of the contribution we have made to this remarkable achievement. Much of it has been financed by British capital. According to the recent survey made by the Union Government, nearly two-thirds of the oversea investment outstanding in the Union at the end of 1956 was British. That is after two staggering wars which have bled our economy white.

But that is not all. We have developed trade between us to our common advantage, and our economies are now largely interdependent. You export to us raw materials, food and gold. We in return send you consumer goods or capital equipment. We take a third of all your exports and we supply a third of all your imports. This broad traditional pattern of investment and trade has been maintained in spite of the changes brought by the development of our two economies, and it gives me great encouragement to reflect that the economies of both our countries, while expanding rapidly, have yet remained interdependent and capable of sustaining one another. If you travel round this country by train you will travel on South African rails made by Iscor. If you prefer to fly you can go in a British Viscount. Here is a true partnership, living proof of the interdependence between nations. Britain has always been your best customer and, as your new industries develop, we believe that we can be your best partners too.

In addition to building this strong economy within your own borders, you have also played your part as an independent nation in the world.

As a soldier in the First World War, and as a Minister in Sir Winston Churchill's Government in the Second, I know personally the value of the contribution which your forces made to victory in the cause of freedom. I know something, too, of the inspiration which General Smuts brought to us in Britain in our darkest hours. Again in the Korean crisis you played your full part. Thus in the testing times of war or aggression your statesmen and your soldiers have made their influence felt far beyond the African continent.

In the period of reconstruction, when Dr. Malan was your Prime Minister, your resources greatly assisted the recovery of the sterling area. In the post-war world now, in the no less difficult tasks of peace, your leaders in industry, commerce and finance continue to be prominent in world affairs today. Your readiness to provide technical assistance to the less well-developed parts of Africa is of immense help to the countries that receive it. It is also a source of strength to your friends in the Commonwealth and elsewhere in the Western World. You are collaborating in the work of the Commission for Technical Co-operation in Africa South of the Sahara, and now in the United Nations Economic Commission for Africa. Your Minister for External Affairs intends to visit Ghana later this year. All this proves your determination, as the most advanced industrial country of the continent, to play your part in the new Africa of today.

Sir, as I have travelled round the Union I have found everywhere, as I expected, a deep preoccupation with what is happening in the rest of the African continent. I understand and sympathise with your interest in these events, and your anxiety about them. Ever since the break-up of the Roman Empire one of the constant facts of political life in Europe has been the emergence of independent nations. They have come into existence over the centuries in different forms, with different kinds of Government, but all have been inspired by a deep, keen feeling of nationalism, which has grown as the nations have grown.

In the twentieth century, and especially since the end of the war, the processes which gave birth to the nation states of Europe have been repeated all over the world. We have seen the awakening of national consciousness in peoples who have for centuries lived in dependence upon some other power. Fifteen years ago this movement spread through Asia. Many countries there of different races and civilisations pressed their claim to an independent national life. Today the same thing is happening in Africa, and the most striking of all the impressions I have formed since I left London a month ago is of the strength of this African national consciousness. In different places it takes different forms, but it is happening everywhere. The wind of change is blowing through this continent, and, whether we like it or not, this growth of national consciousness is a political fact. We must all accept it as a fact, and our national policies must take account of it.

Of course, you understand this better than anyone. You are sprung from Europe, the home of nationalism, and here in Africa you have yourselves created a new nation. Indeed, in the history of our times yours will be recorded as the first of the African nationalisms, and this tide of national consciousness which is now rising in Africa is a fact for which you and we and the other nations of the Western World are ultimately responsible. For its causes are to be found in the achievements of Western civilisation, in the pushing forward of the frontiers of knowledge, in the applying of science in the service of human needs, in the expanding of food production, in the speeding and multiplying of the means of communication, and perhaps, above all, the spread of education.

As I have said, the growth of national consciousness in Africa is a political fact, and we must accept it as such. That means, I would judge, that we must come to terms with it. I sincerely believe that if we cannot do so we may imperil the precarious balance between the East and West on which the peace of the world depends. The world today is divided into three main groups. First there are what we call the Western Powers. You in South Africa and we in Britain belong to this group, together with our friends and allies in other parts of the Commonwealth. In the United States of America and in Europe we call it the Free World. Secondly there are the Communists—Russia and her satellites in Europe and China whose population will rise by the end of the next ten years to the staggering total of 800,000,000. Thirdly, there are those parts of the world whose people are at present uncommitted either to Communism or to our Western ideas.

In this context we think first of Asia and then of Africa. As I see it the great issue in this second half of the twentieth century is whether the uncommitted peoples of Asia and Africa will swing to the East or to the West. Will they be drawn into the Communist camp? Or will the great experiments in self-government that are now being made in Asia and Africa, especially within the Commonwealth, prove so successful, and by their example so compelling, that the balance will come down in favour of freedom and order and justice?

The struggle is joined, and it is a struggle for the minds of men. What is now on trial is much more than our military strength or our diplomatic and administrative skill. It is our way of life. The uncommitted nations want to see before they choose.

What can we show them to help them choose right? Each of the independent members of the Commonwealth must answer that question for itself. It is a basic principle of our modern Commonwealth that we respect each other's sovereignty in matters of internal policy. At the same time we must recognise that in this shrinking world in which we live today the internal policies of one nation may have effects outside it. We may sometimes be tempted to say to each other, 'Mind your own business,' but in these days I would myself expand the old saying so that it runs: 'Mind your own business, but mind how it affects my business, too.'

Let me be very frank with you, my friends. What Governments and Parliaments in the United Kingdom have done since the war in according independence to India, Pakistan, Ceylon, Malaya and Ghana, and what they will do for Nigeria and other countries now nearing independence, all this, though we take full and sole responsibility for it, we do in the belief that it is the only way to establish the future of the Commonwealth and of the Free World on sound foundations. All this of course is also of deep and close concern to you for nothing we do in this small world can be done in a corner or remain hidden. What we do today in West, Central and East Africa becomes known tomorrow to everyone in the Union, whatever his language, colour or traditions. Let me assure you, in all friendliness, that we are well aware of this and that we have acted and will act with full knowledge of the responsibility we have to all our friends.

Nevertheless I am sure you will agree that in our own areas of responsibility we must each do what we think right. What we think right derives from a long experience both of failure and success in the management of our own affairs. We have tried to learn and apply the lessons of our judgement of right and wrong. Our justice is rooted in the same soil as yours—in Christianity and in the rule of law as the basis of a free society. This experience of our own explains why it has been our aim in the countries for which we have borne responsibility, not only to raise the material standards of living, but also to create a society which respects the rights of individuals, a society in which men are given the opportunity to grow to their full stature—and that must in our view include the opportunity to have an increasing share in political power and responsibility, a society in which individual merit and individual merit alone is the criterion for a man's advancement, whether political or economic.

Finally in countries inhabited by several different races it has been our aim to find means by which the community can become more of a community, and fellowship can be fostered between its various parts. This problem is by no means confined to Africa. Nor is it always a problem of a European minority. In Malaya, for instance, though there are Indian and European minorities, Malays and Chinese make up the great bulk of the population, and the Chinese are not much fewer in numbers than the Malays. Yet these two peoples must learn to live together in harmony and unity and the strength of Malaya as a nation will depend on the different contributions which the two races can make.

The attitude of the United Kingdom towards this problem was clearly expressed by the Foreign Secretary, Mr. Selwyn Lloyd, speaking at the United Nations General Assembly on 17 September 1959. These were his words:

> In those territories where different races or tribes live side by side the task is to ensure that all the people may enjoy security and freedom and the chance to contribute as individuals to the progress and well being of these countries. We reject the idea of any inherent superiority of one race over another. Our policy therefore is non-racial. It offers a future in which Africans, Europeans, Asians, the peoples of the Pacific and others with whom we are concerned, will all play their full part as citizens in the countries where they live, and in which feelings of race will be submerged in loyalty to new nations.

I have thought you would wish me to state plainly and with full candour the policy for which we in Britain stand. It may well be that in trying to do our duty as we see it we shall sometimes make difficulties for you. If this proves to be so we shall regret it. But I know that even so you would not ask us to flinch from doing our duty.

You, too, will do your duty as you see it. I am well aware of the peculiar nature of the problems with which you are faced here in the Union of South Africa. I know the differences between your situation and that of most of the other states in Africa. You have here some three million people of European origin. This country is their home. It has been their home for many generations. They have no other. The same is true of Europeans in Central and East Africa. In most other African states those who have come from Europe have come to work, to contribute their skills, perhaps to teach, but not to make a home.

The problems to which you as members of the Union Parliament have to address yourselves are very different from those which face the Parliaments of countries with homogenous populations. These are complicated and baffling problems. It would be surprising if your interpretation of your duty did not sometimes produce very different results from ours in terms of Government policies and actions.

As a fellow member of the Commonwealth it is our earnest desire to give South Africa our support and encouragement, but I hope you won't mind my saying frankly that there are some aspects of your policies which make it impossible for us to do this without being false to our own deep convictions about the political destinies of free men to which in our own territories we are trying to give effect. I think we ought, as friends, to face together, without seeking to apportion credit or blame, the fact that in the world of today this difference of outlook lies between us.

I said that I was speaking as a friend. I can also claim to be speaking as a relation, for we Scots can claim family connections with both the great European sections of your population, not only with the English-speaking people but with the Afrikaans-speaking as well. This is a point which hardly needs emphasis in Cape Town where you can see every day the statue of that great Scotsman, Andrew Murray. His work in the Dutch Reformed Church in the Cape, and the work of his son in the Orange Free State, was among Afrikaans-speaking people. There has always been a very close connection between the Church of Scotland and the Church of the Netherlands. The Synod of Dort plays the same great part in the history of both. Many aspirants to the Ministry of Scotland, especially in the seventeenth and eighteenth centuries, went to pursue their theological studies in the Netherlands. Scotland can claim to have repaid the debt in South Africa. I am thinking particularly of the Scots in the Orange Free State. Not only the younger Andrew Murray, but also the Robertsons, the Frasers, the McDonalds—families which have been called the Free State clans, who became burghers of the old Free State and whose descendants still play their part there.

But though I count myself a Scot, my mother was an American, and the United States provides a valuable illustration of one of the main points which I have been trying to make in my remarks today. Its population, like yours, is of different strains, and over the years most of those who have gone to North America have gone there in order to escape conditions in Europe which they found intolerable. The Pilgrim Fathers were fleeing from persecution as Puritans and the Marylanders from persecution as Roman Catholics. Throughout the nineteenth century a stream of immigrants flowed across the Atlantic to escape from the poverty in their homelands, and in the twentieth century the United States have provided asylum for the victims of political oppression in Europe.

Thus for the majority of its inhabitants America has been a place of refuge, or place to which people went because they wanted to get away from Europe. It is not surprising, therefore, that for many years a main objective of American statesmen, supported by the American public, was to isolate themselves from Europe, and with their great material strength, and the vast resources open to them, this might have seemed an attractive and practicable course. Nevertheless in the two world wars of this century they have found themselves unable to stand aside. Twice their manpower in arms has streamed back across the Atlantic to shed blood in those European struggles from which their ancestors thought they would escape by emigrating to the New World; and when the second war was over they were forced to recognise that in the small world of today isolationism is out of date and offers no assurance of security.

The fact is that in this modern world no country, not even the greatest, can live for itself alone. Nearly two thousand years ago, when the whole of the civilised world was comprised within the confines of the Roman Empire, St. Paul proclaimed one of the great truths of history—we are all members one of another. During this twentieth century that eternal truth has taken on a new and exciting significance. It has always been impossible for the individual man to live in isolation from his fellows, in the home, the tribe, the village, or the city. Today it is impossible for nations to live in isolation from one another. What Dr. John Donne said of individual men three hundred years ago is true today of my country, your country, and all the countries of the world:

> Any man's death diminishes me, because I am involved in Mankind. And therefore never send to know for whom the bell tolls; it tolls for thee.

All nations now are interdependent one upon another, and this is generally realised throughout the Western World. I hope in due course the countries of Communism will recognise it too.

It was certainly with that thought in mind that I took the decision to visit Moscow about this time last year. Russia has been isolationist in her time and still has tendencies that way, but the fact remains that we must live in the same world with Russia, and we must find a way of doing so. I believe that the initiative which we took last year has had some success, although grave difficulties may arise. Nevertheless I think nothing but good can come out of its extending contacts between individuals, contacts in trade and from the exchange of visitors.

I certainly do not believe in refusing to trade with people because you may happen to dislike the way they manage their internal affairs at home. Boycotts will never get you anywhere, and may I say in parenthesis that I deprecate the attempts that are being made today in Britain to organise the consumer boycott of South African goods. It has never been the practice, as far as I know, of any Government of the United Kingdom of whatever complexion to undertake or support campaigns of this kind designed to influence the internal politics of another Commonwealth country, and my colleagues in the United Kingdom deplore this proposed boycott and regard it as undesirable from every point of view. It can only have serious effects on Commonwealth relations, on trade, and lead to the ultimate detriment of others than those against whom it is aimed.

I said I was speaking of the interdependence of nations. The members of the Commonwealth feel particularly strongly the value of interdependence. They are as independent as any nation in this shrinking world can be, but they have voluntarily agreed to work together. They recognise that there may be and must be differences in their institutions; in their internal policies, and their membership does not imply the wish to express a judgement on these matters, or the need to impose a stifling uniformity. It is, I think, a help that there has never been question of any rigid constitution for the Commonwealth. Perhaps this is because we have got on well enough in the United Kingdom without a written constitution and tend to look suspiciously at them. Whether that is so or not, it is quite clear that a rigid constitutional framework for the Commonwealth would not work. At the first of the stresses and strains which are inevitable in this period of history, cracks would appear in the framework and the whole structure would crumble. It is the flexibility of our Commonwealth institutions which gives them their strength.

Mr. President, Mr. Speaker, Honourable Ministers, Ladies and Gentlemen, I fear I have kept you a long time. I much welcome the opportunity to speak to this great audience. In conclusion may I say this? I have spoken frankly about the differences between our two countries in their approach to one of the great current problems with which each has to deal within its own sphere of responsibility. These differences are well-known. They are matters of public knowledge, indeed of public controversy, and I should have been less than honest if by remaining silent on them I had seemed to imply that they did not exist. But differences on one subject, important though it is, need not and should not impair our capacity to co-operate with one another in furthering the many practical interests which we share in common.

The independent members of the Commonwealth do not always agree on every subject. It is not a condition of their association that they should do so. On the contrary, the strength of our Commonwealth lies largely in the fact that it is a free association of independent sovereign states, each responsible for ordering its own affairs but co-operating in the pursuit of common aims and purposes in world affairs. Moreover these differences may be transitory. In time they may be resolved. Our duty is to see them in perspective against the background of our long association. Of this at any rate I am certain—those of us who by grace of the electorate are temporarily in charge of affairs in your country and in mine, we fleeting transient phantoms on the great stage of history, we have no right to sweep aside on this account the friendship that exists between our countries, for that is the legacy of history. It is not ours alone to deal with as we wish. To adapt a famous phrase, it belongs to those who are living, but it also belongs to those who are dead and to those who are yet unborn. We must face the differences, but let us try to see beyond them down the long vista of the future.

I hope—indeed, I am confident—that in another fifty years we shall look back on the differences that exist between us now as matters of historical interest, for as time passes and one generation yields to another, human problems change and fade. Let us remember these truths. Let us resolve to build, not to destroy, and let us remember always that weakness comes from division, strength from unity.

4. Houari Boumediene, *Proclamation of the Council of the Revolution*

Houari Boumediene (1932–1978) was born in a poor peasant family in eastern Algeria, a colony of France. He studied in French and Koranic schools until he was fourteen, but fled to Tunis and then Cairo in 1952 when the

French conscripted him for service in the colonial army. While in Cairo, he gained a strong Arabic training through studies at al-Azhar University.

Boumediene ended his studies in Cairo in 1954 when the Algerian revolution against French rule broke out, and he rose rapidly through the military forces of the Revolution. By 1960, he was the commander of the army general staff, and was able to consolidate his influence in the army. He insisted to his troops the importance of Islam and demanded complete loyalty to himself from them. The influence of Boumediene and his ally, Ahmed Ben Bella, led to a conflict between these military leaders and the civilian leaders of the Revolution. Soon after independence, in 1962, Ben Bella and Boumediene led the army in a coup against the civilian leadership and established themselves in power. Boumediene became the minister of national defense in Ben Bella's first government, and became first vice president in 1963. However, he soon broke with Ben Bella, and during the night of June 18/19, 1965, he led a coup that deposed Ben Bella and established himself in power at the head of a Committee of National Revolution.

The following selection, a statement promulgated by Boumediene after the 1965 coup, explains both his discontents with the preceding regime and his hopes for his country as it attempted to find its way after independence. As president, he emphasized the development of Algeria's oil and natural gas reserves and using the revenues from these industries to foster further industrial diversification. However, in spite of these efforts, at the time of his death in 1978 most Algerians remained in the same poverty they had experienced under French colonial rule.

Proclamation of the Council of the Revolution (19 June 1965)

Algerian people,

November 1, 1954, our country began a revolution that would put an end, by armed struggle and sacrifice, to more than a century of colonial domination.

July 5, 1962, Algeria finally regained its liberty and its independence, at the price of the heaviest sacrifice that History has ever seen.

The political crisis that immediately followed expressed in a violent manner the numerous and inevitable internal contradictions accumulated during eight years of war. The country found itself therefore at the edge of an abyss and once again only the patriotism and disinterest of all sincere militants made it possible to avoid a civil war. The problems were not, however, resolved.

After three years of national sovereignty, the country finds itself in the grip of shadowy intrigues, of conflicting tendencies and of clans revived for the purposes of an old practice of government: divide to rule. Sordid calculations, political narcissism and morbid love of power find their best illustration in the systematic liquidation of the cadres of the country and the criminal attempt to discredit religious leaders and those who resisted the French. The Popular National Army, worthy heir of the glorious Army of National Liberation, will never allow itself—no matter what the maneuvers and attempts—to be cut off from the people from which it sprang and in which it finds both its strength and its reason for existence.

Algerian people,

The men who today have decided to respond to your anguished appeal, persuaded in doing so to understand your dearest wish, have taken it upon themselves to recover for you your lost liberty and your disrespected honor. It was time to discover the evil, to circumscribe it, and to denounce it. It was above all necessary to act, putting an end to this dramatic situation. No matter how important their mission, no one can pretend to incarnate in themselves at the same time Algeria, the Revolution and Socialism. No matter what form the confusion of powers takes, it cannot be allowed to dispose of the country and public affairs of which it has charge as if they are personal and private property.

The balance is heavy and significant:

The bad management of the national patrimony, the weakening of public finances, instability, demagogy, anarchy, deception and improvisation have been imposed as procedures of government. By menace, extortion, theft of individual liberties and uncertianty about the future, it has been attempted to reduce some to docility, others to fear, silence and resignation.

Personal power, today the rule, places all the national and regional institutions of the Party and of the State at the mercy of a single man. He confers responsibility according to his fancy, makes and unmakes directing organs with unhealthy and improvised tactics, and imposes decisions and men according to his moods, caprices and pleasures of the moment.

Algerian people,

Your silence is not an act of cowardice. If the tyrant, today neutralized, permitted himself to believe that you were apathetic, events have taught him already that the punishment of the idols that have been created by mystification will be in the same measure as your confidence, your sincerity and your support.

Algerian people,

A Council of the Revolution has been created. It has taken all the measures to assure, in order and security, the functioning of present institutions and the good conduct of public affairs. It has also undertaken the task of creating the conditions for the institution of a democratic State, governed by laws and based on morality, a State that will know how to survive as government and as men.

The institutions of the Party and of the State function in harmony and within the limits of their respective powers and with strict respect for revolutionary legality. With stability and confidence restored, the Council of the Revolution intends to return our economy to good order. This is possible only if all forms of flowery language and pragmatism are abandoned and if, definitively, the ways and means are objectively spelled out and understood by all.

In this area more than others, it is necessary to substitute probity for the love of luxury, hard work for improvisation, morality of the State for impulsive reactions, in a word a socialism conforming to the realities of the country for a circumstantial and public-relations socialism.

The fundamental positions are irreversible and the gains of the revolution inalienable. Nevertheless, only rigorous measures of cleansing and a firm and clear policy can bring us out of the general malaise that is expressed by reduced productivity, decreasing economic prosperity and unsettling loss of investment.

The radical transformation of our society cannot be accomplished without taking into account our faith and our convictions, the secular traditions of our people and our moral values.

In this new phase of the revolution, the entire nation is unified in confidence and serenity. It must work for the revitalization of our institutions, for political stability in a rediscovered fraternity, for consolidation of revolutionary power on the basis of a truer appreciation of democratic centralism and for the development of a truly socialist society. . . .

Algerian people,

The weight of the long colonial period and of eight years of suffering are today seriously aggravated by the reign of nonchalance, the deterioration of the State and complacent optimism. If the situation is not irreversibly catastrophic, it remains at least serious. Only mobilization around essential goals will permit us to find the way to safety and better hopes for the future.

There will be no recovery and still less any miracle, without work, seriousness, clear objectives and unity. Our country, so many times placed under strain, one more time asks us to rise individually and collectively to the level of our historic responsibilities, for the triumph forever of the Revolution.

For the Council of the Revolution:
Houari Boumediene

Study Questions

1. Discuss the similarities and differences between the bases for Gandhi's opposition to British rule in India and Ho Chi Minh's opposition to French rule in Indochina.
2. Why does MacMillan think that Great Britain should end its colonial rule in Africa?
3. Of the three statements by Gandhi, Ho Chi Minh, and Boumediene, which do you think provides the best basis for an independent state? What criteria did you use to evaluate them?

Suggestions for Further Reading

Ansprenger, Franz. *The Dissolution of the Colonial Empires.* New York: Routledge, 1989.
Chamberlain, Muriel E. *The Longman Companion to European Decolonisation in the Twentieth Century.* New York: Longman, 1998.
Curtin, Philip D. *The World and the West: The European Challenge and the Overseas Response in the Age of Empire.* New York: Cambridge University Press, 2000.
Geismar, Peter. *Fanon.* New York: Dial Press, 1971.
Hargreaves, John. *Decolonization in Africa.* London: Longman, 1996.
von Albertini, Rudolf. *Decolonization: The Administration and Future of the Colonies, 1919–1960.* New York: Holmes and Meier, 1982.

Web Sites

1. After Independence (1962–1999): Algeria

   http://www.arab.net/algeria/history/aa_independence.html

2. The Commonwealth and Australia

   http://www.dfat.gov.au/intorgs/commonwealth

3. Former British colonies and Commonwealth members:

   http://www.sas.ac.uk/commonwealthstudies/library/libcolonies.html

4. French Colonization (1830–1962): Algeria

   http://www.arab.net/algeria/history/aa_french.html

5. Proclamation of the Algerian National Liberation Front, November 1, 1954

   http://www.library.cornell.edu/colldev/mideast/flni.htm

25

The Globalization of the World Economy 1900–1999

TEXTS

The Mediterranean trade with the East, the Atlantic plantation economy, and the informal empires of the late eighteenth century are reminders that there had been economic ties between the European economy and the rest of the world long before the formal empires of the late nineteenth century. Until 1850, however, these ties had been restricted by the relative self-sufficiency of most parts of the world in basic agricultural products. Trade was limited to several distinct commercial areas defined by political association or physical proximity, such as Western and Central Europe, Russia and the Baltic, the North Atlantic, and India and the Far East. This regionalization of trade made for a simplified international economy, as trade accounts within these regions were usually close to balanced, and therefore required little transfer of credit or gold.

The consolidation of empires in the late nineteenth century was a part of a process of globalization of the economies of Europe and the rest of the world. The volume of international trade expanded as Europe and North America industrialized, becoming both more productive and more efficient. Along with the increase in volume came the breakdown of the older barriers between commercial regions. The economic links between the developed north and the less-developed southern hemisphere were important characteristics of the twentieth-century world economy. London was the most important financial center in the world as commercial relations became more complex and its banking community emphasized the maintenance of stable exchange systems. The industrialized economies of Europe and the United States exchanged manufactured goods between themselves in this economic structure, but they also depended on the southern hemisphere for raw materials which were acquired at relatively low prices, then processed and resold into southern hemisphere markets as manufactured goods. In the culmination of the informal and then formal empires of the nineteenth century, it became vital for the industrial economies of Europe to maintain close ties with the south, both to assure a supply of raw materials and also to maintain their markets in these countries. Although imperialism was not the only way of accomplishing this, it remained an important option, especially for powers like Great Britain and France, well into the twentieth century. [1] The economic disruptions caused by war and depression in the 1920s and 1930s seemed to make these imperial ties even more vital for European powers to some observers. [2]

The movements for independence that crossed Asia and Africa after 1945, however, undercut the political supports for these economic arrangements, as colony after colony gained independence from its European master. What followed was the construction of a new international economy that, although it continued many of the trade patterns from before the Second World War, also created new institutions intended to help funnel capital from the developed north to the developing south. Economic relations did not necessarily end with political independence: the world economy remained built around international trade. In the wake of independence, many colonies found themselves in economic relationships with the former imperial powers that severely limited their ability to act independently. [3] At the same time, however, the creation of the International Monetary Fund and the International Bank for Reconstruction and Development at the Bretton Woods conference in 1944, and the International Development Association in 1960, attempted to stabilize exchange rates and provide funds for development.

Such efforts, and the quarter century of economic boom that followed the Second World War, have not eliminated disparities in economic productivity and standards of living between the former imperial powers and the former colonial parts of the world, nor have they reformulated trade patterns that send unfinished commodities from the south to the north and finished goods in the opposite direction. The terms of trade remained in favor of industrial economies during much of the boom, so that even as the economies of the less-developed countries grew at unprecedented rates between the 1950s and the 1970s, they did so at a pace slower than that of the industrial economies. These inconsistencies led to economic difficulties for the former colonies as they struggled to achieve the economic structures and productivity that exist in the developed countries. Some leaders of these newly independent nations have suggested that the former imperial powers continue to exploit the once-colonized world through these economic ties. These relationships of dependency developed in the 1950s as political imperialism declined. They became even more significant in the 1970s and 1980s as a consequence of a worldwide recession which increased Third World debt and increased the interdependence of the economies of the developed countries of the northern hemisphere and those of the less-developed southern hemisphere. [4] More recently, agreements reducing protective tariffs and creating free trade zones have been a focus for attempts to increase the integration of the global economy, as well as the target of protests against the disparities between rich and poor nations that free trade seems, to some, to foster and protect. [5]

1. ROMESH DUTT, THE ECONOMIC HISTORY OF INDIA IN THE VICTORIAN AGE

Romesh Chunder Dutt (1848–1909) was born in the Indian province of Bengal into a Calcutta family whose members were pioneers in Indian participation in government and educational administration. Dutt's early education was in Indian schools, but in 1868, he traveled to England to take the Indian Civil Service examination. While in England, he read English history and undertook legal studies. His experience there convinced him of the value of English democratic political institutions.

In 1871, Dutt returned to India and began a distinguished career in the Indian civil service. By 1894, he had become officiating commissioner of Burdwan, but retired soon after both because of the poor prospects for further advancement for Indians in the British system and also to be able to devote more time to Indian politics and to literary activities. In 1899, he presided over the annual session of the Indian National Congress, the Hindu organization lobbying for greater Indian participation in Indian affairs. After the turn of the century, he was an active participant in projects for economic and political reform in India.

In addition to his career as a public servant, Dutt also produced a significant body of literary and historical writings in the course of his life. These ranged from his account of his first trip to London, *Three Years in Europe* (1872) to a *History of Bengali Literature* (1877) to historical and social romances written in Bengali. He also wrote a number of works that addressed the social and economic problems of the Indian subcontinent. His first essay in this direction was a book published in the 1870s on the *Peasantry in Bengal,* which criticized the land settlement established by the British. In 1899, Dutt settled in London and published several works that dealt with the effects of British colonial domination on Indian agriculture. A series of open letters criticizing the proposals of Lord Curzon, then governor-general, led to a rejoinder from Curzon. Dutt's response came in the form of two volumes on the *Economic History of British India, 1757–1837* (1902) and *India in the Victorian Age* (1904).

Although Dutt never advocated independence for India or the end of the British Empire, he nevertheless appreciated both the strength of the economic relationships between Britain and India that the empire had created and the ways in which these relationships worked to India's disadvantage. In the following excerpt from the *Preface* to *India in the Victorian Age,* he spells out the terms of this relationship in a way that previews many critiques of the increasingly global economy of the twentieth century.

The Economic History of India in the Victorian Age

The late Marquis of Salisbury was Secretary of State for India in 1875. His deep insight in matters to which he devoted his attention is well known. And he condemned the weakness and the one-sidedness of the Indian Fiscal policy in a Minute recorded in 1875, which is often cited. "So far," his lordship wrote, "as it is possible to change the Indian Fiscal system, it is desirable that the cultivator should pay a smaller proportion of the whole national charge. It is not in itself a thrifty policy to draw the mass of revenue from the rural districts, where capital is scarce, sparing the towns where it is often redundant and runs to waste in luxury. The injury is exaggerated in the case of India where so much of the revenue is exported without a direct equivalent. As India must be bled, the lancet should be directed to the parts where the blood is congested, or at least sufficient, not to those which are already feeble from the want of it."

Lord Salisbury's warning has been disregarded. And while we hear so much of the prosperous budgets and surpluses since the value of the rupee was fixed at is. 4d., no advantage has been taken of this seeming prosperity to relieve agriculture. Not one of the special taxes on land, imposed in addition to the Land Revenue since 1871, has been repealed.

It will appear from these facts, which I have mentioned as briefly as possible, that Agriculture, as a source of the nation's income, has not been widened under British administration. Except where the Land Revenue is permanently settled, it is revised and enhanced at each new Settlement, once in thirty years or once in twenty years. It professes to take 50 per cent. of the rental or of the economic rent, but virtually takes a much larger share in Bombay and Madras. And to it are added other special taxes on land which can be enhanced indefinitely at the will of the State. The Land Assessment is thus excessive, and it is also uncertain. Place any country in the world under the operation of these rules, and agriculture will languish. The cultivators of India are frugal, industrious, and peaceful; but they are nevertheless impoverished, resourceless, always on the brink of famines and starvation. This is not a state of things which Englishmen can look upon with just pride. It is precisely the state of things which they are remedying in Ireland. It is a situation which they will not tolerate in India when they have once grasped it.

If we turn from the sources of wealth to its distribution, and to the financial arrangements of India, the same melancholy picture is presented to us. The total revenues of India during the last ten years of the Queen's reign—1891–92 to 1900–1—came to 647 millions sterling. The annual average is thus under 65 millions, including receipts from railways, irrigation works, and all other sources. The expenditure in England during these ten years was 159 millions, giving an annual average of nearly 16 millions sterling. One-fourth, therefore, of all the revenues derived in India, is annually remitted to England as Home Charges. And if we add to this the portion of their salaries which European officers employed in India annually remit to England, the total annual drain out of the Indian Revenues to England considerably exceeds 20 millions. The richest country on earth stoops to levy this annual contribution from the poorest. Those who earn £42 per head ask for 10s. per head from a nation earning £2 per head. And this 10s. per head which the British people draw from India impoverishes Indians, and therefore impoverishes British trade with India. The contribution does not benefit British commerce and trade, while it drains the life-blood of India in a continuous, ceaseless flow.

For when taxes are raised and spent in a country, the money circulates among the people, fructifies trades, industries, and agriculture, and in one shape or another reaches the mass of the people. But when the taxes raised in a country are remitted out of it, the money is lost to the country for ever, it does not stimulate her trades or industries, or reach the people in any form. Over 20 millions sterling are annually drained from the revenues of India; and it would be a miracle if such a process, continued through long decades, did not impoverish even the richest nation upon earth.

The total Land Revenue of India was 17½ millions in 1900–1. The total of Home Charges in the same year came to 17 millions. It will be seen, therefore, that an amount equivalent to all that is raised from the soil, in all the Provinces of India, is annually remitted out of the country as Home Charges. An additional sum of several millions is sent in the form of private remittances by European officers, drawing their salaries from Indian Revenues; and this remittance increases as the employment of European officers increases in India.

The 17 millions remitted as Home Charges are spent in England (1) as interest payable on the Indian Debt; (2) as interest on railways; and (3) as Civil and Military

Charges. A small portion, about a million, covers the cost of military and other stores supplied to India.

A very popular error prevails in the country that the whole Indian Debt represents British capital sunk in the development of India. It is shown in the body of this volume that this is not the genesis of the Public Debt of India. When the East India Company ceased to be rulers of India in 1858, they had piled up an Indian Debt of 70 millions. They had in the meantime drawn a tribute from India, financially an unjust tribute, exceeding 150 millions, not calculating interest. They had also charged India with the cost of Afghan wars, Chinese wars, and other wars outside India. Equitably, therefore, India owed nothing at the close of the Company's rule; her Public Debt was a myth; there was a considerable balance of over 100 millions in her favour out of the money that had been drawn from her.

Within the first eighteen years of the Administration of the Crown the Public Debt of India was doubled. It amounted to about 140 millions in 1877, when the Queen became the Empress of India. This was largely owing to the cost of the Mutiny wars, over 40 millions sterling, which was thrown on the revenues of India. And India was made to pay a large contribution to the cost of the Abyssinian War of 1867.

Between 1877 and 1900, the Public Debt rose from 139 millions to 224 millions. This was largely due to the construction of railways by Guaranteed Companies or by the State, beyond the pressing needs of India and beyond her resources. It was also largely due to the Afghan Wars of 1878 and 1897. The history of the Indian Debt is a distressing record of financial unwisdom and injustice; and every impartial reader can reckon for himself how much of this Indian Debt is morally due from India.

The last items of the Home Charges are the Civil and Military Charges. This needs a revision. If Great Britain and India are both gainers by the building up of the British Indian Empire, it is not fair or equitable that India alone should pay all the cost of the maintenance of that superb edifice. It is not fair that all the expenses incurred in England, down to the maintenance of the India Office and the wages of the charwoman employed to clean the rooms at Whitehall, should be charged to India. Over forty years ago one of the greatest of Indian administrators suggested an equitable compromise. In a work on *Our Financial Relations with India,* published in 1859, Sir George Wingate suggested that India should pay all the expenses of Civil and Military Administration incurred in India, while Great Britain should meet the expenses incurred in England, as she did for her Colonies. Is it too late to make some such equitable adjustment to-day? India's total Civil and Military Charges, incurred in England, come to 6 millions—a sum which would be considerably reduced if it came from the British taxpayer. Is it too much to expect that Great Britain might share this burden, while India paid all the Civil and Military charges incurred in India?

These are the plain facts of the economic situation in India. Given these conditions, any fertile, industrious, peaceful country in the world would be what India is to-day. If manufactures were crippled, agriculture overtaxed, and a third of the revenue remitted out of the country, any nation on earth would suffer from permanent poverty and recurring famines. Economic laws are the same in Asia as in Europe. If India is poor to-day, it is through the operation of economic causes. If India were prosperous under these circumstances, it would be an economic miracle. Science knows no miracles. Economic laws are constant and unvarying in their operation.

The evils suggest their own remedies. The Excise tax on Indian mill industry should be withdrawn; the Indian Government should boldly help Indian industries, for the good of the Indian people, as every civilised Government on earth helps the industries of its own country. All taxes on the soil in addition to the Land Revenue should be repealed; and the Land Revenue should be moderated and regulated in its operation. The Public Debt, unjustly created in the first instance, is now an accomplished fact: but an Imperial Guarantee would reduce the rate of interest; and a Sinking Fund would gradually reduce its volume. Civil and Military Charges, incurred in England, should be borne, or at least shared, by Great Britain, as she shares them in the case of her Colonies. Civil charges in India should be reduced by a larger employment of Indians; military charges in India should be repressed with a strong hand; and India should pay for an army needed for her own requirements. All further extension of railways from State-Loans, or under guarantee of interest from the taxes, should be prohibited. Irrigation works should be extended, as far as possible, from the ordinary revenues. The annual Economic Drain from India should be steadily reduced; and in carrying out these fiscal reforms, representatives of the people of India,—of the taxpayers who are alone interested in Retrenchment in all countries,—should be called upon to take their share, and offer their assistance.

"The Government of a people by itself," wrote John Stuart Mill, "has a meaning and a reality, but such a thing as government of one people by another does not, and cannot exist. One people may keep another for its own use, a place to make money in, a human cattle farm for the profits of its own inhabitants." This statement contains a deep truth. Large masses of men are not ordinarily impelled by a consideration of other peoples' interests. The British voter is as fair-minded as the voter in any other country on earth, but he would not be a British voter, and he would not be human, if he did not ordinarily mind his own interests and secure his own profits. Parliament carries out the mandates of voters; the Indian Secretary, a Member of the British Cabinet, cannot act against the joint wishes of the Cabinet. The Members of his Council are appointed by him, and do not in any sense represent the people of India. The Viceroy of India is under the orders of the Indian Secretary of State; and the Government of India is vested in his Ordinary Council, which, in the words of Sir William Hunter, is an "oligarchy," and does not represent the people. The Members of the Governor-General's Council are generally heads of spending departments, and "the tendency is," as Sir David Barbour said before the Indian Expenditure Commission, "ordinarily for pressure to be put on the Financial Department to incur expenditure. It is practically pressure. The other Departments are always pressing to spend more money: their demands are persistent and continuous." Nowhere in the entire machinery of the Indian Government, from the top to the bottom, is there any influence which makes for Retrenchment, any force which represents the taxpayer. Fiscal reforms are impossible under this Constitution. If Retrenchment is desired some room must be found, somewhere in the Constitution to represent the taxpayer's interests.

The Indian Empire will be judged by History as the most superb of human institutions in modern times. But it would be a sad story for future historians to tell that the Empire gave the people of India peace but not prosperity; that the manufacturers lost their industries: that the cultivators were ground down by a heavy and variable taxation which precluded any saving; that the revenues of the country were to a large extent diverted to England; and that recurring and desolating famines swept away millions of the population. On the other hand, it would be a grateful story for Englishmen to tell that England in the twentieth century undid her past mistakes in India as in Ireland; that she lightened land taxes, revived industries, introduced representation, and ruled India for the good of her people; and that the people of India felt in their hearts that they were citizens of a great and United Empire.

2. C. L. R. JAMES, ABYSSINIA AND THE IMPERIALISTS

C. L. R. James (1901–1989) was born in Trinidad, Jamaica, and spent his entire life studying and writing about the relationship between the European powers and the peoples of Asia, Africa, and the West Indies. He is best known for his history of the Haitian Revolution, *The Black Jacobins* (1938), an analysis of Toussaint L'Ouverture which was strongly influenced by James's Trotskyite loyalties at the time, but which emphasized the ability of non-Europeans to lead a revolution and the possibility of spontaneous leadership for the revolution, both positions at odds with Marxist thought of the time.

Later in his life, James became more focused on culture and human creativity, and is viewed as an early theorist of the postcolonial world. But during the 1930s, he tended to emphasize economic relationships and their political consequences. This is the case in the following article, published in 1936 in *The Keys,* a British journal associated with The League of Coloured Peoples. The crisis brought on by the attempts of the Italian leader Benito Mussolini to conquer the small east African country of Abyssinia provided James with the opportunity to outline the different forms of domination that European powers were able to use against less-developed countries. Although he sees the crisis ending in the imperial domination of Abyssinia by Europe, he also notes the ways in which the rapidly globalizing economy of the period between the world wars allowed a different form of domination.

Abyssinia and the Imperialists

Africans and people of African descent, especially those who have been poisoned by British imperialist education, needed a lesson. They have got it. Every succeeding day shows exactly the real motives which move imperialism in its contact with Africa, shows the incredible savagery and duplicity of European imperialism in its quest for markets and raw materials. Let the lesson sink in deep.

European imperialism has been after Abyssinia for fifty years. What do they want it for? They want it, first of all, for the minerals that are there, to plant cotton, to send some of their surplus population to the highlands, to make the natives buy Lancashire goods, or German goods or Italian goods, as the case might be, to invest money and then tax the native so as to make him pay a steady interest. All this they call developing the country and raising the standard of civilisation. They build a few schools and a few hospitals. Some few of the richer natives get jobs in the government service and come to European universities for education. They are pointed out as evidence of the high standard of civilisation that has been introduced into the native country.

But all the money that the imperialists are making out of the country has to be paid for by labour, and the real sufferers are those millions who, unprotected by trade union organisation or any sort of organised public opinion, are driven off their lands, down into mines at a shilling a day, or working above ground for fourpence a day as in Kenya, with all the special humiliations and degradations that are attached to the African in Africa, not because he is black, but because the imperialist despite his guns and cruisers, is in such mortal fear of the indignation of these people that he builds up in every possible way a wall of defence between himself and them. First of all, he has his cruisers always about, his aeroplanes and his trained soldiers. But in addition he insists always to his own people that they are superior to the exploited races, and he insists always to the exploited races that they are inferior to his own. Thus he reinforces the power of arms by democratizing the mentality of those whom he uses for his purposes both at home and abroad.

Now to this question of Abyssinia. These European imperialists have been after Abyssinia for fifty years. We have to remember that, because the issue before us today is obscured by the mountain of lies and nonsense which are being wrapped around it. They wanted it for the purposes described above, and they have got it. There is no longer any independence of Abyssinia worth a scrap of paper as far as the imperialists are concerned. The moment the Emperor signed the proposals of the Committee of Five in late September the independence of Abyssinia had vanished. All that Italy, Great Britain and France had been quarrelling about among themselves and with Abyssinia was given to them by those proposals, wrapped round with silver paper labelled "assistance to a weaker nation", and blessed with the holy water of the League. European imperialism was determined to get Abyssinia, and it has got it. Let us trace the steps.

Italy tried in 1896 and was beaten at Adowa and driven out. Abyssinia is a high plateau, strategically very powerful. The people are splendid fighters, so that the imperialists saw they could not steal it as easily as they had stolen the rest of Africa. In 1902 Britain asked for the Lake Tana concession. The Abyssinians refused. In 1906 Britain, France and Italy divided Abyssinia in London by the Tripartite Treaty. When they were finished they sent to tell Menelik, the Emperor of Abyssinia, who told them they could write what they liked in treaties, he remained master of his own country. They sheered off.

In 1915 Britain and France brought Italy into the war by, among other promises, a hint of Abyssinian territory. But when the war was over Britain and France grabbed the German colonies and Italy was left out. In 1919 Italy offered Britain to divide Abyssinia with her. The British government said no, that they did not want to have any power near the Lake Tana concession. Whereupon Italy seeing that Britain was not prepared to divide, conspired with France and dragged Abyssinia by the hair into the League of Nations. This was in 1923. This prevented Britain acting single-handed against Abyssinia as she wanted to do. So in 1925 Britain offered to Mussolini to divide on the same terms that she had rejected in 1919. But Abyssinia threatened to fight, and France supported Abyssinia at the League. Britain and Italy apologised, said they had meant no harm. France, it is to be noted, has a railway from Jibuti in French Somaliland to Addis Ababa. She makes an enormous profit from it, and French goods travel along this railway into Abyssinia. So in as much as France cannot attack Abyssinia herself, she was quite prepared to support Abyssinia to keep the others out.

But by January 1935 France is terribly afraid of Germany. Mussolini has a fine army, and in return for a promise of help against Germany, France "disinterests herself economically" from Abyssinia. In other words gives Mussolini a free hand. In Italy the water is up to Mussolini's nose, and he must find some sort of explanation somewhere or perish. So having squared France, he informs the British that he is ready to talk Abyssinia with them. This was on the 29th January last. The British government would not do a single thing. They would not reply to Mussolini because they did not want to say yes—that could be used in evidence against them—and yet they did not want to say no. Because Abyssinia had been blocking them for forty years, and it as time that she was brought to order. Abyssinia kept on appealing to the League of Nations. Laval would not budge, neither would the British Government. Mussolini meanwhile sent his ships packed with men to Africa. But the Abyssinians would not be frightened, and at last the British Government had to take notice. The League met and after some negotiations, they appointed Britain and France to discuss with Italy in Paris.

As can be seen from the *Manchester Guardian* of September, in the notes of the foreign correspondent, Britain and France offered Mussolini vast opportunities for exploitation in Abyssinia, but demanded that he should not dominate the country with an armed force. They all would do that together, and the force would be internalised. But Mussolini said no, and when Britain realised that Mussolini meant to establish himself in Abyssinia as firmly as they, for instance, were established in India, they got thoroughly frightened. For Abyssinia, powerfully situated as it is, is in the heart of the British Empire in East Africa, Mussolini would form an army of these splendid Abyssinian fighters, and from there, in the next war, he could march down into any of the British colonies around.

Britain at once sent the fleet to the Mediterranean, started to mobilise the British Army, and seeing that she might have to fight, decided to make it a League War, in defence of collective security, the independence of Abyssinia and a lot of blather of the kind. All the small nations at Geneva, terribly frightened at what is going to happen when Hitler begins, were glad to see Britain standing up for the League at last and wished to support. "Action now" said Eden, sanctions etc etc. The British Government, however, manipulated a scheme known to the world as the Proposals of the Committee of Five, by which Abyssinia would be delivered to them lock, stock and barrel, disarming of the people, all economic concessions, League advisors to govern the country, control of Budget taxes etc.—in fact all that they had been trying to get for fifty years. The Emperor could get no arms and they refused to give him any until he signed. Between the devil and the deep sea he chose the British Government masquerading as the League. Britain was now in a powerful position. Even although France was unwilling she had Mussolini in a serious hole.

She invited him to come in and share in this League mandate. He refused. The League started to impose sanctions, and worse still, the war went badly for Mussolini. The Abyssinians have been defending themselves with great skill and there is little possibility, in fact none, that Mussolini will dominate the plateau which has made the British government so suddenly enthusiastic for the League. Mussolini, therefore, despite all his noise and bluster, showed himself willing to come to terms and take as much as he could without threatening British interests. Forthwith Britain produces the peace plan, giving half of Abyssinia to Mussolini. Once British interests are no longer threatened and they can get their Lake Tana concession, they have no more interest in the League than they had when Japan stole a large piece of China.

What has caused the trouble is that many well-meaning people in Britain took the British government seriously when it announced itself as converted to the League. This sudden reversal has come as a shock, and Baldwin has had to get rid of Samuel Hoare and dodge and shift around and confess that a mistake has been made. One thing however we can take as certain—the British imperialists were prepared to support the League on behalf of Abyssinia and collective security, and even fight, as long as British imperialist interests were threatened. These are now safe, and all that they are concerned with now is dodging out of their promises as quickly as they can! Public opinion is against them. Public opinion on the whole is not aware that by the proposals of the Committee of Five the imperialists have got what they wanted. It genuinely thinks that the League is protecting Abyssinia, and, that accounts for its indignation.

But British imperialism does not govern only the colonies in its own interests. It governs the British people in its own interests also, and we shall see that imperialism will win. It will talk a lot but it will do nothing for Abyssinia. The only thing to save Abyssinia is the efforts of the Abyssinians themselves and action by the great masses of Negroes and sympathetic whites and Indians all over the world, by demonstrations, public meetings, resolutions, financial assistance to Abyssinia, strikes against the export of all materials to Italy, refusal to unload Italian ships etc.

Mussolini, the British government and the French have shown the Negro only too plainly that he has got nothing to expect from them but exploitation, either naked or wrapped in bluff. In that important respect this conflict, though unfortunate for Abyssinia, has been of immense benefit to the race as a whole.

3. Kwame Nkrumah, *Neo-Colonialism: The Last Stage of Imperialism*

Kwame Nkrumah (1909–1972) was one of the most dynamic and outspoken leaders of West Africa during the period after 1945 in which these former colonies obtained independence from European imperial powers. Born in Nigeria, Nkrumah was educated during the 1920s and 1930s in that country and in the United States. After 1945, he studied in London and became active in the Pan-African political movement. In 1947, he was appointed general secretary of a conservative nationalist movement in the British colony of the Gold Coast, but soon became more radical and in 1949 helped found the Convention People's Party in that country. After a period of imprisonment, in 1951 he became "leader of government business," as the Gold Coast entered a phased move toward independence, which it achieved in 1957 as Ghana. Nkrumah became prime minister, and in 1960, when Ghana adopted a republican constitution, he became its first president. From this position he unsuccessfully pursued a dream of African unity, while attempting to establish a socialist regime in Ghana and developing a marxist-inspired critique of the situation of postcolonial Africa. *Neo-Colonialism: The Last Stage of Imperialism,* published in 1965, represents a part of this activity, although it is not certain that Nkrumah was the actual author of the work. In 1966, he was removed from power in a military and police coup d'état. He died in exile in Guinea in 1972.

Neo-Colonialism: The Last Stage of Imperialism

The neo-colonialism of today represents imperialism in its final and perhaps its most dangerous stage. In the past it was possible to convert a country upon which a neo-colonial regime had been imposed—Egypt in the nineteenth century is an example—into a colonial territory. Today this process is no longer feasible. Old-fashioned colonialism is by no means entirely abolished. It still constitutes an African problem, but it is everywhere on the retreat. Once a territory has become nominally independent it is no longer possible, as it was in the last century, to reverse the process. Existing colonies may linger on, but no new colonies will be created. In place of colonialism as the main instrument of imperialism we have today neo-colonialism.

The essence of neo-colonialism is that the State which is subject to it is, in theory, independent and has all the outward trappings of international sovereignty. In reality its economic system and thus its political policy is directed from outside.

The methods and form of this direction can take various shapes. For example, in an extreme case the troops of the imperial power may garrison the territory of the neo-colonial State and control the government of it. More often, however, neo-colonialist control is exercised through economic or monetary means. The neo-colonial State may be obliged to take the manufactured products of the imperialist power to the exclusion of competing products from elsewhere. Control over government policy in the neo-colonial State may be secured by payments towards the cost of running the State, by the provision of civil servants in positions where they can dictate policy, and by monetary control over foreign exchange through the imposition of a banking system controlled by the imperial power.

Where neo-colonialism exists the power exercising control is often the State which formerly ruled the territory in question, but this is not necessarily so. For example, in the case of South Vietnam the former imperial power was France, but neo-colonial control of the State has now gone to the United States. It is possible that neo-colonial control may be exercised by a consortium of financial interests which are not specifically identifiable with any particular State. The control of the Congo by great international financial concerns is a case in point.

The result of neo-colonialism is that foreign capital is used for the exploitation rather than for the development of the less developed parts of the world. Investment under neo-colonialism increases rather than decreases the gap between the rich and the poor countries of the world.

The struggle against neo-colonialism is not aimed at excluding the capital of the developed world from operating in less developed countries. It is aimed at preventing the financial power of the developed countries being used in such a way as to impoverish the less developed.

Non-alignment, as practised by Ghana and many other countries, is based on co-operation with all States whether they be capitalist, socialist or have a mixed economy. Such a policy, therefore, involves foreign investment from capitalist countries, but it must be invested in accordance with a national plan drawn up by the government of the non-aligned State with its own interests in mind. The issue is not what return the foreign investor receives on his investments. He may, in fact, do better for himself if he invests in a non-aligned country than if he invests in a neo-colonial one. The question is one of power. A State in the grip of neo-colonialism is not master of its own destiny. It is this factor which makes neo-colonialism such a serious threat to world peace. The growth of nuclear weapons has made out of date the old-fashioned balance of power which rested upon the ultimate sanction of a major war. Certainty of mutual mass destruction effectively prevents either of the great power blocs from threatening the other with the possibility of a world-wide war, and military conflict has thus become confined to 'limited wars.' For these neo-colonialism is the breeding ground.

Such wars can, of course, take place in countries which are not neo-colonialist controlled. Indeed their object may be to establish in a small but independent country a neo-colonialist regime. The evil of neo-colonialism is that it prevents the formation of those large units which would make impossible 'limited war.' To give one example: if Africa was united, no major power bloc would attempt to subdue it by limited war because from the very nature of limited war, what can be achieved by it is itself limited. It is only where small States exist that it is possible, by landing a few thousand marines or by financing a mercenary force, to secure a decisive result.

The restriction of military action of 'limited wars' is, however, no guarantee of world peace and is likely to be the factor which will ultimately involve the great power blocs in a world war, however much both are determined to avoid it.

Limited war, once embarked upon, achieves a momentum of its own. Of this, the war in South Vietnam is only one example. It escalates despite the desire of the great power blocs to keep it limited. While this particular war may be prevented from leading to a world conflict, the multiplication of similar limited wars can only have one end—world war and the terrible consequences of nuclear conflict.

Neo-colonialism is also the worst form of imperialism. For those who practise it, it means power without responsibility and for those who suffer from it, it means exploitation without redress. In the days of old-fashioned colonialism, the imperial power had at least to explain and justify at home the actions it was taking abroad. In the colony those who served the ruling imperial power could at least look to its protection against any violent move by their opponents. With neo-colonialism neither is the case.

Above all, neo-colonialism, like colonialism before it, postpones the facing of the social issues which will have to be faced by the fully developed sector of the world before the danger of world war can be eliminated or the problem of world poverty resolved.

Neo-colonialism, like colonialism, is an attempt to export the social conflicts of the capitalist countries. The temporary success of this policy can be seen in the ever widening gap between the richer and the poorer nations of the world. But the internal contradictions and conflicts of neo-colonialism make it certain that it cannot endure as a permanent world policy. How it should be brought to an end is a problem that should be studied, above all, by the developed nations of the world, because it is they who will feel the full impact of the ultimate failure. The longer it continues the more certain it is that its inevitable collapse will destroy the social system of which they have made it a foundation.

The reason for its development in the post-war period can be briefly summarised. The problem which faced the wealthy nations of the world at the end of the second world war was the impossibility of returning to the pre-war situation in which there was a great gulf between the few rich and the many poor. Irrespective of what particular political party was in power, the internal pressures in the rich countries of the world were such that no post-war capitalist country could survive unless it became a 'Welfare State.' There might be differences in degree in the extent of the social benefits given to the industrial and agricultural workers, but what was everywhere impossible was a return to the mass unemployment and to the low level of living of the pre-war years.

From the end of the nineteenth century onwards, colonies had been regarded as a source of wealth which could be used to mitigate the class conflicts in the capitalist States and, as will be explained later, this policy had some success. But it failed in its ultimate object because the pre-war capitalist States were so organised internally that the bulk of the profit made from colonial possessions found its way into the pockets of the capitalist class and not into those of the workers. Far from achieving the object intended, the working-class parties at times tended to identify their interests with those of the colonial peoples and the imperialist powers found themselves engaged upon a conflict on two fronts, at home with their own workers and abroad against the growing forces of colonial liberation.

The post-war period inaugurated a very different colonial policy. A deliberate attempt was made to divert colonial earnings from the wealthy class and use them instead generally to finance the 'Welfare State.' As will be seen from the examples given later, this was the method consciously adopted even by those working-class leaders who had before the war regarded the colonial peoples as their natural allies against their capitalist enemies at home.

At first it was presumed that this object could be achieved by maintaining the pre-war colonial system. Experience soon proved that attempts to do so would be disastrous and would only provoke colonial wars, thus dissipating the anticipated gains from the continuance of the colonial regime. Britain, in particular, realised this at an early stage and the correctness of the British judgement at the time has subsequently been demonstrated by the defeat of French colonialism in the Far East and Algeria and the failure of the Dutch to retain any of their former colonial empire.

The system of neo-colonialism was therefore instituted and in the short run it has served the developed powers admirably. It is in the long run that its consequences are likely to be catastrophic for them.

Neo-colonialism is based upon the principle of breaking up former large united colonial territories into a number of small non-viable States which are incapable of independent development and must rely upon the former imperial power for defence and even internal security. Their economic and financial systems are linked, as in colonial days, with those of the former colonial ruler.

At first sight the scheme would appear to have many advantages for the developed countries of the world. All the profits of neo-colonialism can be secured if, in any given area, a reasonable proportion of the States have a neo-colonialist system. It is not necessary that they *all* should have one. Unless small States can combine they must be compelled to sell their primary products at prices dictated by the developed nations and buy their manufactured goods at the prices fixed by them. So long as neo-colonialism can prevent political and economic conditions for optimum development, the developing countries, whether they are under neo-colonialist control or not, will be unable to create a large enough market to support industrialisation. In the same way they will lack the financial strength to force the developed countries to accept their primary products at a fair price.

In the neo-colonialist territories, since the former colonial power has in theory relinquished political control, if the social conditions occasioned by neo-colonialism cause a revolt the local neo-colonialist government can be sacrificed and another equally subservient one substituted in its place. On the other hand, in any continent where neo-colonialism exists on a wide scale the same social pressures which can produce revolts in neo-colonial territories will also affect those States which have refused to accept the system and therefore neo-colonialist nations have a ready-made weapon with which they can threaten their opponents if they appear successfully to be challenging the system.

These advantages, which seem at first sight so obvious, are, however, on examination, illusory because they fail to take into consideration the facts of the world today.

The introduction of neo-colonialism increases the rivalry between the great powers which was provoked by the old-style colonialism. However little real power the government of a neo-colonialist State may possess, it must have, from the very fact of its nominal independence, a certain area of manoeuvre. It may not be able to exist without a neo-colonialist master but it may still have the ability to change masters.

The ideal neo-colonialist State would be one which was wholly subservient to neo-colonialist interests but the existence of the socialist nations makes it impossible to enforce the full rigour of the neo-colonialist system. The existence of an alternative system is itself a challenge to the neo-colonialist regime. Warnings about 'the dangers of Communist subversion' are likely to be two-edged since they bring to the notice of those living under a neo-colonialist system the possibility of a change of regime. In fact neo-colonialism is the victim of its own contradictions. In order to make it attractive to those upon whom it is practised it must be shown as capable of raising their living standards, but the economic object of neo-colonialism is to keep those standards depressed in the interest of the developed countries. It is only when this contradiction is understood that the failure of innumerable 'aid' progammes, many of them well intentioned, can be explained.

In the first place, the rulers of neo-colonial States derive their authority to govern, not from the will of the people, but from the support which they obtain from their neo-colonialist masters. They have therefore little interest in developing education, strengthening the bargaining power of their workers employed by expatriate firms, or indeed of taking any step which would challenge the colonial pattern of commerce and industry, which it is the object of neo-colonialism to preserve. 'Aid', therefore, to a neo-colonial State is merely a revolving credit, paid by the neo-colonial master, passing through the neo-colonial State and returning to the neo-colonial master in the form of increased profits.

Secondly, it is in the field of 'aid' that the rivalry of individual developed States first manifests itself. So long as neo-colonialism persists so long will spheres of interest persist, and this makes multilateral aid—which is in fact the only effective form of aid— impossible.

Once multilateral aid begins the neo-colonialist masters are faced by the hostility of the vested interests in their own country. Their manufacturers naturally object to any attempt to raise the price of the raw materials which they obtain from the neo-colonialist territory in question, or to the establishment there of manufacturing industries which might compete directly or indirectly with their own exports to the territory. Even education is suspect as likely to produce a student movement and it is, of course, true that in many less developed countries the students have been in the vanguard of the fight against neo-colonialism.

In the end the situation arises that the only type of aid which the neo-colonialist masters consider as safe is 'military aid.'

Once a neo-colonialist territory is brought to such a state of economic chaos and misery that revolt actually breaks out then, and only then, is there no limit to the generosity of the neo-colonial overlord, provided, of course, that the funds supplied are utilised exclusively for military purposes.

Military aid in fact marks the last stage of neo-colonialism and its effect is self-destructive. Sooner or later the weapons supplied pass into the hands of the opponents of the neo-colonialist regime and the war itself increases the social misery which originally provoked it.

4. MIHAJLO MESAROVIC AND EDUARD PESTEL, MANKIND AT THE TURNING POINT, THE SECOND REPORT TO THE CLUB OF ROME

The Club of Rome is a think tank of scientists, business leaders, international civil servants, and politicians from around the world devoted to the discussion of issues of interest to the future of the world economy, and especially to overcoming national barriers to the discussion and solution of these issues. The Club was founded in 1969 by Italian businessman Aurelio Peccei, and gained international prominence in 1972 with the publication of its First Report, *The Limits of Growth,* which called attention to the problem of limited resources in the world. Its Second Report, *Mankind at the Turning Point,* issued in 1974, was an attempt to focus attention on the long-term problems of population growth and economic organization as they appeared in the immediate aftermath of decolonization. Even as that process was breaking up the nineteenth-century empires and creating numerous new nation-states, the Club's *Report* was urging the creation of a system of interdependent and "harmonious" parts, each making its own contribution to the world's economy and culture. The Second Report, therefore, is a vision of how a postcolonial world economy could be organized and of how the former colonies could continue to play a part in the world economic system that was built around the capitalistic economies of the northern hemisphere.

Mankind at the Turning Point, the Second Report to the Club of Rome

Change in the course of world development from undifferentiated to organic growth would have been a matter of choice and good will rather than necessity if the world had not evolved into a state in which nations and regions from all over the globe not merely influence but strongly depend on each other. Contributing to this transition, in addition to the traditional political, ideological, and economic ties, are new global world problems specific for our era such as worldwide dependence on a common stock of raw materials, problems in providing energy and food supply, sharing of the common physical environment on land, sea, and air, etc. The world community appears as a "system" by which we mean collection of interdependent parts rather than merely a group of largely independent entities as was the case in the past. And as a consequence a disturbance of the normal state of affairs in any part of the world quickly spreads all over the world, as many recent events unmistakably show. Let us briefly trace the developments in such an event.

The winter 1971–1972, with its prolonged low temperatures and strong icy winds all over Eastern Europe, effectively destroyed one third of the Russian winter wheat crop. Surprisingly, the government bureaucracy ignored the situation, and the spring wheat acreage allocation remained unchanged. Since the direct per-capita consumption of wheat in that region is rather high (three times higher than in North America), it was urgent that the deficit be eliminated. In July 1972 the U.S. government extended a $750 million credit to the Soviet Union for the purchase of grain over a three-year period. Actually, the value of the purchase increased significantly before the delivery got underway since food prices soared all over the world. The price of wheat doubled in North America—hitherto a bastion of cheap food supply. Public resentment arose because people felt that in effect they were being made to pay for a transaction that did not involve the ordinary citizen. More important, and much more unfortunately, that same year's late monsoon heavily damaged the crops on the Indian subcontinent, resulting in a disastrous loss in food supply, which came in the aftermath of a tragic war. Nowhere was wheat to be found, for most of the world's surplus had been sold. Then a drought hit China and Africa and while China was acquiring whatever foodstuffs were left on the market, hundreds of thousands of Africans faced starvation. In a similar situation several years earlier, millions of tons of wheat had been rushed from North American to avert disaster; but this time only two hundred thousand tons could be made available.

The most outstanding lesson which can be drawn from these events is a realization of how strong the bonds among nations have become. A bureaucratic decision in one region, perhaps the action of just one individual—not to increase the spring wheat acreage—resulted in a housewives' strike against soaring food prices in another part of the world and in tragic suffering in yet another part of the world. If the world is already interdependent to that extent, and interdependence is certain to increase, should regional or national decisions still be made in isolation, in total ignorance of their effects on other parts of the world system?

The world cannot be viewed any more as a collection of some 150-odd nations and an assortment of political and economic blocs. Rather, the world must be viewed as consisting of nations and regions which form a world system through an assortment of interdependences.

However, such interdependence is not the only new feature of the emerging world system. A subtle and very fundamental transformation is taking place. In earlier eras of lesser complexity different cultural or economic aspects, including their effects on technical development and natural environment, could have been considered separately. Today, many of these phenomena have become interdependent which greatly complicates any search for the solution of various critical problems. Traditionally, in order to understand what appeared to him to be diverse aspects of reality, man has developed different scientific disciplines: physics, chemistry, biology, technology, economics, the social and political sciences, philosophy, ethics, theology, etc. And in solving different problems man has relied on experience and expertise in relevant disciplines. But today's problems require knowledge from a number of, if not all, disciplines. For example, the solution of the world food supply crisis is a question not just of agronomy and economics, but of ecology, the physical and social sciences, and many others. How to increase the fertility of the soil, and the acreage of arable land, the question of landownerships, the organization of agriculture, etc., all are now critical and interdependent issues. Furthermore the solution depends on the population growth, since the problem is not in producing foodstuffs as such, but in producing food in the amount required by the existing population. Eventually, the availability of food in one part of the world and the desperate need for food in another will create a new international political situation; the very daily existence of the people in the needy parts of the world will depend on the decisions in other parts and over a long period of time, perhaps indefinitely. Then, the basic individual human values and attitudes of the members of the world community will become a determining factor in deciding whether specific trade-offs and necessary sacrifices will be made. Apparently, the emerging world system requires a "holistic" view to be taken of the future world development: everything seems to depend on everything else. Such a holistic approach is also referred to as the "systems approach," meaning that one looks at the totality of all aspects of a problem rather than focusing attention on an isolated phenomenon, as is the case in the analytic approach traditionally used in scientific inquiry. "You cannot do merely one thing," as G. Hardin has put it. A good example is pollution brought about by anti-pollution devices. The sequence of events started with the explosive growth of industry on the eastern coast of the United States and in Western Europe. Jungles of smokestacks created air-pollution and particle-removing air-cleaning devices were installed to combat that pollution. As a result, smoke pollution was cut down considerably. However, the gases up the smoke-stacks did not carry solid particles and the various nitrogen oxides and sulfur dioxide could freely combine with water in the atmosphere forming sulfuric and nitric acid. Had the escaping gas contained solid particles the acids would not be formed. So now the rain from the supposedly cleaned atmosphere carried the acids on buildings and crops; a case was reported in which the rain was alleged to have been as acid as pure lemon juice: 1000 times the normal level.

Events surrounding other contemporary crises give equally strong indications of the emergence of a global and increasingly complex world system. The energy crisis quite readily provides another such illustration. When the oil crisis broke out in October 1973 efforts were directed toward resumption of supply flow to meet whatever demands would develop. But that turned out not to be the real problem. The real problem is only appearing now when a continuous increase in consumption coupled with an increased price for oil is bringing a major transfer of wealth and economic power. Iran has already acquired what amounts to a "minority" control of Krupp industries—a major steel-producing and engineering company in Germany. The *annual* excess of revenues to the oil exporting countries will amount to 60 billion dollars, which is about two thirds of all overseas investment which United States firms have acquired up to this date. Using such a one-year surplus they could acquire control of an amazing number of companies in the Western developed world including such U.S. giants as American Telephone and Telegraph, Dow Chemical, General Motors, IBM, ITT, U.S. Steel, and Xerox. And what can be acquired in ten years? The oil exporting countries will accumulate $500 billion in less than ten years; an amount which can buy twice the total output of the Japanese economy in the mid-sixties and is of the same order of magnitude as the total world monetary reserves. The developed world could consider interfering in the apparent transfer of economic power if it were not in dire need of both oil and capital; increasing size and complexity of industrial plants, specifically in energy-related sectors, make investment programs more difficult for private companies. Only in May 1974 two major U.S. utilities have announced cancellation of previously planned projects for the construction of nuclear power plants. The estimated cost of such a plant has reached $1.5 billion. With the high interest rates imposed to control inflation and an uncertain economy a long-range investment program going into billions of dollars is simply outside the reach of many companies. The alternative to private investment could be government investment programs, which would require increased taxation and would lead to control or nationalization of the energy industry. Another alternative, however, is foreign investment. In such conditions of interdependence neither of the two sides, oil-exporting or oil-importing countries, can plan long-term development without taking into account the development in other regions and indeed the entire globe.

Global interdependence also appears in other areas of material resources. A confrontation between the raw material producers and consumers on a broader front seems to be in the making amid clear signs of ever closer interdependence between the two sides. The United States, which up to the 1940s was a net exporter of materials, will depend by the year 2000 on imports of around 80 percent for all ferrous metals, excluding iron, and 70 percent for all nonferrous metals. In late 1973 Morocco increased the price of phosphate exports threefold, while in spring 1974 Jamaica increased the taxes on bauxite exports severalfold. The objective was not to inflict economic damage on the bauxite-importing nations but rather to redress the damage done to the balance of payments due to increased oil and food prices.

The reality of the emergence of the world system and its integrative effect on all facets of world development can be also seen by extending the view to the less developed world. The oil import bill of the developing countries will reach $17 billion in 1974, a level more than five times that of 1970. Such an outflow of foreign currency will reduce their total imports by a sizable fraction, cutting into the import of capital goods to build up their industry, and thus hitting where it hurts most: slowing progress toward the goal of reaching the economic takeoff point. Unlike the developed world, the developing countries use imported oil not for the luxuries of individual transportation and home heating, but primarily for agriculture—in mechanization and fertilizer production—and for industry. Whereas the shortage of oil is primarily an inconvenience for the affluent, for underdeveloped countries it means a *direct and immediate* cut in industrial output and food supply. The shortage in oil has already reduced fertilizer production in South Asia in 1973 by hundreds of thousands of tons while over the next three years the tight oil supply situation would certainly lead to an even more dramatic deficit in that region. Regional food production would thereby be curtailed at the time when the demand will have increased considerably. Ten gallons of gasoline, which an average Western citizen uses in one month of pleasure driving—is sufficient to produce the food necessary for the survival of one adult. In a situation of worldwide limited supply an increase in oil use decreases food availability. To be sure, the tradeoffs are global, not local. But can one really ignore that when taking a pleasure ride? Energy and food crises, population growth, and economic developments are all becoming tightly intertwined.

In addition to such a tremendously increased complexity of the emerging world system there is yet another characteristic of that system which makes the search for solutions of various global problems increasingly difficult; namely, the necessity of considering much longer time-horizons, looking twenty, thirty, or even fifty years ahead, rather than one, two, and five years as has been customary in the past. This creates a need to act very much in advance of the full development of a crisis, if its potential impact is to be counteracted successfully.

Historically, crisis situations could be looked upon differently. In the first place, the world system was so weakly coupled that local, national, or regional solutions were feasible. Second, once a problem was recognized, there was sufficient time to find a solution, because the rate of change was slow. Even if a full implementation of a solution were to require ten, twenty, or thirty years, the problem was still essentially the same in quality and magnitude as at the time when the solution had been designed. For example, the population in Europe began to grow faster in the early nineteenth century and the specter of eventual starvation was written on the wall by Malthus; but the agricultural yield could be raised by the introduction of fertilizer sufficiently fast so that the problem was solved even before there was a real food crisis. Today, however, the clocks run faster. Knowledge acquired in school or university and experience gained in practice become quickly obsolete. In an exponentially growing situation, change develops in much less time than the equivalent changes did in the past. For example, if the annual economic growth is 3.3 percent, the next sixteen years will produce the same change as the past forty years. This might help to explain why political and economic decision-makers have consistently underestimated future change, for they too have often marched into the future with their eyes on the past. We are indeed living in a very dynamic world in which we have to look decades ahead when making decisions concerning many vital issues. Such a need cannot but require at least some adjustments within a political system based on a four-year election cycle.

All contemporary experience thus points to the reality of an emerging world system in the widest sense which demands that all actions on major issues anywhere in the world be taken in a global context and with full consideration of multidisciplinary aspects. Moreover, due to the extended dynamics of the world system and the magnitude of current and future change, such actions have to be anticipatory so that adequate remedies can become operational before the crises evolve to their full scope and force.

5. SENATOR DONALD RIEGLE, *SPEECH IN SENATE DEBATE ON RATIFICATION OF NORTH AMERICAN FREE TRADE AGREEMENT (NAFTA)*

The globalization of the world economy led, in the last third of the twentieth century, to a growing number of agreements that created free trade zones in different parts of the world. The success of some of these, notably the European Community first established in 1958, lay in their ability to create large markets for agricultural and manufactured goods, allowing nations to move outside of the restricted opportunities offered in their own domestic markets. The increased competition created within these free trade zones, however, also forced uncompetitive producers to either become competitive or go out of business. The demands of market forces seemed to some to be taking precedence over all other consideration, such as environmental concerns or maintenance of employment and hard-won gains by the labor movement.

In 1992, in the waning days of the presidency of Republican George Bush, the United States negotiated a North American Free Trade Agreement

(NAFTA) with its neighbors Canada and Mexico. The battle for ratification of this treaty took place in 1993, under the new president, Democrat Bill Clinton. The debate made for a confusion of typical political lines: protectionist Republicans opposed the agreement, whereas other members of their party, including former President Bush, remained loyal to it, and still other Republicans saw it as an opportunity to inflict a political defeat on the new president. Clinton's own party was also split: labor unions and environmentalists opposed the agreement as inadequate, likely to lead to the loss of American jobs and environmental damage, whereas other Democrats saw it as an opportunity to adapt the American economy to the demands of the global economy and create jobs for Americans.

In the Senate debate on ratification, Senator Don Riegle, a Democrat from the heavily labor state of Michigan, was one of the speakers who opposed the new president of his own party and spoke against ratification. His concerns, however, went unheard: the treaty was passed by a vote of 61–38 in the Senate, following earlier approval by a 234–230 vote in the House of Representatives.

Speech in Senate Debate on Ratification of North American Free Trade Agreement (NAFTA)

The ACTING PRESIDENT pro tempore. The Senator from Michigan is recognized for 10 minutes.

Mr. RIEGLE. I thank the Chair.

Mr. President, this is a sad and troubling moment in our national history. I am really struck by the disconnection between the debate here and what is really going on across the country at the present time in our communities, and in our national and family life.

The people of America trying to follow this debate and trying to relate it to what is going on in their own personal circumstances must think that we all live on a different planet because we talk in such a grand way about creating jobs in Mexico. There is a desperate need for creating jobs here in the United States, and we are not doing that. In fact, we are moving away from that.

So that is why, fundamentally, this is such a sad and troubling moment in our national history. We have a desperately serious job shortage problem in America today. It is our most important problem. Unemployment is rising in America. More and more workers are finding that they can only find part-time work. In many families both a mother and father are holding two jobs each, four jobs between them, often at or near the minimum wage, to try to generate just enough income to be able to scrape by.

There is very little time for family life, very little time to give to their children or other things because of this steady erosion not only in the sheer volume of jobs but in what our jobs in America are paying.

We have seen the income for our jobs dropping over the last 20 years. As a result, we are seeing a steady grinding down of the middle class in the United States. It used to be that a hard-working person could aspire to get to the middle class, have a middle-class standard of living, and perhaps even go beyond that. Now people are finding that they cannot keep themselves in the middle class. They are sliding back into lower and lower income areas.

The underclass of American citizens, those really in poverty, is growing at a terrifying rate, an absolutely terrifying rate. We see it in our urban centers in a dramatic way. But it is also happening in our rural areas, the rising level of poverty. If you go into the outlying areas of Michigan or any one of the 50 States, you will find in the rural areas people are just barely scraping by, driving old cars, maybe that have had four or five previous owners, that are unsafe. They cannot afford anything else. Many of them cannot even afford that.

Of course, in our urban centers, our urban youth, whether black or white youth, other minorities, are finding the unemployment rates are 50, 60, 70 percent.

So we have an urgent need for a job-growth strategy in America. The disaster of Reaganomics during the eighties, which was this cruel and destructive policy of trickle-down economics, has served to accelerate those trends and create a widening division in America between the rich, who have gotten much, much richer over that period as all the income figures show, and most other families who are working harder and harder and still are slipping backward.

NAFTA is the ultimate expression of trickle-down economics, and it is going to have a terribly damaging effect on our economy, on our working families, and on our social order. Most of the people in this country out beyond the beltway, beyond this insular ring of privilege here, most of the people in the country know that. They understand economics. They know how this is going to work. They have seen the jobs leaving the country before now, and they know this will accelerate those trends.

For our urban youth, who cannot find jobs, they are finding today that it is easier to get a gun than it is to be able to go out and get a job.

That is a prescription for disaster for America. And we are seeing it. We are seeing it in the mayhem, of all of the manifestations of the "Clockwork Orange" society that we are in, the unsafe society across this country that we are seeing today.

I cited recently a story about a mother of three who recently went to a bank teller machine in Detroit and took out some money. She was accosted by three youths. She was shot and killed by a 9-year-old who was accompanied by an 11-year-old and a 14-year-old. That is not an uncommon situation. That is a story in the paper today—another terrifying story of urban violence in our local community here.

It is not surprising that we are seeing our society coming apart, because you have to have enough jobs in society to hold your society together. People have to be able to work. They have to be able to make a contribution. They have to be able to earn, to support themselves, and to support their families. If you do not have a job in America today, you are nobody. You are invisible. You, in effect, disappear.

In fact, even among our homeless population—we have our 500,000 homeless veterans today in the United States—people that wore the uniform of the country, went to serve, many of them in Desert Storm, who have come back and they cannot find work. They have been humiliated to the point where they are out living under bridges and in cardboard boxes because they have not found any way to hook into this economic system of ours.

The people that are going to make the money on NAFTA are the wealthy elite in this country. You can see it in what is happening in the stock market. You can see who stood up to speak for NAFTA; all the pin-striped suit crowd, all of the lobbying money that has been spent on it, the pundits, the people here within the beltway who love to gather in the salons of Georgetown and talk about how wonderful it is to be for free trade. They are out of the line of fire. They have plenty of money. They do not have to worry about their jobs.

The fact that somebody out in Flint, MI, or somebody in Chicago, somebody in some other State across the country is going to take it right between the eyes when they lose their jobs, it is an abstraction. It is a fine point. And it is very easy for them to dismiss because they are out of the line of fire. It does not mean very much to them.

That is what is wrong with America today. We have forgotten about our own people. We are in here now about to pass a job strategy for Mexico. We need a job strategy for the United States. We are about to bring 60 million Mexican workers into our work force who earn one-seventh to one-ninth of what our workers earn.

As Senator METZENBAUM just pointed out, our workers cannot compete with that. We cannot possibly compete with that. That is why we have had so many plants in America close and move to Mexico. We are going to see much more of that in the future. But we are also going to see the grinding down of the wage levels for the jobs that are still left in America because the owners of those firms are going to tell the workers, either you take less in wages and benefits or we are going to have to close and move to Mexico.

That is the inevitable effect of this. Yes; some will make billions. That is why the Mexican Government has spent tens of millions of dollars lobbying this thing through, because they stand to make vast fortunes. They bought and paid for the services of our own former U.S. Trade Ambassador, William Brock, who was hired by the Mexican Government, $30,000 a month they are paying. That is $360,000 a year. That is more than we pay the President of the United States.

He is one of dozens in our country that have sold out and gone to work to help ram this thing through. We saw what happened in the House of Representatives. We had NAFTA defeated 10 days ago. But then we saw the administration take out the checkbook of the American taxpayer and buy the votes they needed to turn that vote around. And every press outlet in the country reported on it. It has been in every newspaper, television, radio show, and program across the country talking about those deals.

That is how this vote got turned around. It has been driven by special interest money, and pressure and privilege, because some people stand to make tens of billions of dollars on moving our jobs to Mexico, and grinding down the wage levels here in the United States.

We desperately need to invest in our own people for a change. That is why Bush and Quayle were thrown out, to put an end to Reaganomics, an end to trickle-down economics. And how ironic it is that George Bush left that poisoned cup on the desk in the White House there, the NAFTA cup, and this administration sadly has come in and decided that they would just drink it right on down. That is what has happened here. It is a great shame. It is a great tragedy. We are going to pay for it in broken lives out across this country over the next several years.

It reminds me very much of Vietnam. We have a wall down there for the Vietnam veterans with 59,000 names.

Most of the names on that wall are not of the families of the economic elite of this country. We are going to have another wall, and it will be an invisible wall on which there will be 500,000, perhaps 5 million or more names of workers in this country—again not of the economic elite—who will lose their jobs or their chances for jobs in America because NAFTA is going to pass. Their job and job opportunity is going to go to Mexico, and it is going to be given to a worker down there working essentially at slave-labor wages. We are going to do without here in this country, and people will wonder how it is—our own people, desperate for work, are going to ask. How can we believe in America, when America does not believe in us?

How do we say to our urban youth: Love and believe in this country, but we have nothing for you? We cannot give you decent education or safe streets or a chance at a job, where you have some prospect of having a life and forming a family of your own and holding it together. No, we cannot do that in America today because we do not have enough job opportunity to go around. But we can go to Mexico with NAFTA and bring in 60 million Mexican workers to compete with our own.

It is wrong and ought to be voted down.

Study Questions

1. What are the characteristics of the world economy as it is viewed by Dutt?
2. For James, what are the principal aspects of the imperial relationship between Great Britain and Abyssinia?
3. How does Nkrumah describe the relationship between the European powers and their former colonies in Africa? What, for him, would true independence involve?
4. What are the principal characteristics of the relationship proposed by the Club of Rome between the former colonies of Asia and Africa and the developed countries of Europe and North America?
5. How does Senator Riegle view the relationship between the United States and areas such as Mexico?
6. Based on these readings, what different explanations are given for the continuing differences of wealth and standard of living between the developed countries of the northern hemisphere and the former colonies of Asia and Africa?

Suggestions for Further Reading

Ashworth, William. *A Short History of the International Economy since 1850.* New York: Longman, 1987.

Bairoch, Paul. *The Economic Development of the Third World since 1900.* Berkeley: University of California Press, 1977.

Barnett, Richard J., and Ronald E. Muller. *Global Reach: The Power of the Multinational Corporations.* New York: Simon and Schuster, 1974.

Seitz, John L. *The Politics of Development: An Introduction to Global Issues.* New York: Blackwell, 1988.

von Laue, Theodore. *The World Revolution of Westernization: The Twentieth Century in Global Perspective.* New York: Oxford University Press, 1987.

Web Sites

1. About the International Monetary Fund:

   http://www.imf.org/external/about.htm

2. The General Agreement on Tariffs and Trade:

   http://pacific.commerce.ubc.ca/trade/GATT.html

3. Global Economy (a Critical Approach):

   http://www.globalexchange.org/economy

4. The World Bank Group:

   http://www.worldbank.org

26

Postcolonialism
1970–Present

TEXTS

1. *Debate on Immigration Control,* House of Commons, December 5, 1958

2. Enoch Powell, *Speech to the Annual General Meeting of the West Midlands Area Conservative Political Centre, Birmingham, 20 April 1968*

3. Margaret Thatcher, *The Path to Power*

4. Mehdi Charef, *Tea in the Harem*

The end of the European empires after World War II dramatically altered the relationships between Europe and the rest of the world. Not only did European diplomats now have to deal with the interests and demands of a host of new nations, but European countries became the destinations of migrants from the former colonies. Many of these migrants were citizens of the former European colonial power, or had immigration rights as a consequence of the independence agreements of their native countries. The influx of non-European immigrants has been one of the most important social and political developments in Europe since the 1960s, introducing greater ethnic diversity into European populations and raising questions about not only immigration policies but also long-standing European policies regarding citizenship.

In Great Britain the focus of the immigration debate was so-called New Commonwealth immigration from the West Indies and South Asia [1,2,3] Under Commonwealth rules, citizens of these former colonies had the right of free entry into the United Kingdom. Beginning in the 1940s, immigration from the West Indies and South Asia began to be significant, although emigration from the United Kingdom to Canada, New Zealand, Australia, and South Africa was even stronger. A series of laws passed since 1962 has limited the citizenship rights of New Commonwealth immigrants. But although there was a general decline in immigration after 1962, the issue remained a charged one in British politics, and immigrants and their children faced significant problems of discrimination. The 1962 Commonwealth Immigration Act began this process of limiting full citizenship rights of Commonwealth residents. As its discussion began in 1961, there was an increase in West Indian, Indian, and Pakistani immigration spurred by the fear that the act would take away the right of entry into the United Kingdom. After the act was passed, immigrants were less often economically active and more often dependents of earlier immigrants. The 1991 census showed an ethnic minority of 5.5 percent in the United Kingdom, with over half British born.

In France immigration has come primarily from the North African colonies of France, Morocco, Tunisia, and especially Algeria, countries that gained independence in the 1950s and early 1960s. The worldwide recession of the 1970s led to tightened immigration controls in France as elsewhere, and this changed the character of immigrants from primarily adult males without families (but often with families remaining behind in their country of origin) to wives and children of earlier immigrants. The immigrant community therefore became more visible, as children of immigrants, many of them born in France, began to impact schools and other facilities, and as the need for apartments led to an increased presence of immigrant families in HLMs, the high-rise moderate income housing projects that marked the perimeters of large urban areas such as Paris, Lyon, and Marseille. By 1990, foreigners made up 6.35 percent of the French population.

The booming postwar West German economy needed labor, especially after 1961 when the Berlin Wall reduced immigration from East Germany, and a bilateral agreement between the German Federal Republic and Turkey in 1961 provide for Turkish migration to West Germany. After 1973, however, official labor recruitment stopped, as the economy slowed. Since then family reunification seems to be the principal characteristic of immigration. As in other West European countries, West Germany placed restrictions on visas and experienced increased xenophobia from the late 1970s to mid-1980s.

It is currently less immigration than the status of existing residents that is creating controversies in Europe. Many immigrants do not wish to return to their country of origin, and the European-born children of immigrants would themselves suffer problems of reintegration should they return to Turkey or North Africa. Their knowledge of Turkish or Arabic is often scanty or nonexistent, and they would face problems of the equivalence of credentials obtained in Europe with those granted in their parents' home countries. At the same time, however, it has proved difficult for European societies to assimilate or accept the differences of these minorities.

Especially in cultural activities, the era after colonialism has given rise to a self-consciousness about the effects of colonialism on the rest of the world, a movement termed "postcolonialism." As with many cultural movements, postcolonialism is difficult to define precisely, but its broadest meaning insists on the disturbances caused by European imperialism both in the preexisting indigenous cultures and in the cultures of the imperial powers. The hybridization of indigenous and imperial cultures has assumed a major place in this movement. More specifically, postcolonial authors, filmmakers, and artists have produced a body of work that reflects on the experiences of the peoples who were colonized, and on the effects of colonization and migration on both migrants and on the countries that have received them. [4] These works have emphasized in particular the experiences of indigenous peoples, women, and migrants. By being critical of and refusing to accept the assumptions of European colonialism, postcolonial authors and artists have created a new perspective on the relations between Europe and the rest of the world.

1. DEBATE ON IMMIGRATION CONTROL, HOUSE OF COMMONS, DECEMBER 5, 1958

In the course of the twentieth century, and especially as colonies gained independence after World War II, their relations with their former imperial masters became an important aspect of global relations. Most former British colonies joined the Commonwealth of Nations after independence, and under Commonwealth rules, their citizens had free entry into the United

Kingdom. These immigrants were usually economically active and were admitted for specific occupations, tending to collect in industrial areas. Racially different from previous immigrants, their presence caused some controversy, such as the Nottingham and Notting Hill race riots in August 1958.

The "race rioting" that occurred in the Saint Ann's Well district of Nottingham on August 23, 1958, and on August 30 and 31 in the Notting Hill district of west London, both areas with high concentrations of West Indian immigrants, were caused by groups of youths from other parts of Nottingham and London going into the West Indian neighborhoods in search of immigrants to attack. These forays generated violent reactions from the residents of those neighborhoods. These incidents brought the issues of immigration and racial discrimination to public attention, and when parliament resumed its sessions in the autumn, the question became a subject of debate. On December 5, 1958, a conservative member of the House of Commons, Cyril Osborne, proposed a motion, calling on the government "to take immediate steps to restrict the immigration of all persons, irrespective of race, colour, or creed, who are unfit, idle, or criminal; and to repatriate all immigrants who are found guilty of a serious criminal offence in the United Kingdom."

Although Osborne's motion declared that "race, colour, or creed" was not an issue, the ensuing discussion quickly focused on the issue of race. His motion brought a rejoinder from members of the Labour Party, especially Charles Grey and A. G. Bottomley, and the debate became an early instance in which the House of Commons openly discussed the possibility of restricting New Commonwealth immigration into the United Kingdom.

Debate on Immigration Control

Mr. Cyril Osborne (Louth): I beg to move,

That, whilst this House deplores all forms of colour bar or race discrimination, it nevertheless feels that some control, similar to that exercised by every other Government in the Commonwealth, is now necessary, and urges Her Majesty's Government to take immediate steps to restrict the immigration of all persons, irrespective of race, colour, or creed, who are unfit, idle, or criminal; and to repatriate all immigrants who are found guilty of a serious criminal offence in the United Kingdom.

I should like, first, to stress what is stated very clearly in the Motion, that this restriction shall apply irrespective of race, colour or creed. I recognise that this subject is political dynamite, and therefore I shall try to handle it with the same care and sense of responsibility that I should observe if it were real dynamite. I also recognise that this country is engaged in trying to build a multi-racial association which, if it succeeds, will be a pattern for the whole world. Therefore, I should like to assure my hon. and learned Friend the Joint Under-Secretary of State for the Home Department that I shall try to say nothing at all that will increase the difficulties either of the Colonial Secretary or of the Home Secretary, who are particularly concerned with this difficult problem.

I should also like to say that, despite what may have been a misunderstanding from a previous speech that I made or an appearance that I made on television, I myself have no racial hatreds or antipathies. I have no colour bar sympathies, and I do not support those who wish to penalise men because of the colour of their skins. I have no sympathy with that point of view at all.

Having made that point clear, I should like the House to realise that this problem, like real dynamite, will not cease to be dangerous by being ignored. Like real dynamite that accumulates in greater quantities, it could become increasingly dangerous. The size of the problem could become really serious and some foolishly applied or accidental spark could ignite the whole lot. We do our country a grave disservice by closing our eyes to what we know to be a very difficult but serious problem. Next to unemployment, which I regard as the gravest problem facing our country at the moment, this is possibly the most important problem with which we are concerned at home.

May I call attention to the fact that the Motion is restrained, moderate and limited? It asks for action to be taken against three categories of people whom I do not think anybody could defend. The Motion asks for fewer powers to be taken by the United Kingdom Government than are possessed already by every other Government in the Commonwealth. When Mr. Manley was in this country just after the unfortunate riots in Nottingham and Notting Hill he was reported as saying that he would not agree to any steps of this kind. Yet I am credibly informed that in the West Indies each island, and especially Jamaica which he represents so ably, has the power, which it exercises, of keeping out persons from other islands. They exercise restraint and restriction against one another. Therefore, it seems to me rather out of place for Mr. Manley to come here and say that he would force upon us a gospel which he himself is not prepared to accept in the case of his fellow West Indians. It seems to me to be the worst form of colonialism in reverse.

I am not asking for panic measures. I am asking for a reasonable consideration of the position.

Why is it that, apart from the social and difficult racial problems that arise, I think that there must be some control of immigration starting with a limitation on the least desirable types? I would remind the House of our basic economic situation. There are more than 50 million people in these islands, and we grow enough food for only 30 million. On the basis of our own food production there are already 20 million too many in these islands. We have no raw materials except coal. Two days ago we discussed the very difficult situation of the coal industry. We have to import 40 per cent. of our foodstuffs and 100 per cent. of our raw materials to keep us fed and employed. These have to be paid for by our exports or we face serious hunger and mass unemployment. That is why it is so important that we should limit the number of immigrants.

Two new dangers are facing us, and especially facing those engaged in the export trade. I fear that at the moment they are only dimly appreciated in the country. The first is that because of what we as white people, the Western world, are trying to do for the Afro-Asian countries in raising their standards of living, we are helping to industrialise them, and by so doing we are setting up new competition against ourselves in world markets. It has been estimated by the United Nations that nine-tenths of the world lives at about one-tenth of our standard of living, and that in these days of automation and semi-automatic machines the labour cost is the most important factor in total cost of production, and if the Afro-Asian peoples are paying only one-tenth of what we are for labour, then their products will destroy us in time in world markets. That will make it more and more difficult for this country to maintain the high standard of living that we are enjoying with the people that we already have here.

In 1954 the United Nations issued a report on the world economic situation, and it was estimated that if there were fair shares between the workers of all countries in the world the average wage would be about 32s. a week. That is the sort of problem that faces us with a population which is already far too large for our own resources. In view of that one fact alone, to allow uncontrolled immigration is just madness.

The other day we had a debate in which contributions were made by hon. Members from both sides of the House who had been to Japan, Hong Kong and India, and they made it clear that competition from newly developing industries in the Far East will cause more unemployment in places like Lancashire. It was also stated that the shipbuilding industry on the North-East Coast was having employment trouble because the Japanese could produce ships more cheaply. Only two days ago we discussed the difficulties of the coal industry caused by the oil coming here from the Middle East. Because of that background it seems sheer madness not to have some control of the number of people coming into these already overcrowded islands.

Another factor even more alarming from the economic point of view is that the countries behind the Iron Curtain are now starting to dump into world markets goods of all kinds at a price far below that at which we can produce them. Our job will therefore be to find work even for the people who are here already without our increasing the number without limit. I was told the other day that the Chinese textile industry is placing certain quality goods in Eastern markets at 10 per cent. below whatever the Bombay price may be, and that the Bombay price is so low that Lancashire cannot live with it.

Our position is difficult enough with the numbers that we have here, and we have a duty to look after our own people. In stating this, I am not doing any injury to other people, because I am merely asking that there shall be done for Englishmen what other parts of the Commonwealth readily do for their own people.

Mr. Martin Lindsay (Solihull): I beg to second the Motion.

The Motion uses the words: "irrespective of race, colour, or creed", but we cannot discuss this matter in such a general context. We all know perfectly well that the whole core of the problem of immigration is coloured immigration. We would do much better to face that and to discuss it realistically in that context.

Mr. A. G. Bottomley (Rochester and Chatham): If I do not follow immediately in my remarks the theme of the speech by the hon. and learned Member for Surrey, East (Mr. Doughty), it is because I want to cut my speech short for the sake of some of my hon. Friends who want to take part in the debate. I will, however, try to pick up some of the hon. and learned Member's interesting comments in the course of my general observations.

It is unfortunate that the hon. Member for Louth (Mr. Osborne) has moved this Motion. It is only a week since the Government lifted certain regulations on the entry of foreigners into the country. I think that, generally, we welcome foreigners, because past experience shows that we have gained a good deal from people coming here from overseas and bringing with them their skills, their culture and a new colour to our national life.

We are talking of plural societies in the British Commonwealth. We are talking of the need to be leaders in a multi-racial world. If we really mean that, we must show signs of believing in it, and we do not do so by restricting the entry into this country of people from other parts of the world. Indeed, no sooner have the Government made that move towards this liberalisation than we find a Government supporter asking us for the first time to impose restrictions on he entry into this country of members of our Commonwealth family.

Let us see what are the numbers involved. When the hon. Gentleman reads his speech he will find that he referred particularly to the coloured population. There are about 190,000 in this country, of which it is estimated that 100,000 come from the West Indies and 50,000 from India and Pakistan. There are many more British people going from the United Kingdom into the Commonwealth, and in India and Pakistan there are 35,000 or more United Kingdom citizens resident there. We want this movement to go on in our great family of nations.

I must say, because I believe it to be true, that in spite of the pious wrappings of this Motion, we cannot escape the fact that it is closely related to colour and race. As my hon. Friend the Member for Durham (Mr. Grey) has shown by his very able speech, certainly it is taken that way in the West Indies and in other parts of the Commonwealth. I ask the hon. Gentleman whether this Motion would have been moved today if it had not been for the shameful events in Nottingham and Notting Hill, three months ago?

Of course, there are faults on both sides. I have never said that all black men are angels and all white men are devils, but I say this to the hon. Gentleman, that he is certainly mixing in very bad company. The people who are concerned with keeping this emotional feeling alive are those who baited the Jews in days gone by, the Fascists—

Mr. Osborne *rose—*

Mr. Bottomley: It is a very bad thing that this Motion has been moved. All I am saying to the hon. Gentleman, and he must take it, is that it will be taken in this way. He is mixing with bad friends. I give due credit to him, and I am not suggesting that he has any such sentiments or feelings for that group, but the fact that he has moved a Motion of this kind gives support to people who share that view.

One hon. Gentleman suggested that immigrants included people with diseases and idlers and criminals. The Government have made their position clear. They say it is not so. Indeed, I refer the hon. Gentleman to the debate in another place when a noble Lord, speaking for the Government, Lord Chesham, said this:

> "It is sometimes said that there is a health problem, but at the moment certainly we are not aware that there is a serious problem." He had said earlier:
> "By and large, they do not present any particular problem to the police, and they are at least as law-abiding as most other inhabitants of this country."—
> [OFFICIAL REPORT, *House of Lords:* 19th November, 1958; Vol. 212, c. 715.]

The hon. Gentleman the Member for Solihull (Mr. M. Lindsay) talked about the numbers on public assistance. The Government spokesman in another place, the Earl of Perth, on the same occasion said that this accusation was very often made, but that it really did not signify because the facts did not justify it.

We on this side of the House recognise that there are numbers of people who come to this country who misbehave themselves. They are to be condemned for this, but already some Commonwealth Governments are taking the trouble to ensure that emigrants are of good character. For instance, I know that Mr. Manley and his Cabinet colleagues in the West Indies now give instructions for careful vetting of applications for passports from those who want to come to this country and anyone with a criminal record is stopped from coming.

Mr. Osborne: Why do we not do something here?

Mr. Bottomley: Because we have always made it a practice not to do so and because this great Mother of Parliaments has established complete freedom and liberty, so we put no restriction on the movement of people. If they are criminal we deal with them in the proper way, judicially. If some get caught in the criminal net we deal with them in the same way as we do with other wrong doers, irrespective of colour, creed or race.

We would do well to remember that a great deal of our standard of living is possible because of our association with these backward peoples. So we cannot shirk our responsibility towards them when they, in their turn, ask for some help. It is natural for them to look to this country for the opportunity of building a decent standard of living, just as the miners did when there was great distress here. They came from the Welsh valleys or from the North-East to London to look for work.

Both the Colonies and the independent members of the Commonwealth are in the process of developing a national economic life. They have to be careful not to overburden themselves with too many immigrants at one time. However, this danger will diminish, and their economies will become stronger and more mature. When that happens they will reduce, and, finally, abolish, their restrictions on immigration from one part of the Commonwealth to another so that, as in this country, there will be complete freedom of movement for Commonwealth citizens within the Commonwealth. We ought to aim at achieving this. We ought to be the leaders instead of limiting in any way entrance into this country.

We have been glad to have immigrants come here since the end of the war. I am sure that there are many who would readily pay tribute to the work done by them as nurses in hospitals and as assistants in public transport. In spite of what the hon. Gentleman has said about one section of a trade union branch apparently causing objections to be made, I can tell him that the Transport and General Workers' Union, which represents that branch, is on record as saying that it is against this kind of discrimination. I can tell him, too, that there are shop stewards in large undertakings throughout the country who have said that these men are their partners, that they want them to work with them, and that this is being done happily and successfully.

2. Enoch Powell, *Speech to the Annual General Meeting of the West Midlands Area Conservative Political Centre, Birmingham, 20 April 1968*

In 1968, a controversial speech by Enoch Powell, a conservative shadow minister, brought the discussion of race and immigration to the foreground in British politics, and in the immediate aftermath, Powell was dropped by Conservative Party leader Edward Heath from the Shadow Cabinet. Enoch Powell (1912–1998) was one of the most powerful and controversial British politicians of the post–World War II era. Educated through scholarships at King Edward's School in Birmingham, his hometown, and at Trinity College, Cambridge University, he was appointed professor of Greek at the University of Sydney, Australia, in 1937. During World War II, he served with distinction in the British army, rising in rank from private to brigadier in the course of the war. In 1946, he joined the Conservative Party, and won election to the House of Commons for the first time in 1950. He rose rapidly, gaining junior ministerial rank in 1955 even though he tended to hold traditional Tory views that were at odds with the increasingly liberal postwar Conservative Party. In 1962, he achieved full cabinet rank as minister of health, but chose not to serve in the government of Harold MacMillan's successor, Alec Douglas-Home. His 1968 Birmingham speech generated controversy for its views on immigration into the United Kingdom, setting Powell at odds with the Conservative Party leadership and especially the party leader, Edward Heath. In subsequent years Powell was to disagree with Heath on other issues, such as the relationship of the United Kingdom to Europe and the policies to be followed in dealing with the disastrous inflation that the country faced in the early 1970s.

Speech to the Annual General Meeting of the West Midlands Area Conservative Political Centre, Birmingham, 20 April 1968

The supreme function of statesmanship is to provide against preventable evils. In seeking to do so, it encounters obstacles which are deeply rooted in human nature. One is that by the very order of things such evils are not demonstrable until they have occurred: at each stage in their onset there is room for doubt and for dispute whether they be real or imaginary. By the same token, they attract little attention in comparison with current troubles, which are both indisputable and pressing: whence the besetting temptation of all politics to concern itself with the immediate present at the expense of the future. Above all, people are disposed to mistake predicting troubles for causing troubles and even for desiring troubles: 'if only', they love to think, 'if only people wouldn't talk about it, it probably wouldn't happen'. Perhaps this habit goes back to the primitive belief that the word and the thing, the name and the object, are identical. At all events, the discussion of future grave but, with effort now, avoidable evils is the most unpopular and at the same time the most necessary occupation for the politician. Those who knowingly shirk it, deserve, and not infrequently receive, the curses of those who come after.

A week or two ago I fell into conversation with a constituent, a middle-aged, quite ordinary working man employed in one of our nationalised industries. After a sentence or two about the weather, he suddenly said: 'If I had the money to go, I wouldn't stay in this country.' I made some deprecatory reply, to the effect that even this Government wouldn't last for ever; but he took no notice, and continued: 'I have three children, all of them been through grammar school and two of them married now, with family. I shan't be satisfied till I have seen them all settled overseas. In this country in fifteen or twenty years' time the black man will have the whip hand over the white man.'

I can already hear the chorus of execration. How dare I say such a horrible thing? How dare I stir up trouble and inflame feelings by repeating such a conversation? The answer is that I do not have the right not to do so. Here is a decent, ordinary fellow Englishman, who in broad daylight in my own town says to me, his Member of Parliament, that this country will not be worth living in for his children. I simply do not have the right to shrug my shoulders and think about something else. What he is saying, thousands and hundreds of thousands are saying and thinking—not throughout Great Britain, perhaps, but in the areas that are already undergoing the total transformation to which there is no parallel in a thousand years of English history.

In fifteen or twenty years, on present trends, there will be in this country 3 ½ million Commonwealth immigrants and their descendants. That is not my figure. That is the official figure given to Parliament by the spokesman of the Registrar General's office. There is no comparable official figure for the year 2000, but it must be in the region of 5–7 million, approximately one-tenth of the whole population, and approaching that of Greater London. Of course, it will not be evenly distributed from Margate to Aberystwyth and from Penzance to Aberdeen. Whole areas, towns and parts of towns across England will be occupied by different sections of the immigrant and immigrant-descended population.

As time goes on, the proportion of this total who are immigrant descendants, those born in England, who arrived here by exactly the same route as the rest of us, will rapidly increase. Already by 1985 the native-born would constitute the majority. It is this fact above all which creates the extreme urgency of action now, of just that kind of action which is hardest for politicians to take, action where the difficulties lie in the present but the evils to be prevented or minimised lie several Parliaments ahead.

The natural and rational first question with a nation confronted by such a prospect is to ask: 'How can its dimensions be reduced?' Granted it be not wholly preventable, can it be limited, bearing in mind that numbers are of the essence: the significance and consequences of an alien element introduced into a country or population are profoundly different according to whether that element is 1 per cent or 10 per cent. The answers to the simple and rational question are equally simple and rational: by stopping, or virtually stopping, further inflow, and by promoting the maximum outflow. Both answers are part of the official policy of the Conservative Party.

It almost passes belief that at this moment twenty or thirty additional immigrant children are arriving from overseas in Wolverhampton alone every week—and that means fifteen or twenty additional families of a decade or two hence. Those whom the gods wish to destroy, they first make mad. We must be mad, literally mad, as a nation to be permitting the annual inflow of some 50,000 dependants, who are for the most part the material of the future growth of the immigrant-descended population. It is like watching a nation busily engaged in heaping up its own funeral pyre. So insane are we that we actually permit unmarried persons to immigrate for the purpose of founding a family with spouses and fiancées whom they have never seen. Let no one suppose that the flow of dependents will automatically tail off. On the contrary, even at the present admission rate of only 5,000 a year by voucher, there is sufficient for a further 25,000 dependants per annum ad infinitium, without taking into account the huge reservoir of existing relations in this country—and I am making no allowance at all for fraudulent entry. In these circumstances nothing will suffice but that the total inflow for settlement should be reduced at once to negligible proportions, and that the necessary legislative and administrative measures be taken without delay. I stress the words 'for settlement'. This has nothing to do with the entry of Commonwealth citizens, any more than of aliens, into this country, for the purposes of study or of improving their qualifications, like (for instance) the Commonwealth doctors who, to the advantage of their own countries, have enabled our hospital service to be expanded faster than would otherwise have been possible. These are not, and never have been, immigrants.

I turn to re-emigration. If all immigration ended tomorrow, the rate of growth of the immigrant and immigrant-descended population would be substantially reduced, but the prospective size of this element in the population would still leave the basic character of the national danger unaffected. This can only be tackled while a considerable proportion of the total still comprises persons who entered this county during the last ten years or so. Hence the urgency of implementing now the second element of the Conservative Party's policy: the encouragement of re-emigration. Nobody can make an estimate of the numbers which, with generous grants and assistance, would choose either to return to their countries of origin or to go to other countries anxious to receive the manpower and the skills they represent. Nobody knows, because no such policy has yet been attempted. I can only say that, even at present, immigrants in my own constituency from time to time come to me, asking if I can find them assistance to return home. If such a policy were adopted and pursued with the determination which the gravity of the alternative justifies, the resultant outflow could appreciably alter the prospects for the future.

It can be no part of any policy that existing families should be kept divided: but there are two directions in which families can be reunited, and if our former and present immigration laws have brought about the division of families, albeit voluntary or semi-voluntarily, we ought to be prepared to arrange for them to be reunited in their countries of origin. In short, suspension of immigration and encouragement of re-emigration hang together, logically and humanly, as two aspects of the same approach.

The third element of the Conservative Party's policy is that all who are in this country as citizens should be equal before the law and that there shall be no discrimination or difference made between them by public authority. As Mr. Heath has put it, we will have no 'first-class citizens' and 'second-class citizens'. This does not mean that the immigrant and his descendants should be elevated into a privileged or special class or that the citizen should be denied his right to discriminate in the management of his own affairs between one fellow citizen and another or that he should be subjected to inquisition as to his reasons and motives for behaving in one lawful manner rather than another.

There could be no grosser misconception of the realities than is entertained by those who vociferously demand legislation as they call it 'against discrimination', whether they be leader-writers of the same kidney and sometimes on the same newspapers which year after year in the 1930s tried to blind this country to the rising peril which confronted it, or archbishops who live in palaces, faring delicately with the bedclothes pulled right up over their heads. They have got it exactly and diametrically wrong. The discrimination and the deprivation, the sense of alarm and of resentment, lies not with the immigrant population but with those among whom they have come and are still coming. This is why to enact legislation of the kind before Parliament at this moment is to risk throwing a match on to gunpowder. The kindest thing that can be said about those who propose and support it is that they know not what they do.

Nothing is more misleading than comparison between the Commonwealth immigrant in Britain and the American Negro. The Negro population of the United States, which was already in existence before the United States became a nation, started literally as slaves and were later given the franchise and other rights of citizenship, to the exercise of which they have only gradually and still incompletely come. The Commonwealth immigrant came to Britain as a full citizen, to a country which knows no discrimination between one citizen and another, and he entered instantly into the possession of the rights of every citizen, from the vote to free treatment under the National Health Service. Whatever drawbacks attended the immigrants—and they were drawbacks which did not, and do not, make admission into Britain by hook or by crook appear less than desirable—arose not from the law or from public policy or from administration but from those personal circumstances and accidents which cause, and always will cause, the fortunes and experiences of one man to be different from another's.

But while to the immigrant entry to this country was admission to privileges and opportunities eagerly sought, the impact upon the existing population was very different. For reasons which they could not comprehend, and in pursuance of a decision by default, on which they were never consulted, they found themselves made strangers in their own country. They found their wives unable to obtain hospital beds in childbirth, their children unable to obtain school places, their homes and neighbourhoods changed beyond recognition, their plans and prospects for the future defeated; at work they found that employers hesitated to apply to the immigrant worker the standards of discipline and competence required of the native-born worker; they began to hear, as time went by, more and more voices which told them that they were now the unwanted. On top of this, they now learn that a one-way privilege is to be established by Act of Parliament: a law, which cannot, and is not intended, to operate to protect them or redress their grievances, is to be enacted to give the stranger, the disgruntled and the *agent provocateur* the power to pillory them for their private actions.

For these dangerous and divisive elements the legislation proposed in the Race Relations Bill is the very pabulum they need to flourish. Here is the means of showing that the immigrant communities can organise to consolidate their members, to agitate and campaign against their fellow citizens, and to overawe and dominate the rest with the legal weapons which the ignorant and the ill-informed have provided. As I look ahead, I am filled with foreboding. Like the Roman, I seem to see 'the River Tiber foaming with much blood'. That tragic and intractable phenomenon which we watch with horror on the other side of the Atlantic but which there is interwoven with the history and existence of the States itself, is coming upon us here by our own volition and our own neglect. Indeed, it has all but come. In numerical terms, it will be of American proportions long before the end of the century. Only resolute and urgent action will avert it even now. Whether there will be the public will to demand and obtain that action, I do not know. All I know is that to see, and not to speak, would be the great betrayal.

3. MARGARET THATCHER, *THE PATH TO POWER*

Although Enoch Powell's views tended to marginalize him in Tory politics (he resigned from the party in 1974), later Tories claimed his views as precursors of their own. Margaret Thatcher (b. 1925) served as a conservative in the House of Commons from 1959 until 1992 and as prime minister for longer than any other prime minister in the twentieth century. As this excerpt from her memoirs shows, she tended to agree with Powell in 1968 during the crisis occasioned by his speech. More than any figure, she led the consolidation of Powell's views within the Tory Party and presided over the Tory dominance of British politics in the 1980s and 1990s. Her policies favored a dismantling of the post–World War II welfare state, close diplomatic ties with the United States, and "Little England" opposition to British integration into the developing European Community.

The Path to Power

The first modern immigration control measure had been introduced by Rab Butler in 1961. Hitherto, Commonwealth citizens had not been subject to the controls which applied to the admissions of alien immigrants from foreign countries. The Commonwealth Immigrants' Act 1962, bitterly opposed by Labour and the Liberals, introduced an annual quota of employment vouchers to limit the inflow, a system subsequently tightened up by the Labour Government in 1965. During 1967 the Kenyan Government's discriminatory policies against Kenya's Asians resulted in a large inflow of immigrants into Britain. This raised awareness both of the scale and impact of past immigration and fears about its unchecked future size. There was particular worry about UK passport holders who were not connected by birth or descent with the United Kingdom. In February 1968 Jim Callaghan announced legislation to deal with this. The issue was also closely linked to the introduction of race relations legislation, which became the Race Relations Act 1968, aimed at curbing discrimination on grounds of colour. This was opposed by many on the right who saw in it a danger of making immigrants a legally privileged community which would have no incentive to integrate fully into British society.

On Sunday 21 April 1968—two days before the debate—I woke up to find the front pages of the newspapers dominated by reports of a speech Enoch Powell had made in Birmingham on immigration the previous afternoon. It was strong meat, and there were some lines which had a sinister ring about them. But I strongly sympathized with the gravamen of his argument about the scale of New Commonwealth immigration into Britain. I too thought this threatened not just public order but also the way of life of some communities, themselves already beginning to be demoralized by insensitive housing policies, Social Security dependence, and the onset of the 'permissive society'. I was also quite convinced that, however selective quotations from his speech may have sounded, Enoch was no racist.

At about eleven o'clock the telephone rang. It was Ted Heath. He said: 'I am ringing round all the Shadow Cabinet. I have come to the conclusion that Enoch must go.' It was more statement than enquiry. But I said that I really thought that it was better to let things cool down for the present rather than heighten the crisis. Ted was having none of it. 'No, no,' he said. 'He absolutely must go, and most people think he must go.' In fact, I understood later that several members of the Shadow Cabinet would have resigned if Enoch had not gone.

Yet for several reasons it was a tragedy. In the short term it prevented our gaining the political credit for our policy of controlling immigration more strictly. This was an issue which crossed the political and social divide, as was demonstrated when London dockers marched in support of Enoch. Moreover, in practical terms there was very little to choose between the policies of Ted and Enoch on the matter. Although it is true that as a result of the speech the official Conservative line on immigration became more specific, essentially we all wanted strict limits on further New Commonwealth immigration and we were all prepared to support financial assistance for those who wanted to return to their country of origin.

4. MEHDI CHAREF, *TEA IN THE HAREM*

Mehdi Charef (b. 1952) was born in Algeria, but moved to France in 1963 with his parents. Arriving at the age of eleven, he experienced the disruptions of migration acutely, and although he had learned some French in Algeria, the war for independence had limited his educational opportunities. In France, he lived in a high-rise suburb of Paris, Nanterre, and in the *cités de transit* that French authorities built as temporary housing for immigrants. He worked in a factory as a teenager, but was arrested at the age of eighteen and served two years in prison. Upon his release, he once again worked in a factory, beginning to write fiction and screenplays in his spare time. *Tea in the Harem* was published in 1983 to critical acclaim, allowing him to escape the world he wrote about. It was translated into Spanish, German, and Basque, and in 1985, he directed a film based on it which won several French film prizes. He subsequently made several other films, and in 1989 published a second novel, *Harki*.

Charef's work has been profoundly influenced by his experience of being separated from his Algerian origins and living in a country in which he is considered a foreigner. It reflects a broader movement in France in the 1970s and 1980s of cultural expression by North Africans living in France. Helped by the liberal policies of the Socialist government of François Mitterand, who was elected president of France in 1981, this community was able for the first time to form organizations, performing plays and rock music, and making films. *Le cinéma du banlieu* (films of the suburbs) and *beur fiction* are expressions of the particular sensibilities of these immigrant communities in France. *Beur* is a slang term used by youths in the immigrant community to describe themselves. It uses Verlan, a kind of slanging used by the French underworld, involving inverting syllables, in this case of the French word for arab, *arabe*. In 1981, a radio station, Radio Beur, began broadcasting in the Paris area, and in the last two decades, both novels and films have described the lives of North African immigrants and their families.

Tea in the Harem

Lessons and homework took second place.

At the time, Majid and his parents were living in the Nanterre bidonville—the rue de la Folie—the largest and the cruellest of any in the Paris suburbs. Shantytowns that could equal anything in Brazil, but without the sun and the music. When Majid's dad had sent for his wife and son to come from Algeria, he'd not told them in his letter that they'd be coming to live in a cold, smoky barracks. When she first saw the place, Malika burst into tears, and Majid wondered if it was some kind of practical joke, because back home there was never enough to eat, but at least you had your little stone-built house; at least you had a home. You can always hide an empty stomach, but a hovel is there for all to see. Whatever happened to dignity? Malika used to clutch her little boy in her arms and wish she'd never made the voyage. His father used to say:

'They're going to rehouse us somewhere decent. . .I've been down to see them at the Town Hall. . .'

Months, years, spent living on their nerves—and always on the alert for fires, because in the shanty town the fires were a weekly event. Sometimes they were huge and lasted for hours. People would finally go back to bed in the early hours of the morning, with the flames dying down and the firemen exhausted.

Majid was seven years old when he and his mother found themselves waiting, one November morning, on the platform of a Paris station. His father was supposed to be meeting them, but he wasn't there. They waited for him, wandering around the station as the early editions hit the news stands and commuters stood drinking their morning coffees. Malika was still wearing her veil—as if caught between two civilizations. The suburban commuters on their way to clock in at the office eyed her curiously. This was the first time she'd left her village in Eastern Algeria, and here she was, all of a sudden, catapulted to the other side of the Mediterranean. Everything seemed so very huge here. 'This must be progress,' she told herself behind her veil. She had bought a new *haik* specially for the trip. It was her best outfit, and she wore it only to discover that women don't wear them here. Finally Majid's dad arrived, dressed in his fez. Majid didn't recognize him—when his father had emigrated, he had been too young to know him. He let himself be kissed by the man, because Malika told him that this was his father.

Then came the taxi, and then the shanty town. Young Majid went out looking for kids, and there were kids everywhere. 'Don't go getting lost,' Malika would tell him when he went out.

He was surprised by the Arab children—they all spoke French! And the kids weren't worried by this slum city, with its mud and its piles of rotting garbage. They spent their time—the Arab kids, with the Portuguese and the French—playing among the wrecked cars.

The football pitch is a sight to see. It's next to the street, and the goalposts are four big oil drums filled with stones. It's cold here. Majid's cheeks are blue and his lips are trembling, but nobody pays any attention to him. He wanders round the village. It's a real labyrinth, but it's organized. It's got a butcher's, a grocer's, a café-bar, a restaurant, and even a hairdresser's. A letterbox at the side of the road serves as a target for the kids' catapults. The one who gets his stone through the slot is the winner.

The children seem happy enough as they play in among the mud and the poverty and the thick smoke from people's stoves. Kids always seem to make out somehow—they'd find themselves somewhere to play even in a minefield. . .!

Majid enrols at the local school. His pals from the shanty town are easily recognizable by the mud on their shoes. It's not even worth cleaning shoes like that. You'd have to be an acrobat to avoid the mud—there was a long trek between the shantytown and the main road, and you could hardly do it on your head!

God, the playground is huge on your first day at school when you don't know anyone! It's like a football game—you have to mark out the opposition if you don't want to end up screwed. Majid is one of those with a will to fight. A survivor. He can never sit at the back as part of a herd—he has to be in front, at the top, all the time, even if it is exhausting, because it's not a lot of fun out there on your own. If you don't want to be on your own, then you have to take others along with you—but they're usually such losers that you're better off going it alone.

That evening, when Majid returns home, he finds his mother sitting at the kitchen table peeling potatoes. Malika's sitting on a chair, but Majid hasn't got used to chairs yet. In Algeria, everyone used to sit on the floor to eat and talk. But not here, because what will the neighbours think. . . ?

His mum is deeply unhappy. She can't keep the walls clean, because they're made of board. Can't clean the floor either—no point in using a floor-cloth because it's a dirt floor, and if you sweep it, all you get is clouds of dust. She doesn't even dare go out, because women don't wear veils here, and she's scared to go out without her *haik*. She still can't find the courage to do it, so it's left to Majid to go and fetch the water from the communal tap. There's just one tap for the whole shanty town. In winter it freezes solid and has to be thawed out. The inhabitants bring newspaper, strips of wood, cardboard boxes and crates, and they build a fire round it. And while they wait they sit on jerry-cans, making the most of the warmth and talking of this and that.

Every now and then someone fiddles with the tap to see if any water's coming through. To get it to run, you have to heat it up, say a prayer, and wait for a miracle. You might as well call in a witch doctor or do a rain dance round it, for all the good it does.

All this provides an entertaining spectacle for the residents of the surrounding tower-blocks. They're all right—they've got hot water on tap. You can see them looking out at you. There's probably one of Majid's classmates up there somewhere, watching him . . . well fed, freshly bathed and warmly dressed in clean pyjamas and slippers. He doesn't like to look up; he turns back to the fire.

The tap remains frozen for most of the winter and has to be thawed out two or three times a day. As for the toilets, they're just a big hole with two planks over it, inside a hut that has no roof.

It took Malika a long time to get used to all this. Sometimes, though, on a Sunday afternoon, they'd invite their relations round for a meal in their shack. Then she was happy, because the conversation turned to life in the old country. When friends criticized her for not going out, she'd just shrug her shoulders. What's the point? It's so cold in this country . . . the sky is always so grey . . . Majid used to do his homework sitting on his bed, next to a little coal stove, using a chair for a desk.

Study Questions

1. Why do Osborne, Powell, and Thatcher perceive the New Immigration into the United Kingdom as a threat? What justifications do they give for this view of the immigrants?
2. What is the basis for the position taken by the opponent of Osborne in the parliamentary debate?
3. In Charef's novel, Majid moves as a child from Algeria to the Paris region. What are the principal characteristics of Paris as Majid saw them?
5. How do you think Majid would respond to the comments by Osborne, Powell, and Thatcher about immigrants?

Suggestions for Further Reading

Ashcroft, Bill, Gareth Griffiths, and Helen Tiffin. *The Empire Writes Back: Theory and Practice in Post-Colonial Literatures.* New York: Routledge, 1989.

Feldblum, Miriam. *Reconstructing Citizenship: The Politics of Nationality Reform and Immigration in Contemporary France.* Albany: State University of New York Press, 1999.

Hargreaves, Alec G. *Voices from the North African Immigrant Community in France: Immigration and Identity in Beur Fiction.* New York: Berg, 1997.

Young, Robert. *White Mythologies: Writing History and the West.* London: Routledge, 1990.

Web Sites

1. International Human Rights Association

   http://www.humanrights.de/congress/2000/04/23/9.html

2. Muslims (noncitizens) in France:

   http://www.bsos.umd.edu/cidcm/mar/frmuslim.htm

3. Windrush Carnival Theme Celebrates the 50-year Caribbean Presence in Modern Britain:

   http://www.thechronicle.demon.co.uk/archive/laroscar.htm

CREDITS

Anglo-American Treaty of Peace, 1783. From William M. Malloy, *Treaties, Conventions, International Acts, Protocols and Agreeements between the United States of America and Other Powers.* Washington: Government Printing Office, 1910, Vol. I, pp. 586–589.

Arnold, Matthew. *On the Study of Celtic Literature.* New York: E. P. Dutton, 1910, pp. 23–28.

Baker, Samuel White. *The Albert N'Yanza: Great Basin of the Nile and Explorations of the Nile Sources.* Reprint; New York: Horizon Press, 1962 (1866), pp. 351–356, 359–360.

Beddoe, John. *The Races of Britain.* Reprint; London: Hutchinson, 1971 (1885), pp. 2–8.

Behn, Aphra. *Oroonoko.* London: Methuen, 1986, pp. 27–34.

Bird, Isabella. *The Yangtze Valley and Beyond.* Reprint; London: Virago Press, 1985 (1899), pp. 496–504.

Boas, Franz. *The Mind of Primitive Man.* New York: Macmillan Company, 1913, pp. 99–105.

Boswell, James. *Life of Johnson.* Edited by George Birkbeck Hill. New York: Harper & Brothers, 1891, Vol. III, pp. 8–9, 57–58.

Boumediene, Houari. *Proclamation of the Council of the Revolution.* Translated by James R. Lehning. Original French version in *Discours du Président Boumediene, 19 juin 1965–19 juin 1970.* Constantine: Ministère de l'Information et de la Culture, 1970, Vol. I, pp. 7–10.

Burton, Richard Francis. *Personal Narrative of a Pilgrimage to Al-Madinah and Meccah.* London: Tylston and Edwards, 1893, Vol. II, pp. 160–162, 165–172.

Charef, Mehdi. *Tea in the Harem.* London: Serpent's Tail, 1989, pp. 96–100. Reprinted courtesy of The Serpent's Tail.

Chateaubriand, Francois-René, Vicomte de. *Travels from Paris to Jerusalem, and from Jerusalem to Paris.* Translated by Frederic Shoberl. London: H. Colburn, 1835, Vol. II, pp. 181–184.

Conrad, Joseph. "Heart of Darkness". In *Youth and Two Other Stories*. New York: Doubleday, Page and Co., 1924, pp. 106–113.

Constitution of the French Colony of Saint-Domingue. From: *La Révolution française et l'abolition de l'esclavage*. Translated by James R. Lehning. Paris: Editions d'histoire sociale, 1968, T. XI, document 18.

Dampier, William. *A Voyage to New-Holland in the Year 1699*. From: *Dampier's Voyages*. Edited. by John Masefield. New York: E. P. Dutton, 1906, Vol. II, pp. 381–387.

Darwin, Charles. *Beagle Diary*. New York: D. Appleton and Company, 1896, pp. 376–378, 393–398.

Debate on Immigration Control, House of Commons, December 5, 1958. Parliamentary Debates, Fifth Series, Volume 596, pp. 1552–1553, 1555–1557, 1561–1562, 1574–1576.

Decree of the National Convention, 16 Pluviose Year II. From: *La Révolution française et l'abolition de l'esclavage*. Translated by James R. Lehning. Paris: Editions d'histoire sociale, 1968, T. XII, document 8.

Defoe, Daniel. *Robinson Crusoe*. Boston: Ginn and Company, 1916, pp. 221–228, 237–238.

Diderot, Denis. *Supplement to Bougainville's Voyage*. Translated by James R. Lehning. Original French text in *Oeuvres Complètes de Diderot*. Paris: Garnier Frères, 1875, Vol. 2, pp. 213–214.

Durkheim, Emile. *The Elementary Forms of the Religious Life*. New York: MacMillan Company, 1915, pp. 9–13.

Dutt, Romesh. *The Economic History of India in the Victorian Age*. London: Kegan Paul, Trench, Trubner and Co., Ltd., 1916, pp. xii–xix.

Ellis, Havelock. *A Study of British Genius*. London: Hurst and Blackett, 1904, pp. 51–57.

Falconbridge, Alexander. *An Account of the Slave Trade on the Coast of Africa*. London: Phillips, 1788, pp. 12–15, 19–20.

Flaubert, Gustave. *Salammbô*. New York: Albert & Charles Boni, 1919, pp. 48–58.

Forster, E. M. *A Passage to India*. New York: Harcourt, Brace and Company, 1924, pp. 41–47.

Gandhi, Mohandas K. *Hind Swaraj*. From *The Collected Works of Mahatma Gandhi*. Ahmedabad: Navajivan Trust, 1963, Vol. 10, pp. 47–53. Reprinted courtesy of the Navajivan Trust.

Gilbert, W. S. *The Mikado*. London: G. Bell and Sons, 1911, pp. 73–76, 81–89.

Gobineau, Joseph Arthur Comte de. *The Inequality of Human Races*. Translated by Adrian Collins. Reprint; Torrance, CA: Noontide Press, 1983 (1854), pp. 168–174, 179–181.

Hobson, J. A. *Imperialism: A Study*. New York: James Pott & Company, 1902, pp. 76–78, 85–87, 91.

Huc, Evariste-Régis. *A Journey through the Chinese Empire*. New York: Harper & Brothers, 1855, Vol. 2, pp. 47–52.

Humboldt, Alexander von, and Aimé Bonpland. *Personal Narrative of Travels to the Equinoctial Regions of America during the years 1799–1804.* Translated by Thomasina Ross. London: George Bell & Sons, 1908, Vol. III, pp. 70–75.

The Interesting Narrative of the Life of Olaudah Equiano, Written by Himself. London: Printed for and Sold by the Author, 1789, pp. 45–52, 70–74.

James, C. L. R. *Abyssinia and the Imperialists.* From *The Keys* (1936). Reprinted courtesy of the Estate of C. L. R. James.

Jones, Sir William. *Preface* to *Grammar of the Persian Language.* From The Works of Sir William Jones. Delhi: Agam Prakashan, 1799, Vol. V, pp. 165–170.

A Journal of a Voyage Round the World in His Majesty's Ship Endeavour, in the Years 1768, 1769, 1770, and 1771. London: T. Becket and P.A. De Hondt, 1771, pp. 35–36, 38–39, 41–43, 46–47, 51–53.

Kingsley, Mary. *Travels in West Africa.* London: Macmillan and Co., 1897, pp. 215–220, 226.

Lander, Richard. *Records of Captain Clapperton's Last Expedition to Africa.* Reprint; London: Frank Cass & Co., 1967 (1830), pp. 73–82.

Lane, Edward William. *An Account of the Manners and Customs of the Modern Egyptians, Written in Egypt during the years 1833, 1834, and 1835.* London: Charles Knight and Co., 1842, Vol. II, pp. 105–113.

Ledyard, John. *A Journal of Captain Cook's Last Voyage.* Reprint; Chicago: Quadrangle Books, 1963 (1783), pp. 143–148.

Lenin, V. I. *Imperialism: The Highest Stage of Capitalism.* From *V. I. Lenin, Collected Works.* Moscow: Progress Publishers, 1964, Vol 22, pp. 265–267, 298–302.

Letter to South Carolina Gazette Concerning Slave Trade. From Elizabeth Donnan, ed., *Documents Illustrative of the History of the Slave Trade to America.* Washington, D.C.: Carnegie Institution of Washington, 1935, Vol. IV, pp. 291–294.

Livingstone, David. *The Last Journals of David Livingstone in Central Africa.* New York: Harper & Brothers, 1875, pp. 59–66.

Loti, Pierre. *Aziyadé.* Translated by Marjorie Laurie. New York: Kegan Paul International, 1989, pp. 60–63, 70–72. Reprinted courtesy of Kegan Paul International.

MacMillan, Harold. *The Winds of Change.* From *Pointing the Way 1959–1961.* London: Macmillan, 1972, pp. 473–482.

Malinowski, Bronislaw. *Argonauts of the Western Pacific.* London: George Routledge & Sons, 1922, pp. 387–391.

Malinowski, Bronislaw. *A Diary in the Strict Sense of the Term, 1914–15.* Stanford, CA: Stanford University Press, 1966?, pp. 243–245. Excerpted from *A Diary in the Strict Sense of the Term* by Bronislaw Malinowski. Translated by Norbert Gutermann. With the permission of the publishers, Stanford University Press. Text © 1967 by Valetta Malinowska.

Melville, Herman. *Omoo.* Boston: L. C. Page & Company, 1892, pp. 289–295.

Mesarovic, Mihajlo, and Eduard Pestel. *Mankind at the Turning Point, The Second Report to the Club of Rome*. New York: E. P. Dutton & Co., 1974, pp. 18–31. Reprinted courtesy of Mihajlo Mesarovic.

Minh, Ho Chi. *Declaration of Independence of the Democratic Republic of Vietnam*. From Viet-Nam Delegation in France, *The Democratic Republic of Viet-Nam*. Paris: Imprimerie Centrale Commerciale, 1948, pp. 3–5.

Nkrumah, Kwame. *Neo-Colonialism: The Last Stage of Imperialism*. London: Heinemann Educational Books Ltd., 1965, pp. ix–xvi. Reprinted courtesy of Panaf Books Ltd.

Powell, Enoch. *Speech to the Annual General Meeting of the West Midlands Area Conservative Political Centre, Birmingham, 20 April 1968*. From *Reflections of a Statesman: The Writings and Speeches of Enoch Powell*. London: Bellew Publishing, 1991, pp. 373–374, 379.

Riegle, Donald. *Speech in Senate Debate on Ratification of North American Free Trade Agreement, Congressional Record* Vol. 139 #163 (November 20, 1993), S16615-16616.

Rousseau, Jean-Jacques. *Discourse on the Origins of Inequality*. Toronto: E. P. Dutton, 1913, pp. 207–215.

Roy, Rammohun. *Letter on Education*. From *The English Works of Raja Rammohun Roy*, Bahadurganj, Allahabad: The Panini Office, 1906, pp. 471–474.

Shelburne, Lord. *Debate in the Lords on the Preliminary Articles of Peace*. From *The Parliamentary History of England*. London: Hansard, 1814, Vol. 23, pp. 408–410.

Speke, John Hanning. *Journal of the Discovery of the Source of the Nile*. New York: Harper & Brothers, 1864, pp. 423–429.

Thatcher, Margaret. *The Path to Power*. New York: HarperCollins, 1995, pp. 145–147. Reprinted by permission of HarperCollins Publishers, Inc. Copyright © 1995 by Margaret Thatcher.

Treaty Concluded between Albert Dolisie and the Chiefs of Alima, 17 October 1884. From *Brazza et la prise de possession du Congo*. Translated by James R. Lehning. Paris: Mouton & Co., 1969, pp. 327–329.

Tylor, E. B. *Primitive Culture*. New York: Henry Holt and Company, 1877, Vol. I, pp. 26–32.

"War with the Ashantee." *Annual Register 1824*. London: Baldwin, Craddock, and Joy, 1825, pp. 134-136.